ISRAEL, PALESTINE, AND THE POLITICS OF RACE

ISRAEL, PALESTINE AND THE POLITICS OF RACE

Exploring Identity and Power in a Global Context

Yasmeen Abu-Laban and Abigail B. Bakan

BLOOMSBURY
NEW DELHI • LONDON • OXFORD • NEW YORK • SYDNEY

BLOOMSBURY INDIA
Bloomsbury Publishing India Pvt. Ltd
Second Floor, LSC Building No. 4, DDA Complex, Pocket C–6&7,
Vasant Kunj, New Delhi 110070

BLOOMSBURY, BLOOMSBURY ACADEMIC INDIA and the Diana logo are trademarks of Bloomsbury Publishing Plc

First published in India 2024
First published in Great Britain 2020

Cover design: Ian Ross www.ianrossdesigner.com
Cover image from the public domain

This edition published with permission from Bloomsbury Publishing Plc,
50 Bedford Square, London, WC1B3DP, UK

A catalogue record for this book is available from the British Library.
A catalog record for this book is available from the Library of Congress.

ISBN: 978-93-56406-78-0

Typeset by Integra Software Services Pvt. Ltd.
Printed at Manipal Technologies Limited, Manipal

To find out more about our authors and books
visit www.bloomsbury.com and sign up for our newsletters

CONTENTS

Acknowledgments vii
List of Abbreviations ix

Prologue: Why the politics of race? 1
Introduction 9

PART ONE SOCIAL SCIENCES AND THE ISRAEL/PALESTINE RACIAL CONTRACT

1 The idea of Israel and the absence of Palestine: Limits and possibilities for scholarship 23

2 The racial contract and Israel/Palestine 49

3 Israel/Palestine from local to global: Palestine in the POST-9/11 ERA 81

PART TWO GLOBAL POLITICS AND THE ISRAEL/PALESTINE RACIAL CONTRACT

4 The paradox of the United Nations: Human rights, Israel, and Palestine 109

5 Indigenous Palestine: Contested origin stories and the UN Declaration on the Rights of Indigenous Peoples 129

6 Global civil society and a "United Nations from below": The BDS movement 147

PART THREE THE ISRAEL/PALESTINE RACIAL CONTRACT: REBRANDING AND RESISTANCE

7 Israel's rebranding campaign and the politics of gender 177

8 Environmental racism and contested territory: Land, water, and air in Israel/Palestine 205

9 Israel/Palestine and the apartheid analysis: Toward a one-state solution? 225

Conclusion: Global response to the Israel/Palestine racial contract: BDS from South Africa to Palestine 247

Epilogue: Toward a politics of solidarity 263

References 272
Index 329

ACKNOWLEDGMENTS

The completion of this volume would not have been possible without the support and services of multiple institutions and individuals. Funding for this research and the publication of its findings were made available through the Social Sciences and Humanities Research Council of Canada, Queen's University, the University of Alberta (including the Office of the Vice-President, Research), and the University of Toronto. Thanks are owed to our publisher, I.B. Tauris/Bloomsbury; the anonymous reviewers of the original manuscript; and to our editor, Joanna Godfrey.

We have been supported in the completion of this research by: the Department of Political Studies and the Department of Gender Studies at Queen's University; the Department of Political Science at the University of Alberta; and the Department of Social Justice Education, Ontario Institute for Studies in Education (OISE), at the University of Toronto. We are grateful for the expertise and generosity of Kathryn Arbuckle and Amanda Wakaruk and other staff of The University of Alberta Library Systems, and to the staff at the United Nations Archives and Dag Hammerskjold Library in New York. The outstanding support of our copyeditor and all-round professional wordsmith, Angela Pietrobon, has been pivotal to the successful completion of this volume.

We are grateful to a superb group of graduate research assistants, who are also our colleagues: Katrina Bland, Kyle Jackson, Rusa Jeremic, Emrah Keskin, Nicole Lugosi, Elizabeth Macve, John McCoy, Nisha Nath, Elim Ng, Maria Relucio, Celia Romulus, and Siavash Saffari.

We are immeasurably grateful to many people who contributed to providing intellectual spaces for the conversations that surrounded the preparation of this book: Nahla Abdo, Ghada Ageel, Sharryn Aiken, Emily Andrew, Bruce Baum, Aziz Choudry, Roland Sintos Coloma, George Sefa Dei, Chandni Desai, Susan Drummond, Enakshi Dua, Dan Freeman-Maloy, Judy Garber, Joyce Green, Adam Hanieh, Paul Kellogg, Catherine Kellogg, Andy Knight, Kiera Ladner, Margaret Little, David

Lyon, Mojtaba Mahdavi, Mazen Masri, Charles Mills, Scott Morgensen, Ester Reiter, Mary Jo Nadeau, Diana Ralph, Shereen Razack, John Riddell, Alan Sears, Sid Shniad, Daiva Stasiulis, Vannina Sztainbok, Rick Szostak, Njoki Wane, Suzanne Weiss, Cynthia Wright, Rafeef Ziadah, and Elia Zureik.

Parts of this book build on arguments that were previously published by the authors, jointly and equally. Chapter 2 draws from Yasmeen Abu-Laban and Abigail B. Bakan, "The Racial Contract, Israel/Palestine and Canada," *Social Identities* 14, 5 (September 2008): 637–60. Chapter 9 draws from Abigail B. Bakan and Yasmeen Abu-Laban, "Israel/Palestine, South Africa and the 'One-State Solution': The Case for an Apartheid Analysis," *Politikon: South African Journal of Political Studies* 37, 2–3 (December 2010): 331–51. We thank Taylor and Francis (www.tandfonline.com) for permission to use these materials. Chapter 3 extends our previous work in Yasmeen Abu-Laban and Abigail B. Bakan, "The 'Israelization' of Social Sorting and the 'Palestinianization' of the Racial Contract: Reframing Israel/Palestine and the War on Terror," in *Surveillance and Control in Israel/Palestine: Population, Territory and Power*, eds. Elia Zureik, David Lyon, and Yasmeen Abu-Laban (London and New York: Routledge, 2011), 276–94. We thank Routledge. We also acknowledge that sections of Chapter 5 were reprinted with permission from the publishers from Yasmeen Abu-Laban and Abigail B. Bakan, "Contested Origin Stories and the Case of Israel/Palestine: 'Dialogue' in the Context of Unequal Power," in *Towards the Dignity of Difference?*, eds. Mojtaba Mahdavi and W. Andy Knight (Farnham: Ashgate, 2012), 261–79. Finally, Chapter 6 builds on Abigail B. Bakan and Yasmeen Abu-Laban, "Palestinian Resistance and International Solidarity: The BDS Campaign," *Race and Class* 51, 1 (2009): 29–54.

Our families have endured countless hours of distractions and have been endlessly supportive. It is an understatement to extend our gratitude, appreciation, and love to Paul Kellogg, Rachel Kellogg, Michael Stephens, Gabriel Stephens, Adam McNally, and Christine Tardif; Zachary Jericho Couture; Baha, Riyad, and Max Abu-Laban; and to Carol Shaben and Sharon McIrvin Abu-Laban.

The courage and tireless commitment to overcome the violences that are inherent in the Israel/Palestine racial contract—in the region, in the diaspora, and in the global movements for solidarity—have been our steady inspiration. We hope this volume can serve to give back in some modest way. With all this support, the analysis presented in the following pages and any errors associated with this analysis are ours alone.

LIST OF ABBREVIATIONS

9/11	September 11, 2001, the date of four air-based attacks against the United States
AFN	Assembly of First Nations
ANC	African National Congress
APSA	American Political Science Association
BDS movement	boycott, divestment and sanctions movement
BNC	BDS National Committee
CAIA	Coalition Against Israeli Apartheid
CJC	Canadian Jewish Congress
CPCCA	Canadian Parliamentary Coalition to Combat Antisemitism
CPSA	Canadian Political Science Association
GUPW	General Union of Palestinian Women
ICCA	Interparliamentary Coalition for Combating Anti-Semitism
ICJ	International Court of Justice
IJV	Independent Jewish Voices (Canada)
I/P racial contract	Israel/Palestine racial contract
IR	international relations
I/P	Israel/Palestine
OPT	Occupied Palestinian Territories
PLO	Palestine Liberation Organization

PA	Palestinian Authority
UN	United Nations
US	United States of America
WCAR	UN World Conference Against Racism, Racial Discrmination, Xenophobia and Related Intolerance; also called Durban conference

PROLOGUE: WHY THE POLITICS OF RACE?

In 2014, then Prime Minister Stephen Harper became the first Canadian head of government to speak in the Israeli parliament, the Knesset. He used the occasion to signal Canada's support for Israel as a specifically "Jewish state" and to criticize Canadian university campuses as places where "most disgracefully of all, some openly call Israel an apartheid state" (Harper 2014). Harper (2014) said it reflected "outright malice" because the country was based on "freedom, democracy and the rule of law." As scholars based in Canadian universities who are fully versed in campus debates concerning Israel and Palestine, we knew that the prime minister was not in fact fairly representing the diversity of views expressed by the Canadian public on the political entity frequently termed "Israel/Palestine" in an effort to capture its complexity. Nor was the prime minister of Canada fairly representing the professors, students, and staff from universities and colleges across Canada who have participated in events aimed at challenging the human rights consequences of Israel's policies, through what has become, since 2005, an annual educational event called "Israeli Apartheid Week." And, as those who identify with both the Palestinian (Yasmeen Abu-Laban) and the Jewish (Abigail Bakan) cultural and diasporic experiences, upon Harper's speech in the Knesset, we were reminded of the importance of the work we were conducting, which has culminated in this book.

The Harper moment in the Knesset was not exceptional, however. Rather, a highly charged Canadian and international political atmosphere surrounding Israel/Palestine has been characteristic of our initial and continued scholarly work in this specific field. Such an atmosphere draws attention to the foundational and continued exceptionality of the idea of Israel in contemporary political discourse, and to the related exclusion of the political realities that have transformed the Palestinian people into stateless refugees, second-class Israeli citizens, and the occupied. Not least, in July 2018, the Israeli government approved—by a vote in the Knesset of 62 in favor, 55 opposed, and 2 abstentions—the "Basic Law: Israel—The Nation State of the Jewish People." The law enshrines the "Land of Israel" as "the historical homeland of the Jewish people," thereby unambiguously excluding the one in five citizens who are Indigenous Palestinians from membership in the nation. It also declares Jerusalem as the capital of Israel, universalizes Jewish immigration, and upholds the development of settlements as a "national value" (Basic Law 2018; Wootliff 2018).

This book is the outgrowth of our shared conviction that some of the most pressing questions of social and political life today concern race and power, and yet asking such questions in relation to Israel is commonly painfully difficult and charged. The Middle East is a key conflict zone and often the subject of the nightly news. However, certain perspectives about Israel/Palestine are apparently off limits. This gap in discursive understanding has been and remains starkly clear. It is the background against which we began our discussions together in the winter of 2006 and continued working through to our final completion of this manuscript.

In particular, several events made the questions and perspective we wished to advance about "race" seemingly untouchable—at least for the archetypical rational and career-minded Canadian university professor attuned to the patterns of reward and advancement in and outside the academy. What happened? The United Nations World Conference Against Racism, Racial Discrimination, Xenophobia and Related Intolerance (WCAR) held in Durban, South Africa, between August 31 and September 8, 2001, had derailed precisely over Israel/Palestine. Specifically, criticisms of Israel's treatment of Palestinians had led the United States and Israel to withdraw from the conference on the grounds of anti-Semitism, here meaning anti-Jewish racism. By the time of the 2009 review conference of the WCAR held in Geneva, it was the Canadian government that had taken the lead among all countries (particularly many Western countries) in boycotting the entire United Nations (UN) event on grounds that the Durban conference had provoked an "anti-Semitic hate fest," according to Jason Kenney, then immigration minister, cited in 2010 in *The Toronto Star*.[1] Unusually, when compared with other UN conferences, there was almost no critical scholarly conversation about the WCAR events. Pundits and academics were not lining up to ask whether an event that had held so much promise—occurring as it did on the soil of postapartheid South Africa—actually merited the sweeping negative charge of serving to advance anti-Jewish hatred and of advancing a global event that was "anti-Semitic." One of the very few persons to raise doubts was Canadian journalist and writer Naomi Klein. Klein drew attention to the complex issues being addressed in an important article in *Harper's Magazine* (Klein 2009c). In actuality, the UN WCAR advanced global conversations surrounding multiple forms of racism, which included reparations for the transatlantic slave trade, migration, intersectional anti-racist feminism, and the treatment of such varied groups as the Roma, the Dalit, and the Palestinians (Klein 2009c). However, the hostile climate surrounding reasoned conversations that challenged racism regarding Israel/Palestine reverberated widely.

Additionally, the fallout from the September 11, 2001, attacks on New York and Washington in the United States proved to be fertile ground for Samuel Huntington's "clash of civilizations" perspective, first published in an essay in 1993, and then in book-length form in 1996. In the post-9/11 political era, issues related to race, religion, culture, and security were often conflated and came to form a new priority in many social science analyses, often closely tied to funding agencies and state goals. Moreover, responses to the "war on terror" saw the advance of unique challenges to scholarship that drew from a postcolonial frame of reference regarding the Middle East, particularly frameworks pioneered by those such as the late American-Palestinian scholar Edward Said (see Said 1979a on Orientalism) or that challenged a dominant Zionist narrative, such as the work of Jewish scholar Norman Finkelstein (see Finkelstein 2000). As contemporary politics associated with state security were increasingly framed in relation to religion and "civilization," new challenges arose to bringing in issues of power inequalities, such as those relating to race and colonialism. Significantly, when then US President George W. Bush ushered in the global "war on terror," Palestinians implicitly and explicitly were once again signaled as the world's leading "terrorists." This not only encouraged broad identification with the Israeli state by Western liberal democracies but also paved the way for a new scrutiny of academic analyses that were critical of Israel, the United States, and Western interests (see Thobani 2002). Certain feminists were quick to support the new normal, asserting Western interests to be particularly pro-gender equality, while Muslim women in the world's East were stereotyped as victims of exceptional patriarchy (see Chesler 2003).

In Canada, the administrations of Conservative Prime Minister Stephen Harper between 2006 and 2015 posed a particularly stark dimension to the new post-9/11 global reality. Since the end of the Second World War, Canada has had a history of consistent support for Israel. Consequently, both of the main political parties that have formed national governments—the Conservative Party and the Liberal Party—have shown little sympathy for the demands of generations of Palestinians for the minimal recognition of their human rights (Freeman-Maloy 2016). However, abandoning even a nominal position of balance, Harper led Canada on a decidedly more overt "pro-Israel" stance, symbolized clearly in his visit to the Knesset in 2014, but also exemplified in many elements of domestic and foreign policy. This unilaterally and staunchly pro-Israel orientation carried direct implications for the ability of nongovernmental organizations, arms-length agencies, and even academics to raise questions relating to Israel's record of human rights violations in relation to the Palestinians or to consider different models of statehood for Israel/Palestine (Abu-Laban and Bakan 2012a).

As feminist, anti-racist scholars in Canada, for us, these particular twenty-first-century conditions certainly provoked a sense of nervousness in talking about Israel and Palestine, but they also renewed our commitment to responsible scholarship. We committed to press on with our shared research agenda, to unpack and analyze the politics of race in relation to Israel/Palestine. Indeed, we reasoned that if we—as two tenured, full professors, and as political scientists trained in comparative politics with an arsenal of scholarship in other areas—could not do work on Israel, Palestine, and race, then who could? However, even though each of us had never shied away from controversial topics in our published work, this topic was, in our experience, particularly fraught. Each time we forwarded an argument in a conference paper, journal article, grant application, or classroom, anxiety levels would rise. To relieve the anxiety that we felt—in others more than in ourselves—we turned to self-identifying. In all our writing and our commentaries together since, we have chosen to position ourselves to indicate that we reflect two different cultural and diasporic experiences, as we have in introducing this prologue: Jewish in the case of Abigail Bakan and Palestinian in the case of Yasmeen Abu-Laban. We considered this when we first presented a jointly written paper in 2007 at a major academic conference in Canada, noting how unusual it was for our colleagues to hear a conversation addressing race in relationship to Israel/Palestine. Our audience surprised us with exceptional praise and gratitude, noting a particular and deep appreciation not only for our argument but also for sharing our backgrounds and family histories. This positioning has become a standard feature of our work on this project, even though we have frequently revisited this and pondered its relevance in light of the fact that we do not draw attention to our identities in our other academic scholarship and publications. In doing this, we wondered, were we inadvertently feeding into the odd dynamic in many North American universities, which holds that to achieve "balance," a Palestinian speaker must always be heard alongside an Israeli—or at least Jewish—speaker? Because this issue of balance is typically not raised when an Israeli (or Jewish) speaker appears alone to speak on the Middle East, were we reinscribing all the ways in which Palestinian voices have been silenced due to the power inequities that have produced "Israel" and "Palestine"? Were we perpetuating essentialized misunderstandings of the complex peoples and histories contained within, and stemming from, Israel/Palestine, bereft of considerations of power?

In answering these questions for ourselves, we came to view our joint work together as setting a foundation for advancing anti-racist discussion across all manner of divisions. Indeed, when we self-identified and spoke together, we found that others would often heave a sigh of relief. Perhaps somehow the specter of a conflict about to erupt had been removed—or, if a conflict had emerged in the audience, we had positioned ourselves at the outset as unsurprised and prepared to address queries. We came to consider that we were perhaps providing a model for how to have a conversation. In this, it was our many commonalities, not our differences, that were evident. One of these similarities includes that each of us are dual US and Canadian citizens—two countries where there are strong formal commitments to free speech and academic freedom.

The work that follows in this volume is the product of research, analysis, and writing that is jointly and equally shared. We write not as the product of an artificially constructed so-called dialogue based on essentialized difference, but as collaborators and coauthors working within a common paradigm and on a common project of advanced research. What we say and what we write are based on a series of shared assumptions from political scientists who traverse disciplinary boundaries. Our commonalities are that: (1) we study power, which we understand to be both materially and ideologically grounded; (2) we see value in the comparative study of politics and states; (3) we see value in the multidisciplinary and interdisciplinary study of race, gender, class, and citizenship; and (4) we embrace the perspective of anti-racist feminism. It is these commonalities that led us to work collaboratively along with others to advance a new section of the Canadian Political Science Association in 2008–9, specifically devoted to the study of "Race, Ethnicity, Indigenous Peoples and Politics." Similarly, this book is the outcome of these same commonalities, of turning our attention specifically to the study of Israel/Palestine.

In the pages that follow, we draw on an anti-racist, feminist method to advance a discussion of the narratives and discourses that "Israel" and "Palestine" provoke both for people in the region and internationally. We turn to the work of Charles Mills and Antonio Gramsci to theorize how a politics of race has structured power relations both in and outside the region and how it can be challenged. And, not least, we reflect analytically on the promising sites of nonviolent resistance and praxis, paying special attention to the ideas signaled in the boycott, divestment, and sanctions (BDS) movement and to the apartheid analysis of the state of Israel.

Unlike any other state context where we have conducted scholarly work, even when we have addressed challenging and difficult issues associated with class inequality, racism, sexism, marginality, and exclusion, we have found that to speak about and theorize race, power, and inequality in Israel/Palestine has exposed us to forms of harassment, scrutiny, and censorship that are vividly distinct. They are too numerous to name. Suffice it to say, however, we have fretted over the implications for our students and their future careers when they have been inspired to study Israel/Palestine; we have anticipated disruptions with every conference presentation and sometimes experienced them; and we have read between the lines in every anonymous review, always mindful of the exceptionally overwrought context in which we write. In this experience, we know we are not alone. Indeed, we have been fortunate in the comparatively minimal harm that we have encountered and overwhelmed with the ongoing encouragement and support that has inspired us to carry on. And, in doing this work, we have witnessed the growing strength of the BDS movement globally and seen the power and hope activists derive from approaching Israel/Palestine in new ways. We have also been reminded, through the many positive responses we have received about our joint work, of the joy and value of the tools on offer in meaningful social science research.

We have written this book in an effort both to continue and to reframe a conversation about the politics of race in Israel/Palestine, within the scholarly community and beyond. As this work was nearing completion, we witnessed major changes in the countries where we both have the right to vote: Canada and the United States. In October 2015, Justin Trudeau, leader of the Liberal Party, was elected as prime minister of Canada and a new administration came to office, amid great optimism that there would be significant change. Indeed, some welcome reforms have been initiated in terms of issues such as gender and minority representation, refugee policy including more openness toward the now millions of Syrian refugees, and a verbal commitment to reconciliation with Canada's significant Indigenous population involving an ongoing, if contested, process of recognizing and redressing past and present harms. However, regarding Israel/Palestine, it is the notable consistency with the past rather than change that marks the new administration. In February 2016, only a few months after Trudeau's majority government was elected, Liberal Party members of parliament voted overwhelmingly in support of a motion introduced by the opposition Conservative Party, to reject and condemn the BDS movement. The motion drew upon a standard misguided and inaccurate narrative—that this movement, which is grounded in international law, "promotes the demonization and delegitimization of the State of Israel" (Hansard 2016; Martin 2016). Clearly, as journalist Antonia Zerbisias (2015) has noted, "Harper may have left the building but, when it comes to Israel, he haunts us still."

In the United States, the November 2016 presidential election and rise of Donald J. Trump to the highest elected office in the country came as a surprise to many pollsters and pundits. His campaign rhetoric set off a flurry of speculation domestically and internationally about what his victory would mean. In Canada, leading newspapers raised concerns precisely because Trudeau's agenda and style were so markedly different from those of Trump. To exemplify:

> These are two leaders going in different directions: on refugees, borders, trade, climate change, even international security, on ideological inclination, political base and personal style. Mr. Trudeau played on the notion that he's the anti-Trump. And his supporters liked it. (Clark 2016)

Yet, if Trudeau came to power by promising to welcome more refugees, and Trump by saying he would build a wall to keep out Mexicans (along with many other claims and promises that have threatened to undo conventional and established policies and alliances), it is notable that, on the question of Israel, Trump differs little from Trudeau in terms of clearly supporting Israel and silencing critics of its policies. Indeed, during the course of his campaign, Trump moved from wanting to be a neutral "deal maker" to supporting settlements, opposing any sanctions on Israel, and pledging to punish those who support the BDS movement as well as investigate purported intimidation of students who support Israel on US college campuses (Maltz 2016). Not least, in 2018, Trump announced that the US embassy would be moved to Jerusalem, a move that gave symbolic recognition to Israel's claim to the undivided capital, ignoring the long-held and present claims of Palestinians.

This volume, then, is part of a continuing conversation relevant in a wide international context. We hope it will serve as a modest contribution to the work of a growing community of scholars who are finding the spaces and supports to address Israel/Palestine in a manner that is consistent with how scholars address other states in the social sciences and humanities. The year 2017 marked the centennial of the famous 1917 Balfour Declaration, which so dramatically impacted the fate of the peoples in that area of the world called Palestine. Now, into the second century, the multigenerational toll exerted by the ongoing crisis in Israel/Palestine is a reminder that the time has never been better for new thinking about Israel, Palestine, and the politics of race.

Note

1 *Toronto Star*, "Canada Skipping UN Racism 'Hatefest' Again, Ottawa Says," *The Star.com*, November 25, 2010, http://www.thestar.com/news/canada/2010/11/25/canada_skipping_un_racism_hatefest_again_ottawa_says.html.

INTRODUCTION

Introducing Israel, Palestine, and the politics of race

Alice Walker, the first African American woman to win a Pulitzer Prize for Literature, refused in 2012 to give permission for publication rights for an Israeli edition of her famous book *The Color Purple*.[1] While authors typically want their books to reach global audiences, her refusal in this case was because of her support for the Palestinian boycott, divestment, and sanctions (BDS) movement. Her statement, written on June 9, 2012, merits quotation in full:

> *Dear Publishers at Yediot Books,*
>
> *Thank you so much for wishing to publish my novel THE COLOR PURPLE. It isn't possible for me to permit this at this time for the following reason: As you may know, last Fall in South Africa the Russell Tribunal on Palestine met and determined that Israel is guilty of apartheid and persecution of the Palestinian people, both inside Israel and also in the Occupied Territories. The testimony we heard, both from Israelis and Palestinians (I was a jurist) was devastating. I grew up under American apartheid and this was far worse. Indeed, many South Africans who attended, including Desmond Tutu, felt the Israeli version of these crimes is worse even than what they suffered under the white supremacist regimes that dominated South Africa for so long.*
>
> *It is my hope that the non-violent BDS (Boycott, Divestment, Sanctions) movement, of which I am part, will have enough of an impact on Israeli civilian society to change the situation.*

In that regard, I offer an earlier example of THE COLOR PURPLE's engagement in the world-wide effort to rid humanity of its self-destructive habit of dehumanizing whole populations. When the film of The Color Purple was finished, and all of us who made it decided we loved it, Steven Spielberg, the director, was faced with the decision of whether it should be permitted to travel to and be offered to the South African public. I lobbied against this idea because, as with Israel today, there was a civil society movement of BDS aimed at changing South Africa's apartheid policies and, in fact, transforming the government.

It was not a particularly difficult position to hold on my part: I believe deeply in non-violent methods of social change though they sometimes seem to take forever, but I did regret not being able to share our movie, immediately, with (for instance) Winnie and Nelson Mandela and their children, and also with the widow and children of the brutally murdered, while in police custody, Steven Biko, the visionary journalist and defender of African integrity and freedom.

We decided to wait. How happy we all were when the apartheid regime was dismantled and Nelson Mandela became the first president of color of South Africa.

Only then did we send our beautiful movie! And to this day, when I am in South Africa, I can hold my head high and nothing obstructs the love that flows between me and the people of that country.

Which is to say, I would so like knowing my books are read by the people of your country, especially by the young, and by the brave Israeli activists (Jewish and Palestinian) for justice and peace I have had the joy of working beside. I am hopeful that one day, maybe soon, this may happen. But now is not the time.

We must continue to work on the issue, and to wait.

In faith that a just future can be fashioned from small acts,
Alice Walker

Alice Walker's careful words tellingly highlight the kinds of linkages that can be identified among the goals of the United States' Black civil rights movement, the struggle to end apartheid in South Africa, and contemporary anti-racist politics in relation to Israel/Palestine. The emergence of a movement for boycott, divestment, and sanctions, of which

Walker's statement is a part, counters what has been referred to as Israel's apartheid policies toward Palestinians. This movement, like Walker's statement, conveys an emerging form of global anti-racist politics. However, as we note in the prologue of this volume, analytical conversations about Israel/Palestine are persistently contentious. Here, we suggest this is due largely to a deeply entrenched hegemonic discourse in international politics, and relatedly in social science. This hegemonic discourse is grounded in a certain idea about what Israel is and what it means. Israel is considered as a unique state without international comparison, exceptional in its "Jewish" character and founded in the context of redress for the Nazi Holocaust of the Second World War. Concomitant with this idea about a state is the erasure of another population rendered stateless, resulting in the absenting of Palestine and Palestinians. The latter are outside of the "Jewish" state, as Palestinians are overwhelmingly Muslim and Christian. However, these ostensibly religious identifiers have very little to do with belief or spiritual identities; the Palestinians have encountered systemic violence, the redrawing of geographic boundaries, and colonial dispossession from 1948 to the present time.

How are we to think about these realities? This book challenges this hegemonic understanding of Israel/Palestine from the standpoint of critical political science (Abu-Laban 2007; Bakan and MacDonald 2002). Our perspective, among other things, foregrounds the politics of race. The work seeks to challenge the legitimacy of repressive and silencing dominant narratives and to expand the conceptual space for productive, critical, and comparative analysis (Abu-Laban and Bakan 2012a). Specifically, we employ a number of core analytical tools in relation to method, theory, and praxis that have led to increased understandings of varying colonial settler states and relationships regarding race, racism, and racialization in civil society. These, we argue, can helpfully serve to advance the central issues of race and power regarding the politics of Israel/Palestine. These analytical tools can be summarized under the headings of: anti-racist feminism, the racial contract and hegemony, and praxis related to the BDS movement. Below, we briefly elaborate each of these analytical tools.

Anti-racist feminism

Our method of analysis is grounded in our common commitment to, and advance of, anti-racist feminism (see, for example, Abu-Laban 2008a; Abu-Laban and Gabriel 2002; Bakan and Dua 2014; Bakan and Kobayashi

2000; Bakan and Stasiulis 1997; Bannerji 1993, 1995, 2000; Davis 2016; Lourde 1984; Stasiulis and Bakan 2005; Razack 1998, 2015). Anti-racist feminism has many diverse strands, and there is no single definition of such an approach. However, such a perspective centrally "analyzes contemporary theoretical and political issues within the framework of the historically racialized and gendered power structures ... and the ongoing colonial practices that demonstrate that race and gender are constitutive of the structures and subjectivities that shape the nation and the global order" (Razack, Smith, and Thobani 2010: x). Consistent with critical race theories, anti-racist feminism challenges the embedded marginalization, or erasure, of racialized and Indigenous subjects in the construction of liberal notions of state power (Bakan and Dua 2014). And, consistent with feminist theories, anti-racist feminism centers a methodology that is innovative in its data collection and interpretation, reflexive about the role of the researcher in seeking situated knowledge, and concerned with social change and social justice (Doucet and Mauthner 2006). Such an approach has stressed the significance of listening deeply to marginalized discourses and, rather than turning away from fraught topics, attempting to engage and "trouble" them (Butler 2006a), with a view to attending to deeper and more meaningful analysis.

Anti-racist feminism has also played a particularly significant, and unique, role in advancing the understanding of Canada as a colonial white settler state (Abele and Stasiulis 1989; Monture-Angus 1995; Razack, Smith, and Thobani 2010; Thobani 2007b). Our analysis draws upon our perspective and familiarity with Canadian politics and scholarly debates concerning race and racialization and their interface with larger international issues. Canada is the place where the term "multiculturalism" was coined, traceable to the federal government's 1971 policy. Canada has been upheld in a United Nations Educational, Scientific and Cultural Organization (UNESCO) study as the country that comes closest to embodying the "aspirations" flowing from "various United Nations instruments on cultural, linguistic and religious diversity" (Inglis 1996: 18). International leaders such as the Aga Khan IV have also called Canada a model for the world because its governing practices are considered to reflect the ideal of cultural pluralism.[2] Canadian discourse also frequently counterposes the United States' "race problem" and "violence" with Canada's apparent "tolerance" and "peacefulness" (Croucher 1997). However, the rhetoric of multiculturalism has been subject to extensive critique—a critique which we have ourselves forwarded—demonstrating that the promise of multiculturalism belies Canada's position as a constitutional monarchy bounded in colonialism and colonization (see Abu-Laban 2007; Bakan 2008a, 2016; Dhamoon 2009).

Grounding our approach to Israel/Palestine and the politics of race from such a vantage point has supported our comprehension and respect for the extensive literature written by Palestinians or about Palestinian experiences, and the related sustained accounts of colonialism, dispossession, and occupation (Ageel 2016; Said 1992). Anti-racist feminism has also attended to the politics of subjectivity, identity, and emotion (Ahmed 2004; Lourde 1984), which are central in addressing the context and content of the politics of race in Israel/Palestine.

Racial contract and hegemony

Our theoretical framing considers issues of power, centering the multilayered relationships of race and the state by drawing on the contributions of Charles Mills' theory of the racial contract (Mills 1997; Pateman and Mills 2007). While Mills himself does not actually discuss this region, our reading of racial contract theory as a feature of state hegemony helps us in explaining Israel, Palestine, and the politics of race within and beyond the Middle East region. Charles Mills' (1997) notion of the racial contract challenges the purported equality principle of the social contract, which has been dominant in Western liberal democratic theory. He suggests that a way to re-conceptualize the notion of the "contract" is to recognize the lived, or nonideal, experiences of racialized inequality embedded in the development of Western states. These developmental processes serve to bring to the fore such terms as conquest, slavery, colonialism, imperialism, apartheid, and reparations (Mills 1997: 4). For Mills, the racial contract is not a contract between individuals who are equal, but rather one between those who count and those who do not—a difference that he expresses in distinguishing "we the people" from "we the white people" (1997: 3). We adopt the notion of the racial contract to explain the relationship of Israel's privileged position both to other states internationally with a history of white settler colonialism (including Canada and the United States) and to the Indigenous Palestinian population—within 1948 Israel proper, in the Occupied Palestinian Territories, and in the diaspora. The normalization and universalized acceptance of the exclusion of Palestinians from

Israeli institutional norms and practices, as exemplified in the areas covered in the chapters that follow, is reflective of entrenched patterns of racialization associated with colonialism, imperialism, and white (European) settlement of Indigenous lands and peoples.

For Mills, racial contracts are embedded in the social and political relations of dominant liberal democratic discursive practices, where whiteness serves as an ostensibly superior modality, as "white supremacy," and acts as an "unnamed political system that has made the modern world what it is today" (Mills 1997: 1). However, while the racial contract framing assists in describing the underlying structural interconnections linking race, state, and power within Israel/Palestine, and between Israel/Palestine and the West, it is Antonio Gramsci's (1971) historical materialist concept of hegemony that brings in the dynamic contradictions and potential for resistance. Gramsci's original concept of hegemony stresses the reliance of capitalist economic power on dominant ideology, even as this reliance is contested and complicated by dynamics of consent and coercion. A neo-Gramscian approach also addresses the role of civil society in the social relations of power.

The relevance of Gramsci's notion of hegemony to global contexts and domestic state practices has been the subject of debate (Cox 1983; Germain and Kenny 1998; Gill 1993); moreover, it has not been a standard in considering Israel/Palestine. However, the original framework has been applied to global processes as well as national states (Gramsci 1971; Ives and Short 2013; Katz 2006; Morton 2003, 2007a, 2007b, 2011). We suggest that it is useful to consider the continual tension between dominant state policies and related ideologies, and the variegated impact of international factors and events, when considering the politics of race in the context of Israel/Palestine. Further, emergent counterhegemonic claims made by marginalized groups can be usefully understood in the context of a neo-Gramscian approach (Gill 2000; Hall 1986; McKay 2005, 2008). A Gramscian, or more accurately neo-Gramscian, approach is one that considers contexts and conditions in contemporary global politics and retains the elements of agency contained in the concept of hegemony (Bates 1975; Demirovic 2003). It therefore recognizes the continually contested character of power. A neo-Gramscian framework is therefore useful in understanding how the racial contract in the case of Israel/Palestine is both evident and challenged.

The specific nature of the Israeli state clearly complicates racial hierarchies. Often such complexities are seen as too challenging to allow for effective comparative political analysis, and Israel/Palestine is removed from standard discourse. We suggest, alternatively, that the specific nature of what we refer to as the *Israel/Palestine racial contract* be considered. In this volume, we elaborate how this Israel/Palestine racial contract has been advanced, the specific features that simultaneously give it definition and render it elusive, and why it has become hegemonic in the post–Second World War era in political policy and discourse.

Israel was established at the end of the Second World War in response to the racialized genocide of Jews in Europe under the Nazi regime in Germany (see Bakan 2014a). Jews, specifically Ashkenazi (European) Jews, have been historically treated as "less than white" in Western states (Brodkin 1998); however, in the context of Israel/Palestine, they have moved to a position more closely comparable to the white elite of apartheid-era South Africa. This marks a dramatic transition over a generation and can be understood to contribute to the heightened emotional tenor that accompanies considerations of the politics of race in Israel/Palestine. However, the complexities do not end here. While legacies of racial prejudice against Jews, or anti-Jewish racism (usually termed anti-Semitism), persist internationally, other prejudices associated with Orientalism and Islamophobia, or anti-Arab/Muslim racism, have been institutionalized in the Israel/Palestine context. This has long impacted the unequal relations experienced by Mizrahi (Oriental), Ethiopian, and other non-European Jews in Israel, as well as Palestinian Arabs (both Christian and Muslim). In the post-9/11 context, the particular form of racialization of Palestinians characteristic of Israeli state practices has been advanced globally, on the heels of new assertions of security concerns. This politically and socially constructed, racialized model of the "dangerous Other" contrasts with another trajectory—one toward a formal advance of multiculturalism, with all its contradictions, which is expected to minimize racial difference and is commonly assumed to be associated with modern liberal democracies.

In the United States and Canada, dominant paradigms guiding post–Second World War knowledge production display a discernible silence on Palestinians. This is consistent with a similar dominant historic silence about Indigenous peoples, as both the US and Canada have longstanding and ongoing conditions as settler-colonial states. This condition of silence has only been partially, and recently, addressed in Canada through the publication of the report of the Truth and Reconciliation Commission, which exposed the foundational role of the "Indian" residential school system in advancing the "cultural genocide" of Indigenous peoples in Canada (TRC 2015). Notably scant are analyses that consider the domestic and international implications of Israel/Palestine from the vantage point of race and racism. These intellectual lacunae are significant, not least given contemporary political debates in the lived world of race and ethnic conflict, and the centrality of the Middle East in politics and political science today. The Israel/Palestine racial contract includes, therefore, a mythologized exceptionalism regarding the state of Israel (making it difficult to compare with other states) and a simultaneous absenting of Palestine and Palestinians (making it difficult to see their humanity).

More recent events in the twenty-first century, within states and globally, have continued to be shaped by the Israel/Palestine racial contract. In an event we will discuss further, the 2001 United Nations World Conference on Racism, Racialization, Xenophobia and Related Intolerance (WCAR) and the 2009 WCAR Review Conference saw delegations from the United States, Israel, and Canada withdraw from participation on ostensible grounds of objections to a "new anti-Semitism," taken to mean anti-Jewish racism. This analytic is contentious, though little scholarly attention has attempted to explain the divergent interpretations, including a problematic conflation of criticisms of the state of Israel's policies with anti-Semitism. Also notable is the rise of anti-Arab racism, or Islamophobia, which targets the Arab/Orientalized "other" in ways modeled on the stereotyped "terrorist" in the Middle East context (Razack 2008). The silence in mainstream academic scholarship—not least in the dominant political science and ethnic studies framings—on the Palestinian reality and the attendant patterns of racialization suggest considerable risk in the capacity of analysts to offer explanations of, or remedial approaches to, contemporary political concepts and debates.

Praxis and the BDS movement

There are, however, counternarratives that are especially strong in civil society and global fora. Beyond the elected offices of governments, in post-9/11 social movements, in the work of United Nations rapporteurs, and among some critical scholars, attention has been drawn to the significance of race and racialization in Israel/Palestine. The Israel/Palestine racial contract remains hegemonic, but it is also contested. Turning to praxis, or politically informed action for social change, our work has been both inspired by and committed to advancing the Palestinian call for boycott, divestment, and sanctions (BDS) against the state of Israel. As repeated peace plans brokered by international and local actors have failed, the BDS movement gestures toward an alternative strategy. The movement is proactive, with a call directly from Palestinian civil society to global civil society and with a focus on building an international movement of economic, political, and social pressure from below aimed at isolating Israel as a "pariah state" comparable to apartheid South Africa (Barghouti 2004).

The BDS campaign, addressed in more detail in this volume, while calling for the implementation of international law through peaceful means, continues to face distinctive challenges that render its claim to progressive space contentious. This movement has been hampered, we maintain, by an international racial contract, which, since 1948, has drawn a common interest between the state of Israel and powerful international political allies, while absenting the Palestinians as both "non-white" and stateless. The unique role of Zionism as an ideology that lays claim to anti-racist ideological space as a response to anti-Semitism in the history of Europe, the United States, and Canada, while at the same time advancing racialized interests of colonial expansion in the Middle East, renders the ideological terrain of the BDS movement in the West complex (see Honig-Parnass 2003: 68–75).

This complexity is augmented by the near absence of normalized discourses regarding Israel/Palestine in mainstream academic and policy circles. That the Israel/Palestine racial contract is unnamed is in keeping with Mills' understanding of the racial contract as "non-ideal theory." In the case of the Israel/Palestine racial contract, the effect is to place the state of Israel beyond and outside of standard comparison with other states. The charged atmosphere of dialogue and critique is significantly rooted in an ideology of entrenched Orientalism, constructing a framework where "as human beings the Palestinians do not exist" (Said 2004a: 180). The uniquely challenged context of debate on this issue in global politics has been widely identified by writers critical of Israeli politics, including established scholars who are also Jewish, such as Norman Finkelstein, Ilan Pappe, and Uri Davis (see, for example, Davis 2003; Finkelstein 2003a; Pappe 2007). Recently, this exceptional atmosphere has also been identified by conservative theorists who align their views, for example, with the likes of the late Samuel Huntington, the foundational intellectual architect of the post-9/11 framing of a "clash of civilizations" (1996).[3]

Accordingly, Mearsheimer and Walt, who have challenged the role of the Israel lobby in shaping US foreign policy, maintain that discussion of US support for Israel has been made impossible in "polite company" and is commonly met by moral arguments in an effort "to stifle or marginalize serious discussion" (2007: 9–10).

The BDS movement, however, suggests a new way of framing Israel/Palestine and challenges the hegemony of the Israel/Palestine racial contact. The movement has continued to attract supporters, even in the face of persistent efforts to confuse and distort its message and despite notable repression. Included in the BDS call from Palestine is an effort to challenge the idea that the state of Israel defies comparison. Alternatively, a new discourse is suggested, if not explicit, in the call's demands, where Israel can be understood in terms of a racialized hierarchy associated with, for example, the concept of "apartheid." We will closely examine the concept of apartheid in this volume and show why it is applicable to Israel by considering state practices and international contexts where race and power are linked in specific ways.

The BDS movement has found resonance in civil society organizations that have emerged in the context of a renewed period of resistance to neoliberalism and opposition to US militarism associated with the Iraq war. The anti-apartheid movement that successfully challenged the institutionalized racism of the South African state has also served as a source of inspiration. Moreover, that the BDS movement is associated with a new generation of Palestinian, Jewish, and other activists from diverse backgrounds in Western countries is significant.[4] This challenges the racial contract that has divided social justice activists and works to replace a politics of division with one of solidarity. The BDS movement has emerged in the post–September 11, 2001 climate, where fear, racial profiling, and the detention of Arabs and/or Muslims have become more salient, with its proponents participating in and bolstering a global movement against war and racism (see Abu-Laban 2004: 17–40; Bakan 2005b: 269–82).

Israel, Palestine, and the politics of race

In the following chapters, we address the underlying epistemological assumptions that frame a hegemonic, but inaccurate, understanding of the idea of "Israel" and the related and similarly inaccurate absenting of "Palestine" as subsumed within the Israel/Palestine racial contract. We address this as a process that arises from constructed forms of knowledge associated with racialization, a phenomenon referred to by Sullivan and Tuana (2007), following Mills on the racial contract, as an epistemology of ignorance. We maintain that this is not merely the result of misinformation or lack of familiarity but flows directly from an active process of generating mythologies and absences that is consistent with a Gramscian notion of hegemony. These mythologies and absences also serve to legitimize and maintain specific patterns of state power and unequal social relations.

This volume seeks to account for this epistemology of ignorance and to revive the analytic contribution of critical scholarship by engaging conceptual categories utilized in multidisciplinary fields to specifically address racialization in Israel/Palestine. Expanding from Achille Mbembe's (2001) argument that the ideas associated with certain geographic places (such as Africa) serve to construct self and other in specific ways, we argue that the "idea" of Israel has served as a powerful signifier of Western/universal redress for the Nazi genocide. This idea has suggested an ascribed identity, a sense of "our" civilization that is part of a postwar hegemony (see Bakan 2008b). In this context, "Palestine" and "Palestinians" have come to assume a role of "absolute otherness," as the representatives of a constructed imaginary that is either entirely disembodied and absented or distorted as the uncivilized/Muslim/terrorist. Further, we consider an alternative conceptual framework as a way to advance a conversation regarding race and racialization in Israel/Palestine. We suggest that contemporary scholarship and popular knowledge can benefit from moving what Edward Said (1992) called "the idea of Palestine" more centrally to our understanding of the construction of "race" in the twentieth and twenty-first centuries.

The argument proceeds in three parts, with each considering the hegemonic, or dominant, framework regarding Israel/Palestine and the politics of race in specific ways. In Part One, we consider "Social Sciences and the Israel/Palestine Racial Contract." In terms of hegemonic discourses, we suggest a close look at political science and ethnic studies, and the application of the racial contract to Israel/Palestine. We then look at how such hegemonic ideas are expressed in state security and surveillance in Israel/Palestine, and indicate the persistence of Palestine as a reality that refuses to be absented, not least in the post-9/11 era. In Part Two, we consider "Global Politics and the Israel/Palestine Racial

Contract," with a more focused consideration of the United Nations and the framework of human rights regarding Israel/Palestine and the politics of race. We also consider the relevance of the 2007 United Nations Declaration on the Rights of Indigenous Peoples and how it has been the subject of contested views regarding land claims in the region. Also in this part, we consider the BDS movement and its relationship to the United Nations in more detail, suggesting how the movement has resisted the racial contract and centered the presence of solidarity with Palestine. Finally, in Part Three, "The Israel/Palestine Racial Contract: Rebranding and Resistance," we move to consider the politics of race within contemporary conversations about the environment, gender, and efforts to "rebrand" the idea of Israel in the face of growing opposition to the established racial contract. We end the part with a focus on the contested notion of apartheid and highlight a renewed optimism regarding a future unified, democratic state of all citizens. We conclude the volume with a review of global responses to the Israel/Palestine racial contract from South Africa to Palestine, followed by reflective epilogue, considering the claims of stateless refugees from the Holocaust to the present-day situation of Palestinians, and of the new refugees from Syria and beyond.

Notes

1 Allison Flood, "Alice Walker Declines Request to Publish Israeli Edition of The Color Purple," *The Guardian*, June 20, 2012, http://www.guardian.co.uk/books/2012/jun/20/alice-walker-declines-israeli-color-purple?newsfeed=true.

2 Haroom Siddiqui, "Why the Aga Khan Loves Canada and We Love Him: Siddiqui," *The Star*, February 26, 2014, https://www.thestar.com/opinion/commentary/.

3 For a summary of alternative frameworks and an analytical critique, see Bakan's "Imperialism and Its Discontents" (2005b).

4 See Rafeef Ziadah, "Sixty Years of Nakba: Palestinian Refugees and the New Anti-Apartheid Movement," *Left Turn*, April 9, 2008, http://www.leftturn.org/60-years-nakba-%E2%80%93-palestinian-refugees-and-new-anti-apartheid-movement.

PART ONE

SOCIAL SCIENCES AND THE ISRAEL/ PALESTINE RACIAL CONTRACT

1 THE IDEA OF ISRAEL AND THE ABSENCE OF PALESTINE: LIMITS AND POSSIBILITIES FOR SCHOLARSHIP

The challenge of knowing "race" in the Israel/Palestine context

As authors with dual Canadian and US citizenship and as academics based at Canadian universities, we are especially attuned to what we call the challenge of knowing "race" in Israel/Palestine. By this we mean that, while universities in Canada and the United States have often been at the center of debates regarding Israel/Palestine (Abu-Laban and Bakan 2012a; Ageel 2016; Butler 2006b; Dawson and Mullen 2015; Masri 2011; Nadeau and Sears 2010; Salaita 2015; Stewart 2010; Thompson 2011), terms like "race," "racism," and "racialization" are not a widely accepted means through which academics or students understand this conflict zone. However, as pivotal arenas of knowledge production, universities have actually been central to the Israel/Palestine racial contract. In this chapter, we examine the underlying ideas broadly considered in the social sciences that render conversations regarding Israel/Palestine notably fraught. We suggest that central to this outcome are contemporary understandings of race and the relevance of such understandings to the Israel/Palestine racial contract in the North American (here meaning US and Canadian) traditions of academic scholarship.[1] To better illustrate this, we focus on two important fields of knowledge: the discipline of political science and the interdisciplinary area of ethnic studies. "Race" is not frequently addressed in much work in political science, and when it is, it is often subsumed under or beside notions of "ethnicity." The processes of racialization in Israel/Palestine have received particularly scant attention in the discipline. In the area of ethnic studies, while race is more readily addressed, the case of Israel/Palestine similarly remains largely unstudied.

In what follows, the elision of race in the context of Israel/Palestine in both political science and ethnic studies is addressed, followed by a more detailed consideration of the idea of Israel and the absenting of Palestine. The chapter concludes with a consideration of the contribution of concepts such as racial contracts, Indigeneity, and apartheid in the context of Israel/Palestine. These are suggested as valuable conceptual tools in advancing a more comparatively informed and productive critical discourse that contributes to part of our understanding of the Israel/Palestine racial contract, the elaboration of which is developed in subsequent chapters.

Absences: Political science and race and ethnic studies and Palestine

Political science, as the study of states and power, is an academic discipline arguably well suited to the study of race and racialization in Israel/Palestine. However, political science has not generally developed as a welcoming intellectual home for critical race analyses regardless of geographic region or country case study (see Thompson 2008). As a discipline, political science has its origins in the developments of modern social science, and it was given renewed prominence in the decades following the Second World War. Developments in the United States since the mid-twentieth century have heavily shaped the discipline, not least because estimates show that some 75 to 80 percent of the world's political scientists were located in the United States by the 1990s (Taylor 1999). Moreover, commonly American narratives of the discipline are drawn upon both within and outside of the US context (Gunnell 2002; see also Adcock and Bevir 2005; Klingemann 2007).

This is not to suggest that the subject of race and politics has gone unnoticed. In the case of comparative politics—one of the main subfields in the discipline—there was sporadic attention for much of the postwar period to issues of race and ethnicity, which was further advanced in 1995 with the creation of a new section dealing with race/ethnicity in the American Political Science Association (APSA). However, even with this section in place, analyses of racialization as a historically and socially constructed process were marginal (Taylor 1999) and tended not to intersect with other interdisciplinary approaches that foreground race (Walton, Miller, and McCormick 1995). The complex intersections of race, gender, and class among other forms of inequality also remained marginal (Dawson and Cohen 2002: 503). In 2004, Hanchard and Chung noted, "there has been little discussion of the conceptual and methodological implications of the comparative study of race and ethnicity on contemporary debates and discussion in comparative politics in the US, though a more serious undertaking of these issues in cross-national perspective could greatly enhance the literature" (320). As Dawson and Cohen noted in reviewing the study of race at the beginning of the 2000s:

> One central theme ... is the need to understand the process of racialization and racial orderings throughout history and from the perspective of different racial and ethnic groups. More often than not political science seems oblivious to the different methods, times, and reasons groups become racialized subjects. Further, the dynamic trajectory of racial ordering and its consequences for not only policy areas such as immigration but also the evolution of state operations and orientations seems noticeably absent from our analyses. Exploring the historical and specific processes of racialization should provide greater insight into such staples of political science inquiry as electoral realignment, public opinion shifts, and interest group proliferation. (2002: 489)

Throughout the 2000s, US and Canadian political scientists identified similar problems with the study of race. Watts, for example, noted that the serious study of Afro-American politics was hampered by mainstream political science approaches, which defined politics in narrow terms, lacked theorization about white domination, fixated on electoral politics, and reified race (2007: 406–28). More broadly, Wilbur Rich (2007) suggested that it was a lack of deep understanding about race in the United States that compounded the problem of political scientists attending to race adequately elsewhere in the world. Debra Thompson (2016) has noted that methods of determining and assessing census data regarding race have varied greatly across states, rendering the most basic comparative analyses notably fraught.

Given this backdrop, there are some welcome recent advances of note. These include the formal creation in 2009 of a "Race, Ethnicity, Indigenous Peoples and Politics" section in the Canadian Political Science Association (CPSA) and the production of a new journal entitled *Journal of Race, Ethnicity and Politics* through the Race, Ethnicity, and Politics section of the American Political Science Association (APSA). It is significant that in its inaugural March 2016 issue, the journal's editor observed that, despite the APSA section, "research in race and ethnicity retained a curious place in the discipline" (Ramakrishnan 2016). To quote:

> many departments did not know how to evaluate political science publications that were getting published in interdisciplinary journals such as *Ethnic and Racial Studies, International Migration Review,* and *American Indian Quarterly*. In addition, many excellent articles were getting rejected from flagship political science journals because their work was seen as too narrow, and scholars who managed to publish in such journals were encouraged to frame their scholarship in ways that would appeal to mainstream audiences. (Ramakrishnan 2016: 2)

As a remedy, the openness of the journal to work that engages subfields across the discipline as well as diverse methodologies and intersectional approaches is a nascent, but encouraging, sign of disciplinary shift (Ramakrishnan 2016: 3).

As it stands, however, other subfields of the discipline have different challenges. In the subfield of political theory—the area within postwar US political science charged with considering normative questions (Gunnell 2006: 484–5)—scholars of democratic theory have turned to the politics of multiculturalism and inclusion, which tends to frame racialization as a feature of illiberal attitudes and premodern practices. In the face of what has been termed the "behavioral revolution," and the related privileging of certain kinds of research that could inform (US) policy makers, political theory continues to retain a surprising influence (Kettler 2006). In this regard, US political theorists, like their empiricist colleagues, have a strong concern for democratic theory (Berndston 1987). Over the 1970s and 1980s, democratic theory came to be characterized by the debate between liberals and communitarians. However, since 1989 and the attendant waning of the historic Cold War binary between "democracy" and "communism," political theory has more seriously taken up issues of national identity and multiculturalism. This turn is symbolized significantly with the rising international influence of Canadian political theorists Will Kymlicka (1989, 1995, 1998) and Charles Taylor (1994).

In short, dominant strands of political theory have gone multicultural (May, Modood, and Squires 2004: 3–8). The focus on cultural minorities—largely national minorities within liberal democratic nations—has tended, however, to in effect downplay and/or make less possible a focus on race and processes of racialization, as well as other forms of social differentiation and power relations, through a privileging of "culture" (Dhamoon 2006, 2010). Much of this work theorizes at a very abstract level, with limited attention to empirical realities in distinct contexts (May, Modood, and Squires 2004: 5–6) or historical specificities. The significant exceptions (Carens 2000, 2013) are important, but they have not penetrated the hegemony of liberal multiculturalism. And despite the impressive contributions of Canadian political scientists to studies of multiculturalism, the absence of attention to racialization, as both socially constructed and historically specific, has hampered the study of politics in Canada (Abu-Laban 2007). This is despite analyses of hegemonic multiculturalism within the field of political theory that have foregrounded race and racism (Coulthard 2014; Dhamoon 2010; Galabuzi 2006; Johnson and Enomoto 2007; Kernerman 2005; Tully 1995).

In her article "Is Race Political?," Debra Thompson addresses the awkward disconnect between the realities of race as factors in power and the near-absence of attention to race in Canadian political science. She writes:

> English Canadian political science has been ignoring all the signs that point to the relevance of race: demographic data point to the increasing racial population of Canada; the link between race and politics is clear both in terms of the production of race itself and the political and social barriers faced by racialized populations; and other disciplines in the social sciences have been far more successful than political science at publishing and presenting journal articles that take race as an important subject of research.... Similarly, the

> dominant approaches to the study of English Canadian political science are unlikely to acknowledge race as a political production or phenomenon.... [I]nstitutions, state parties, and "official politics" are dominant ... where racial minorities are currently underrepresented in institutions like the House of Commons and the formal bureaucracy of the Canadian government. Also, political participation in Canada often concerns the activities of citizens, and only of citizens, and until recently political science has not considered the liminal positioning of new immigrants, permanent residents and refugee claimants, the majority of whom belong to racial minority groups. This is not to say that racial minorities are politically passive, but rather that their access to power and decision makers is limited. (Thompson 2008: 534–37)

A legacy of "colonial amnesia" (Choudry 2010), which is characteristic of countries with settler histories and ongoing structures such as Canada's, bears heavily on contemporary mainstream political science. Other subfields in the discipline, notably in the influential field of international relations (IR), have similarly largely elided a focus on race and racialization. In the context of the Cold War and the interests of US policy makers, as well as the particular dominance of US-based academics in state security, the areas of focus have included issues of national security, nuclear deterrence, and military strength. As an area of study closely linking state policy to research, IR has been described variously as a field or subfield of political science, or as a discipline in its own right. Regardless, it is clear that IR was shaped by the postwar development of political science as a discipline, and it is closely associated with liberal democratic state military policy. As McSweeney points out, "measured in terms of growth since 1945, the study of security is probably the most prestigious sub-field of international relations" (1999: 25). Moreover, at least until the mid-1980s, many questions of international security were framed strictly within the boundaries of the discipline of political science and its objectivist tradition (McSweeney 1999: 33).

Many writers contributed to new directions, including post-Cold War discussions of "new security" and the constructed character of security within IR (Buzan and Waever 2003; Buzan, Waever, and de Wilde 1998; Waever, Buzan, Kelstrup, and Lemaitre 1993). Nonetheless, in practical application, these authors have tended to address the construction of global and regional security threats with scant attention to how processes of racialization impact, define, or affect definitions of security or its risks. Thus, as Chowdhry and Nair state, such "understandings of power relations render invisible or inconsequential the racialized, gendered, and class nature of power in IR" (2013: 6).

The case of Israel figures uneasily in approaches to global security, and similarly within political science. The claimed "Jewish" character of all the significant political institutions in that state is normalized and accepted in international arenas. Moreover, Israel's exceptionality is widely taken as a given. As Whitaker notes, this exceptionality has dramatically escalated in the post-9/11 context, not least associated specifically with airline security and antiterrorism (2011: 371). The inattention to the construction of racialization has enabled the state's claimed Jewish identity and representation to be accepted as a fact, rather than as a feature of state hegemony and an ideological project that is subject to intellectual and analytical scrutiny and critique. This dominant and accepted framing of Israel as a normalized "Jewish state" has simultaneously effectively absented Palestinian experience, history, and identity claims. At its most problematic, this absenting is replaced with an assumed stereotype of the "Palestinian" as "terrorist" (Lentin 2008c; Massad 2006). In this process, political science has been consistent with the social sciences generally, presuming Israel to be "a pioneering, settler-immigrant society that is democratic and has little in common with European-colonial ventures" (Zureik 2011: 5). Comparative studies that address Israeli politics tend to presume the place of Israel to be on the same footing as Western liberal democracies (Haklai 2011; Migdal 2001). If history is brought to bear in the analysis, it is commonly according to the hegemonic narrative of a desert "land without a people" brought to bloom by Western settlement in a way that is consistent with Zionist framings. This narrative places European Jewish victims of anti-Semitism (anti-Jewish racism) as benevolent, innovative, and industrious colonists. This frame absents Palestine and Indigenous Palestinians and fails to view Zionism, as Said (1992) starkly poses the question, from the standpoint of its victims.

In recent years, political science associations internationally and in Canada have developed area studies focusing specifically on the politics of race and racism (Dawson and Cohen 2002; Taylor 1999), and political scientists have addressed the significance of race in state policies and practices domestically and internationally (Abu-Laban 2000; Chowdhry and Nair 2013; Saleé 2004; Stasiulis and Bakan 2005; Thompson 2008, 2012, 2016). However, the specific nature of anti-racism as a political project remains largely unaddressed. If political science tends to absent or diminish the significance of race and racialization, arguably ethnic studies should serve as an alternative natural home. But here too, the study of race and racialization regarding Israel/Palestine remains absent or marginal.

In the United States, ethnic studies "as a discipline, emerged in the post-Civil Rights era" (Prashad 2006: 158). It developed in the context of struggles for academic legitimacy, where historic exclusions of "non-white intellectuals" and features of "faculty hesitancy" mitigated the more rapid scholarly development demanded by the subject matter (Clarke 1977: 124). However, by the twenty-first century, ethnic studies had come of age as a recognized disciplinary focus. Combining a series of diverse studies of the minority "other" under a common rubric, the emergent discipline did not "disavow the importance of racialization and of racial oppression," even when possibly risking becoming "invested in the frozen tundra of identity" (Prashad 2006: 157). Critical challenges, not surprisingly, have arisen concomitant to the mainstreaming of ethnic studies.

> Every time the identity of the American people in this continent is celebrated today as a uniquely composite blend of European immigrants who settled the Atlantic colonies or passed through Ellis Island, a political decision and a historical judgment are being made. A decision is being made to represent the Others—American Indians [*sic*], African Americans, Chicanos, Puerto Ricans, Asians, other peoples of colour—as missing, absent or supplemental. (Juan 1991: 467)

Efforts to theorize differences and linkages among various types of racialized experiences generated distinct disciplinary foci and complex debates regarding the relationship between critical scholarship and social justice practices (Juan 1991; Prashad 2006). Notably fraught in this context, and relevant to the study of Israel/Palestine, is the association of "Jewish studies" with both historic exclusion of Jewish minorities comparable to other minority groups and the common ascendance of Israel as a powerful militarized state, closely associated with US imperialist interests in the Middle East. A series of debates regarding the ascribed "model minority" status of American Jews (Glazer 1964), and relationships between African Americans and Jewish Americans, with noted contributors including James Baldwin, have generally not found easy resolution (Feldman 2015: vii–xi; Prashad 2006: 166).

More recent developments in Jewish cultural studies (Boyarin and Boyarin 2002) hold greater promise, as they are premised explicitly on delinking Jewish diasporic cultural identity from a defense of, or association with, the Zionist political ideology of the state of Israel. However, these issues are inextricably linked in contemporary discussions, in both scholarship and public discourse, with the complex geopolitics of the Middle East. Without in any way minimizing the centuries-long legacy of anti-Semitism, particularly in European and North American polities, we argue that the colonial history and apartheid conditions of Israel demand theoretical attention. A method that incorporates the contributions of a more critical approach, with an emphasis on processes that construct and deconstruct patterns of racialization as part of state hegemonic practices and political ideologies, can help to advance such a conversation. And further, political science, and not least the field of comparative politics, arguably has an essential contribution to make in moving this discussion forward. To this end, the unequal power relations of states that are embedded in, and that in turn advance, racialization demand attention, without *a priori* methodological assertions of state exceptionalism.

If the scholarly absence of a focus on race and racialization in Israel/Palestine is clear, moving to redress this absence in the vast area of North American social sciences poses complex challenges. This is not a simple case of "add and stir," to borrow a common feminist critique of the absence of women as subjects in the social sciences. This brings us to a discussion of the deeper epistemological issues that have supported a sustained distortion of the idea of Israel and the concomitant absenting of Palestine.

The idea of Israel

"Israel" is not only a state but the concept or idea of a state. While Ilan Pappe (2014) has addressed the idea of Israel as a constructed notion within the state of Israel itself, we consider this "idea" differently, from the perspective of the racial contract and on a global scale. Established in 1948, the idea of Israel marks the effective culmination, like a symbolic victory flag, of the Allies' success in defeating the Axis powers during the Second World War. The ideological frame of the United States, Canada, and Western Europe was defined not only by the Cold War—claiming "democracy" in its liberal Western modernist form as the high point of humanity, and "communism" in its Stalinist bureaucratic form as the low point—but also by the United Nations Declaration of Human Rights (also adopted in 1948). The ascribed liberal democratic accomplishment of overcoming the racist and authoritarian global vision of Hitler's Nazis is enmeshed within the idea of Israel. Reclamation of Jewish victims of Nazi genocide over time became embedded in the normative assumptions of the day. US hegemony became asserted as a given, and with it came a new assertion that the previously understood Christian Protestant mission of humanity and a sound work ethic dedicated to protecting "God's good earth" (Connolly 2008; Weber 1977) was now to be understood as an amended mission of the "Judeo-Christian." Enter the state of Israel. With this came the ascendance of designated Jewish Americans, formerly subject to strict quotas in the university system (Soares 2007), in one of the most dramatic moments of upward class mobility known in liberal democracies (Brodkin 1998; Feldman 2015; Goldstein 2006).

The construction of this geopolitical epistemology, ultimately expressed in a new racial contract regarding Israel/Palestine, depended upon a number of important absences. This period saw the advance of a specific epistemology of ignorance (Sullivan and Tuana 2007), which also served to cover over the racialized logic and legacy of the atomic bombing of the Japanese in Hiroshima and Nagasaki and the racist treatment of Asian Americans and Asian Canadians that was endemic to the security regime of the Second World War (Miki 2005). It also, significantly, absented the lived experiences of anti-Semitism of Jews in Europe, the United States, and Canada and the long traditions of progressive, anti-racist organizing that united Jewish workers with other immigrant and minority populations in labor and socialist organizing (Bakan 2014a; Reiter 2016). This new Israel/Palestine racial contract also absented the disturbing concessions made to the Nazi genocide by the same states that claimed victory against the Nazis. This was starkly marked by a major international conference in Evian, France, in 1938 that resulted in the refusal of asylum to Jewish refugees (Sacher 2005: 516). Also absented were the international corporate links that tied Western businesses to the German genocide machine (Black 2011).

The hegemonic status of the idea of Israel is dependent upon historical and material conditions in a way that blends fact and fiction. This analytical point of view is consistent with a neo-Gramscian approach. The idea of Israel indeed depends upon the establishment of Israel on land that was claimed to be uninhabited, rendering the Indigenous Palestinian population invisible in the most enduring and significant absence. Yet for them, the moment of establishment of Israel, projected and memorialized in the Zionist narrative as an achievement of "independence" from the period of the British Mandate, is the *Nakba*, Arabic for catastrophe. The establishment of the state of Israel was the result of the forced removal of tens of thousands of Palestinian people from their homes in a violent moment of ethnic cleansing (Pappe 2007). This is not merely a well-documented historic event, however, but a continuing process of absenting that includes the denial of the right of return, the occupation of Palestinian territories, and the denial of equal citizenship claims of Palestinians in Israel.

The enduring idea of Israel is also grounded in a specific geopolitical context. It feeds into notions of "democracy" and "human rights" constructed as part of the ideological hegemony of the United States in the aftermath of the Second World War. Israel was and is imagined and understood as a progressive, humanistic state, emblemizing liberal and even social democratic norms. The entrenchment of this idea as hegemonic was not a simple or linear process. It is notable that this idea has included a variety of formative moments on a number of levels, from media spectacles such as the Eichmann Trial (Arendt 2006), to war and occupation such as Israel's Six Day War of 1967 (Gordon 2008b), to an extensive, international, intellectual, and political "branding" exercise on the part of Zionist advocates regarding interpretations of the Holocaust and linkages to Israeli state practices (Finkelstein 2003a, 2005). Some of the central elements of the construction and maintenance of this idea are elaborated in our discussion of the United Nations (Chapter 4), contested ideas of who is Indigenous (Chapter 5), and rebranding and gender (Chapter 7).

The constructed idea of Israel, however, consistently relies on a series of absences that render the claimed democratic and humanistic referents into distortions of the actual practices of the Israeli state. The idea of Israel also rests on the dismissal of the legitimacy of a counternarrative that could alter or correct such distortions. What we term "the Israel/Palestine racial contract," associated with the idea of Israel, includes the notion that Israel is so exceptional that it is without comparison internationally. This idea of Israel is based on a mythologized exceptionalism. The constructed uniqueness is circular in logic. This idea challenges comparative politics as an approach, presuming a variety of discursive objections to critiques of the mythology of exceptionalism itself. Principal among these objections is the claim that any challenge to the hegemonic idea of Israel is tantamount to anti-Semitism, or anti-Jewish racism. A variant of this takes on a particularly virulent affective form when the proponents of a critique are of the Jewish faith, culture, or identity. Commonly, the invective turns to the person—rather than the argument—who is charged with willfully suffering from the symptom of being "self-hating," ascribing a particular psychological dimension to the conversation. The idea of Israel is rendered hegemonic in part through the silencing of critiques that could, if allowed discursive legitimacy, shift the focus to a more accurate comparative political or historical context. The Israel/Palestine racial contract associated with the idea of Israel is, therefore, based on the implicit, and at times explicit, assumption that racism toward all Jewish people (anti-Semitism) is inevitably suggested or embedded within any substantive critique of Israel's policies or practices as a state.

Regarding this claim, the charge of anti-Semitism has emerged in several distinct phases. The most recent iteration asserts that a "new" anti-Semitism has been advanced in the twenty-first century. This body of claims notably emerged, as Norman Finkelstein states, "just as Palestinians renewed their resistance to occupation" (2005: 21), as the second Intifada (uprising) welcomed the new millennium. As the extreme repression that followed from the Israeli state came under challenge, there was

> a vast proliferation of books, articles, conferences, and the like alleging that—in the words of the Anti-Defamation League (ADL) national director Abraham Foxman—"we currently face as great a threat to the safety and security of the Jewish people as the one we faced in the 1930s—if not a greater one." (Finkelstein 2005: 21)

The literature included an array of authors finding a new common cause (Berenbaum 2008; Chesler 2003; Perry and Schweitzer 2008). From this perspective, international arenas for challenging racism attending to the threats to survival and rights faced by Palestinians under occupation have been identified as outlets of this new form of racism, not least the 2001 World Conference Against Racism, Racial Discrimination, Xenophobia and Related Intolerance (WCAR) held in Durban, South Africa, and the subsequent 2009 Durban Review Conference held in Geneva, Switzerland. In these instances, major states, including the United States, Canada, and, not surprisingly, Israel, withdrew from the conference process on the grounds that these UN events were in fact not anti-racist, but racist, expressed through anti-Semitic racism. With the withdrawal of these key states, delegates were urged to follow suit, and thereby abandon the goal of advancing a common plan or even a common statement to oppose racism globally.

The WCAR has earned scant attention in both scholarly and policy analysis (Jackson and Faupin 2008). The intellectual climate associated with explorations of the politics of anti-racism has been, arguably, rendered chilly. The confused assignment of critiques of Israel's racialized practices as equivalent to anti-Jewish racism has been central to this challenging discursive context. The falsely assigned charge of anti-Semitism has also served to trivialize the reality of actual anti-Jewish racism in the context of anti-racist studies generally. Rather than advancing solidarity and common opposition to racism, the misplaced claim is divisive, isolating those who seek to develop a more general, universalized response to racism in its various forms (Masri 2011; Salaita 2015).

In the example of the World Conferences Against Racism, for instance, a number of important civil society representatives from Canada and the United States, and among Palestinian delegations, who were involved in the preparatory process and in the conferences and related nongovernmental organization (NGO) forums, expressed dismay regarding the role of their respective governments. A joint statement signed by a broad range of organizations, including the African Canadian Legal Clinic, Canadian Arab Federation, Canadian Labour Congress, and Independent Jewish Voices (Canada), which was presented in 2009 by a delegation of Canadian observers noted: "Canada's refusal to participate in the UN process is a demonstration of its failure to acknowledge the persistence of racism and state responsibility to address it." Many stakeholders who remained involved in the WCAR process and shaped the final declarations, while acknowledging expression by some delegations of anti-Semitic comments, maintained that such expressions were sharply challenged and were not reflective of the totality of the conferences (Robinson 2012).[2] These stakeholders were disappointed by the absence of states bearing considerable stature on the global stage, notably the United States, Canada, and Israel (Klein 2009c).

Among those expressing deep concern about this view of the WCAR process were African and African diasporic groups, including delegations of African Americans and African Canadians (Bakan and Abu-Laban

2015). For these groups, the 2009 Durban Review Conference was seen as an opportunity to continue a conversation begun at the 2001 WCAR about the legacies of the injustices of the transatlantic slave trade, including the potential advance of a movement seeking various forms of reparation. The lack of engagement in the dialogue regarding reparations for the impact of slavery and the slave trade was taken as a hurtful minimization of the continuing legacy and violent effects of racism toward peoples of African origin and descent (Winbush 2003). The interpretation of the WCAR as a conference process that, in its totality, treated anti-Semitism as "less deserving" than other forms of racism (Zafer-Smith 2003: 104), however, is misleading[3]. Many media accounts focused on the withdrawal of delegates from 23 European Union countries attending the 2009 WCAR review conference, during a speech of then Iranian President Mahmoud Ahmadinejad—a figure infamous for having so dangerously referred to the Holocaust as a "myth,"[4] but one hardly representative of the majority of delegates to the United Nations event. Mary Robinson, presiding officer for the WCAR in Durban in 2001, and then UN high commissioner for Human Rights, acknowledged that this was a difficult conference (Robinson 2012), noting US withdrawal and charges of anti-Semitism. However, she also has noted that the United States withdrew before the deliberations were finalized, and that the final declaration was devoid of anti-Semitic language or meaning (Robinson 2012: 233–48).

Following the withdrawal of Western states, such as the United States and Canada, from the WCAR process, however, this charge of a "new anti-Semitism" was further embedded in various institutional forms. This is consistent with hegemonic assumptions of the Israel/Palestine racial contract. For example, in February 2009, the Interparliamentary Coalition for Combating Anti-Semitism (ICCA) was convened among international parliamentarians and government representatives in a conference in London, UK. The ICCA (2009) produced the "Declaration on Combating Anti-Semitism," calling on governments and the United Nations to resolve to "never again" be party to or witness of "another gathering like" the 2001 World Conference Against Racism, which was stated to include the "singling out of Israel for discriminatory treatment." Subsequently, the Canadian Parliamentary Coalition to Combat Antisemitism (CPCCA) (2009) was launched according to the same mandate. Canada, under the then minority government of Conservative Party leader Stephen Harper, was particularly aggressive in leading the international "challenge" to this apparently virulent form of racism

(Cairns and Ferguson 2011).[5] Despite official policies of multiculturalism, the Canadian government, and the Conservative Party in particular, in fact has a long and shamefully poor record regarding anti-racist politics (Dhamoon 2010; Stasiulis and Bakan 2005; Thobani 2007b). However, the wave of challenges is international, with ample examples of attacks on the legitimacy of those who attempt to criticize Israel's policies, and with the result being that they are faced with charges of anti-Semitism (Butler 2008, 2014; Finkelstein 2005; Mearsheimer and Walt 2007; Salaita 2015; Schiffer and Wagner 2011). Arguably, what in fact motivates the claim is an effort to silence challenges to the hegemonic idea of Israel's mythologized exceptionalism (see Nadeau and Sears 2011).

Included among those targeted with the charge of anti-Semitism are Jewish critics of Israeli state policy who are further labeled "self-hating." A discursive method that moves away from substance, regardless of agreement or disagreement, to a discrediting of the person is not commonly accepted in normal protocols associated with the higher goals of liberal democracy. This is indicative of standards formally associated with educational, legal, social, medical, and journalistic norms and practices, for example. However, when the issues are associated with race and racialization, another set of rules seems to come into play (Bakan and Dua 2014; Razack 1998, 2008, 2015). There is a curious legitimacy to the widespread acceptance of the charge of anti-Semitism when it is leveled by politically motivated defenders of the state of Israel, who may or may not be Jewish, against others who challenge Israel's policies and who are also Jewish. While the origins of this strangely accepted logic are not entirely obvious, some clues to its normative positioning are indicated in the epistemological foundations of modern Zionism, which is a political strategy or ideology rather than a marker of Jewish identity. Zionism is therefore distinct from Judaism, as a religion, or Jewishness, as a cultural identity. Uri Davis puts forward the same argument in different terms:

> Judaism is not Zionism. Judaism, as a confessional preference, should be strictly an individual matter, and generally speaking, like other individual preferences ... should not be the concern of the law. Zionism, a political programme, is a matter of public debate ... The political Zionist school of thought and practice is committed to the normative statement that it is a good idea to establish and consolidate in the country of Palestine a sovereign state, a Jewish state, that

> attempts to guarantee in law and in practice a demographic majority of the Jewish tribes in the territory under its control. (2003: 12)

Zionism is traceable as a modern political ideology to its founder, Theodore Herzl. Glenn Bowman identifies in Herzl's work two contesting, ideal types of Jews—one to be uplifted as a model that could overcome the prejudice of the European gentiles, and another to be reviled and essentially deserving of anti-Semitic disdain. The former is the "new Jew" of Zionist colonial settlement (originally with an indeterminate geographic location). Bowman summarizes Herzl's "discursive splitting of the Jew into two distinct personifications":

> One type of Jew, with which he identified, was the enlightened cosmopolitan who carried his Jewishness in the same way as an Austrian or a Frenchman bore his national origin—as an evident yet fundamentally irrelevant aspect of an all-round educated person deporting himself with grace and self-possession. The other Jew, whom he loathed and in whom he believed anti-Semites found the font of their stereotypes of the Jew, was the *Ostjude* ("Eastern Jew") who dwelled in and had been shaped by the ghetto. For Herzl, the ghetto Jew—isolated from participation in European national movements as well as from modernization and enlightenment—had developed a self-serving mentality focused on economic gain and manifest in an obsessive money hunger and a self-debasing humility behind which lurked a crafty arrogance. (2011: 68)

The specific genealogy of the charge of "self-hating Jew" for those who adopt a critical view of Zionism and the policies and practices of the state of Israel is unclear. However, the notion that there is a bifurcation of Jews—one group to be admired and advanced in the Zionist vision and another to be disdained and dismissed—is reflected in Herzl's original forwarding of political Zionism.

One of the most high-profile and public examples of the charge of "self-hating Jew" was expressed in the treatment of Hannah Arendt's (2006) journalistic analysis of the trial of Adolf Eichmann in 1962. The capture, kidnapping, and arrest of the Nazi administrator by the Israeli police secret service (agents of Mossad and Shin Bet), where he had been living and hiding in Argentina, was seen as a moral and political triumph for the still young Zionist government of the state of Israel. Eichmann had escaped from Germany to avoid facing charges at Nuremburg and was taken to Israel after his capture, tried by the Israeli court, and ultimately sentenced to death and hanged in 1962. Arendt, a Jewish survivor of the German Nazi Holocaust and living in the United States at the time, offered to cover the trial for *The New Yorker* magazine. In her coverage, she objected to the process of kidnap, maintaining that this was "a clear violation of international law" (Arendt 2006: 263). Moreover, she described the event as less about justice and more about the construction of a show trial by the Israeli government under Ben Gurion. Arendt maintained that the effort to present Eichmann as a central mastermind in the Holocaust was unfounded and that the evil manifest was less demonic than "banal," systemic in the Nazi political and industrial machine. In this system, she identified processes that involved a complex interconnection of race and power, including the cooperation under the Nazis of the "Jewish councils" (*Judenrate*) as both victims and victimizers. Moreover, Arendt identified a cynical attempt by the Zionist government of Israel to use the trial to shape the memory of the Holocaust as a crime against the "Jews," rather than a crime against "humanity," the latter of which she saw as the more accurate account initiated by the Nuremburg trials (Arendt 2006; Bakan 2014a).

The response to Arendt's analysis among leading Jewish Zionist writers was vitriolic. According to Arendt's biographer, Elisabeth Young-Bruehl, writing in 2004, such attacks continued in the press for "nearly three years, and it [i.e., the atmosphere of these attacks] continues to simmer even now when the book made from the articles is in its twentieth reprinting" (2004: 339). Arendt was referred to, significantly, as a "self-hating" Jew. In her clear and dignified reply, Arendt notes the particular attention leveled toward her identification of the role of the Jewish councils. Among certain reviewers, the alleged charges were that she had, in Arendt's words, "claimed that the Jews had murdered themselves. And why had I told such a monstrously implausible lie? Out of 'self-hatred', of course" (Arendt 2006: 284).

In a more recent discursive deconstruction of another Jewish academic, Jennifer Peto, a graduate of the University of Toronto's Ontario Institute for Studies in Education's (OISE) MA program, the charge of "self-hating" attracted national attention in Canada. While any further association between Peto and Arendt would, of course, be unfair to both scholars, it is significant that the charge continues to be used to discredit scholarly research on Israel and Zionism in contemporary circumstances.

Peto's thesis, "The Victimhood of the Powerful: White Jews, Zionism and the Racism of Hegemonic Holocaust Education," addresses, as the title suggests, the links between education about the Holocaust and the politics of Zionism.

As Nadeau and Sears summarize:

> In December 2010, Jenny Peto's Master's thesis at OISE was the topic of at least five articles or commentaries in the *National Post*, as well as discussion on the floor of the Ontario Legislature. The attention that Peto's work attracted was not in the form of a serious engagement with the thoughtful and provocative arguments she makes. It was simply another salvo in the ongoing silencing campaign aimed at shutting down criticism of Israel. (2011: np)

Regardless of the specific nature of the challenges, however, when academics encounter such an atmosphere when conducting scholarly research, it sends a message to others who might consider entering into the conversation. The Israel/Palestine racial contract is thereby perpetuated, enabling the hegemonic construction and further reproduction of the idea of Israel and the absenting of Palestine. This brings us to consider the nature of such absenting in more detail.

The absence of Palestine

> *There was no such thing as a Palestinian. When was there an independent Palestinian people with a Palestinian state? ... It was not as though there was a Palestinian people in Palestine considering itself as a Palestinian people and we came and threw them out and took their country away from them. They did not exist.*
>
> **—ISRAELI PRIME MINISTER GOLDA MEIR**[6]

The profound discursive absence of the Palestinians since 1948 is graphically illustrated by Prime Minister Golda Meir's insistence, in a leading British newspaper, that Palestinians did not "exist." Her 1969 statement, in effect, echoed the much earlier erasure of Palestine's Indigenous Arab (Christian and Muslim) population, contained in the infamous early Zionist motto calling for the settlement of Palestine since it was a "land without a people" (Zangwill 1901). Even today, it is notable that considerable energy is invested in attempts to sever Palestinian claims to the British mandatory geographic space of Palestine. This is perhaps most commonly encountered in the long-enduring suggestion, still popular among some Israeli politicians, that Jordan should be the homeland of the Palestinian people (Peter and Prusher 2009). This is a proposal rejected not only by Jordan (Peter and Prusher 2009) but by Palestinians themselves (Ryan and Hallaj 1983).

To be clear, through their oral as well as written histories, Palestinians have "established" not only their presence in Israel/Palestine from antiquity but also the ways in which their population self-identified as "Palestinian" in the nineteenth and early twentieth centuries, including, therefore, the period long before 1948 (Farsoun and Aruri 2006; Khalidi 2010). Additionally, for over a decade, a "post-Zionist" historiography has utilized archival documents made public in Israel to further evidence the militarized violence that produced and sustained the *Nakba* (Pappe 2007). This historiography challenges the official Israeli narrative of state founding, which, to paraphrase Golda Meir, holds that no one was "thrown out" but rather that the Palestinians voluntarily elected to depart. Not least, the work of the late Columbia University professor Edward Saïd, a literary scholar widely read across disciplines of the social sciences and humanities, powerfully illuminated the peoples and societies of the Middle East and Palestine and provided a means to understand their experiences in relation to human history and power differentials in the *lingua franca* of English (Abu-Laban 2001). This came out through Said's now-classic discussion of the relevance of Orientalism to colonialism, including the Zionist settler-colonial project in Palestine (1979a). It is also expressed in his work *The Question of Palestine*, which explicitly aimed to articulate for an American/Western audience "the Palestinian experience, which to all intents and purposes became a self-conscious experience when the first wave of Zionist colonialists reached the shores of Palestine in the early 1880s" (Said 1979b: ix).

Said's (1979b) account is premised on the geopolitical realities of occupation, exile, and absenting that generated Palestine's "non-existence" from 1948; nonetheless, he simultaneously reveals Palestine's relevance to the political imaginary and the experience of the Indigenous Arab population. This population was, and is, despite current assumptions of an Arab-equals-Muslim association, Christian and Muslim. Said recognized the difficulty of even finding ways to articulate Palestine as an experience, memory, or idea, especially in the West. In his words, "the sheer impossibility of finding a space in which to speak for the Palestinians is enormous; indeed, every statement on behalf of Israel intensifies and concentrates pressure on the Palestinian to be silent, to accept repression" (Said 1979b: 39–40). As Said put it, with a clarity that continues to resonate: "The fact of the matter is that today Palestine does not exist, except as a memory or, more importantly, as an idea, a political and human experience, and an act of sustained popular will" (1979b: 5).

The difficulty in speaking as, or in solidarity with, what might be bluntly called "the Palestinian voice," as well as the difficulty in hearing "the Palestinian voice," is one that we attribute to the Israel/Palestine racial contract. There are, of course, multiple and varied Palestinian voices, and the aim here is not to essentialize or to reduce these voices to a singular expression. However, in terms of Israel, Palestine, and the politics of race, there is a sustained, systemic, and hegemonic racialized process of discrimination, repression, and exclusion that generates a commonality of experience among Palestinians internationally, and across generations. It is the cumulative effect of these racialized processes, combined with the challenges inherent in even naming these processes as racialized, that sustains the absence of Palestine and the Palestinians. This is a central element in the Israel/Palestine racial contract, and it is inextricably linked to the idea of Israel.

The racialized processes that have led to the absenting of Palestine and Palestinians may be seen to stem from a number of factors. First among them is the physical absence of Palestinians from mandatory Palestine. The *Nakba* itself served to all but obliterate Palestinian society, since over half the people in what became Israel were made refugees outside of mandatory Palestine. The continued physical absence of Palestinians from the land remains, and today Palestinians make up one of the world's largest and oldest refugee populations.

Moreover, Palestinians are, collectively, the targets of extreme repression. Historian Ilan Pappe (2007) has described in detail the process of "the ethnic cleansing of Palestine" preceding Israel's establishment as a state in 1948. It was militarized repression that sustained the denial of return for Palestinians, despite the fact that as early as 1948, UN Resolution 194 called for the return of refugees. For the small minority of Palestinian Arabs who remained in the new state, they were and are treated as a perceived and permanent threat. As such, Palestinians in

Israel are the main objects of "emergency regulation," as well as a host of measures aimed to count their presence specifically in relation to the Jewish population—regulating their actions, movements, and ownership of land (see Zureik 2011). Indeed, Mahmoud Darwish, who was during his lifetime frequently referred to as Palestine's national poet, highlighted the militarized encounters that Arabs in Israel endured in his defiant 1964 poem titled "Identity Card." To quote its opening stanza:

Record!
I am an Arab
And my identity card is fifty thousand
I have eight children
And the ninth is coming after a summer
Will you be angry?

After the 1967 war, the Israeli military occupation of the West Bank, Gaza, and East Jerusalem furthered the means through which Palestinians experienced militarized repression. This included control over their land, resources, mobility, and daily activities—from education, to access to services, to travel and employment (Gordon 2008b). Since those under occupation lack Israeli citizenship, the racialized character of differential treatment is especially obvious. The first Intifada (which may be dated from 1987 to 1993) brought to the world the image of Palestinian youth resisting the Israeli military with nothing but stones. It was in this context that Hanan Ashrawi wrote her 1988 poem "From the Diary of an Almost-Four-Year-Old," based on the true story of a young child who, while standing on the balcony of her grandmother's house, lost an eye due to a rubber bullet fired by an Israeli soldier. As this incident was followed by infants also losing eyes in similar ways, the poem's powerful last stanza (Ashrawi [1988]: 341) shows the almost-four-year-old narrator musing:

I hear a nine-month old
has also lost an eye,
I wonder if my soldier
shot her too—a soldier
looking for little girls who
look him in the eye—

I'm old enough, almost four,
I've seen enough of life,
but she's just a baby
who didn't know any better

The Israel/Palestine racial contract relies on the absenting expressed graphically in such lived experiences. The violence against Palestinians that is embedded in Israeli state practices is perpetual, but also rendered invisible. This absenting is, however, politically and socially constructed; for Palestinians, the frustration in the absence of acknowledgment or redress generates the necessity of resistance, which takes multiple forms. Since the second Intifada (dating from 2000), the building of the separation wall has further compounded the racialized experience of Palestinians living under occupation. Although deemed to be in contravention of international law by the International Criminal Court, the wall—dubbed, significantly, the "apartheid wall"—has further restricted the mobility of Palestinians and, in many instances, access to their land, while further segmenting their experience in relation to Israeli Jewish settlers. As such, Palestinians living under Israeli occupation, as well as those who hold Israeli citizenship, experience discrimination as non-Jews by the Israeli state. For Palestinians outside of mandatory Palestine, their "right" of return has been continually denied.

Palestinians have faced unique challenges in being able to narrate their own history and experiences. The hegemonic Israel/Palestine racial contract is dependent upon the perpetuation of active processes to render Palestinians nonexistent. While attention to "ethnic" history has been important to the evolution of "ethnic studies" in both the United States and Canada, rendering the history of the Palestinians knowable continues to be a challenge. This is not only because stateless Palestinians have no national archive but also because refugees commonly lost their own private materials in the forced removal from Palestine during the *Nakba* (1947–9), and in other wars in the region (Khalidi 2006: xxxv). Thus, while the Israeli state and the Israel/Palestine racial contract have helped to articulate a particular history, fostering the idea of Israel's millennial ties to the "holy land," Palestinians, lacking a state, are denied a parallel ability to articulate their own history. Moreover, while there are many Palestinian writers, historians, and artists, such figures often face repressive conditions in presenting their works. This would include Palestinians in the diaspora. For example, consider the spurious attacks on Edward Said, who in life was charged with being a "Professor of Terror" because he was Palestinian, while simultaneously he was also accused of lying about his claim to Palestinian identity since he also spent time in Egypt as a child (for a response, see Shuraydi 2001). In short, the Israel/Palestine racial contract perpetuates conditions where Palestinians are materially and ideologically denied the cultural capital to systematically break through these attempts at silencing and delegitimization. In addition, those taking up the cause of Palestine solidarity can themselves face a unique climate of repression, not least within the academy (Abu-Laban and Bakan 2012b; Bakan and Abu-Laban 2016; Dawson and Mullen 2015; Nadeau and Sears 2011; Salaita 2015; Thompson 2011).

The Israel/Palestine racial contract is thus ideological as well as material. Another factor in the absenting process is quite literal, on the very ground of Israel/Palestine, where the Palestinians' historic presence has been subject to erasure through Israel's state-sponsored process of "Judaization" in policies relating to settlement, land, planning, and development (Yiftachel 2006). However, this has not prevented what many Palestinians experience as an appropriation of elements of Palestinian culture. This is indicated, for example, when North Americans or others outside the region come to associate the origins of such foods as falafel, hummus, and "Israeli couscous" with "Israel," or more broadly the "Middle East," rather than with "Palestine." In this way, the cultural erasure of Palestinians may be seen to occur, with different degrees of intensity, both inside and outside Israel/Palestine.

A final factor contributing to the absenting of Palestine in the Israel/Palestine racial contract is that Palestinians have been compelled to endure and defend themselves against a recurrent pattern of dehumanizing and derogatory imagery. This stems from a very particular interpretation and usage of biblical imagery in which modern Israel is identified as a "biblical land" or "holy land," and a solely and singularly "Israelite" identity of this land is deemed beyond assail (Masalha 2007: 310–11). Such imagery is furthered through the discourse ascribing Palestinians to be the world's premier "terrorists" since the time of the 1967 war. This linking of biblical interpretation, history, and contemporary politics is noted in David Theo Goldberg's discussion of racial states, wherein he observes:

> *Identified as the direct kin of biblical Philistines,* by the mid-twentieth century Palestinians as a people were often seen as Philistines as much in characterization as in scriptural name, conceived in the representational struggle as bloodthirsty and warmongering, constantly harassing modern-day Israelites, debauched and lacking altogether in liberal culture. *Terrorists, it seems, historically all the way down to the toenails of time. Goliath cut to size by David's perennial craftiness and military prowess.* (2009: 107–8; emphasis added)

In Goldberg's particular choice of phrasing around "direct kin," what is left out is that even if the word "Philistine" appears to be an etymological predecessor of the word "Palestine," there is no clear ethnic or hereditary connection between modern Palestinians and the ancient Agean "Sea People" known as the Philistines (Hare 2009; Masalha 2007: 99).[7] Moreover, any precise identification of "ethnic" boundaries among ancient cultures (Canaanites, Israelites, Philistines, etc.) has been argued to be "highly problematic and completely fictional in the critical period of 'Israelite origins' (Iron I Age)" (Masalha 2007: 255). Archeological evidence, in fact, suggests that the original inhabitants of Israel/Palestine (i.e., Mizrahi Jews, Palestinian Christians, and Palestinian Muslims) are products of the same shared Canaanite culture (Boyarin 2004; Qumsieh 2004; Sand 2009).

Still, that "Palestinians" and "Philistines" are so easily connected is significant in relation to racialization, which is at the heart of Goldberg's argument. In particular, as Masalha notes, the Philistines played the role of the archetypical enemy "other" in the story of the Israelites, and most emphatically in the story of David and Goliath, as Goldberg also suggests (Masalha 2007: 99). Indeed, in subtle ways, the biblical story of David and Goliath is continually repeated in the imagery surrounding discussions of Israel/Palestine. This may be seen in the oft-repeated phrasing of "little" Israel surrounded by "large" (and hostile) Arab states. More recently, Israel is claimed to be uniquely and unfairly "singled out" for human rights violations by ascribed "anti-Semitic" supporters of the WCAR process, or of the boycott, divestment, and sanctions (BDS) movement. Israel's mythologized exceptionalism as a claimed victim state is consistent with the hegemonic idea of Israel and the absenting of Palestine. To quote from Masalha, who in turn draws from the work of John McDonagh (2004):

> In the Bible the Philistines became the archetypical Other, whose sole function in the text was to plot the destruction of civilization, and whose activities provided justification for the expansion of the Israelites. The Philistines—not unlike the modern Palestinians—had become the Other as a result of the challenge they posed to the bourgeoning collective Hebrew identity, within the parameters established by the biblical narrative. The "ignorant" and "demonic" Philistines, then, fulfilled a role in the construction of the great colonial edifice of Otherness that was later to be played by, among others, Arabs and Muslims, Africans, Indians, Aboriginals, this role furthermore ironically played out to tragic effect by the Jews themselves over centuries of persecution in the West. (Masalha 2007: 99–100)

We see here a construction of the direct linkage of Palestinians and Philistines (however historically debatable) grounded in the fear of the enemy Other, in this case in Orientalized form.

This is a fear that feeds ideological justification for the repression of the Palestinians, who are perceived as entirely Muslim even if there is a sizable minority that is Christian. It also feeds an ideological justification for Israel's continued colonial rule, occupation, and operations outside the rule of international law. This brings us to consider in more detail the applicability of the racial contract framework regarding the Israel/Palestine context. This follows in the next chapter, which takes up national, international, and temporal contexts.

Notes

1 It is important to note that the land upon which present day Mexico, the United States and Canada are situated has been, and still is, referred to as "Turtle Island" by Indigenous peoples. This feature, along with deepening economic relations as a result of the North American Free Trade Agreement, changed under US President Donald Trump in 2018 as a United States-Mexico-Canada Agreement, has spawned understanding emphasizing that "North America" includes Mexico, the United States and Canada (see Abu-Laban, Jhappan, and Rocher 2008). Our focus here, however, is on the US and Canada specifically.

2 Danny Glover, "Race and the Obama Administration," *The Nation*, April 20, 2009, http://www.thenation.com/article/race-and-obama-administration.

3 African Canadian Legal Clinic et al., "Find out the Real Reason Canada Skipped out on UN Anti-Racism Gathering," *Rabble.ca*, April 27, 2009, http://www.rabble.ca/news/2009/04/find-out-real-reason-canada-skipped-out-un-anti-racism-gathering.

4 Michael J. Jordan, "Ahmadinejad Polarizes UN Racism Conference," *The Christian Science Monitor*, April 20, 2009, https://www.csmonitor.com/World/2009/0420/p06s07-wogn.html.

5 Scott Maniquet, "Excerpt: Harper's Speech on Israel, Anti-Semitism," *National Post*, November 8, 2010, http://news.nationalpost.com/2010/11/08/excerpt-harpers-speech-on-israel-anti-semitism/.

6 Frank Giles, "Interview with Golda Meir," *The Sunday Times*, June 15, 1969.

7 Amiran Barkat, "Dig Backs Biblical Account of Philistine City of Gat," *Haaretz*, August 5, 2009, http://www.haaretz.com/culture/arts-leisure/dig-backs-biblical-account-of-philistine-city-of-gat-1.166315; *Seattle Times*, "Two Peoples, One Land: Understanding the Israeli-Palestinian Conflict," May 12, 2002, http://old.seattletimes.com/news/nation-world/mideast/roots/.

2 THE RACIAL CONTRACT AND ISRAEL/PALESTINE

Introducing the racial contract

It is impossible to avoid the realities of race and racism as part of the fabric of international political economy, not least after the events of 9/11 (Frankenberg 2005). The "war on terror" that animated the US administration of George W. Bush in 2001 resonated in Canada, especially under a federal government led by staunch conservative (lower case "c") and Conservative (upper case "c"; the name of the then governing political party) Prime Minister Stephen Harper. Bush and allies like Harper (as well as those in Canada's Liberal Party in the 2000s) implicitly lent greater institutional legitimacy to racial profiling, and simultaneously politicized and racialized the borders of every country, including that which divides the United States and Canada (Abu-Laban 2004; Bakan 2005b). While there have been changes in administrative styles in the United States under Presidents Barack Obama (2009–17) and Donald Trump (inaugurated in 2017), and in Canada under Liberal Prime Minister Justin Trudeau (elected in 2015), the racialized security regimes associated with the post-9/11 era have remained institutionally entrenched (Perera and Razack 2014).

Despite the pervasiveness of race and racism as an integral element of state policies and practices, the analytical tools on offer in both mainstream scholarly and public discourses have tended to minimize the realities of racialization. Instead, global relations in the twenty-first century have often been reduced to Samuel Huntington's "clash of civilizations," where race and culture are rendered synonymous and are also obscured in racialized stereotypes associated with the language of "culture" (see Huntington 1996; for critiques, see Arat-Koç 2014; Nath,

Tungohan, and Gaucher 2018). Moreover, the Israel/Palestine conflict, though significantly pre-dating 9/11, has become subsumed in post-9/11 ideological and political framings.

It is in this context that the analytical framework suggested originally in Charles W. Mills' *The Racial Contract* (1997) is particularly helpful. Rather than identifying racism and racialization as exceptional interruptions in an otherwise race-neutral polity of democratic liberalism, Mills maintains that systemic racism is embedded in the fabric of Western society. More pointedly, Mills theorizes the entrenchment of "white supremacy," identifying this as an "unnamed political system that has made the modern world what it is today" (1997: 1). As indicated in the previous chapter, the study of "race" has been unevenly taken up across disciplines of the modern academy. It has also served as an unclear and confusing topic of discussion in what Antonio Gramsci would call the "common sense" ideologies in civil and political society (Gramsci 1971; Hall 1986; Herman and Chomsky 1988). In light of this complex and unclear terrain in the mainstream and multisited conversations attending to race and racism, the theory of the racial contract marks a significant contribution. It serves to underscore how "races" come into existence and change, and how they are continually socially and politically reconstructed through a series of formal and informal agreements between those defined as white and those defined as nonwhite.

In this chapter, we consider how the work of Charles Mills is useful in focusing on the fraught context of Israel/Palestine and its interface with other states, in particular Canada. Reference to Canada offers a unique vantage point for advancing the idea of a racial contract, because of the country's strong formal commitment to human rights. Notably, it was Canadian John Humphrey who drafted the 1948 United Nations Universal Declaration of Human Rights. After the Second World War, the Canadian state embraced the claimed status of "helpful fixer" in the international political economy, and multiculturalism has been an official national policy since 1971. The former was furthered through an ideological commitment of Canada as a "peacekeeper," which retained popular saliency despite the former Harper Conservative government's elevation of military history and war victory in public institutions, ceremonies, and commemorations (Abu-Laban 2014). In fact, the Israel/Palestine racial contract is relevant in the enduring Canadian peacekeeper trope because Canada emerged in the modern era as the generator of official international state "peacekeeping" where relations with the United Nations and the Middle East were central to the project (Freeman-Maloy 2016).

In light of the centrality of the Middle East to Canada's foreign policy image, the relevance of attending to the Israel/Palestine racial contract in relation to Canada is clear. At the same time, Canada is far from an obvious case for contemplating racism or racialization. For Mills, it is precisely the lack of explicit, or obvious, attention to racism in liberal democratic theory that compels the argument of the racial contract. To demonstrate the salience of the racial contract in the context of Israel/Palestine, we proceed in four parts. First, we address how the racial contract is a useful analytical tool that can contribute to a better understanding of the contemporary internal dynamics of countries formed as settler colonies, as well as international politics. Second, following from this general discussion, we turn to address how concepts such as anti-Judaism, Orientalism, and anti-Semitism are key historic components of the racial contract in Canada and internationally. Third, we consider the Israel/Palestine racial contract specifically, indicating how it has defined the state of Israel since 1948, which posits the nonidentity of Palestinians while asserting the democratic contractarian nature of an Israeli state grounded in "Jewish nationality." This is effectively, however, a noncontractarian, or nonegalitarian, relationship, one that is not based on consent but on coercion through force, exile, occupation, and imprisonment. Since 1948, this pattern has been blurred through the establishment of an international Israel/Palestine racial contract that assigns a common interest between the state of Israel and international political allies, including Canada, while absenting Palestinians simultaneously as nonwhite, the subjects of extreme repression, and stateless. This feature is addressed in the fourth part of the chapter, which considers a series of United Nations votes and accords. We argue that in order to understand these varied dimensions, the racialization of categories commonly considered to be race neutral—including citizenship, religion, and democracy—must be explicitly recognized as part of the continued exercise and reproduction of state power, imperialism, and an ideological privileging of a constructed and hegemonic whiteness (Bakan 2014b).

Our aims are to understand the significance of thinking about the racial contract in addressing Israel/Palestine and to bring Canada's racial contract with Israel into the purview of anti-racist analysis. This approach is consistent with a growing literature that attempts to explain the linkages among race, class, political economy, imperialism, colonialism, hegemony, and ideology (Abu-Laban 2005; Abu-Laban and Gabriel 2002; Bakan 2014b; Bakan and Dua 2014; Bakan and Stasiulis 1997; Bannerji 1993, 1995, 2000; Baum 2006; Bolaria and Li 1988; Bristow et al. 1994; G. E. Clarke 2006; Cooper 2005; Galabuzi 2005; Henry et al. 1995; Henry and Tator 2002; James 1989; Lawrence 2004; McKittrick 2006; Mills 1997; Razack 1998, 2002, 2004, 2015; Roediger 2007; Said 1979a; Stasiulis and Bakan 2005; Williams 1944). We believe that a perspective that is anti-racist legitimately challenges Zionism—as an ideology that has supported the practices of Israel as a settler state—but is in no way grounded in a view that renders any legitimacy to anti-Semitism (anti-Jewish racism). Similarly, analyses that identify the ethnicized "whiteness" of the Israeli state and put forward analogies with the apartheid state of pre-1994 South Africa are consistent with such an anti-racist perspective (an argument developed more fully in Chapter 9) (Carter 2006; Cook 2006; Davis 2003; Finkelstein 2003b; Karmi 2007; Neumann 2005; Pappe 2007; Rodinson 1973; Tilley 2005b).

The racial contract as a category of analysis

Charles Mills' work *The Racial Contract* takes as its starting point the way that the discipline of philosophy has been, both demographically and conceptually, one of the "whitest" of the humanities (1997: 2). As such, Mills argues that much work in the discipline cannot adequately deal with the contributions of Indigenous, African American, Third World, and Fourth World (stateless) political thinkers (1997: 3). Mills offers the "racial contract" with its emphasis on social contract theory—which grounds the core set of assumptions regarding individual and group relations in liberal democratic thought—as a way to conceptually bridge mainstream political ethics and philosophy. He also suggests the value of more critical work that explicitly takes up themes such as history, conquest, slavery, colonialism, imperialism, apartheid, and reparations (1997: 4). For Mills, the racial contract is not a contract between individuals who are equal, as presumed in the social contract, but rather a contract between those who count. The latter is a difference that he expresses succinctly in distinguishing the phrase "we the people" from "we the white people" (1997: 3). As such, the racial contract is both a "nonideal" theory and a way of explaining the genesis of state and society with the aim of generating criticism. In Mills' words:

> If the ideal contract is to be endorsed and emulated, this nonideal/naturalized contract is to be demystified and condemned. So the point of analyzing the nonideal contract is not to ratify it but to use it to explain and expose the inequities of the actual nonideal polity and to help us to see through the theories and moral justifications offered in defence of them. It gives us a kind of X-ray vision into the real internal logic of the sociopolitical system. Thus it does normative work for us not through its own values, which are detestable, but by enabling us to understand the polity's actual history and how these values and concepts have functioned to rationalize oppression, so as to reform them. (1997: 5–6)

For Mills, then, "the modern world was … expressly created [through contracts over slavery, colonialism, and the like] as a *racially hierarchical* polity, globally dominated by Europeans" (1997: 27; emphasis original). In essence, Mills offers a way to grapple with "race" in Western societies and modernity, by showing how nonwhites have been subordinated. *The Racial Contract* is a work of philosophy forwarding a way of thinking through and analyzing relationships, not one of political science intended to describe concrete state processes. It does not, therefore, offer a theory of how particular groups come to be categorized or outline the abundance of categories that might be constructed. Understandably, Mills acknowledges that the "white/nonwhite divide does not fully deal with 'borderline' Europeans, white people with a question mark—the Irish, Slavs, Mediterraneans, and above all, of course, Jews" (1997: 78–9). Similarly, he also notes that "other subordinate Racial Contracts exist which do not involve white/nonwhite relations" (1997: 127). In the end, however, Mills maintains that the white/nonwhite dichotomy carries a simplicity that is all the more important because "*Whiteness is not really a color at all, but a set of power relations*" (1997: 127; emphasis original).

With these provisos, Mills' foundational work does provoke, we suggest, a series of important questions when we move to consider particular states and the international arena. There is now an extensive literature in the area of critical whiteness studies, and there is room to debate the specific nature of the relationships among race, class, gender, and state power in advanced capitalist societies and within global relations (Allen 1994, 1997; Bakan 2008a; Bakan and Dua 2014; Baum 2006; Galabuzi 2007; Hale 1998; Roediger 2007, 2017). In this context, Mills' contribution compels questions that explore racialized contractual relations that have become embedded in the hegemonic liberal capitalist project of Western ruling elites and between such elites and other regions and states. Such a perspective can explain the way in which racism, though formally illegal and in violation of commonly accepted principles of human rights, continues to be systemic, perpetuated, and reproduced in conditions of modern democracies. As a category of analysis, therefore, the notion of the racial contract can usefully serve to focus attention on the intersections of state power and systemic racism that would otherwise escape critical, analytical scrutiny.

Two states that are the subject of our investigation here are particularly prone to escaping such analysis: Canada and Israel. Indeed, Canada became notably distinguished internationally for its uniquely uncritical relationship to the Israeli state during the administrations of Conservative Prime Minister Stephen Harper (2006–15) (Freeman-Maloy 2016). This is expressed in a government-sponsored promotional video shared on YouTube titled "Through Fire and Water," in which then Prime Minister Harper's visit to the Israeli Knesset, on January 20, 2014, is featured.[1] The 2015 Canadian election of a Liberal Party government brought notable changes in many areas by unseating the previous Conservative government. These included a focus on gender and Indigenous and minority representation in the cabinet, a commitment to the rights of same-sex couples, and a policy of welcoming significant numbers of Syrian refugees.[2] However, importantly, the exceptionally uncritical foreign policy vis-à-vis Israel has remained consistent between the two governments of Harper and Trudeau.[3]

A specifically Israel/Palestine racial contract is starkly revealed in considering this relationship. Canada is commonly seen as race-neutral space, a state founded in the afterglow of the "rescue" of fugitive Black slaves from the United States in a mythologized ideological legacy of the Underground Railroad (Bakan 2008a; McKittrick 2006; McKittrick and Woods 2007). Canada's establishment as a white settler state, though well documented, continues to be obscured in this widely accepted notion of democratic neutrality (Baum 2006; McKittrick 2006; Razack 2004; Stasiulis and Yuval-Davis 1995). Israel is a state established on the grounds of separate citizenship for those defined as "Jewish," who in turn receive privileged status on the basis of a legally defined ethnic-religious identity.

Israel's version of modernity therefore fuses theology and politics. It has commonly been seen as a uniquely democratic nation in the Middle East, even though post-Enlightenment democratic traditions have emphasized the separation of religion and the state. More specifically, even though the Israeli state has no record of equality in relation to Palestinians or even Palestinian Israelis, academic scholars have "explained" this contradiction by employing the qualifier of "ethnic democracy" (Smooha 1997; for a critique, see Sa'di 2000).

It is useful to consider an amended and specific notion of a racial contract to unpack the normalized conditions of racism in both Canada and Israel, where the settler character of each state has been obscured. This is one that draws upon a neo-Gramscian notion of hegemony, where a dominant set of ideas and related practices are elemental to state rule in capitalist societies. This dominance, while advancing the interests of the minority ruling elite, is contradictory in that it is enforced not only through coercion but also by consent, and is relevant to both national and international political governance (Germain and Kenny 1998; Gill 1993; Gramsci 1971). In this perspective, racial contracts are endemic to the hegemonic state projects of capitalist elites and have extended across nationally defined borders to construct a type of international racial contract where there is an assumed commonality of interests between states. The specific Israel/Palestine racial contract is an example of this.

Taking the Canadian and Israeli states as examples of the Israel/Palestine racial contract demonstrates the process, noting the recent history over the twenty-first century. Canada was the first state to cut off aid to the democratically elected government of the Palestinian Authority in the Occupied Territories in March of 2006. During Israel's war on Lebanon in July of the same year, Prime Minister Stephen Harper identified Israel's violent response as "measured," while the actions of Hezbollah were termed "genocidal" (Weiss 2007). In January 2008, Canada distinguished itself as the sole country to vote against a resolution of the United Nations Human Rights Council (UNHRC), calling for Israel to "lift immediately the siege that it has imposed on the occupied Gaza Strip, restore continued supply of fuel, food and medicine and reopen the border crossings," and for the "immediate protection of the Palestinian civilians in the Occupied Palestinian Territory in compliance with human rights law and international humanitarian law and to refrain from violence against the civilian population" (UNHRC 2008). In the same month, Jason Kenney, then the Conservative government's secretary of state for multiculturalism, announced that Canada would decline participation in the second United Nations World Conference on Racism, Racial Discrimination, Xenophobia and Related Intolerance (UN WCAR), scheduled to take place in Geneva, Switzerland, in 2009. The grounds for the refusal to participate were related to criticisms of Israel in the first UN WCAR, held in Durban, South Africa, in 2001. These discussions were identified by Kenney as "a circus for intolerance and bigotry" that was particularly "directed at the Jewish people."[4] And, in March 2008, the Department of Public Safety and Emergency Preparedness of Canada signed a "Declaration of Intent" with the Ministry of Public Security of the Government of the State of Israel. The two governments agreed to prioritize and "manage cooperation" in several sectors, including border management and "security," correctional services and prisons, illegal immigration, and "terrorist financing." The two governments further agreed to establish a joint "Management Committee," which would monitor the exchange of information and expertise and establish "clear lines of communication" in pursuit of "common goals."[5] And, Canada has distinguished itself internationally as among the most aggressive in repressing freedom of expression for the boycott, divestment, and sanctions movement.[6] This list, while not exhaustive, illustrates a persistent pattern of increasingly close relations between Canada and Israel in the post-9/11 period (Abu-Laban and Bakan).

While criticisms of its racist practices are readily dismissed by governments such as Canada's, Israel continues to act in defiance of international law and the standard human rights norms associated with liberal democracies. At the same time, the hegemonic discourse associated with the racial contract serves to deny the reality and applicability of critical notions of racism; it marginalizes or silences discussions grounded in critical anti-racism of Israel's role in the Israel/Palestine conflict. Instead, such critical views are challenged by a hegemonic discourse that adopts a select anti-racist narrative based on charges of anti-Semitism, or anti-Jewish racism, calling attention to the historic oppression of Jews in Eastern Europe and Nazi Germany.

The claim commonly presented is a Zionist response, where a state in the land of Palestine is described as the only viable and permanent antidote to European and global anti-Semitism. The combination of a highlighted emphasis on the experience of European racism toward the Jewish population with a minimization or absenting of Israel's apartheid-like and settler-colonial structure has tended to diminish the level of scholarly and public discourse regarding the racialization of Palestine and the Palestinians.

The Israel/Palestine racial contract is, however, unstable and subject to challenge. A politics of anti-racist opposition to Israel's oppressive policies has been introduced through analogies with the apartheid system of pre-1994 South Africa. Analyses that follow from such an analogy identify the ethnicized "whiteness" of the Israeli state and are consistent, moreover, with a more universalistic anti-racist perspective that challenges both anti-Semitism and anti-Arab racism (Carter 2006; Cook 2006; Davis 2003; Ferguson 2007; Finkelstein 2003b; Karmi 2007; Neumann 2005; Pappe 2007; Rodinson 1973; Tilley 2005a, 2005b).

The Israel/Palestine racial contract is therefore an arena of intense, ongoing contestation. However, the assertion of a tight association between the state of Israel and the interests of all Jewish people, inside Israel and in every country of the world, inhibits constructive exchange among scholars and activists alike. The Zionist response has rendered the racialized whiteness and apartheid character of the Israeli state the subject of a fraught and emotionally charged atmosphere. The emphasis placed here on the racial contract between Canada and Israel is suggested as a means to normalize scholarly critical discourse. We also intend to shine a light on the conditions and rights of the Indigenous Palestinian population within the boundaries of Israel proper, in the Occupied Territories, and in the Palestinian diaspora. Such an analysis is consistent with a growing field of scholarship that is premised on recognition of the capitalist and racist character of the Canadian state, contrary to the mythologized image of a race-neutral and multicultural "peacekeeper" (Engler and Fenton 2005; Kellogg 2004, 2005, 2015; Razack 1998, 2002, 2004).

This general formulation we present is, in broad strokes, perhaps rather obvious. The relationship between Israel and the Palestinian population is not dissimilar from many settler-colonial experiences, where conquest, war, occupation, legislated discrimination, and the systemic violation of human rights have been endemic to the structure of the state and civil society. For those who have studied the realities of the region from a critical anti-racist or Marxist perspective, there is no room to maintain that this is a conflict of two equal and equivalent "sides." It is complicated, however—as referred to above—by historic forms of racialization, as well as the particular racialized character of the Israeli state.

The history of the Nazi Holocaust and the decades of experience of anti-Semitism in Europe create another dimension to our understanding of the role of an Israel/Palestine racial contract and its place in global politics. Following from Mills' analysis, the Jewish population of Germany and Eastern Europe were clearly racialized and scapegoated on the basis of assigned phenotypical characteristics and the nonwhite victims of the Tsarist and Nazi regimes. Moreover, liberal democratic reforms in Western Europe, the United States, and Canada did not moderate such racialization, as indicated starkly by the uniform rejection of the claims of Jewish refugees for asylum in the face of threatened genocide. Over this period of time, Jews in the United States and Canada, for example, clearly were "less than white" (Brodkin 1998: 23; also see Abella and Troper 2012; Bakan 2014a). But this pattern is not a static one. In liberal democracies, from the post–Second World War period through to the present, a notable and dramatic transition in the socioeconomic and racial positioning of Jewish citizens is traceable. Jewishness—as a cultural and ethnic identity distinct from a religious identity with Judaism—in liberal democracies (and here we are not including Israel) rests in a position of unstable and non-Christian whiteness (Brodkin 1998; Goldstein 2006; Levine-Rasky 2007). The association of whiteness with hegemonic power structures includes not only domestic socioeconomic positioning but also changes in Western foreign policy and new renditions of Orientalism (Said 1979a). The historic experiences of anti-Jewish oppression and racialized patterns of discrimination in Europe and North America have been artificially used in part to justify Western imperialist foreign policy in the Middle East (Finkelstein 2000). The Israel/Palestine racial contract therefore influences, and has been influenced by, discourse regarding racism and anti-racism, both domestically and internationally.

The relationship between Zionism and anti-racism has thus become complicated by these conflations and is central to the hegemony of the Israel/Palestine racial contract as well as to contestations of this hegemony. Modern Zionism developed in close association and identification with colonialism and imperialist expansion. Zionism is therefore a nationalist ideology, but it is simultaneously a conservative ideological response to European anti-Semitism. The claim that Israel is an exclusively and ethnically defined "Jewish state," even in an age of ostensibly enlightened Western secularism, has arisen in the context of extensive, strategic geopolitical interests in the non-Western Middle East. Through this process, Zionism—a political strategy and response against anti-Semitism through the construction of an ethnically defined and exclusively "Jewish" modern capitalist national state—has moved from a marginal view to one that is hegemonic in global politics. Concomitantly, Zionism has become falsely identified as equivalent to, and has been conflated with, Jewish identity and Judaism (Hertzberg 1997; and from a critical perspective, see Bakan 2014a; Cook 2006; Finkelstein 2000, 2003b, 2005; Rose 2004; Said 1992). Further, the mythologized notion of a Jewish "return" to a land that was far from unpopulated was grounded in the parallel myth of an absented Palestinian reality. The forced removal, punishment, and occupation of the Indigenous Palestinian population in the aftermath of the Second World War (Pappe 2007; Siegel 1986) has coincided with an unstable and tenuous "whitening" of the Jewish population in the West. The road to "whiteness" for ethnically defined "Jews" has been associated with an assumption of an ideological acceptance of Zionism and a related uncritical stance toward the state of Israel, including its origin, historical claims, and domestic and international politics and linkages. It has also ascribed Jewish nationality in the state of Israel to those who reside anywhere in the world, while Indigenous Palestinians are displaced and denied the right to return.

Unpacking these various constructed conflations demands a critical approach drawing on a Gramscian understanding of states, power, and hegemony in connection with patterns of racialization. Following from Charles Mills' work in *The Racial Contract* and using our own understanding that "race" is socially produced and historically variable, in what follows we explain in more detail the Israel/Palestine racial contract. We employ the idea of the racial contract, and its particular categorization of white and nonwhite, as an analytical category for understanding relations of state and power in Israel/Palestine and its European and global dimensions, both historically and today.

Situating the "questions": The rise of the racial contract

We situate our understanding of the emergence of "the Jewish question" as well as "the question of Palestine" in relation to the rise of a European-based racial contract, which drew from preexisting strains of anti-Judaism and Orientalism and had far-reaching consequences both in and outside of Europe. As Bruce Baum has pointed out, the idea of "the Caucasian race" (and its more informal popular offshoot, "white") is socially constructed, historically specific, and the product of specific relations of power (2006: 7–8). Emerging from the seventeenth century and becoming more firmly rooted in the eighteenth century, European race scientists (and race-thinking) variously distinguished "white" (European) people from "nonwhite" (non-European) people in a hierarchical way. Dividing humanity into imaginary "races" not only was a process intimately tied to nationalism but also served to sustain the real inequities produced through capitalism, colonialism, and imperialism. Put differently, race-thinking helped to justify the perception of "white" privilege in economic, cultural, and political spheres within countries of Europe and globally. Whether or not such perceptions of privilege coincided with real material advantage, or in fact served to cover for material disadvantage, was variable and contingent, depending on specific historical circumstances (Bakan 2008b).

By the eighteenth century, in the very "era when European peoples were increasingly rallying behind new liberal and egalitarian ideas concerning 'the rights of Man,'" pseudoscientific discourses on race asserted that there were "natural (i.e. racial) limits to which peoples were suited for freedom and equality" (Baum 2006: 59). Such hierarchical thinking about the world's people clearly expressed the ideological justification for colonialism and was closely connected to the European expansion of Atlantic slavery (Bakan 1987; Blackburn 1997; Robinson 2000, 9–24). Colonialism was "literally" represented in Rudyard Kipling's famous 1899 poem about the "white man's burden." Colonialism was materially represented in the complex privileges (and denial of privileges) ascribed by virtue of race, ethnicity, gender, and class in the formation of settler colonies (Stasiulis and Yuval-Davis 1995). Thus, for example, the historic project of modeling Canada after Britain politically, economically, culturally, socially, and demographically as a white settler colony frequently led to prohibiting the entry of "non-white" groups, and to assimilative and discriminatory measures directed at Indigenous peoples and other "non-whites" (Stasiulis and Jhappan 1995).

To understand the distinctive character of discourses animating "the Jewish and Palestine questions," it is important to note that the development of modern scientific racism in Europe meshed with earlier, or premodern, ideas. A central one, as argued by Harle (2000), was the idea of "the enemy" rooted in Western conceptions of "good" versus "evil." As a result, for example, anti-Judaism was prevalent in the ancient world, and when Christianity became Rome's official religion, Jews were prohibited from marrying Christians and owning property (Harle 2000: 63). Myths reached a new level from the time of the first Crusade, when "Jews were presented as children of the Devil, agents employed by Satan for the express purpose of harming Christians" (Harle 2000: 63). Moreover, Muslims, as pointed out by Said in his classic discussion of Orientalism, served from the time of the Crusades as "Europe's Other" (1979a). As Harle also notes, Muslims formed the quintessential foe:

> The religious and political patterns of Enemy thinking were strengthened by historical experiences. Among the enemies that have threatened Europe and against which Europe has fought, the Arabs have kept the major place—together with their religion, Islam. Due to this religious nature of the threat, we can speak of Muslims as the Enemy of Europe. Their role is connected to a more general role of the Orient; therefore we have a rather long tradition here. (2000: 67)

Given the interrelationship between the rise of race-thinking and imperial power, as Arabs and Jews came to be depicted as "Semites" in many "race" classifications, it is notable that they were variably placed both as a branch of and as completely outside of the "Caucasian race" (Baum 2006: 113, 133). Questioning the "Caucasian identity" of Jews grew as anti-Semitism (here meaning the belief in the specifically racial inferiority of Jews, or anti-Jewish racism) deepened in Europe in the nineteenth and early twentieth centuries (Baum 2006: 154–61). Similarly, the tendency to view Arabs/Muslims as biologically inferior increased with the rise of imperialism and the subjugation of ostensibly "backward" races, cultures, and societies (Said 1979a: 206). In this way, adherence to Islam, even apart from a perception of ascribed "dark skin," emerged as a critical marker of nonwhiteness (Massad 1993: 108).

The globalizing context of imperialism and colonialism as well as the deepening of nationalism and persecution of Jews in Europe—from the pogroms of the 1880s to the infamous 1894 Dreyfus trial in France to the forgery of the Protocols of the Elders of Zion—form the backdrop to the emergence of political, or modern, Zionism, as noted a Jewish nationalist movement originally inspired by Theodor Herzl (1988). Although the nationalist project may have conceivably taken different forms, after Herzl convened the first World Zionist Congress in Switzerland in 1897, it was clear that land acquisition and settlement—in particular securing a state in historic Palestine, then under Ottoman control—would emerge as the ultimate goal (John and Hadawi 1970: 1).

While the Zionist movement was a response specifically to anti-Semitism and its violence in the context of Europe (Khalidi 1985: 37), the movement initially did not have more than minimal support among European Jews. Some European Jews saw Zionism's overt political agenda as incompatible with religious and/or spiritual practice; others saw it as further threatening their precarious status in the countries in which they lived (Mallison 1971: 61; Rabkin 2006). Alternative strategic and political responses to anti-Semitism were much more influential, including socialist organizations such as the Bund, the Mensheviks, and the Bolsheviks (Bakan 2014a; Rose 2004). Zionism also failed to garner the mass support of Jews living outside Europe in Palestine, at the time less than 10 percent of the population (Chomsky 1982: 461). Nonetheless, the Zionist movement came to synergize with European, and specifically British, race-thinking and colonial aspirations over those deemed less worthy to form part of state and ruling-class ideology. Consider, for example, the 1903 "offer" by the British government of the Jewish settlement in East Africa. While this proposed option was ultimately rejected, it was not passed over without debate between Theodor Herzl and his eventual successor, Chaim Weizmann (Mallison 1971: 63). Moreover, Arthur James Balfour, who, as British foreign secretary, penned the 1917 letter that came to be known as the Balfour Declaration, promised "the establishment in Palestine of a national home for the Jewish people," and he was himself "uncomfortable" with the place of Jews within British (Christian) society (Stein 1961: 165). Underscoring this discomfort, in 1905, as British prime minister, Balfour enacted immigration laws aimed to curb the entrance of Jews, who were deemed "undesirable foreigners" (Tibawi 1978: 1).

Zionism as a political movement was not monolithic in the early years of the twentieth century (Habib 2004: 27–28). However, the Zionist movement did coalesce ultimately around the particular claim to Palestine based on ostensible historical and/or religious interpretations (as in "a chosen land for a chosen people") that served to make the Indigenous Muslim and Christian Arabs in Palestine, and their claims, invisible. Their invisibility as human beings and as political and social claims-makers in the Zionist imaginary was perhaps most graphically exemplified in various phrasings of the well-known refrain of "a land without a people for a people without a land." There is some debate concerning the attribution of the original phrase, as well as the extent to which this phrasing was believed literally among early Zionists (Garfinkle 1991). It remains, however, fair to say that British-born playwright Israel Zangwill was instrumental in originating the phrase in the early 1900s (Garfinkle 1991: 540). Moreover, just as Zangwill was important to popularizing the idea of the United States as a "melting pot," even if it was not always taken literally in the context of vexed politics about race and immigration in America (Abu-Laban and Lamont 1997), he was also instrumental in popularizing the idea that Palestine's Indigenous population could be discounted. As Hani Faris (1975: 81) notes of Zangwill's article in the December 1901 issue of the British publication *New Liberal Review*:

> Zangwill claimed in his article "The Return of Palestine," written in 1901, that the country had "remained comparatively empty for eighteen hundred years," that its land was unexploited, and that at the time the country was without a people, waiting for a people without a land.

In its European roots and in its erasure of Indigenous people, Zionism can be understood as an ideology associated with a settler-colonial movement, and the state of Israel as a settler colony akin to South Africa (Abu-Lughod and Abu-Laban 1974a; Khalidi 2010; Rodinson 1973; Said 1992) or other settler colonies, such as Canada, the United States, New Zealand, and Australia (Stasiulis and Yuval-Davis 1995). The European Zionist tradition also notably treated Palestinian Arabs in classically Orientalist fashion. Thus, Herzl himself spoke critically of Palestine's "dirty Arabs," as well as "blackened Arab villages whose inhabitants looked like brigands"; and Chaim Weizmann spoke of "the desert" (i.e., Arabs) "against civilization" (i.e., European Jews) (Massad 1993: 101–2). Through the assertion of Zionism, it could be understood that the less-than-white Jewish victims of anti-Semitism could assert a bridge to whiteness, if they identified with European global hegemony, Orientalism, and colonial settlement of coveted lands in the global South. An alternative anti-racist strategy grounded in challenging imperialism and colonial structures, and in forging bonds of solidarity with non-Jewish allies in the workers' and socialist movements, initially proved more attractive to the largely poor and working-class Jewish European population and continued to inspire a secular Jewish tradition (Reiter 2016; Riddell 1993: 282–91).

The Zionist nationalist project and the Balfour Declaration, in particular, were also to be countered by Arab nationalism. The exact date of emergence of the Arab nationalist movement can be debated, but certainly by the early 1900s, there were strong sentiments in favor of empowering all Arabs, regardless of religion, to stave off foreign domination. These aspirations for self-rule are reflected in the correspondence (from July 14, 1915) between Sherif Hussein from Mecca and Sir Henry McMahon, the British high commissioner for Egypt. Hussein offered to assist the British Empire in its war effort against Turkey with the expectation that the British would acknowledge the independence of the Arab countries, which included the area of Palestine (John and Hadawi 1970: 35–52).

The Balfour Declaration was intentionally vague, giving some recognition to the majority of "existing non-Jewish communities in Palestine" and their "civil and religious rights," but failing to endorse the principle of national self-determination. This did not stop the Balfour Declaration from acquiring approval from the League of Nations, including Canada (at that time as Britain's Dominion). After the First World War, the text was incorporated into the British Mandate for Palestine, now freed from Ottoman rule. In light of the British government's ambiguity as reflected in the Balfour Declaration and the Hussein–McMahon correspondence, it is sometimes said that Palestine was the "twice promised land." That Britain was in a position to "promise" (or not) had much to do with colonialism and the whiteness associated with state power in and outside Europe; this was power that left those outside—Arab Muslims, Arab Christians, and Jews—ultimately pitted against each other.

Until 1939, the British Mandate was marked by increasing Jewish immigration to Palestine, a practice that garnered support from Zionists and signaled the beginnings of a demographic transformation. Throughout the mandatory period, Arab-Palestinian resistance to British colonial rule continued, taking the form of strikes, demonstrations, and sporadic violent clashes (Swedenburg 2003). By May 1939, the British government issued a White Paper (report), restating, with an aim of clarifying, its policy on Palestine. The White Paper refuted the basic interpretation previously established in the Balfour Declaration, arguing that the framers of the mandate "could not have intended that Palestine should be converted into a Jewish state against the will of the Arab population of the country" (Britain 1939). Additionally, it called for a decrease in Jewish immigration and an independent state in Palestine for both Arabs and Jews. After the issuing of the White Paper, Zionist groups began to militarily resist the British. However, the horrendous conditions in Europe that triggered migration (even after the White Paper) also need to be situated in relation to the historic racial contract.

The racial contract that gave rise to "the Jewish Question" in Europe took a genocidal turn with the installation of Germany's Adolf Hitler in 1933, Nazism's embrace of "Aryan" supremacy, and death camps as the "final solution." Throughout the 1930s, extreme racism against the Jewish population and threatened genocide led to emigration, and by the culmination of the Second World War, there were more than 400,000 Jewish refugees (Lilienthal 1978: 50). By 1938, international pressure to accept Jewish refugees led to the convening of an international conference in Evian, France, where delegates from 32 countries were represented. However, refuge in other countries, particularly the United States and Canada, was not forthcoming (Habib 2004: 29).

Indeed, the case of Canada is especially illustrative here. For much of its history, Canada maintained its status as a white settler colony by enforcing a preference for white Protestants of British origin in its immigration intake (Abu-Laban 1998). As Irving Abella and Harold Troper (2012) have shown, the prevailing attitude of Canadian elected and immigration officials toward Jewish refugees in the period 1933–48 was that "none is too many," an attitude reflected in a policy of negligible intake. Indeed, Canada (along with Cuba and the United States) in 1939 refused entry to the M.S. St. Louis, forcing over 900 Jews fleeing Nazi persecution to turn back to Europe, and for many to face imminent death.

The Nazi Holocaust contributed to widespread despair about the prospect of normalizing Jewish life in the context of liberal Western European states. The failure of any major state to accept Jewish refugees was a testimony to this reality. While Nazi racism toward the Jews of Germany and Eastern Europe was extreme in its use of modern capitalist technology and its systemic nature, anti-Jewish racism was not new to the region or Europe generally. Earlier generations of European Jews had turned to other strategies to challenge racism, particularly in the socialist and labor movements. There is an extensive literature regarding socialist and labor responses to anti-Semitism that forged a tradition that was originally far more influential than the marginalized Zionist strategy (Bakan 2014a; Reiter 2016; Rose 2004). However, with the consolidation of Stalinism in Russia in the late 1920s and early 1930s, a capitulation to patterns of pre-revolutionary, state-led anti-Semitism developed in the Soviet Union. The combined rise of Nazism and Stalinism in Europe and the failure of liberal democracies in the West and North America to embrace Jewish refugees opened the door to the isolationism and xenophobia that would fuel the Zionist settlement of Palestine (Bakan 2014a). Moreover, this ideological current was met with an interest in colonial expansion, from Britain and then the United States, providing a tragic combination in the post–Second World War period of *realpolitik* that absented the reality of Palestine and the Palestinians (Rose 2004; Shlaim 2002).

As the continuing revelations concerning the Nazi treatment of Jews unfolded after the Second World War, a new perceived legitimacy became attached to the Zionist goal of a "Jewish state" in Palestine. The Partition Plan (Resolution 181), which sought to create a Jewish and an Arab state, was passed on November 29, 1947, through a majority vote in the United Nations General Assembly (with Canada, the United States, and the Soviet Union in favor and Britain abstaining). The newly emergent United Nations, like the League of Nations before it, reflected the historic, global racial contract insofar as member countries were heavily from the West and many parts of the developing world were still under colonial rule. It is questionable whether such a plan would have ever passed in a General Assembly composed of newly independent states. Indeed, the Partition Plan was challenged by Palestinian Arabs on grounds that noted, "whereas Jewish ownership of land amounted to only 5.67 per cent of the total land area of Palestine, more than half of the country was allotted to the Jewish state, including the majority of the fertile and highly developed coastal and other plains" (John and Hadawi 1970: 268).

Nonetheless, on May 15, 1948, an independent state of Israel was declared and the British Mandate came to an end. As a result, open warfare between the surrounding Arab states and Israel erupted. Sections of the Israeli military conducted a systematic campaign of ethnic cleansing to ensure that land previously held by Indigenous Palestinians could be declared vacant and open to permanent Jewish-only settlement (Pappe 2007). By the end of the war, more land had been taken by Israel than was even allotted under the earlier Partition Plan. Israeli leaders, immediately upon the founding of the state of Israel, indicated that the new state belonged to all the Jewish people around the world and invited immigration with the promise of immediate citizenship, ushering in a new era of racial contract, and a specific Israel/Palestine racial contract.

The Israel/Palestine racial contract

The events of 1948 are subject to conflicting national narratives on the part of Palestinians and Israelis. For many Israelis whose sense of citizenship entitlement was forged in the Zionist and colonialist occupation of Palestine, the years 1947 and 1948 are seen as a period of the birth of an independent national state. The establishment of Israel became intimately connected to the Holocaust in this national narrative, shaped both as a form of implicit reparation for European Nazism and as a regionally based "War of Independence." In contrast, for Palestinians, the year 1948 represents a catastrophe (in Arabic, *Al-Nakba*) characterized by half of the Arab population losing their homes and property and becoming stateless refugees outside of historic Palestine. Indeed, from 1949, Palestinian national identity crystallized around the loss of homeland, the longing to return, and the desire for self-determination. This identity found institutional support with the creation of the Palestine Liberation Organization (PLO) in 1964, and the organization's political and social institutions (Rubenberg 1983). A series of wars in the region (in 1956, 1967, 1973, and 1982) served to reconfigure control of the land in favor of the state of Israel. For example, after the 1967 war, the territories of the West Bank and Gaza (known as the Occupied Palestinian Territories) came under Israeli control. The Oslo agreement, signed in 1993 by Israel and the PLO, allowed for parts of these two territories to be handed over to Palestinian rule (the Palestinian Authority). Hopes in the promise of peace accorded by the Oslo agreement have, however, proven to be tragically misplaced. In effect, from its inception in 1948, Israel's relationship to Palestine and Palestinians has been marked by conditions of "intensified state sanctioned practices of coercion ... rationalized through the multivalent figure of permanent war" (Feldman 2015: 5).

We suggest that, just as the geographic boundaries of the Israeli state have been extended over historic Palestine, the legal-juridical framework of the state has worked to propel Jews—ethnically defined (and more specifically Ashkenazi Jews originating from European and/or western countries)—to the apex of economic, cultural, and political power. This legal-juridical framework has allowed for state expropriation of land through a variety of "legal" means as well as three "fundamental laws" that work to provide separate and preferential legal statuses for Jewish as opposed to non-Jewish citizens (Tekiner 1991: 48–51). These fundamental laws are: (1) the Law of Return (which grants all Jews, and Jews alone, nationality status in

Israel with the right to settle), (2) the Law of Citizenship (which provides means for acquiring Israeli citizenship on specific terms for Jews and non-Jews), and (3) the World Zionist Organization/Jewish Agency (Status) Law (which charges this organization and its subsidiaries with "gathering in the exiles" through a partnership with the Israeli state) (Tekiner 1991: 48–51). These, in summary, form the historic juridical basis of the Israel/Palestine racial contract and serve to codify the racialized, apartheid character of the Israeli state. More recent laws and state practices have only intensified this ethnic privileging of Jewish nationals and the exclusion of Palestinians from civil and social rights (Masri 2017).

Of course, the basis of social power in a capitalist and demographically diverse society like Israel, which continues to receive immigrants, is complex. As Abu-Saad notes in regard to race and racism in Israel in the twenty-first century:

> Israeli society is comprised of a diverse population in which multi-layered ethnic, racial, religious and national identities intersect on a number of levels. This mix includes Ashkenazi Jews (of European and American background), Mizrahi Jews (North African and Middle Eastern background), new Jewish immigrants (from places such as the former Soviet Union and Ethiopia), a Muslim/Christian/Druze Palestinian Arab minority, and non-citizen foreign labourers. (2004: 7)

It is beyond the scope of this work to address comprehensively all of these dimensions of Israeli society (Sela-Sheffy 2006), but for our purposes, the cases of Israeli Palestinians and Sephardic/Mizrahi Jews are particularly important. These examples highlight the social, economic, and political power of Jews (in relation to non-Jews) and the power of Ashkenazi (European/western) Jews in particular. The legal and institutional premise of a state defined by the ethnically and racially ascribed character of its empowered citizens serves to enforce and reproduce racial separateness, or apartheid (Davis 2003; Tilley 2005b).

A starting point for understanding 1948-era Israel and its present-day reverberations relates to how the area was demographically transformed, going from being characterized by an Arab majority before the war into being an area in which Arabs were a minority (Hadawi 1967: 194). Palestinian Israelis continue to be a demographic minority, as well as a minority in relation to power. This is due to their subordinate class and citizenship positions, which also take on complex gender dimensions

(Herzog 2004; Zureik 1979). Additionally, it should be noted that this group has been the subject of a particularly tenacious form of cultural racism (evident in school texts and popular culture) that highlights negative themes relating to their "intrinsic" thieving, dirtiness, corruption, untrustworthiness, and violence (Bar-Tal and Teichman 2005; El Asmar 1986). Peled-Elhanan (2012) has also found that Israeli schoolbooks present Palestinians/Arabs in drab and primitive surroundings, rather than as relatable contemporary people.

Within the Israeli Jewish majority, there are also complex class, race, and gender dimensions that have served to advantage the Ashkenazi Jewish population. As noted, the Zionist movement, both in its conception and its eventual application through legal-juridical state structures, was a response to the experience of Western/European racism against Jews. After the creation of the state of Israel in 1948, however, large waves of immigration came from Middle Eastern and North African countries. Uri Davis notes that "many of the Jews from Asia and Africa were in fact part of the cultural elite of their countries—but when they emigrated to Israel they were confronted by the racism implicit in the fear of 'Orientalization' which so animated the Ashkenazi establishment who controlled the state" (1977: 39). The experience of this grouping has led Ella Shohat to speak of the "Jewish victims" of Zionism.

> The Zionist denial of the Arab-Moslem [*sic*] and Palestinian East, then, has as its corollary the denial of the Jewish "Mizrahim" (the "Eastern Ones") who, like the Palestinians, but by more subtle and less obviously brutal mechanisms, have *also* been stripped of the right of self-representation. Within Israel, and on the stage of world opinion, the hegemonic voice of Israel has almost invariably been that of European Jews, the Ashkenazim, while the Sephardi voice has been largely muffled or silenced. (1988: 1)

Further adding to the complexity of the Israel/Palestine racial contract is the ongoing occupation as well as the broader Palestinian diaspora. In other words, the events of 1948 produced more than "Israeli Palestinians"—they also produced Palestinian refugees, some of whom became citizens of other Arab, Western, and non-Western countries, and many of whom to this day live in refugee camps.

Statistics on the refugee population are notoriously difficult to collect, but an increasing body of research reveals a consistent pattern, summarized by Ilan Pappe as "the ethnic cleansing of Palestine" (2007). This reality is captured by Brynen and El-Rifai as "the twin misfortunes" befalling Palestinians as both the largest and one of the oldest refugee populations globally (2007: 1). A 2014 survey reports that there are approximately 7.98 million Palestinian refugees and internally displaced persons; this continues to constitute the largest and the most longstanding group of forcibly displaced persons globally (BADIL Resource Center 2015: iii–34). Of these, the largest group comprises Palestinians and their descendants displaced or expelled from their places of origin as a result of the war of 1948, approximately 5.09 million of whom have registered for assistance from the UN Relief and Works Agency for Palestine Refugees, while a further 1 million did not register or are not eligible for UN assistance. The second largest group comprises Palestinians displaced for the first time as a result of the 1967 war (more than 1 million). The third group, mainly from the Occupied Palestinian Territories, is made up of those who are outside of historic Palestine and unable to return owing to revocation of residency, denial of family reunification, or fear of persecution (numbering 720,000). Internally displaced Palestinians include those in Israel displaced after 1948 due to population transfer, land expropriation, and house demolition, as well as Palestinians internally displaced in the Occupied Territories during or after the 1967 war (BADIL Resource Center 2015: 33).

It is the reality of the forced displacement, transfer, and collective punishment of Palestinians that compels to the fore issues relating to the right of return for refugees. Resolving these issues, which in turn reproduce the conditions that generate the Israel/Palestine racial contract, includes recognition of the legal right of return as well as the need for compensation for lost property and a "truth and reconciliation" style commission. In contrast, the approach of the Israeli state has been to reject outright any historical responsibility for the refugee problem. Israel has called on Arab states to implement measures to address the permanent settlement of Palestinians, while rejecting in principle the Palestinian refugees' right of return to their original homeland (Hammer 2005: 88–92). This stands in contrast with Israel's Law of Return, which grants all Jews worldwide the right to settle permanently.

For those Palestinians living in the West Bank and Gaza Strip, the 1967 war created a new era in the economic situations of these territories. Over the 1970s and 1980s, these areas became both increasingly dependent on the Israeli economy and a source of expendable labor for Israel in increasingly marginalized regions. Additionally, and coinciding with the occupation, land was expropriated for the building of settlements for Jewish settlers and water was expropriated for Israel (Aruri 1983). These developments were not only fundamentally unaltered by the Oslo Accords but in fact augmented. In May 1996, then Israeli Prime Minister Binyamin Netanyahu declared a localized war on terror and shattered any remnants of the Oslo Accords. As Hammer notes:

> The closure of the territories, their re-occupation and other Israeli measures during the Second Intifada have reversed the slow economic growth that the West Bank and Gaza had experienced [post-Oslo] and have virtually destroyed the Palestinian economy. (2005: 98)

Indeed, it is in this context of closure that Israel turned to seek international temporary workers for jobs previously performed by Palestinians. The occupation since 1967, along with the subsequent exile of Palestinians, has therefore been a further key dimension of the Israel/Palestine racial contract. The 1967 occupation has worked to entrench the hegemony of Jews over non-Jews in ways that have played on racialized Orientalist themes of inferiority, incapacity for self-rule, and the constructed "enemy," that is, the Muslim other. In light of this, van Teeffelen's (1994) analysis of bestselling English language novels over the 1970s and 1980s on the Israeli-Palestinian conflict is instructive. The study finds that these novels have made use of metaphors that distinguish Israelis/Europeans from Palestinians/Arabs according to racialized stereotypes grounded in Orientalism. Thus, the metaphor of desert (Palestinian) is contrasted with civilization (Jew), the metaphor of attack (Palestinian) is contrasted with nonviolence (Jew), and the metaphor of threat (Palestinian) is contrasted with vulnerability (Jew) (van Teeffelen 1994).

This brings us to a consideration of Canada and its non-neutrality regarding both racism within Canadian society and its own racial contract and in regard to the Israel/Palestine racial contract.

Canada and the Israel/Palestine racial contract

As noted, there is a long history that has shaped Canada's formation as a settler-colonial state and the complex and inequitable dimensions this has taken. This history has included close identification with European colonial projects, including the Atlantic slave trade and the threatened genocide of and extreme racism toward the Indigenous population (Bakan 2016; Lawrence 2004). It has also included specifically racialized patterns of immigration, along with a hierarchy of institutionalized state preference for white Anglo-Celtic settlement defined as "Canadian," while Black Canadians and people of color from points of origin in the global South are treated as cheap and/or expendable labor (Bakan and Stasiulis 1997; Galabuzi 2005; Stasiulis and Bakan 2005; Thobani 2007b; Razack 1998, 2002). This is despite important changes over the post–Second World War period, from the removal of the overt legal racism governing immigration, to the introduction of "multiculturalism" as official state policy, to public discussions of forms of Indigenous self-government and reconciliation. The continued reality of racism and the perpetuation of racialized inequality in contemporary Canada is, however, well documented (Galabuzi 2005; Razack 2015; Smith 2007). Despite this reality, Canada has tended to be seen as a model internationally of multicultural formal democracy. This operates in contradictory ways. The projected image obfuscates the racial contract but does not eliminate it. Instead, it serves to hide the reality of racism in a deep ideology of denial or mythologized equality. It also, however, provides a normative standard against which overtly undemocratic, racialized practices can potentially be challenged. These nuanced relationships between systemic racism and legal equality contrast with the more overtly racialized character of the state of Israel.

There is also, however, a way in which racial contracts in other countries are supported by ostensibly "race" neutral countries like Canada. This is a particularly interesting case to consider, as Canada, both during and after the Cold War, has maintained a nominal peacekeeping tradition and an image of "quiet diplomacy," projecting a state identity as the helpful fixer, both internationally and domestically (Razack 2004). This image of middle power statesmanship has provoked ongoing debates among scholars of Canadian foreign policy and the Middle East. Issues of contention include: whether policy makers have been merely noncommitted or actively prudent in regard to Israel (Kay 1978, 1996), whether particular individuals made a difference in fostering support for an Israeli state (Tauber 2002), whether policy was forged in relation to national self-interest (Bercuson 1985), and whether the Canadian state and its Middle Eastern policy have been profoundly and increasingly shaped by American dominance in the region and over Canada (Ismael 1994). Added to this, there is debate about the relative weight of "the

Jewish" and "the Arab" lobbies in Canada in shaping foreign policy (Freeman-Maloy 2016; Goldberg 1990; Tauber 1999).

Rather than entering into the existing terms upon which the debates over Canada's peacekeeping image have been structured, we alternatively stress that Canada's particular constructed international image belies the underlying racial contract, generally, and the specific international racial contract between Canada and Israel/Palestine. There is no demonstrable basis for claimed global neutrality, as we have argued, when it comes to the Israeli-Palestinian issue. Indeed, as the discussion suggests thus far, both the relevance of race-thinking and the racial contract have infused global power relations. And, the state of Israel and the stateless plight of Palestine are both very much outgrowths of the international order, including the United Nations and the League of Nations that preceded it.

Over the course of the post–Second World War period, Canada's position on some key dimensions of the Israeli-Palestinian debates has placed the country squarely in a complicit role regarding the dispossession of the Palestinian people through the creation of the state of Israel as well as, post-1948, the Israel/Palestine racial contract. Canada not only voted in favor of the Partition Plan, despite Britain's abstention, but also played a central role in developing this option (Jacoby 2000: 84). Further, as symbolized by its admission into the United Nations in 1949, Israel rapidly gained the recognition of the two extant global superpowers: the United States and the Soviet Union. Despite the abstention of Britain, Canada also voted in favor (UN General Assembly Resolution 273 and UN Security Council Resolution 69, in 1949). Decades later, in 1968, a year when Canada had membership on the Security Council, Canada was the only country to join the United States in abstaining on a resolution condemning the acquisition of territory and the occupation of East Jerusalem through military conquest (UNSC Resolution 252). Canada again abstained (with the United States and Denmark) from the vote requesting that the United Nations Secretary General send a representative to the Occupied Territories and that Israel cooperate with this representative (UNSC Resolution 259).

Some General Assembly resolutions are also notable. In 1974, in the context of a General Assembly that now contained countries that were formerly European colonies, the PLO was granted observer status in the United Nations General Assembly. It was in this period that a divide between ("white") countries of the West and ("nonwhite") countries of the developing world became more obvious. In the words of PLO leader

Yasser Arafat in his first address to the Assembly: "Today's United Nations represents 138 nations, a number that more clearly reflects the will of the international community" (Arafat 1975). On the resolution granting the PLO observer status (Resolution 3237), while 95 countries voted in favor, 17 voted against it (including Canada, the United States, and Israel) and there were 19 abstentions.

In 1975, the General Assembly passed a resolution calling Zionism "a form of racism and racial discrimination" (Resolution 3379), which similarly reflected a divide between countries of the West and countries of the developing world. This resolution was adopted through 72 votes in favor, 35 against (including Britain, Canada, the United States, and Israel), and 32 abstentions. In the words of then adviser to the League of Arab States, A.M. El-Messiri, in explaining this outcome, "From the perspective of an Afro-Asian, it is not difficult to see Israel as yet another manifestation of a racist form of colonization—namely, settler colonialism" ("The UN Resolution on Zionism" 1975). It should be noted that Israel's precondition for participation in the Madrid peace conference was the revocation of this resolution, which occurred on December 16, 1991, with Canada voting in favor (Resolution 4686).

The impact in Israel is important to consider. Arie Dayan observes that in 1975 "all Israel rose up in arms" and that the "local 'Avenue of the United Nations' was suddenly renamed 'Avenue of Zionism'" (1993: 96). In contrast, the response to the revocation of the resolution was silence, leading Dayan to reflect:

> One possible explanation [for the difference] is that the Israel of 1991 was very different from the Israel of 1975. Back then, for example, who would have imagined that a man such as Meir Kahane, whose political program called for the outlawing of marriage between a Jewish woman and an Arab man, could be elected to the Knesset? And who would have believed at the time that a man like Rehavam Zeevi, whose sole political credo is the "transfer" of Arabs out of the country, could become a government minister in Israel? Is it possible that most Israelis preferred not to exult too noisily when the resolution was revoked so as not to alert those who might be tempted to reexamine the UN's comparison? (1993: 96–97)

In more recent years, the trend has continued. On March 16, 2006, Canada was one of only two countries (the other being the United States) to vote against a nonbinding resolution adopted by the United Nations Economic and Social Council calling on Israel to allow all Palestinian refugee women and children to return to their homes. This was the first resolution regarding the Middle East to come before a UN body after the swearing in of Conservative Prime Minister Stephen Harper's government in the previous month. One year earlier, the same resolution had been put forward and the Liberal government under then Prime Minister Paul Martin abstained. However, the right of return of Palestinian refugees has been repeatedly passed by the United Nations General Assembly. While only the United States and Israel have opposed this, Israel has faced no sanctions for its failure to recognize this right or to adhere to the UN resolution (Resolution 194, December 11, 1948). Moreover, the general shift to a more overtly uncritical stance taken by Canada toward Israel in the United Nations has continued since the election of Liberal Prime Minister Justin Trudeau. In November 2015, the United Nations voted on a series of nonbinding resolutions relating to the rights of Palestinians and critical of settlements and occupation, most of which were either adopted or soon to be adopted by committees of the UN. Canada either abstained or voted against all of these at the committee level and ultimately at the General Assembly (Csillag 2015). As a consequence of this position, the takeaway message in an article in *Canadian Jewish News* was that Trudeau was not deviating from the "Israel-friendly" stance of the Harper Conservatives and the previous Liberal government of Paul Martin at the UN.[7]

The positioning of the Liberal government of Paul Martin was quite telling because it involved a ruling made by the International Court of Justice (ICJ). Specifically, it is of note that, on July 9, 2004, a historic ruling of the ICJ found that the so-called separation wall under construction in the Occupied Territories was illegal. The ICJ also ruled, by recurrent votes of 14 to 1, that the Israeli state must stop further construction, remove the parts of the wall already constructed, and compensate Palestinian families for losses of land and livelihood resulting from the construction of the wall. The ICJ's press statement from July 9, 2004, included a note on the importance of international law:

> By a majority of 14 to 1, the judges found that the barrier's construction breaches international law, saying it violated principles outlined in the UN Charter and long-standing global conventions that prohibit the threat or use of force and the acquisition of territory that way, as well as principles upholding the right of peoples to self-determination.

> Observing that 80 per cent of Israeli settlers in the occupied Palestinian territory now live between the barrier and the so-called Green Line marking the 1949 boundary of Israel, the Court said the structure's route could "prejudge the future frontier between Israel and Palestine." The ICJ—the UN's principal judicial organ—said construction "would be tantamount to de facto annexation" as it explained that the barrier could create a potentially permanent "fait accompli" on the ground.

On July 20, 2004, the UN General Assembly voted that Israel must comply with the court's decision: 150 nations voted in favor, including 25 from the European Union. Six nations voted against the resolution, including Israel and the United States. Canada was one of ten countries to abstain on the vote. Significantly, Israel has refused to recognize the ruling and the illegal construction of the wall has continued unabated. While international law is clear, the notion that Israel is a race-neutral democracy—and not subject to the scrutiny applied to other countries in the Middle East and other parts of the developing world—has in practical terms rendered the ICJ ruling moot. This is an indication of the Israel/Palestine racial contract and of Canada's role in ensuring its continuation in the international arena.

Our point in highlighting the place of Canada in these deliberations of the United Nations is to suggest that the racial contract as it has existed regarding post-1948 Israel/Palestine finds both support and points of resistance in the UN itself. The Canadian government has operated to further entrench the realities of racism against the Palestinians in Israel and in the diaspora, extending the racial contract internationally. We conclude this chapter by suggesting that the Israel/Palestine racial contract, in keeping with Gramsci's understanding of hegemony, has not only points of support but also resistance in both Canadian and Israeli civil societies. It is these points of resistance that provide guideposts for considering a consistent anti-racist response that can challenge the Israel/Palestine racial contract.

In conclusion: Toward breaking the contract?

Though the notion of a "clash of civilizations" was not a creation of the events on September 11, 2001, this framing of world politics gained popularity in the post-9/11 period. The "war on terror," ostensibly in retaliation for 9/11 and in the prevention of a repeated attack, has shaped US foreign policy and global politics in the aftermath (Bakan 2005b; Huntington 1996). For example, in one typical post-9/11 textbook that is circulated to instructors of political science for consideration in university teaching, the phrase "clash of civilizations" is used in the introduction. The way it is used suggests it is a common-sense feature of global politics today. As Joel Krieger observed just a few years after September 11, while previously economic dimensions of globalization, including the growing gap between North and South, dominated concerns, this quickly shifted following the attacks. To quote:

> Since the attacks of September 11, 2001, concern about the "clash of civilizations" between the West and the Muslim world, the problem of security against terror, and questions about how American power will recast global alliances and affect both national politics and people's lives throughout the world, have partially refocused our thinking about globalization. (Krieger 2005: x)

In this context, many social and political constructs that appear to be race neutral have in fact become racialized. Samuel Huntington (1996) explicitly traces the "clash" to a "demographic" challenge posed by the populations of "Islam and Asia," who threaten "Western civilization." The latter in this view are presumed to be non-Islamic and, ostensibly, white. This perspective is extended in Huntington's later works to incorporate the apparent threat of Latinx ("Hispanic") Americans (Huntington 2005). It also serves in many instances as a guideline for states to enforce borders, construct barriers, and limit or permit access to a wide variety of services and rights. This phenomenon is not new, but its increasing transparency is notable (see Brown 2010). From this perspective, Israel's constructed wall is not an entirely unique example. Another case of the erection of walls in the name of security has been encroaching on the US-Mexico border. While this has been a hallmark of the presidency of Donald Trump, US President George W. Bush called for the development of 698 miles of new fencing along the US-Mexico border. Congress budgeted US$1.2 billion toward the project and, notably, the Department of Homeland Security committed to completing 370 miles of the fence by the end of 2008.[8] Though expansion was controversial and ordered to be halted by US President Barack Obama in March 2010, strict regulation of the US-Mexico border has continued.

The racialization of social and political categories has been normalized in ideological and popular usage, however, as reflected, for example, in the 2016 US election campaign rhetoric of Republican President Donald Trump and his commitment to building an immigration wall between the United States and Mexico (and have Mexico pay). The 2000-mile border between the United States and Mexico already features fencing along more than 500 miles and is the object of intense surveillance, and therefore the proposal raises issues regarding human rights, as well as practical issues of sovereignty, governance, and costs.[9]

The construction of walls in the name of security runs counter to the generalized impulse toward globalization, or even regionalization, that has marked post–Cold War world politics. However, in the aftermath of 9/11, and with widespread emergence of governments advancing stricter immigration controls, the politicization and racialization of borders are becoming more common. This is consistent with the notion of a separation of peoples whose "civilizations" inevitably "clash." The risk is that the racialized divisions that are presented to be race neutral in Israel/Palestine are becoming further normalized internationally as an acceptable standard. There is a problematic acceptance of an approach to relations among citizens that is consistent with the racial contract, where complicity with racialized norms and practices becomes compatible with conditions of liberal democratic ideology and related institutions.

Charles Mills usefully suggests that a widening critical analysis of the ideas suggested in the notion of a racial contract can be extended to explain a racial polity, framed by a paradigm that "takes race, normative whiteness, and white supremacy to be central to US and indeed global history" (1997: 119). It is significant that in Mills' original framework, along with an insistence on the systemic nature of racism in modern society, there is also a substantial place for agency and resistance.

Canada's role as an international ally of Israeli state practices can be and is being challenged by a growing social movement. The Coalition Against Israeli Apartheid (CAIA) and Independent Jewish Voices (Canada) (IJV), as well as the Stop the Wall Campaign in Palestine, and, in Israel, Women in Black and the movement of "refuseniks"—Israeli conscripts who refuse to serve in the Israeli Defense Force—are only some of the organizational expressions of anti-racist solidarity. A global movement for boycott, divestment, and sanctions against Israel is raising international awareness and provoking extensive debate, and it is comparable to the movement that challenged the apartheid regime of

South Africa. The contradictory notion of a racial contract that cultivates systemic inequality and is at the same time posited as part of an open democracy in countries like Canada offers political space for those who choose to challenge, and eventually break, the racial contract. There is space afforded, therefore, to challenge the racialized practices not only of the state of Israel but also of the Canadian state and other examples of Western democracies that are complicit in international racial contracts.

Such spaces of resistance have not fundamentally dislodged the Israel/Palestine racial contract grounded in a close association of Zionism with Western hegemony and the simultaneous absenting of Palestine. There are indications, however, that even among elite pro-Western theorists, there is growing concern to provoke an atmosphere of legitimacy for debate. An important example is the publication of John Mearsheimer and Stephen Walt's *The Israel Lobby and US Foreign Policy* (2007). The analysis is consistent with the most conservative views of empire but attempts to challenge the normalization of the deep historic ties between Israel and the United States. In its failure to see the role of hegemony and reject arguments that point to geopolitical strategic alliances as explanatory factors, the study relies on a traditional interest group framework. The authors arguably give undue import to the activities of specific lobby groups in shaping US state policy. The consistency of the approach with contemporary neoliberalism is clear; the authors dedicate their book to none other than the late Samuel Huntington. However, the widespread attention Mearsheimer and Walt have received, beginning with their article on the same theme in the *London Review of Books* (2006), suggests the possibility of a crack in the hegemonic bloc regarding the racial contract between countries like the United States and Canada with Israel. Divisions such as these are important indicators of a potential weakening in the hegemonic state practices and ideologies, which could allow greater scope for social movements to break the Israel/Palestine racial contract and to build new bonds of anti-racist solidarity within and beyond state borders.

Notes

1 YouTube.com, "Through Fire and Water," July 18, 2014, https://www.youtube.com/watch?v=hq8MN0OBEO4.

2 Jeremy Keehn, "What Justin Trudeau's Victory Means for Canada," *The New Yorker*, October 20, 2015, http://www.newyorker.com/news/news-desk/

what-justin-trudeaus-victory-means-for-canada; Daniel Leblanc, Steven Chase, and Gloria Galloway, "Trudeau Sets Fresh Tone with Cabinet Ready to Tackle Thorny Issues," *The Globe and Mail*, November 4, 2015, http://www.theglobeandmail.com/news/politics/trudeau-sworn-in-at-rideau-hall/article27096353/; Tonda MacCharles, Les Whittington, and Bruce Campion-Smith, "Prime Minister Justin Trudeau Unveils Diverse Cabinet in Touching Ceremony," *TheStar.com*, November 4, 2015, http://www.thestar.com/news/canada/2015/11/04/trudeaus-cabinet-prospects-found-for-rideau-hall.html.

3 Patrick Martin, "Parliament Votes to Reject Israel Boycott Campaign," *The Globe and Mail*, February 23, 2016, https://www.theglobeandmail.com/news/world/parliament-votes-to-reject-campaign-to-boycott-israel/article28863810/; Antonia Zerbisias, "Israel Need Not Worry About Justin Trudeau," *Aljazeera*, November 11, 2015, http://www.aljazeera.com/indepth/opinion/2015/11/israel-worry-justin-trudeau-151109061056908.html.

4 CTV.ca News Staff, "Canada Pulls Support for UN Anti-Racism Conference," January 23, 2008, https://www.ctvnews.ca/canada-pulls-support-for-un-anti-racism-conference-1.272485.

5 Government of Canada, "Canada and Israel Sign Declaration to Cooperate on Public Safety," March 23, 2008, http://www.marketwired.com/press-release/canada-and-israel-sign-declaration-to-cooperate-on-public-safety-835257.htm.

6 Palestinian BNC, "Palestinian Civil Society Condemns Canadian Government Disinformation and Repression against Boycott Movement," February 5, 2015, https://bdsmovement.net/2015/palestinian-civil-society-condemns-canadian-government-disinformation-and-repression-against-boycott-movement–13051.

7 Ron Csillag, "Trudeau Government Votes Against UN Anti-Israel Resolutions," *Canadian Jewish News*, November 26, 2015, http://www.cjnews.com/news/canada/trudeau-government-opposes-annual-un-onslaught-against-israel.

8 Lynn Brezosky, "Another Side to the Border Fence," *The Seattle Times*, May 25, 2007, https://www.seattletimes.com/nation-world/another-side-to-the-border-fence/.

9 Leanna Garfield, "Trumps $25 Billion Wall Would Be Nearly Impossible to Build, According to Architects," *Business Insider*, November 13, 2016, http://www.businessinsider.com/trump-wall-impossible-build-architects-2016-11.

3 ISRAEL/PALESTINE FROM LOCAL TO GLOBAL: PALESTINE IN THE POST-9/11 ERA

Social sorting and Israel/Palestine

There is an increasing legitimacy of state-supported and state-promoted surveillance as an acceptable form of maintaining "security" (Agamben 2005; Ong 2006), broadly framed in terms of a post-9/11 model. This security model is ostensibly motivated to protect an innocent public citizenry associated with states of the global North from "terrorists." These "terrorists" ostensibly originate from and/or find safe haven in states of the global South or seek, or have sought via immigration, to enter states of the global North. Exceptional scrutiny of borders and of designated subjects within borders considered to be suspect has been accompanied by a new period of heightened surveillance. The relationships among security, surveillance, and state regimes that extend the racial contract that has advanced in the Israel/Palestine context are the focus of this chapter.

Surveillance is ubiquitous, particularly in the contemporary information age, where both corporations and states make use of new technologies that allow for the rapid collection and flow of data within and across national boundaries (Lyon and Zureik 1996: 4–5; Whitaker 1999: 80–122). As a consequence, while surveillance may be understood as a characteristic of various communities across time and space, in the current period there is both a qualitative and quantitative escalation (Lyon 2007: 100; Perera and Razack 2014). Moreover, while the ubiquity of surveillance was established well before September 11, 2001, the post-9/11 period has allowed for a steep intensification of surveillance processes (Abu-Laban 2015; Lyon 2003; Todd and Bloch 2003; Zureik and Salter 2005).

Our focus on surveillance relates to understanding unequal power relations and sites of resistance in the context of the Israel/Palestine racial contract. From this perspective, the concept of "social sorting" (rather than merely "privacy") serves as a compelling point of entry into contemporary surveillance studies, not least in relation to Israel/Palestine and the post-9/11 period. As David Lyon argues, social sorting underscores the fact that surveillance is not a neutral process, and that people may be categorized and treated differently as a result of gender, race, ethnicity, religion, class, and age among other forms of difference (2007: 177). We would note, significantly, that the relevance of the concept of social sorting based on disability is also relevant to these surveillance practices (Erevelles 2011).

Considering the post-9/11 period as a pivotal marker, we examine the manner in which a particular form of social sorting has moved from an apparently unique condition in the context of Israel/Palestine, often seen as *sui generis*, to one that has "gone global." We suggest that what could be considered as a certain "Palestinianization" has occurred in liberal democracies, generalizing a sense of fear or threat in response to those who are socially sorted as "terrorists." This sorting, similar to the manner in which Palestinians have been separated out and socially sorted from Israelis in the Middle East context, is ideologically constructed to be marked by Islamic beliefs, Arabic origins, and/or racial stereotypes on the basis of ascribed phenotypical characteristics. These racialized patterns of social sorting are not the invention of states since 9/11; rather, they are consistent with established ideologies and practices associated with the racial contract. However, the particular association and legitimacy of racialized social sorting with Islamophobia, or anti-Muslim racism, in the post-9/11 period can be understood to have particular roots in, and relevance to, the Israel/Palestine context.

Palestinianization arises in relation to the hegemonic state that depends upon its construction. We argue that a parallel "Israelization" of surveillance and social sorting has developed in the same liberal democratic states that have relied on Palestinianization. While Israel has commonly been identified as an exceptional state without comparison, in the post-9/11 context, there has been a shift. Now the United States—and by association, other liberal democracies in the global North including Canada—has come to identify the need for uniquely repressive measures in the face of a purported "terrorist" threat similar to that encountered by Israel since its inception as a state.

To demonstrate this argument, we suggest a reframing of the post-1948 period of Israel's historical narrative to illustrate how the Israeli military state came to rely on the figure of the "Palestinian terrorist" and how this now serves as a microcosm for the "war on terror." As such, the racialization of security that defines Israel's apartheid-like system has moved in the post-9/11 period further from the local to the global, as have the actual and potential sites of and forms of resistance to surveillance and social sorting. We present an interpretive chronological reading based on an understanding of contemporary "terrorism" as a racialized category, derived significantly from the context of Israel/Palestine. We demonstrate how this has become more firmly entrenched in security responses in liberal democratic countries of Europe and North America, feeding policies and practices that bypass liberal norms of projected racial and ethnic neutrality, due process of law, and human rights. Israel's surveillance practices and its particular form of social sorting have influenced, in the terms of Agamben (2005), "exceptional" responses in liberal democracies, wherein provisional measures are transformed into a technique of governance. While these measures are presented as a temporary state of emergency, in fact they have become entrenched as permanent (Bakan 2014b).

The argument that follows proceeds in six parts. In the first part, we address the nondemocratic character of the Israeli state and consider the applicability to Agamben's (2005) notion of a "state of exception" in the case of Israel/Palestine. We contextualize and challenge the claim to exceptionality of the state of Israel and frame its particular form of racialization in the context of the Israel/Palestine racial contract.

The next four sections cover specific time periods: the establishment of the state of Israel in 1948 to the end of the 1967 war, 1967 until the end of the Cold War in 1991, the Oslo and post-Oslo contexts between 1992 and 2000, and the contemporary post-9/11 period. Through this periodization we demonstrate how the move from the local to the global has been heavily buttressed not only by technological developments that may enable greater means for social sorting ("Israelization"), but also by an aggressive ideological campaign constructed around the notion of the Palestinian "terrorist" ("Palestinianization"). This ideological construction is shown to posit Israel, artificially, as a victim state, thereby justifying the use of violent measures that subvert human rights and normalize US and Western patriotism, security, and exceptional measures in relation to the ascribed threat of "Islamic" and/or "Arab" terrorism. This political assertion of Islamophobia (or anti-Muslim racism) in conjunction with security and the "war on terror" (Fekete 2004; Mamdani 2004; Razack 2008) impacts the nature of social sorting, affecting both noncitizens and citizens.

The sixth and final section of this argument turns to consider sites of resistance. Despite the extreme and repressive apparatus that maintains Israel's racialization and oppression of Palestinian resistance, the context remains unstable and subject to challenge. There are important points of resistance articulated within civil society, both within and outside of Israel/Palestine, that can inspire a response grounded in principles of anti-racism and human rights.

Israel as a state of exception? Theorizing race and racial contracts

Georgio Agamben's (2005) concept of the "state of exception" rests ambiguously with regard to its applicability to the Israeli state. At issue is the implication of Israel's unproblematic membership in the community of Western liberal democracies (see Zriek 2008 on applicability; for the critique, see Pappe 2008). As Pappe rightly notes, if Israel is conceptually included in this community, it would be the only so-called democracy, where citizenship is overtly defined through ethnicity and religion (2008: 160). Put differently, apartheid regimes are normally counterposed rather than equated with liberal democratic systems of governance. Moreover, as Pappe continues, since 1948 violence has characterized the Israeli state's relations with Palestinians (whether they hold Israeli citizenship or not); violence is the norm rather than, as implied in Agamben's understanding, the exception in an otherwise liberal consensual model (2008: 165).

This exchange is useful in illustrating an important aspect of exception not considered by Agamben, namely the specific manner in which Israel has been treated as "democratic" despite considerable evidence to the contrary (see, e.g., Cook 2006; Davis 2003; Rodinson 1973; Yiftachel 2006; Zureik 1979). This is consistent with our notion of mythologized exceptionalism. Israel is commonly identified as a state without comparison, framed in international politics as the only "Jewish" state, and one that is claimed to be exceptionally "democratic" in the context of the Middle East (Cook 2006; Rose 2004). There is also a mythologized history, addressed earlier in Chapter 2, subsumed in the notion of a "chosen people" and a specific framing of the origins and current hegemonic positioning of Zionist ideology that emphasizes this exceptionality. This mythologized exceptionalism serves to render practices otherwise considered unacceptable in international law and basic human rights practices to be legitimate, and legitimated, that is, beyond normative challenge. Such an artificially elevated exceptionality is complicated, however, and sustained by other conditions. There is in fact, in historical terms, a unique origin to the state of Israel, as a modern state envisioned in the United Nations (through its Partition Plan) and, after 1948, recognized by powerful states and brought into the UN system. Moreover, Israel holds a unique place in terms of its high rate of per capita military aid from the United States, a fact that has emerged as the subject of contested debate even among mainstream analysts (Mearsheimer and Walt 2007; Ruff 2007; Zureik, Lyon, and Abu-Laban 2011).

The elements of mythologized exceptionalism and its sustaining conditions introduce distinct complications into the study of Israel/Palestine, with implications for how we might think about surveillance, social sorting, and racialization. In particular, Israel's close association with Zionist ideology has created an informal but sustained atmosphere of surveillance in the Western academy, where comparison between Israel and other colonial states is uniquely subject to challenge. Those advancing criticisms of Israeli policies or practices can face intense scrutiny of their motivations (Salaita 2015), underscoring what Virginia Tilley refers to as "Zionist exceptionalism" (2005b: 134). The latter is a dimension, we would argue, of the mythologized exceptionalism common in Israel studies generally. Assertions of this unique form of exceptionalism have therefore limited the capacity of modern scholarship to identify cross-national comparative patterns in the settlement and conquest of, and violence directed at, Palestinians in the establishment and ongoing conduct of the Israeli state.

This mythologized exceptionalism is elemental to the Israel/Palestine racial contract, belying an underlying commonality in the origin of the modern state of Israel as a settler colony. This blurs the reality of racism in the context of Israel/Palestine today and compromises the legitimacy of theorizing race in fully comparative terms. Given these important challenges regarding the appropriateness of Agamben's "state of exception" in relation to Israel, we instead draw on Agamben's idea of exception to highlight how, within Western liberal democracies today, being profiled or labeled a "terrorist" carries with it a high probability of "being taken to a place of law without law" (Razack 2008: 34). It is, we suggest, the racialization of Palestinians as "terrorists" that demands critical attention both in the context of Israel/Palestine and, as we argue below, with regard to its implications in other locales where Agamben's concept of exception may be more readily applied, including the United States, Canada, and countries of the European Union.

From such a vantage point, Israel is unique in its deep ideological claim to exceptionality, but in other respects, it is notably, and importantly, comparable. The racial contract provides a way of being able to name what is so often bypassed in real-world politics. Applied to Israel/Palestine, the focus on the racial contract makes explicit Israel's core features as a state grounded in the absenting or subordination of the Palestinian "other." This Israel/Palestine racial contract has, as we have maintained, since 1948, constructed Palestinians as nonwhite, as the subjects of extreme repression, and as stateless. Attention to the Gramscian notion of hegemony can place the racial contract framework in a larger context of class and ideological dominance.

What David Theo Goldberg calls "racial Palestinianization" is, in his estimate, "among the most repressive, the most subjugating and degrading, the most deadly forms of racial targeting, branding, and rationalization not least in the name of racelessness" (2009: 130). Gargi Bhattacharyya (2008) argues that the Palestinian struggle has become a cipher for both the "clash of civilizations" and the "war on terror" in ways that reverberate outside of Israel/Palestine. As such, "Israel offers a model for transforming the justified demands of the racialized other into evidence that this otherness is innate, impassable and can only be contained and disciplined in the interests of the enlightened western state and its (full) citizens" (Bhattacharyya 2008: 49).

In what follows, we identify the development of Israel's particular form of social sorting. This is a mode of governance that has become hegemonic and fixated on the perceived and permanent threat of "terrorism." We trace the development of some of the ways in which a growing Israelization of surveillance practices has emerged, along with a Palestinianization of the racial contract, moving from the local context of Israel/Palestine *per se* to the wider global context, with a particular emphasis on liberal democracies.

1948–67: Ethnic cleansing, the making of a military settler state, and the construction of an enemy

As Ilan Pappe has documented, the state of Israel was established through a process of forced exile and transfer of Palestinians, and occupation of Palestinian land, consistent with recognized definitions of ethnic cleansing (2006b: 1–29). This is the foundational element in a process of social sorting defined through the construction of the Indigenous Palestinian as the "enemy." Relatedly, resistance to this process has been treated as an existential threat to the territory redefined as the "Jewish state" of Israel, constructed by the state as exclusively and ethnically Jewish. The Zionist vision of an ethnically exclusive "Jewish" state coincided with a European political project associated first with imperial Britain and second with US interests in the Middle East. These imperial projects included the demographic transfer and "casting out" (Razack 2008) of Arab Palestinians. This process of dispossession, the "colonization of Palestine," was explicit in the visioning of early Zionist thinkers. As Bein (1939) discussed:

> Our thought is that the colonization of Palestine has to go in two directions: Jewish settlement in Eretz Israel and the resettlement of the Arabs of Eretz Israel in areas outside the country. The transfer of so many Arabs might seem at first unacceptable economically, but is nonetheless practical. It does not require too much money to resettle a Palestinian village on another land. (as cited in Pappe 2006b: 7–8)

Despite efforts to bury and distort the history of the origins of the state of Israel as an ethnically defined, colonial-settler state, and to absent Indigenous Palestinian culture and history, the records are clear. Pappe summarizes the early chronology and course of events:

> The [United Nations] Partition Resolution was adopted on 29 November 1947, and the ethnic cleansing of Palestine began in early

> December 1947 with a series of Jewish [Zionist] attacks on Palestinian villages and neighbourhoods in retaliation for the buses and shopping centres that had been vandalised in the Palestinian protest against the UN resolution during the first few days after its adoption. Though sporadic, these early Jewish assaults were severe enough to cause the exodus of a substantial number of people (almost 75,000).
>
> On 9 January, units of the first all-Arab volunteer army entered Palestine and engaged with the Jewish forces in small battles over routes and isolated Jewish settlements. Easily winning the upper hand in these skirmishes, the Jewish leadership officially shifted its tactics from acts of retaliation to cleansing operations. Coerced expulsions followed in the middle of February 1948 when Jewish troops succeeded in emptying five Palestinian villages in one day. On 10 March 1948, Plan Dalet was adopted.... About 250,000 Palestinians were uprooted in this phase, which was accompanied by several massacres, most notable of which was the Deir Yassin massacre.... The British left on 15 May 1948, and the Jewish Agency immediately declared the establishment of a Jewish state in Palestine, officially recognised by the two superpowers of the day, the USA and the USSR. (2006b: 40)

The documentation supporting Pappe's research is extensive and has further supported a new school of Israeli "post-Zionist" historiography. Though it is beyond the scope of this chapter to fully chronicle the case, it should be noted that elements of this historiography are reflected in the work of both Palestinian and Jewish scholars (see Abu-Lughod and Sa'di 2007b; Davis 2003; Karmi 2007; Khalidi 1987; Pappe 2006b; Rose 2004; Said 1992; Tilley 2005b). Our intent here is to emphasize the violence behind the process of social sorting, where occupation, transfer, and the denial of the right of displaced Palestinians to return to their land were grounded on a differentiation between the ascribed Jewish settler (and eventually Israeli national) and the constructed security "threat" of the Palestinian Arab (and eventually Palestinian refugee or Arab Israeli). Put differently, Palestinian Arabs were perceived and treated as a threat whether or not they held Israeli citizenship, defining a specific racialization in this foundational social sorting. This process of social sorting is elemental to the Israel/Palestine racial contract.

Beginning under the British Mandate in the 1930s and 1940s, the arming of the Zionist military organization Hagana by Britain (Ben-Gurion 1963), the arming of illegal armed organizations such as the Irgun and Stern Group (Great Britain 1971/1987), and the covert operations smuggling Jewish refugees to Palestine in the face of British quotas (Kimche and Kimche 1955) laid the basis for the military and intelligence apparatus of the Israeli state, specifically the Israeli Defence Forces and Mossad. In the lead-up to the establishment of Israel, a pattern emerged where initial settlement was met by local resistance, which was in turn described as an "enemy" attack meriting militarized retaliation on a scale far greater and more violent than the provoking incident and culminating in the forced exodus of Palestinians (Childers 1961).

This pattern of violent occupation followed by local resistance, only to be met by immeasurably greater and more violent "retaliation," has characterized Israel's pattern of continued expansion in Palestinian territory. This process demanded a highly militarized state on one side, associated with the newly established state of Israel, and the concomitant perception of a blameworthy (Said and Hitchens 1988) and dangerous, Indigenous, racialized Palestinian population, sometimes supported by neighboring enemy Arab states. The establishment of militarized borders, heightened monitoring of Palestinian activity at every level of social interaction, and regulated movement to prevent return became a normalized, permanent feature of Israel's state structure and security practices. Suspicion, surveillance, and sorting through state identification systems in order to prevent the return of Palestinians to their homes (as Zureik [2001: 213–18] shows in his discussion of "present absentees" in the 1948 Israeli Census), along with more general forms of racial profiling, became standard features of Israel's treatment of displaced Palestinians. Israel continued to maintain, for example, the legislative "emergency status" developed under the British mandatory government, creating a "permanent war footing" and allowing violence to be used in controlling Palestinian resistance (Cook 2004a). Additionally, in its first decade, the Israeli state passed a series of new laws premised on "security" and the need to "cultivate" the land, which effectively removed more land from Palestinian Arabs inside Israel (Adams 1977: 27–8).

The established pattern of interaction with the state of Israel for Arab Palestinians became clearly differentiated from that experienced by and normalized for Jewish "nationals" (Zureik 1979). For the former, "the main, and perhaps the only, contact of Israeli Arabs with the state was through the army, the police and the criminal justice system" (Korn 2000: 159), sites of the modern state prone to relying upon both surveillance and repression. Based on an extensive study of available criminological analyses regarding the Arab population of Israel, Korn finds three principal features that can be understood to characterize relationships between Jews and Arabs in post-1948 Israel (referred to as "Arab Israelis"): Arab Israelis are separated and distinct from the dominant Jewish Israelis as a group, geographically and socially; Arab Israelis are subjected to differential access to resources, power, and status relative to Jewish Israelis; and Arab Israelis are subject to heightened levels of political and social control relative to the Jewish majority (2000: 161).

The necessity to hold conquered territory by force and to maintain a militarized system of regulation and control to ensure power over a conquered Indigenous population followed from the original settler character of the Israeli state. The process of racialized social sorting associated with the original *Nakba*, and later extended to the occupation of greater Palestinian territory during the 1967 war, can be understood as part of a continuum in the maintenance of the Israel/Palestine racial contract, entrenching a militarized settler state. The permanent acceptance and institutionalization of this level of separation between the Jewish/European national as the normalized, "democratic" citizen and the Palestinian/Arab non-national as the normalized, threatening "enemy" other have become inscribed in the reality of Israel/Palestine. "Israel," and hence Israelization, demanded the subordination of Palestine, and hence Palestinianization. The initial boundaries were sustained through extensive processes of surveillance, securitized borders and policing, and these boundaries were deepened in the periods that followed, described below.

1967–91: Expansion, occupation and the construction of the terrorist threat

It was in the period following the 1967 war and occupation of Palestinian territories that the construction of the threat of the "Palestinian terrorist" became more firmly embedded in Israeli discourse, with international reverberations. If the period from 1948 to 1967 was characterized by Israel seeming to solve what Usher (2005: 10–11) calls its "native problem" through ethnic cleansing, violence to prevent the return of Palestinians, asserting control over the remaining Arab population of Israel, and settling new Jewish immigrants as preferred citizens, then 1967 marks the period when the "native problem" returned via occupation. Moreover, its return created new public relations issues for the Israeli state, in regard to both its own citizens and the global community.

"Terrorism" as a discourse has its roots in the French Revolution and was advanced primarily in relation to resistance in European colonies (such as Algeria) after the Second World War (Bankoff 2003: 418). Of course, as David Lyon notes, the term "terrorism" is "notoriously slippery, not least because one person's 'freedom fighter' is another's 'terrorist,'" citing the Israeli-Palestinian conflict as one among several cases in point (2003: 49). Consequently, "terrorism," as Noam Chomsky has argued, can be read into the 1948 foundation and ongoing actions of the state of Israel and earlier in the lengthy record of bombings, massacres, and expulsions targeting civilians committed by Zionist groups in Palestine (1986: 110–13). Yet, until recently, there has been a condition of virtual immunity in these acts of violence in Western and especially US elite opinion (Chomsky 1986: 113). In dramatic contrast, by the 1980s, the categories of Palestinian, Arab, and Muslim were frequently conflated and the Palestinian/Arab/Muslim "terrorist" came to be treated as a central risk to the United States, and by extension the West (Said 1994: 310). Rather than simply reflecting an uneven application of the terms "terrorism" and "terrorist" in both the US mainstream media and government (Kapitan and Schulte 2003), we suggest the significance of understanding how these terms are racialized and work in accordance with the Israel/Palestine racial contract.

The 1967 war symbolized a turning point in the perception of Israel in many Western countries and especially in Europe; it also heightened awareness of the Palestinian case. The Western ideological fixation on the "Palestinian terrorist" may in part be attributed to the transition that occurred in Israel/Palestine through the 1960s, when the despised other could not be simply depicted as a regional military enemy. The rapid and decisive victory of the capture of the Golan Heights, the Sinai Peninsula, the West Bank, East Jerusalem, and the Gaza Strip, coupled with the military occupation of Palestinians, led to new questioning of which side would be most appropriately characterized as the "David" or the "Goliath." At the same time, the power and validity of the national claims of Palestinians for recognition and statehood were given a new boost with the creation of the Palestine Liberation Organization (PLO) in 1964, and the observer status accorded the PLO in the United Nations in 1974. Not least, as Usher also points out, "unlike the 1948 territories, in and from which the transfer of Palestinians had been hidden and/or justified by the imperatives of war and Jewish survival, there was no Israeli consensus, post-1967, over the fate of the newly acquired territories" (2005: 12–13).

In practical terms, however, the situation was not ambiguous. When it came to the Occupied Palestinian Territories, the Israeli state was able to exercise violence more bluntly as the Palestinian inhabitants were not formally considered to be Israeli citizens. A regime of military governance was institutionalized and with it came detentions without trial, deportations, the destruction of homes, and curfews (Adams 1977; Aruri 1989; Gordon 2008b). Other forms of collective punishment were also institutionalized, including militarized checkpoints controlling the mobility of Palestinians, with identity cards coming to occupy "the symbol of surveillance *par excellence*" (Zureik 2001: 224).

In short, against key elements of the 1978 Camp David Accords (Carter 2006: 224–28), throughout this period, what Neve Gordon calls the "colonization principle" (2008b: 27–9) came increasingly to the fore—it was openly recognized and institutionalized. This colonization involved the management of the lives of Palestinian subjects and the extraction of resources, including water and land, for the use of growing numbers of Israeli settlements in the Occupied Palestinian Territories. Nonetheless, Palestinians did engage in forms of resistance to surveillance and colonization, most clearly in the first Intifada. This brought to the world the image of Palestinian children challenging the Israeli military with stones (Gordon 2008b).

Moreover, the military became increasingly integrated into the economic fabric of the state of Israel. It is widely acknowledged that beginning in 1967 and accelerating after 1973, military production—often with US technical, financial, and corporate assistance—was a major engine of growth in the Israeli economy (Hanieh 2003: 8; Maman 1999: 96; Pieterse 1985: 20). As one example, in 1977, and perhaps not coincidentally foreshadowing the construction of the "separation barrier" (also dubbed the apartheid wall), an electrified wall was built by Israeli technicians at the border of Namibia and Angola to deter the South West Africa People's Organisation (SWAPO) resistance forces from gaining entry into Namibia (Pieterse 1985: 18). By the 1980s, Israel had assumed an important place in "all the dimensions of the global counter-insurgency business" (Pieterse 1985: 9), a feature also related to its interface with the PLO. As the PLO emerged as a national liberation organization committed to armed resistance, as well as the government-in-exile for the Palestinians both in historic Palestine and in the diaspora (Rubenberg 1983), successive Israeli leaders termed it a "terrorist" organization. In the United States and the Western world, "Palestinians became the premier terrorists" (Bovard 2003: 7).

The 1979 Jerusalem Conference on International Terrorism marked a significant event in the internationalization of responses to Israel's discourse on terrorism (Ralph 2006: 273) and also can serve as a marker in the Palestinianization of the racial contract. The conference was convened, in the words of future Israeli Prime Minister Binyamin Netanyahu, to "begin the formation of an anti-terror alliance in which all the democracies of the West must join" (Netanyahu 1982: 2). This position was echoed by future US President George H.W. Bush, who argued "terrorism must be combated ... by the free nations of the world" (Bush 1982: 335). The common element underlying this perspective, also evident in US government definitions, was "that only private citizens and private groups can be guilty of terrorism," not state actors (Bovard 2003: 228).

The racialized construction of "terrorists" emerging from the context of Israel/Palestine also laid the basis for a new focus on "international terrorism" in the United States in the 1980s under President Ronald Reagan, at the time steeped in the rhetoric of the Cold War (Bovard 2003: 8–30; Chomsky 1986: 1–10). In its most obvious policy application outside Israel/Palestine, the focus on terrorism made its way into the treatment of noncitizens via immigration and refugee discussions, and through legal applications in Western countries (Huysmans 2000; Macklin 2001: 391–2). This pattern reasserted itself after September 11, 2001, with greater resiliency and with more serious consequences; after 9/11, it was applicable not only to immigrants but also citizens. The period preceding 9/11 served to lay the groundwork for the logic and deepening global extension of the Israel/Palestine racial contract and related surveillance.

1992–2000: From Oslo to the second Intifada

By the late 1980s and early 1990s, a number of factors had converged to shift the dynamic between Israel and the PLO—including the end of the Cold War, the 1991 US-led Gulf War, diminished support for the PLO by

Gulf States, and renewed questions about the morality of the Occupation following the first Intifada. In 1988, the PLO, under the leadership of Yasser Arafat, had effectively abandoned the earlier call for armed struggle and a secular and democratic Palestine, moving to a strategy where a two-state solution became the goal. This marked a change in that Palestinians living within the 1948 borders were now politically seen as distinct from those in the Occupied Palestinian Territories, as were the Palestinian refugees in the diaspora. This helped lay the basis for the 1993 news that "shocked" the world: Israel and the PLO had held secret negotiations in Oslo designed to bring a peaceful resolution to the Palestinian–Israeli conflict. The political rhetoric pivoted on Israel's "right to exist," and when this was recognized by the PLO, what also emerged was a concession to the institutionalization of the Israel/Palestine racial contract by a section of Palestinians, under the leadership of the PLO. On September 13, 1993, Prime Minister Yitzhak Rabin and Yasser Arafat famously shook hands after a signing ceremony in Washington presided over by US President Bill Clinton. The Oslo process and the Oslo Accords (The Declaration of Principles on Interim Self-Government) fostered a series of agreements in the 1990s that led to the Israeli withdrawal from parts of the West Bank and Gaza and to the creation of the Palestinian Authority.

Much could be addressed about the shortcomings of both the Oslo process and the Accords when it came to the role of both the United States and Norway (Sanders 1999), not least their failure to deal with Palestinian refugees, Palestinian statehood, and other "final status" issues. However, a detailed consideration goes beyond the scope of this discussion. It suffices that, as Gordon points out:

> If one reads the eight different Oslo agreements the Israelis and Palestinians signed over the years, not as part of a peace process (i.e., the way they were presented to the public), but rather as texts that depict the attempt to outsource responsibility for the occupied population to a Palestinian Authority (PA), the strategy Israel adopted becomes clear.... The overarching logic informing the different agreements is straightforward: transfer all responsibilities relating to the management of the population to the Palestinians themselves while preserving control of Palestinian space. (2008b: 35)

As such, the Oslo Accords cantonized Palestinian spaces in the West Bank and Gaza and introduced new paradoxes into constructions of paradigms of surveillance. The social sorting process that established Israel and that expanded in the 1967 war was now to be embedded in the vision of a permanent "peace." Israelization in the Middle East now earned international recognition, including a defined responsibility of a section of Palestinian society in enforcing the social sorting process. For example, Palestinian police had as a main duty, implicitly in the agreements, the responsibility to ensure "the protection of Israeli security and colonial interests in the Occupied Territories" (Lia 2006: 2–3).

By May 1996, Israeli Prime Minister Binyamin Netanyahu had declared a localized war on terror and simultaneously declared war on the Oslo Accords. With no repercussions from the United States, it is not surprising that later attempts to revive the Oslo process failed, including the Camp David 2000 Summit orchestrated by US President Bill Clinton. Nor is it surprising that at the same time, there was greater state violence, with massive increases in the destruction of Palestinian homes and the extrajudicial killings of Palestinians. This process coincided with increased Israeli surveillance of the air and ground via military satellites and unmanned armed drones (Gordon 2008a: 37; Gordon 2008b: 202–3). By 2000, the Al-Aqsa Intifada ushered in a new spiral of desperation and violence involving Palestinian suicide bombers. This "ignited the cultural imagination of western societies" (Naaman 2007: 941) in combining perceptions about religion (specifically, Islam) with a certain perceived role of women, men, and family life in so-called "traditional" societies. These constructions—of ostensibly dangerous, suicide-driven men and now women, who were motivated by religion to destroy the innocent—were foundational in the later construction of post-9/11 moral panic about both noncitizens and citizens, well beyond Israel and the Middle East (see Razack 2008). The pieces were now all in place for the global Israelization of surveillance and the Palestinianization of the Israel/Palestine racial contract—a tinderbox to be lit by the events of 9/11.

2001–08: The "victim state" model and liberal democratic exceptions

Since September 11th, the representation of the Palestinian/Arab/Muslim terrorist has assumed greater transhistorical and transnational proportions. In the context of Israel/Palestine, the website of the Israeli

Ministry of Foreign Affairs has depicted "Arab and Palestinian terrorism against Israel [*sic*]" as "predating" the establishment of the state in May 1948 (Israel Ministry of Foreign Affairs 2002: 1). Its transnational characteristics are contained in how notions like "sleeper cells" have made their way into the popular lexicon of Western countries. As Bankoff notes, "just as the non-Western world was previously portrayed as disease-ridden, poverty-stricken and hazard-prone, more or less the same regions are now depicted as 'terrorist-spawning'" (2003: 418).

Since 9/11, such representations have been aided by a new ideological framing of the West, and concomitantly Israel's place in the racial contract. This marks a moment of redefining hegemony in the international racial contract. In shaping the response to 9/11, the US administration under the presidency of George W. Bush presented the crisis in terms that identified the United States and American "values" as victims of a global enemy that was neither a state nor the policy of a state. Rather, the "enemy" was perceived to be Arab or Muslim "terrorism" specifically, later elaborated as the values of a perceived system of extremism, sometimes bearing the term "Islamofascism." As Sunera Thobani has aptly summarized:

> As the Bush Administration (with the support of its allies, including Canada) launched the War on Terror to reassert its dominance, the battle to control the meaning of the attacks was no less intense than the one waged on the bodies of the Muslims named as the enemy.... The Bush Administration has described Western societies as gravely threatened by the murderous violence of the Islamists, and in effect, whiteness has been recast as vulnerable, endangered, innocent and the subject of irrational hatred of this fanatic non-Western Other. (2007a: 169–70)

Among those who accepted various elements of this basic and racialized framing of the 9/11 attacks were a number of leading North American and European mainstream feminists (for a critique, see Razack 2008: 83–106; Thobani 2007a). As an example, consider Phyllis Chesler, author of *The New Anti-Semitism: The Current Crisis and What We Must Do About It*. Chesler notes that upon learning of the attacks of September 11, 2001, she typed the sentence: "Now, we are all Israelis"; the rest of the manuscript followed (2003: 1). The argument develops a comparison between the United States after 9/11 and Israel since its inception. Israel is posited as a state historically victimized by Arab extremists, but, until

9/11, largely isolated, with only the Jewish population to really defend it in an embattled and defensive war of survival. The events of 9/11, according to Chesler, need to be understood as extending the experience of Israel and its Jewish citizens to the global scale. Notably, in constructing this analysis, Chesler accepts the mythologized exceptionalism in the Zionist narrative, where Israel is perceived to be fundamentally unique in its democratic character in the Middle East, in its advanced values, and in its protection of the "Jewish people." Those who challenge the state of Israel and its policies are, she maintains, ultimately anti-Semitic and implicitly defending a "reactionary Islamic" worldview. The latter is understood to be both undemocratic and barbarically sexist.

The mythologized exceptional character of Israel as a victim state, rooted in the original Zionist colonial project, is thus extended to encompass the United States and the West. The social sorting that generates violent measures to secure a constructed and settler, non-Arabic, and non-Muslim public from the threat of "terrorism" is elevated in this framing of the events of 9/11. Moreover, the analogy of victimization is extended and enhanced with a parallel analogy, developing associations first between "extreme" Islam and a "new anti-Semitism" that challenges Israeli policies, and in turn draws further parallels with Hitler's Nazis. In Chesler's words:

> The new anti-Zionist and anti-Semite does not distinguish between Jew and the Jewish state and finds both objectionable in the same way that Nazi-era or Christian-era propagandists found individual Jews objectionable. (2003: 192)

This view of Israel as a victim state that is comparable to a post-9/11 United States claimed greater ideological space, particularly throughout the two terms of the George W. Bush administration. It has also become normalized intellectually, summarized in the notion of "Islamofascism." The term has been used by writers such as the late Christopher Hitchens in the media, and during the 2006 Israeli attack on Lebanon both by then UK Prime Minister Tony Blair and then US President George W. Bush.[1] But it is also being advanced at a more theoretical level, presented as a concept based on an assumed association of Zionism and the state of Israel with the interests and beliefs of Jewish people in all historical periods and in all social and political circumstances. The argument is that Jewish people are the victims of both Islam and fascism, as two sides of the same anti-Semitic coin, and that the two sides are really one and the same. Telos Press, for example, has published the English translation of Matthias Küntzel's 2007 book, *Jihad and Jew Hatred: Islamism, Nazism and the Roots of 9/11*. The book won the London Book Festival grand prize (2007) and the Independent Publishers Book Awards' Gold Award for Religion (2008). The argument hangs on the idea that any challenge to Zionism and the establishment and activities of the state of Israel is equivalent to anti-Semitism. From there, it asserts a linear analysis of the history of the Muslim Brotherhood and global politics from the Second World War to 9/11, highlighting the significance of close linkages between Islam and fascism.

This reframed global context was matched by, and in turn supported, the further entrenchment of the Israeli state's resolve to manage the "conflict" with Palestinians according to a racialized hegemonic project. The period following 2001 witnessed one of the most violent in Israel's history of apartheid-like practices against Indigenous Palestinians. The restrictions on the mobility rights of Palestinians, endemic in the original forced settlement and establishment of the state of Israel as a "Jewish only" territory (Korn 2000), intensified, justified on the grounds that there were heightened security risks associated with the second Intifada (Cook 2006).

Israel's refusal to adhere to international law continues to be, after 9/11, virtually ignored by the major powers in global politics. While this pattern was in place before 9/11, it is perhaps more notable in recent rulings. For example, the continued extension of the "separation barrier," ruled illegal by the International Court of Justice (ICJ) in 2004, continues, with no consequences or sanctions for the violation (Dolphin 2006). Moreover, the massive Israeli attack in the West Bank in March 2002 (cynically dubbed "Defensive Shield") is, according to Neve Gordon, paradigmatic of a new form of control, wherein "the occupying power adopt[s] more intense and remote mechanisms of violence" while destroying the civil and administrative institutions (2008b: 205). The same parameters of violence and destruction—in contravention of international law—can also be seen in the December 2008–January 2009 Israeli attack in Gaza (cynically dubbed "Operation Cast Lead") as well as the July–August 2014 Israeli attack in Gaza (the so-called "Operation Protective Edge"). The lost lives of Palestinians in Gaza climbed into the thousands with these attacks, with little by way of diplomatic consequences for Israel from powerful states. In essence, the global accommodation of the

Israelization of surveillance and the accompanying violent enforcement of social sorting, and of the Palestinianization of the Israel/Palestine racial contract with the accompanying dehumanization of the ascribed "terrorist," has apparently enabled the Israeli state to assume a wider remit in its actual oppression of Palestinians. It is therefore unsurprising that Mbembe calls the Israeli occupation "the most accomplished form of necropower" in its creation of death worlds (2003: 27). To quote:

> Everywhere, the symbolics of the *top* (who is on top) is reiterated. Occupation of the skies therefore acquires a critical importance, since most of the policing is done from the air. Various other technologies are mobilized to this effect: sensors aboard unmanned air vehicles (UAVs), aeriel reconnaissance jets, early warning Hawkeye planes, assault helicopters, an Earth-observation satellite, techniques of "hologrammatization." Killing becomes precisely targeted. (Mbembe 2003: 29)

Post September 11th, the assertion of the (Muslim/Arab) terrorist as the common enemy of Israel and other Western states has entailed in the latter, even more aggressive, immigration laws and practices, border controls, and forms of increasingly digitalized surveillance over noncitizens (Abu-Laban 2015; Broeders 2007; Cole 2002–3; Fekete 2004: 16–17; Razack 2008: 31). It has also entailed a reconstruction of the threat of "foreigners" such that not only noncitizens but also "suspicious" citizens may be viewed as dangerous and treated differentially (Abu-Laban 2004; Bigo 2005; Dhamoon and Abu-Laban 2009; Fekete 2004). For example, a new legitimacy for overt racial profiling was established as a feature of advanced security measures associated with technologically advanced surveillance and connected to practices and ideas of responsible democratic governance (Abu-Laban 2004, 2005; Lyon 2003: 49–60; Razack 2008). This contrasts with the post–Second World War and pre-9/11 period, where such practices were commonly considered ideologically, if not in practice, to be a relic of an archaic past and where discriminatory practices were assumed to be overcome with the expansion of modernity (Cairns 1999). At the extreme, after September 11th, citizens of liberal democracies were subject to rendition for torture, as suffered by dual Canadian and Syrian citizen Maher Arar. US authorities falsely accused Arar of being a member of Al Qaeda and chose to deport him to Syria, where he was imprisoned and tortured between 2002 and 2003. An independent Canadian commission cleared Arar of any wrongdoing, and the Canadian government under Prime Minister Stephen Harper offered an apology for the role Canadian officials may have played and 10.5 million dollars (Canadian) in compensation. However, the case in fact shows the relevance of Agamben's (2005) concept of exception even in Canada (Abu-Laban and Nath 2007). Collectively, these post–September 11th practices, often advanced through antiterrorist legislation, speak to the Palestinianization of the racial contracts of liberal democracies. Such practices are differentially directed at noncitizens as well as citizens in the name of security and combating "terror," resting upon a deep and racialized acceptance of the unnamed Islamic/Arab dangerous other.

In the heightened climate of antiterrorism surveillance following 9/11, the Israeli state has increased its international profile as an "expert" in "resisting" the threat of the constructed "Muslim terrorist." The results of this expertise—a clear feature of the Israelization of surveillance—were tragically indicated in the response of the London police system to the July 7, 2005, incidents. On that day, a horrific attack on innocent citizens took place on the London Underground when three bomb explosions erupted within fifty seconds of each other. On July 9, the BBC reported 49 confirmed deaths, 25 missing people, and at least 700 injuries.[2]

On July 22, 2005, a 27-year-old man, Jean Charles De Menezes, was shot and killed by police in the Stockwell Underground station on suspicion of terrorism. De Menezes was innocent of the crime, but the police shooting to kill on suspicion of terror was not accidental. De Menezes was a Brazilian national living in south London. He had lived with his uncle in Sao Paulo from the age of fourteen to further his education, and had arrived in Britain in 2002, living there first as a visitor and then as a student. He was not of Arab origin, nor of Islamic faith. But the fact that he fit the ascribed profile of a "Muslim terrorist" and was perceived to be a potential suicide bomber was sufficient grounds to render him vulnerable to police. This was a moment of articulation of the specific Palestinianization of the racial contract, moving from the localized notion of the threatening "Arab terrorist" in the Middle East to the British liberal democratic context. De Menezes, a Latino person of color and hence already treated as "other" in the British/European racial contract, became a suspected suicide bomber on site, perceived as such by police trained in antiterrorist activity, significantly, by the Israeli state. As Jude McCulloch and Vicki Sentas summarize:

That the shooting of Jean Charles was represented as a "regrettable necessity" for which no one is held accountable underlies the low value placed on the lives of "suspected others" sacrificed in the pursuit of "national security".... The failure to prosecute his death as a crime, announced almost a year after his killing, fits with the pattern of impunity in cases of police shooting deaths at the hands of the state more generally. The relegation of the killing to the status of collateral damage echoes the war's international front. (2006: 1)

The *Financial Times* reported on July 25, 2005:

> Senior police officers said guidelines giving armed officers specific instructions on how to deal with suspected suicide bombers were circulated secretly for the first time, though never published, in 2003. A Met [Metropolitan police] team had visited Israel and Sri Lanka and produced a confidential report on tackling an Al-Qaeda threat in the UK. Instructions ... are thought to have covered disabling the nervous system with a shot to the head.... According to minutes of a meeting that have been made available to the FT [*Financial Times*], David Venessa, then head of anti-terrorist operations, told ... his officers they were facing a very different threat from suicide bombers than they had faced from the IRA [Irish Republican Army].[3]

Venessa is quoted further to state: "Clearly the experience of Israel and some of its responses to suicide bombings would not be suitable as a response to the UK." But he also stated that it would be "foolish not to try to draw on their experience." As Massoud Shadareh of the Islamic Human Rights Commission of the UK stated: "No one told us the police had been given effective carte-blanche to shoot dead on suspicion."[4]

This example illustrates the changed context of post-9/11 security, surveillance, and social sorting. The capacity of Israel to present its colonialist occupation of the Indigenous Palestinian population as a defensive posture against "Arab terrorism" was enhanced in the framing of the United States and the West in general as victims of 9/11. As McCulloch and Sentas state:

> Tactics developed by the Israeli forces for use in the Occupied Territories and inside Israel directly influenced the development of the firearms tactics that led to the death of Jean Charles. The shooting of

> Jean Charles happened under the remit of "Operation Kratos," a policy developed in consultation with the Israeli security officials. A national steering group on dealing with suicide bombers was set up shortly after September 11; it involved the British Home Office, MI5, Special Forces, the attorney general, and the Director of Public Prosecution, among other agencies.... Kratos recommended "shooting to kill" suspected suicide bombers by firing at their heads so that bullets do not detonate explosives strapped around bodies. (2006: 5)

Israel has seen fit to market more aggressively its services in the training of police in the aftermath of 9/11 on the grounds that it holds expertise in the science of controlling "Palestinian terrorists," considered comparable to those responsible for the events of 9/11. Police training missions to Israel have been organized among Ontario provincial police in Canada and across the United States. This has included tours of Israeli commanders to US cities to train federal and local law enforcement officials, as well as visits to Israel directly for training. According to a 2005 statement by US Capitol (Washington, DC) Police Chief Terrance W. Gainer, "Israel is the Harvard of antiterrorism."[5]

The ideological positioning of Israel as a victim state—apparently comparable to the United States on the world stage, and under siege from purportedly dangerous and collectively suspicious citizens who "look like" Arab/Palestinian/Muslim terrorists—has moved an historic "conflict" once noted for its acclaimed exceptionality into a realm of heightened universality. Naomi Klein (2007) has identified the manufacture and export of the Israeli security industry in the aftermath of 9/11 as not only ideologically opportune but also profitable for Israeli capitalism. The infamous Apartheid Wall (separation barrier) has been identified as a prototype for increasing surveillance in other parts of the world in the post-9/11 era. Klein notes a list of Israeli companies (including Elbit, Magal, and Verint Systems) that have been central to the wall's construction. Israel's capacity to specialize in apparently apartheid-sensitive technological devices that enhance "security" based on racial profiling has proven a boon to Israel's version of "disaster capitalism." This builds on Israel's contemporary global economic strength in high technology (Hanieh 2003: 14). Klein notes that:

> "Security barriers" may prove to be the biggest disaster market of all. That's why Elbit and Magal don't mind the relentless negative publicity

> that Israel's wall attracts around the world—in fact, they consider it free advertising. "People believe we are the only ones who have experience testing this equipment in real life," explained Magal CEO Jacob Even-Ezra. Elbit and Magal have seen their stock prices more than double since September 11, a standard performance for Israeli homeland security stocks. Verint—dubbed the "granddaddy of the video surveillance space"—wasn't profitable before September 11, but between 2002 and 2006 its stock price has more than tripled, thanks to the surveillance boom. (2007: 528)

Israel's ascribed commonality with the United States as a post-9/11 victim state has, however, also revealed contradictory ramifications in the hegemony of the Israel/Palestine racial contract. While serving to hide the racialized and settler character of the state of Israel and thereby cultivating global tolerance and even sympathy for its specific racial contract, this image also challenges the historic notion of Israel as a peaceful and democratic haven in an otherwise barbaric Orientalized Middle East (Said 1992). The close association between Israel and a besieged post-9/11 United States, in other words, has also served to expose the mythologized exceptionalism that has historically surrounded Israel's aggressive and racialized practices toward the Palestinian people.

The international campaign on the part of the Israeli state to "re-brand" its public image as an attractive tourist site testifies to the challenges and contradictions of the post-9/11 hegemonic moment (developed further in Chapter 7). Cities targeted for the rebranding campaign include Toronto, Tokyo, London, Boston, and New York.[6] According to a September 2006 report in *Israel Today*, this entailed a $20-million, multi-year plan "to re-brand Israel and to improve its image."

> The purpose of the plan is to rid Israel's image around the world as an aggressor and warmonger, and to expose the international media and the public to Israel's more attractive sides such as the contributions to medicine and science, great achievements in high tech, conquering of the desert, contribution to world culture, the extraordinary number of Nobel Prize Laureates, and Israel as a great place for foreign investments.[7]

But the surveillance and racialized social sorting targeting Palestinians has continued and intensifies. Potential sites of resistance to Israel's oppressive practices have, however, also arisen in this context.

Conclusion: Sites of resistance

Our interest in surveillance and social sorting relates to what these processes reveal about state power, regionally and internationally, and about resistance in Israel/Palestine and the global solidarity movement. In the discussion to this point, the power of the Israeli state vis-à-vis the Indigenous Palestinian population has been apparent, illustrative of what we call the Israel/Palestine racial contract. Consistent with Gramsci's conception of the relationship between the state and civil society, we conclude this chapter by considering the ways in which the current conjuncture is one where new forms and locations of resistance to Israel's oppressive practices have come to the fore.

The ongoing daily struggles of Palestinians on the ground indicate a pattern of continual resistance. This is expressed in multiple ways, including through the words, images, and stories of children living with the consequences of the Apartheid Wall and navigating the surveillance and violence to which they are subject in this conflict zone (Shalhoub-Kevorkian 2006). It includes the Israeli refuseniks, who would rather face arrest for resisting conscription than "dominate, expel, starve and humiliate an entire people" (Grossman and Kaplan 2006: 189). It includes the Israeli women of Machsom Watch, who go to checkpoints to monitor the operation of the army and in some cases intervene (Naaman 2006). And it includes multiple forms of cultural production and creative reconfigurations of space, law, and history in artistic and creative expressions (Desai 2015).

These new sites of resistance have developed both within and outside of the conflict zone of Israel/Palestine. They have advanced further in response to the united call that has arisen from Palestinian civil society organizations for a comprehensive movement of boycott, divestment, and sanctions against the Israeli state for its continued illegal military occupation of Palestine, and for its repressive policies (Palestinian BNC 2005). This is an emerging international social movement that brings together Arabs and non-Arabs, Jews and non-Jews, spanning countries of Europe and North America and reaching to nations in the global South, including postapartheid South Africa (see Chapter 6). It is notable that in this movement, the analogy between contemporary Israel and Apartheid South Africa has become a standard point of reference. In articulating this comparison—one that is now established in scholarly research as well as popular works, such as former US President Jimmy Carter's book

Palestine: Peace not Apartheid (2006)—the mythologized exceptionalism of the Israeli state is implicitly challenged. Instead, the racialized nature of the Israeli state is suggestively, and strategically, compared to the racialized apartheid state of South Africa, a state that is now seen to be at least legislatively on the other side, as it were, of a particularly heinous racial contract, including legitimation of racialized social sorting and the accompanying processes of surveillance.

Another potential contribution of the apartheid comparison regarding sites of resistance is related to the construction of the racialized Palestinian as the classic, post-9/11 "terrorist." The processes we have referred to as the Palestinianization of the racial contract and the Israelization of social sorting and surveillance depend largely on a particular set of stereotyped constructions that conflate ascribed religious, racial, and cultural identities within a security framework threatened by "terrorism." During South Africa's apartheid period, the African National Congress (ANC) was similarly treated as a "terrorist" movement, and its leader, the late Nelson Mandela, was imprisoned for life. Despite continuing and extreme challenges, the fact that South Africa has moved into a postapartheid phase, where Nelson Mandela was not only released from incarceration but became the first democratically elected president in postapartheid South Africa, indicates that change can happen, even when conditions seem insurmountable. Despite the continuity of state practices in Israel/Palestine, which indicates the complexity of the local and global hegemony, the comparison with South Africa gestures to the possibility of a more optimistic outcome to the current conjuncture in Israel/Palestine.

Notes

1 Tony Blair, "Speech to the Los Angeles World Affairs Council," August 1, 2006, Available at http://news.bbc.co.uk/2/hi/americas/4785065.stm; Richard Allen Greene, "Bush's Language Angers US Muslims," *BBC News*, August 12, 2006, http://news.bbc.co.uk/2/hi/4785065.stm; Christopher Hitchens, "Defending Islamofascism: It's a Valid Term and Here's Why," *Slate*, October 22, 2007, https://slate.com/news-and-politics/2007/10/defending-the-term-islamofascism.html.

2 *BBC News*, "Tube Bombs 'Almost Simultaneous,'" July 9, 2005, http://news.bbc.co.uk/2/hi/uk_news/4666591.stm.

3 Jimmy Burns, "Met Adopted Secret Shoot-to-Kill Policy in the Face of a New and Deadly Threat," *FT.Com*, July 25, 2005, http://archive.li/GCgYa.

4 Ibid.

5 Sari Horwitz, "Israeli Experts Teach Police on Terrorism: Training Programs Prompt Policy Shifts," *Washington Post*, June 12, 2005, http://www.washingtonpost.com/wp-dyn/content/article/2005/06/11/AR2005061100648.html; Khaled Mouammar, "Khaled Mouammar's Complaint Re: Ontario Provincial Police's Trip to Israel." *Address to Professional Standards Bureau, Ontario Provincial Police*, August 11, 2005, http://www.montrealmuslimnews.net/khaled.pdf.

6 David Brinn, "Israel's Rebranding Efforts to Focus on Toronto." *Jerusalem Post*, March 16, 2008, https://www.jpost.com/International/Israels-rebranding-efforts-to-focus-on-Toronto.

7 *Israel Today*, "Israel to Re-brand Itself in the World," September 12, 2006, http://www.israeltoday.co.il/default.aspx?tabid=178&nid=9460.

PART TWO

GLOBAL POLITICS AND THE ISRAEL/ PALESTINE RACIAL CONTRACT

4 THE PARADOX OF THE UNITED NATIONS: HUMAN RIGHTS, ISRAEL, AND PALESTINE

The UN has been the central global arena for addressing issues of human rights. The 1948 Universal Declaration of Human Rights is seen as a foundational element in the cascading significance of this frame, ultimately inspiring what has been deemed the "human rights revolution" (Ignatieff 2007; Iriye, Goedde, and Hitchkock 2012). The institutional historiography of the UN is intimately linked to the post–Second World War context, and the relevance of the Holocaust, and Holocaust memory, is central to the idea of human rights as a universal principle (Galligan and Larking 2009; Simon, Rosenberg, and Eppert 2000). However, the so-called "question of Palestine," brought onto the international stage by Edward Said in his classic book of the same title (1981), continues to escape Western understanding. It has been curiously excluded from a consistent human rights frame, a central issue in the international movement calling for justice for Palestinians (Palestinian BNC 2005). In this chapter, we link these typically disconnected strands to argue that the UN has served as a paradoxical site regarding the Israel/Palestine racial contract, as a means to both advance institutional support for rights and simultaneously legitimize rights denial. The paradox is messy, even chaotic, and nonlinear. The pivotal centering of the Holocaust, and the commitment to remember the devastating slaughter of millions of Jewish people, is placed uncomfortably in relation to the *Nakba* and the ongoing denial of Palestinian refugees' right to return to the homes and land from which they were exiled in 1948, the same year that the UN embraced the Universal Declaration of Human Rights.

The argument in this chapter is presented in two parts. The first part considers the relevance of the development of an international framework and discourse pertaining to human rights, particularly in the wake of the Holocaust and the Second World War. In the second part, the "question of Palestine" is considered as a window into the exclusionary aspects of the UN, rooted in its organizational predecessor, the League of Nations, and the mandate system set up after the First World War. Both of these dimensions, one inclusionary and the other exclusionary, are deeply embedded in longstanding, often polarized, international discussions pertaining to race, racism, and ideas surrounding anti-racist practice. As a consequence, it is perhaps not surprising that these dimensions have continued to play out in the twenty-first century, most evident in the United Nations World Conference Against Racism (WCAR) process.

The WCAR process is addressed here by way of conclusion to the chapter. The process began with the 2001 world conference held in Durban, South Africa, and continued with the 2009 review (held in Geneva, Switzerland) and the 2011 tenth anniversary commemoration (held in New York, US). All of these events have been, significantly, sponsored by the UN and bear an explicit mandate to address the persistence of racism internationally. While not the first moment of such conferences, or the only space in the UN lexicon to address racism specifically in the context of human rights, the WCAR process has been an important forum for expressing some of the most prominent tensions in the twenty-first century, not least the challenge of considering race in the context of Israel/Palestine.

Chaotic inclusion: The human rights revolution

The "human rights revolution" spans a period that is commonly understood to have expanded, unevenly and not without considerable resistance, over two phases in the post–Second World War era. The first period covers the institutionalization of the Universal Declaration of Human Rights in 1948 until the early 1990s; the second extends from the early 1990s to the present. The turning point of the 1990s was marked by the changing borders and emergent new dialogues that accompanied the end of the Cold War. It was also marked by the reform of human rights instruments in the UN as the principal site of the global political and legal organization of states and nonstate actors. In the lead-up to 1988, marking the fortieth anniversary of the Universal Declaration of Human Rights, the UN General Assembly unanimously committed to launching a public information campaign regarding human rights and to developing and strengthening human rights awareness and support in complementary activities among UN bodies, member states, and nongovernmental organizations (see UN General Assembly 1992).

The UN review process that accompanied this transitional moment recognized that human rights activities and awareness had expanded dramatically in the forty years following the UN Declaration of Human Rights (UN General Assembly 1992: 4). In the period following 1948, there was, despite controversy, increasing international support for various levels of human rights protections. As of 2010,

> Fundamental international treaties in the human rights sphere were adopted in close succession; today there are nine of them, one of which (On the Protection of All Persons from Enforced Disappearance) has not yet been enacted. Since 1948 (the year the Universal Declaration of Human Rights was adopted), all UN members have ratified at least one of the human rights treaties, and 80 percent ratified four and more. It resulted in creation of eight committees of independent experts to monitor implementation of the fundamental international human rights treaties: the Committees on Human Rights; Economic, Social and Cultural Rights; Elimination of Racial Discrimination; Elimination of Discrimination against Women; Committee against Torture (in 2007 it acquired a Sub-Committee on Prevention of Torture and Other Cruel, Inhuman or Degrading Treatment); Committee on the Rights of the Child; Committee on the Protection of the Rights of All Migrant Workers and Members of Their Families and Committee on the Rights of Persons with Disabilities. (Lyapichev 2010: 143)

In the period coinciding with and following the forty-year anniversary mark of the Universal Declaration of Human Rights, although the earlier period of institutional and legislative inclusion was not considered complete, the identified focus of UN activities shifted toward building up a "universal culture of human rights" through a World Public Information Campaign for Human Rights (UN General Assembly 1989: 4). This universal culture was premised on the idea that "human rights and fundamental freedoms were inherent in the human person without any distinction as to race, colour, sex, language, religion, political or other opinion, national or social origin, property, birth or other status" (UN General Assembly 1989: 4).

The UN approach to human rights policies and practices changed from the late 1980s. The UN Commission on Human Rights (UNCHR), originally established in 1946, was replaced by the UN Human Rights Council, formed in 2005. A brief summary of the transition indicates the shift:

> In March 2005, Kofi Annan in his report "In Larger Freedom: Toward Development, Security and Human Rights for All" suggested that the UN Human Rights Commission should be replaced with a smaller permanent UN Human Rights Council, which should inherit from its predecessor the system of special procedures and, at the same time, take measures to become a more efficient instrument of promotion and protection of human rights all over the world. On 14–16 September 2005, in New York heads of state and government passed a decision on reforming the UN human rights activities; on 15 March 2006, the UN GA specified this in Resolution 60/251. The resolution replaced the UN Human Rights Commission with the UN Human Rights Council. The status of the latter was promoted to a subsidiary body of the UN GA [General Assembly]. Its membership was decreased while membership criteria were tightened with an understanding that it was open for all UN members. (Lyapichev 2010: 145)

During both the first and second periods of human rights recognition at the UN, the application of a framework regarding anti-racism was particularly challenged. Moreover, among numerous points of contention, a perpetual and continuing issue was the application of a consistent anti-racist human rights approach to the Israel/Palestine conflict. The effectiveness of human rights policies is uneven and chaotic, not least due to concerns to address and redress the overtly racist policies of the Nazi regime and the Axis powers that backgrounded the Second World War. Indeed, the genocidal policies of the Nazis toward Jewish people and the explicit, entrenched state defense of a eugenicist argument for the superiority of the white Christian "Aryan" race were pivotal in shaping the discussions that led to the development and widespread approval of the Universal Declaration of Human Rights. Following the failed experiment of the League of Nations, the emergent UN was originally imagined as an extension of the influence of the Allied forces. It was later understood in the context of the contested terrain of the Cold War.

> The UN's General Assembly adopted the Universal Declaration of Human Rights (UDHR) in 1948 and, in Article 1, proclaimed: "All human beings are born free and equal in dignity and rights". This international consensus of noble ideals, forged by nations emerging from the horrors of a second World War and shocked by the atrocities committed against civilian populations in that war, was soon fractured by Cold War differences and disagreement over combining civil and political rights, championed by Anglo-American and European countries, with economic, social and cultural rights, supported by communist states and developing countries. (Galligan and Larking 2009: 1)

The post-Nazi relationship to the Holocaust was therefore embedded in the original framework of the UN, specifically its human rights framework. However, this stood in contrast to the absence of such a humanitarian impulse among the Allied powers regarding the human rights of Jewish victims of Nazi genocide during the actual events of the war. One of the most striking examples is indicated in the outcome of the international conference convened on the initiative of US President Franklin D. Roosevelt in July 1938, at Evian, France, specifically to address the issue of increasing numbers of Jewish refugees seeking asylum from Nazi persecution (Estorick 1939). Delegates from thirty-two countries met over a period of nine days; ultimately, all the major powerful states, including the United States and Britain, refused to open their borders to the calls for refuge. As noted earlier, the Canadian government's wartime policy regarding Jewish refugees was explicit, summarized simply by Frederick Blair, the minister responsible for immigration in the government of William Lyon Mackenzie King, as "None is too many" (Abella and Troper 2012).

With the victory of the Allied forces, however, and the expansion of trade and aid to post–Second World War Germany, an "invented tradition" (Hobsbawm and Ranger 1983) of Jewish rescue and assimilation in a renewed "Judeo-Christian" Western imaginary emerged and eventually gained hegemonic influence (Bakan 2014a). This was a complex and chaotic process. It included pragmatism and *realpolitik* with an aim to secure a stable new world order, but the process was mired in ideological inconsistency. While ongoing elements of anti-Semitism (here meaning anti-Jewish racism) in the West were minimized, efforts were increased to enhance liberal inclusion of religious and ethnic minorities in the nominal structures of international institutions. Ultimately, the memory of the Jewish Holocaust was captured particularly by the emerging Israeli state, and among its international advocates, especially US Zionist organizations. The effect was to deny, forgive, and forget Western European racism toward the Jewish population and to ascribe Jewish survival to the colonial state-building project associated with Israeli military occupation of Palestinian land, first in 1948 and then with further reach in 1967.

Significant moments in the construction of what can be considered a chaotically inclusive process of human rights at the level of the UN can be identified. These moments reveal an inconsistent pattern regarding racism, which, while certainly not unique to the context of Israel/Palestine, starkly demonstrates a specific emerging racial contract. Even as the formal institutions and normative influence of human rights at the level of the UN were advancing, a parallel frame of Israel's exceptionality and its exemption from accountability to international law in relation to the racialized occupation of Palestinian lands was solidified. A formative element of this paradox at the interface of human rights and anti-racism on the global stage was the capture and monopolization of a certain narrative. This narrative held that the extreme suffering of the Jewish people in the face of Nazi genocide was grounds for establishing a new form of postwar colonialism in the Middle East. The narrative provided justification in the new era of "human rights" for the violent origins of the Israeli state. Pivotal moments in this process include, particularly: the Nuremburg Trials, Israel's original recognition and status in the UN, the Eichmann Trial, and the 1967 Israeli-Arab War. While an extensive historical review of these elements would take us beyond the scope of this discussion, each is briefly addressed below to indicate how the pattern of institutionalization of the Israel/Palestine racial contract was foundational to the UN framing of human rights.

In the years immediately following the Second World War, a diplomatic process was initiated that included the establishment of criteria by which senior Nazi officers could be held to account, establishing the grounds for an international system of justice. The trials of Nazi officers ultimately took place in Nuremburg, Germany, in military tribunals held between

November 20, 1945, and October 1, 1946. The location, territory under the occupation of the Allied forces, was agreed upon by three major wartime allies—the United States, the USSR, and the UK—with the addition of France. The grounds for the choice of Nuremburg were that it had previously been a recognized center for Nazi rallies and events. The Palace of Justice, including an attached prison complex, was a large and relatively undamaged symbolic venue. Significantly, diplomatic efforts that generated the conditions for the Nuremburg Trials also led to the development of the Universal Declaration of Human Rights and the UN Charter.

> The diplomatic process that led to the adoption of the Universal Declaration of Human Rights (or the Declaration) began in 1946 in New York City, where the "nuclear" UN Commission on Human Rights met for the first time and set out the guidelines for drafting the text adopted by General Assembly resolution in 1948. Together with two other diplomatic events—the San Francisco Conference of 1945, which adopted the UN Charter (or the Charter), and the London Conference that same year, at which the Allies agreed on the legal contours of the postwar Nuremberg prosecutions—the Declaration laid out the normative underpinnings of an international system governed by the rule of law and respect for human rights. This founding trifecta would be relied on by future generations of lawyers and diplomats to create institutions aimed to prevent and limit war, hold accountable the political and military leaders responsible for violating core principles of internationally recognized law, and support the development and enforcement of international human rights norms. (McGuinness 2011: 749)

These trials indicated the formal commitment of the international community to try and prosecute Nazi military and political leaders, though in fact many senior Nazi personnel proceeded to be welcomed into European and North American society without restriction. However, in the trials, the crimes of Nazi genocide were framed in the context of crimes against humanity as a whole. The Nazi war machine was considered to include genocide and anti-Semitism but was not read to be reducible to or explicitly focused on this issue. Consideration of anti-Semitism in the context of international justice, however, elevated the interests of the European movement for the establishment of an ethnically defined state that would privilege Jewish nationality, or political Zionism.

The relationship of Israel to the UN is obviously significant in terms of human rights and anti-racist agendas, and it prefigures the discussion below regarding the contested exclusion of Palestine and Palestinians. It is notable that Israel was established as a state with a particular political frame grounded in a Zionist response to European anti-Semitism. This included the 1894 Dreyfus Affair in France, on which Theodor Herzl reported (Begley 2009). Zionism, as noted earlier, is a political perspective, and therefore it should not be equated with Jewish cultural or religious identity or with Judaism as a theology. It was, until the events of the Second World War, a marginal perspective. In order to advance, Zionist adherents demanded links with European power and colonialism, accounting for Herzl's admiration for Cecil Rhodes and the project of imperial settlements in southern Africa (Bakan 2014a).

The next formative event was the establishment of the state of Israel. A variety of geopolitical and ideological factors combined in 1948 to produce a new state in the Middle East characterized by a number of features of exceptionality. The foundational story of Israel's "independence" from colonial Britain was rendered consistent with an origin story associated with the aftermath of the Second World War. However, there was an inherent contradiction in terms of human rights. Israel's Zionist narrative exclusively privileged Jewish identity and "nationality"—especially European, or Ashkenazi and white, Jewish identity—which was particularistic. Internationally, however, the desire to redress the severe violation of the human rights of the Jewish population in Europe and internationally expressed a universalistic perspective. The violence and colonial dispossession that accompanied the establishment of the state of Israel contradict the principles of universal human rights, pointing to the Israel/Palestine racial contract. Regarding the uneven and chaotic inclusiveness of the UN, it is notable that, as Ilan Pappe has summarized:

> An inexperienced UN, just two years old in 1947, entrusted the question of the future of Palestine's fate into the hands of a Special Committee for Palestine, UNSCOP [UN Special Committee on Palestine], none of whose members turned out to have any prior experience in solving conflicts or knew much about Palestine's history.... [T]he UN accepted the nationalist claims the Zionist movement was making for Palestine and, furthermore, sought to compensate the Jews for the Nazi Holocaust in Europe. (2006b: 31)

Gilbert Achcar notes the polarization of perspectives that emerged within and beyond the UN.

> Even on the territory attributed in November 1947 to the "Jewish state" by a UN General Assembly in which the future "Third World" was barely represented—a territory that would be substantially enlarged *manu military* in the course of the first Arab-Israeli war—close to half the resident population received Israel's declaration of independence as an outrage. At the time, a yawning gulf separated those who regarded the creation of Israel as an act of liberation of the first importance—the redemption of European Jewry's centuries-old history of oppression—and those who perceived it as the establishment of a colonial entity at the cost of the Indigenous population. (2009: 27)

While established on the territory of historic Palestine, among a diverse population that included a majority of Indigenous Muslim and Christian Palestinians, as well as a minority of Mizrahi (Arab or Oriental) Jews and some Ashkenazi (European) Jews, it was framed as a uniquely "Jewish" state in the aftermath of European Jewish genocide. With its explicit association with European colonial settlement, and as the product of considerable advocacy from Jewish Zionist civil society organizations, Israel's establishment could be framed as a form of reparation for the Holocaust. The expectation of mass emigration of the remaining surviving European Jewish population was, however, consistent with the historic anti-Semitism that sought elimination of Jewish life and citizenship from Christian "civilized" society. The interface of issues of race, hegemony, and power associated and intersecting with both anti-Semitism (as anti-Jewish racism) and Orientalism (as anti-Arab racism) is elemental to the Israel/Palestine racial contract.

On May 11, 1949, one year after its establishment, Israel was recognized by the General Assembly and accepted into the UN with Resolution 273. The resolution, importantly, recalls the resolutions of November 29, 1947 (Resolution 181), and December 11, 1948 (Resolution 194). The former recognizes both a Jewish and Arab state based on the partition of Mandatory Palestine; the latter recognizes the right of displaced Palestinian refugees to return to their homelands and receive compensation. These conditionalities were associated with the vote to accept Israel into the UN as a voting member state. They remain unmet, however, to this day. At the same time, the recognition of a state that was specifically associated with a single religious-ethnic community posed particular challenges in terms of human rights and anti-racism. Israeli historian Shlomo Sand summarizes the contradictory tensions, naming Israel as an "ethnos state":

> In 1947 the UN General Assembly resolved by a majority vote to establish a "Jewish state" and an "Arab state" in the territory that had previously been known as "Palestine/Eretz Israel". At that time, many thousands of displaced Jewish persons were wandering in Europe, and the small community that had been created by the Zionist settlement enterprise was supposed to take them in. The United States, which before 1924 had taken in many Yiddish Jews, now refused to open its gates to the broken remnants of the great Nazi massacre. So did the other rich countries. In the end, it was easier for those countries to solve the troublesome Jewish problem by offering a faraway land that was not theirs. (2009: 280)

The framework for attending to international human rights in the UN was clearly, then, contradictory and inconsistent from its earliest, foundational years. Hannah Arendt, a German Jewish-American scholar and a survivor of the Holocaust, as noted earlier, famously documented and analyzed the Eichmann trial in 1961 (2006). Israel was only thirteen years past its origins at the time of the trial. The Israeli state's identification of the original moment as Israel's "war of independence" was a narrative still in the making.[1] Arendt maintained that the trial served as a turning point in international processes regarding human rights, an analysis consistent with consideration of the Israel/Palestine racial contract. With this trial of one particularly infamous Nazi war criminal, Adolf Eichmann, the frame of international justice regarding Germany's role in the Second World War established at Nuremburg was to shift. Arendt maintains that, rather than the trial taking place under the terms of the Nuremburg international military court, Eichmann's trial was placed in a uniquely distinct venue and jurisdictional context. Arendt understood the Eichmann trial as a moment of Israel's political assertion of its claim to represent the Jewish survivors of the Holocaust, as the charges were shaped fundamentally as "a crime against the Jewish people," rather than, following the Nuremburg trials of 1945–6, crimes against humanity. Through this process, the high-profile trial served not as a model for challenging war crimes against humanity based on the principles of universal human rights, but as an instrument of nation building for the still-young state of Israel. The trial was significant in developing a specific interpretation of the events of the Second World War, framing the postwar order within a distinctly Zionist understanding of anti-Semitism.

Arendt suggested that the trial was less about justice than performance. She challenged the event as a "show trial," where "David Ben-Gurion, Prime Minister of Israel … rightly called the 'architect of the state,' remains the invisible stage manager of the proceedings" (2006: 5). Eichmann had fled Germany to avoid facing charges at Nuremburg and was living and hiding in Argentina. There, he was kidnapped by the Israeli police secret service and taken to Israel, where he was tried by the Israeli court. Ultimately, Eichmann was sentenced to death and hanged in 1962. While she recognized that the "justification was the unprecedentedness of the crime and the coming into existence of a Jewish State," she noted:

> In this instance, Israel had indeed violated the territorial principle, whose great significance lies in the fact that the earth is inhabited by many peoples and that these peoples are ruled by many different laws, so that every extension of one territory's law beyond the borders and limitations of its validity will bring it into immediate conflict with the law of another territory. (2006: 264)

The next significant moment linking the Israel/Palestine racial contract to the UN and human rights was the 1967 Six-Day War. Following the earlier moments, the war solidified the association between Israeli state practices and the constructed memory of the Holocaust. As David MacDonald (2008) has noted, the 1950s and 1960s were a period of Israel's nation building, which became tightly linked to a constructed insistence on international Holocaust commemoration. The 1967 war became a "rallying call for American Jews to come together in defence of the homeland, and the war marked a profound 'Israelization'" (MacDonald 2008: 19). The links between Israel and the United States were also, and not coincidentally, more profoundly forged in the events and aftermath of the 1967 war. Israel proved a valuable ally in opposing Arab states that were challenging US hegemony in the world's most oil-rich region. The 1967 war was significant also in shifting global attention away from Europe's role in advancing genocidal anti-Semitism during the Second World War. Israel claimed to be a victim of hostile Arab neighbors and emphasized association in the Middle East with European Nazis, effectively minimizing numerous links between Nazis and allied powers (see Black 2011).

The UN, while repeatedly calling for the withdrawal of Israel's occupation of territories seized in the 1967 war, at the same time tolerated the continuous expansion of permanent Israeli settlements. The process of chaotic inclusion associated with the UN human rights framework has therefore simultaneously restricted the expansion of Israel as a settler-colonial state in terms of resolutions and policies, while enabling and institutionalizing the occupation in practice. Efforts to call Israel to account in this anomalous situation have generated claims of Israeli victimhood on the world stage (Patten 2013). These claims are relevant specifically in the constructed charge of a "new anti-Semitism," which has been amplified in the post-9/11 period (Abu-Laban and Bakan 2011).

Israel's exceptionalism, however, is not readily traceable to its ascribed claim to represent Jewish people and interests, a representation that is widely challenged by Jewish critics within and beyond Israel's borders (Burg 2008; Pappe 2006b; Piterberg 2008; Sand 2009). Rather, what is exceptional are Israel's contradictory claims to adhere to universal human rights while enacting grave violations of the human rights of Palestinians—within the boundaries of Israel proper, in the Occupied Territories, and in the diaspora. The invented tradition that links Palestinian victims of colonial occupation and apartheid practices with redress for crimes of Nazis during the Holocaust has contributed to this contradictory and challenging discursive terrain.

Notably, and as developed further in Chapter 9, apartheid policies have historically been a particular focus in the UN regarding human rights violations. South African apartheid policies were repeatedly challenged by UN resolutions, legislative and policy instruments and conferences. The successful transition away from apartheid in South Africa has been hailed as, at least in part, the product of a persistent campaign grounded in the UN human rights system (for partial summaries, see Brits 2005; Dubow 2008; Malhotra 1964; Narang 2001; Reddy 1974). This was not, however, a unanimous movement among member states. The resistance of UN efforts against South African apartheid has been noted, and it is perhaps not insignificant that Israel maintained links with South Africa despite pressures to support limitations on South African state practices (Polakow-Suransky 2010).

Contested exclusion: The question of Palestine redux

Palestinians—as a people who have been denied statehood, and who are dispersed, colonized, fragmented across many state boundaries, and subject to a persistent pattern of anti-Arab racism consistent with entrenched Orientalism—have long been treated in the UN as a "question." In the League of Nations, they were treated as not worthy of self-determination. Yet, it is clear that, over the course of the post–Second World War era, the "question of Palestine" has not had any real "answer" or resolution. Neither the UN nor the Palestinians are static entities. In the years since the UN was founded, its more representative nature has afforded Palestinians a greater avenue for attempting to secure their own form of representation in this international organization. The UN has also been a place where the language of human rights can be mobilized to support the Palestinian experience and claims. At the same time, and as underscored by various actions and inactions—from the Partition Plan, to the lack of sanctions against Israel for failing to comply with international law, to the lack of enforcement of the Palestinian right of return—the UN has also been a place where Palestinian self-determination and rights have been denied. The Palestinian interface with the UN, one that may be characterized as ongoing contested exclusion, therefore deeply underscores the paradoxical character of the UN's politics of universal human rights. This paradox also accounts for ongoing attempts to utilize other means of enabling support, most recently a global movement for boycott, divestment, and sanctions directed at Israel. This movement is increasingly appealing to unions, students, churches, and other civil society activists in countries of the West (Bakan and Abu-Laban 2009).

The relationship of Palestine to the UN is a relationship of a stateless people to an international organization made up of states. This inherent tension cannot be fully addressed without recognizing the role of the League of Nations before the formation of the UN in 1945. Reviewing the historical evolution of the Israel/Palestine racial contract from a different lens, with a focus on Palestinian exclusion, demonstrates how the frame of human rights was advanced rhetorically while failing to address the rights of racialized, colonized, and Indigenous populations, of which the Palestinians were and are a part. Significant for the future of Palestine was the fact that the League of Nations established a system for transferring control of territories under Ottoman rule at the end of the First World War. Hence, Britain was given the Mandate over Palestine in 1922, and British authorities subsequently incorporated the 1917 Balfour Declaration into the Mandate. The Balfour Declaration—a document written in the form of a letter from Foreign Secretary Arthur Balfour to British Zionist leader Walter Rothschild—indicated:

> His Majesty's Government view with favour the establishment in Palestine of a national home for the Jewish people, and will use their best endeavours to facilitate the achievement of this object, it being clearly understood that nothing shall be done which may prejudice the civil and religious rights of existing non-Jewish communities in Palestine, or the rights and political status enjoyed by Jews in any other country. (United Kingdom 1917)

As Edward Said (1981) noted, the Balfour Declaration was pronounced by a European country about a non-European territory. The policy ignored both the presence and the wishes of the majority of the population. Indeed, it is notable that the Indigenous Palestinian (Christian and Muslim) population is merely referred to as "existing non-Jewish communities" and that the quest by Arabs for self-rule was ignored by the British state. As noted in Chapter 2, this quest was evident in the 1915 correspondence between Mecca's Sharif Hussein and Egypt's High Commissioner for Egypt (John and Hadawi 1970: 35–52). Moreover, the Zionist movement was, in the first place, a European-based movement responding to racism in Europe, but at the same time reflected Orientalist ideas and assumptions that rendered the Indigenous Muslim and Christian population both invisible and othered (Abu-Laban and Bakan 2008: 646). The Balfour Declaration was a document responding to the Zionist movement and also reflected the interests of colonial state power associated with racialized whiteness, both within and beyond the borders of Europe in the early twentieth century (Abu-Laban and Bakan 2008: 647). Further reflecting these aspects of state and colonial power informed by a strategy of divide and conquer, during 1915–16, then British Prime Minister David Lloyd George also "promised" Palestine to the Ottoman Empire in exchange for a separate peace (Schneer 2010: 252), seemingly making Palestine not the "twice" but "thrice" promised land, as British state officials offered it, variously, to Arabs, Jews, and Turks.

The relevance of colonial thinking and racialized power is further illustrated in the fact that, on November 29, 1947, the General Assembly of the newly created UN passed the Plan of Partition, aiming for it to be implemented upon termination of the British Mandate for Palestine. This plan sought to create "Independent Arab and Jewish States and the Special International Regime for the City of Jerusalem" (UN General Assembly 1947). It is noteworthy that, in this period, vast areas of the world were still under colonial rule; only fifty-seven states belonged to the UN in 1947 (in contrast to the 193 sovereign states in 2019). Of these fifty-seven states, thirty-three voted in favor of the partition plan, including the majority of European states (although Britain abstained). Due to its allotment of more land for a Jewish state and its favoring of what were viewed as settler-colonial aims of the Zionist movement, the plan was seen as unfair and rejected by the Indigenous Palestinian population. The plan, of course, never came to pass. In the context of mounting hostilities, or civil war, between Arabs and Jews in Palestine, on May 14, 1948, the British Mandate came to an end and an independent state of Israel was declared. Following this, open warfare broke out between Israel and other Arab states. By the end of the 1948 war, more land went to Israel than previously allotted in the partition plan. Nonetheless, as noted above, through General Assembly Resolution 273, Israel was admitted into the UN on May 11, 1949, and its claim to statehood was largely embraced by the international community. Further, a series of additional wars in the region (1956, 1967, 1973, and 1982) and the building of settlements in the Occupied Palestinian Territories, held to be illegal under international law, led to more land being expropriated from Palestinians and falling under Israeli control, generating still more Palestinian refugees.

By way of contrast, the *Nakba* occurred in the very same year that the 1948 Universal Declaration of Human Rights was passed, emblematically underscoring the tension that Palestine/Palestinians exhibit in relation to the UN. Thus, while Palestinian statelessness is treated as a problem and is subject to numerous resolutions in the UN, it has also assumed a form of almost structural permanence in the many decades since 1948. For example, General Assembly Resolution 194 (December 11, 1948) establishes a right of return for Palestinian refugees by resolving that:

> refugees wishing to return to their homes and live at peace with their neighbours should be permitted to do so at the earliest practicable

date, and that compensation should be paid for the property of those choosing not to return and for loss of or damage to property which, under principles of international law or in equity, should be made good by the Governments or authorities responsible.

For Palestinian refugees, the right of return to lands controlled by Israel has not been enforced, even though the General Assembly's Resolution 273 of 1949 premised Israel's admittance into the UN on both the partition plan and the right of return of Palestinians (UN Resolution 194). Further, a similar institutionalization of exclusionary practices associated with the rights of Palestinians is linked with the United Nations Relief and Works Agency for Palestine Refugees in the Near East (UNRWA). UNRWA was created by the General Assembly in December 1949. It is a social and educational program dedicated to "Palestine refugees," and now also to their descendants. It confines eligibility to register to those who lost their livelihood and homes as a result of the 1948 war, between June 1946 and May 1948. Not all Palestinian refugees, therefore, are covered under UNRWA—an estimated three million fall outside of eligible status, including those stemming from new waves of expulsion and dispossession following the 1967 war. UNRWA is tasked with providing "assistance, protection and advocacy for over 5 million registered Palestine refugees in Jordan, Lebanon, Syria and the occupied Palestinian territory pending a solution to their plight" (UNRWA 2016). UNRWA's Syrian operations have been further complicated by the fact that there has been armed civil conflict in that country since 2011, and Syrians themselves have become a major refugee group (UNHCR 2016).

UNRWA is a program that must be continually renewed, and it relies on donor states, making its status and its work in relation to refugee services precarious and highly vulnerable to financial commitments from international sources. For example, in Canada, the Conservative government of Prime Minister Harper first reduced funding to UNRWA and then eliminated it entirely by 2010, but the Liberal government of Prime Minister Justin Trudeau restored funding in 2016. Conversely, in the United States, President Donald Trump eliminated American funding for UNRWA in 2018, a much bigger issue, as the United States accounted for about one-third of UNRWA's budget in 2017 (De Young, Eglash, and Boulasha 2018). It is evident that there would be a humanitarian crisis if UNRWA did not exist. The need for its continuation rests on the tragic reality that both peace and the return of Palestinian refugees have proven elusive (Lindsay 2012).

The Palestinian population has thus been rendered stateless, but in a contradictory manner. Their right of return as refugees has been clearly recognized in recurrent UN resolutions, and, importantly, implies original statehood. Moreover, as of 2012, Palestine has obtained nonmember observer state status (comparable to the Holy See) in the UN General Assembly (UN Resolution 67/19). The earlier admittance of the Palestine Liberation Organization (PLO) with observer status into the UN in 1974, retained in the 2012 UN resolution, marked a turning point for Palestinians, both in terms of their attempts to achieve a form of international representation in the absence of statehood and to utilize the instruments associated with human rights to draw world attention to their ongoing conditions and claims. The condition of statelessness, however, continues. It is indicated both in the process of dispossession and the tolerance of ongoing enforcement of this dispossession. This reflects the entrenched Orientalism and anti-Arab racism that is elemental to the Israel/Palestine racial contract. Until the formation of the PLO in the 1960s, the Palestinians as a people did not have a direct voice, but were spoken for by others—such as Arab states or the Arab League. The PLO introduced a different point of reference into the interface between Palestinians and the UN.

The PLO is central to the history and organization of Palestinians after their diaspora. It is an organization committed to liberation and one that has operated like a government in exile in terms of providing social assistance and support to Palestinians (Rubenberg 1983). In particular, the PLO insisted it was the "sole and legitimate representative of the Palestinian people," a challenging claim to make given that, as a people, by 1967, Palestinians were characterized as being dispersed, stateless, occupied and—in the case of the small Palestinian population in Israel that held Israeli citizenship—subject to a kind of internal colonialism (Zureik 1979). The PLO claim to be the representative also met hostility from powerful states because it was treated as a "terrorist" organization. This was not only a view advanced by Israel, but also the US and other Western states. However, the admittance of the PLO into the UN General Assembly and its accordance of observer status in 1974 by the vast majority of world states served to give symbolic credibility to the claim that the PLO was the voice of the Palestinians.

As noted in Chapter 2, the admission of the PLO as observer to the UN General Assembly was a reflection that this UN body was changing with the independence of numerous countries that had previously been under colonial rule through the 1950s and 1960s. Additionally, the 1960s and 1970s saw the solidification of the Universal Declaration of Human Rights into a more full-blown "international bill of rights," the 1965 adoption of the UN's International Convention on the Elimination of All Forms of Racial Discrimination (ICERD), and the growing attention paid by the General Assembly to South African apartheid. This climate of recognition of the rights of racialized and colonized peoples saw Palestine and the Palestinians, for the first time, come to be placed in a framework explicitly naming racism.

It is in this context that, on November 10, 1975, the General Assembly passed a resolution identifying Zionism as "a form of racism and racial discrimination" (Resolution 3379). This resolution brought to the surface the multiple issues associated with the Israel/Palestine racial contract and was challenged particularly by Israel as well as the United States and Canada, among other Western countries. It should be noted in this case that there was also a link established between apartheid South Africa and Israel. Hence, Resolution 3379 is prefaced as "taking note" of Resolution 77 (XII) of 1975, which held "that the racist regime in occupied Palestine and the racist regimes in Zimbabwe and South Africa have a common imperialist origin, forming a whole and having the same racist structure and being organically linked in their policy aimed at repression of the dignity and integrity of the human being" (UN General Assembly 1975). From the vantage point of political analysts attuned to Palestinian inequality, passage of this resolution (3379) in 1975 was seen as a victory. In the words at the time of the late Palestinian political scientist Ibrahim Abu-Lughod:

> If the General Assembly's resolution identifying Zionism as a form of racism and racial discrimination does nothing more than stimulate an informed public discussion of Zionism and Israeli practices, it will render a unique service. Yet there is no doubt that it will accomplish much more; it has already begun to produce searching questions on future policies towards a political entity that effectively and unashamedly treats its non-Jewish population with racial contempt, a state that bases its very existence on such an ideology. (1975: 311)

Indeed, it is notable that in two UN world conferences, held in 1978 and 1981 respectively, the issue of racism directed at Palestinians was raised. Although these particular conferences primarily took as their focus the need to overcome apartheid in South Africa, the United States and Israel did not participate in these events because of the focus on Israel and the Palestinians. In many ways, this foreshadowed the stance that was taken in 2001 at the World Conference Against Racism held in Durban, South Africa.

As noted in Chapter 2, the resolution equating Zionism with racism was short-lived, and rescinded in December 1991 as part of the 1991–3 Oslo process involving Israel and the PLO. Following Oslo, the newly created Palestinian Authority did achieve observer status in the General Assembly (Resolution 250; July 7, 1988), and more recently, after a failed bid for statehood, as noted the Palestinian Authority achieved the status of "nonmember observer state" in 2012. This has allowed for the symbolic affirmation of "the State of Palestine" having a nonvoting seat in the General Assembly. However, the Oslo peace process has clearly failed. The absence of full statehood has been accompanied by continued and deepening forms of repression experienced by Palestinians in the post-Oslo period. There have been other attempts, utilizing various means, to draw attention to the Palestinian experience of oppression and lack of rights in Israel, under Israeli occupation, and in the diaspora. The 2001 World Conference Against Racism, Racial Discrimination, Xenophobia and Related Intolerance (WCAR), significantly taking place in Durban in postapartheid South Africa, emerged as one global arena where Palestinians and their supporters, among delegations of racialized peoples from all over the world, took an opportunity to reaffirm their lived experience in relation to racism and to attempt to use UN instruments associated with human rights to draw world attention and seek redress.

Moreover, given the active participation of postcolonial states and global civil society delegates in the 2001 WCAR, discussions of Palestine were also related to the emergent Palestinian call by global civil society to enact a systematic campaign of boycott, divestment, and sanctions against Israel (Bakan and Abu-Laban 2009). This call is related to the fact that the UN has been unable, or unwilling, to effectively deal with Palestinian claims and experiences of injustice. This sense was poignantly reignited in the aftermath of the 2004 International Court of Justice (ICJ) ruling on the illegality of the so-called "separation wall" winding through Palestinian land in the West Bank. Not only did Israel refuse to recognize the ruling, but it faced no serious international sanction from other states for this violation.

The UN commitment to human rights offers, in sum, a paradox, one that has affected states as well as civil society regarding the Israel/Palestine racial contract. There are increasing voices within the Jewish community internationally objecting to an assumed association of their interests with the policies and practices of the state of Israel and the related political ideology of Zionism. Moreover, the longstanding pattern of the Israel/Palestine racial contract backgrounds more recent movements among Palestinians to identify with Indigenous peoples globally, and to call for an international campaign for boycott, divestment, and sanctions against Israel. These issues are addressed in the following chapters.

Note

1 Note that the paragraphs relevant to Arendt and the Eichmann trial in this section draw largely from Bakan (2014b).

5 INDIGENOUS PALESTINE: CONTESTED ORIGIN STORIES AND THE UN DECLARATION ON THE RIGHTS OF INDIGENOUS PEOPLES

Framing narratives, claiming discourses

As presented in the previous chapters, multidisciplinary work on Palestinian identity and history suggests the appropriateness of framing this collectivity in relation to colonial subjects and placing Israel's relationship to Palestine and Palestinians in the context of European settler colonization. The framing of Palestinian identity, however, is complicated by a counterframing grounded in a particular Zionist political narrative. As indicated throughout this volume, Zionism is understood to refer to a political perspective that sees anti-Semitism (or anti-Jewish racism) internationally as remedied only through the development and defense of an ethnically defined "Jewish" state. In the Zionist framing, the Jewish diaspora is presented as an exiled community with a claim to Indigenous, or original, rights in historic Palestine. Zionism is, therefore, understood in this context to assume that the "Jewish people" are a single, unified, ethnically defined group, distinct from adherence to the Jewish religion or theological tenets or to Jewish cultural identity (Hertzberg 1997).

This framing has been consistent with the hegemony of Western political thought in the post–Second World War era noted in the UN human rights model. It has, however, been understood to extend deeply into historic temporal boundaries, depending strongly on origin stories consistent with dominant traditions in Western thought. Such stories are common not only in creationist theologies but also in defining scientific enquiry and grounding relations of citizens and states (Wright 2004). The relationship of the post–Second World War Zionist framing of the geopolitics of Israel/Palestine is therefore significant. In this chapter, we demonstrate that this understanding is an ideological construct associated with the Israel/Palestine racial contract and the Zionist project of colonial state-building, rather than a valid rendition of the historical record. Significantly, the claim to uncomplicated and uniform Jewish Indigeneity presumes that the territory of pre-1948 Israeli settlement was "a land without a people," uninhabited by human society prior to the establishment of the state of Israel. This claim is contested in multiple literatures, including Palestinian historical records, recent historiography advanced by Israeli scholars, and contemporary Jewish cultural studies.

We argue that while the claim to Indigeneity on the part of Palestinians is clear, the Israel/Palestine racial contract renders this claim particularly fraught. In this chapter, we consider the contested claims to Indigeneity through three distinct entry points. First, we consider recent policy discussions that address Indigeneity claims in the UN, and the relationship of these discussions to the inclusion or elision of Palestinian claims. Second, we review and unpack the arguments surrounding Zionist claims to Indigeneity. And third, we review the longstanding claims to Palestinian Indigeneity based on a history of ongoing Israeli colonization and the legitimization of such colonization in contemporary Western narratives. Such a view provides a link between Palestinian identity and contemporary international debates on Indigeneity. We conclude the chapter by considering the contribution and some of the challenges of a clear understanding of the claims of Palestine and Palestinians as consistent with Indigenous peoples internationally.

United Nations and Indigenous rights

When the UN General Assembly passed the UN Declaration on the Rights of Indigenous Peoples (UNDRIP) in 2007, it was to bring an end to "nearly 25 years of contentious negotiations over the rights of native people to protect their lands and resources, and to maintain their unique cultures and traditions" (UN General Assembly 2007). Within such a context, the UNDRIP marks an historic moment in which, despite limitations, the rights and claims of Indigenous peoples were formally recognized on an international scale (Tawhai 2016). For example, the UNDRIP figures prominently in the calls to action of the report of the Truth and Reconciliation Commission (TRC) of Canada, the mandate of which was to address and redress the legacy of residential schools that enforced decades of institutional racism in the name of providing "education" to Canada's Indigenous peoples and contributed to cultural genocide (TRC 2015). In the contested territory of Israel/Palestine, the histories and claims made by Indigenous peoples globally have had considerable resonance for Palestinians (see Jamal 2011; Salaita 2006).

The strong efforts to support the internationalization of Indigenous rights came from popular groups among multiple states, including such settler-colonial societies as Australia, New Zealand, Canada, and the United States. However, the state representatives of these same countries originally voted against the UNDRIP (Merlan 2009). These states objected to "provisions on self-determination, land and resource rights and, among others, language giving Indigenous peoples a right of veto over national legislation and State management of resources" (UN General Assembly 2007), though all eventually endorsed the UNDRIP. The implications of this original rejection by the "Anglo-American" settler states as well as the meaning and potential efficacy of the Declaration on the Rights of Indigenous Peoples have been the focus of a great deal of scholarly commentary (Davis 2008; Merlan 2009; Ochman 2008).[1] In contrast, even given the general recognition that there is a lack of international consensus on what defines an Indigenous people (Daesig 2008: 9), there has been scant attention to the question of Indigeneity in the context of Israel/Palestine.

This apparent absence of Palestinian claims to Indigeneity in mainstream Western hegemonic discourse is even more notable when contrasted with the salience of this association in Palestinian scholarship and civil society discourse, where it was firmly established well before the extensive "lobbying in the corridors of power" (Stavenhagen 2009: 352) for the UN Declaration on the Rights of Indigenous Peoples even began. The definition of Indigeneity established by José Martinez Cobo, and adopted by the UN as its working definition, highlights the following:

> Indigenous communities, peoples and nations are those which, having a historical continuity with pre-invasion and pre-colonial societies that developed on their territories, consider themselves distinct from other sectors of the societies now prevailing in those territories, or parts of them. They form at present non-dominant sectors of society and are determined to preserve, develop and transmit to future generations their ancestral territories, and their ethnic identity, as the basis of their continued existence as peoples, in accordance with their own cultural patterns, social institutions and legal systems. (as cited in Daes 2008: 9)

In light of the experience of generations of Palestinians, Amal Jamal finds this definition resonant with the Palestinian minority in Israel who hold citizenship. As he writes:

> The Palestinian community in Israel is an Indigenous community on account of its descent from the population that inhabited Palestine at the time of colonization and before the establishment of Israel. The Palestinians have clear priority in time when compared with the Jewish community, whose members have mostly emigrated from several countries in the last 120 years and moved to settle in the country. The self-consciousness of the Palestinians as a group was established and remains connected to their historical experience in concrete territorial space. The political and cultural reality established by Zionism has not broken the sentimental, cultural, moral and legal bond that Palestinians have to their homeland. (2005: 2)

The gap in Western discourse between international policy and Palestinian historic identity regarding Indigeneity does not negate the fact that reference may also be made to a series of unique features in the UN governance of Israel/Palestine. These include, for example, as discussed above, UN Resolution 194 governing the right of return of Palestinian refugees, and the UN Relief and Works Agency providing assistance to these same refugees in and outside of historic Palestine. The UN Declaration on the Rights of Indigenous Peoples opens a further space in which human rights claims may be advanced and allows a window through which to reconsider other claims to Indigeneity, not least the Zionist framing of Israel and its biblical reference points.

Zionist claims to Indigeneity in Occupied Palestine

If Palestinians are the Indigenous residents of the land currently defined as Israel, how is this reality hidden, silenced, and altered by the hegemonic state system? Maintaining the balance between its Jewish-only ethnic privileging and the absenting and marginalization of the Palestinian population is highly dependent on a cultivated public image, historically rooted and adaptive to changing conditions (Slabodsky 2014: 145–75). The organization of tours to Israel is a standard activity among Zionist advocates in Canada and other Western states, and it is accompanied by a complex narrative combining regulated storytelling and selective visits to designated sites (Habib 2004) that are consistent with the Israel/Palestine racial contract. The tours and narratives associated with them are structured to confirm the messaging of Israel's hegemonic Zionist political national discourse.

The early 2000s featured some significant moments. On February 17, 2006, the Canadian Jewish Congress (CJC), ostensibly representing "the Jewish communities of Canada," and the Assembly of First Nations (AFN), "the national organization representing First Nations citizens in Canada," issued a joint press release announcing the "largest-ever mission to Israel by a North American First Nation group [to] learn how their Israeli counterparts preserve their historic languages and culture" (AFN and CJC 2006).[2] The release alerted the media and the public of a six-day "educational journey" (February 17–22, 2006), co-chaired by CJC's then national president, Ed Morgan, and AFN's then national chief, Phil Fontaine. According to Fontaine:

> Indigenous people in Canada have much in common with the people of Israel, including a respect of the land and their languages. (AFN and CJC 2006)

And, according to Morgan:

> We share values and similar historical experiences with our First Nations friends ... This trip presents an exceptional challenge and opportunity to learn about what each of our communities holds most dear—our culture and our history. (AFN and CJC 2006)

Two years after this AFN-CJC tour, another visit followed, launched with less fanfare but concluding with more accountable results. This time, seventeen First Nations women from Canada participated in an eleven-day "study tour" in Israel, based at the Golda Meir Mount Carmel Training Centre. This encounter was organized by the CJC and the Larry and Judy Tanenbaum Foundation Fellowships. It was an eminently Canadian cultural moment; the named associate of the funding foundation, Larry Tanenbaum, was then chair of Maple Leaf Sports and Entertainment (see Mackey 2002). The visit was led by selected representatives who advanced Israel's vision of its own, ostensibly unique, "democratic values" in the Middle East (see Slabodsky 2014). Significantly, the tour did not include travel to the Occupied Palestinian Territories (Ross 2008). The visit was designed to ensure a specific reading of Israeli reality. The articulated assertion expressed in these regulated tours is that the role of Jews in the Israeli state-building process is one of Indigeneity, comparable to the positioning of First Nations in Canada and cultivated through direct linkages with community members and leaders. The view is supported by some of Canada's most high-profile Zionist advocates. Human rights lawyer, former elected Member of Parliament (MP) for Mount Royal, Quebec, and then senior ranking Liberal Party representative Irwin Cotler stated in 2008:

> Israel, rooted in the Jewish people, as an Abrahamic people, is a prototypical First Nation or aboriginal people, just as the Jewish religion is a prototypical aboriginal religion, the first of the Abrahamic religions. In a word, the Jewish people is the only people that still inhabits the same land, embraces the same religion, studies the same Torah, harkens to the same prophets, speaks the same aboriginal language—Hebrew—and bears the same aboriginal name, Israel, as it did 3,500 years ago. Israel, then, is the aboriginal homeland of the Jewish people across space and time.[3]

The particular timing of the 2006 AFN-CJC trip to Israel can perhaps be explained in part by the context of the overtly anti-Semitic public statements of David Ahenakew, a leading First Nations spokesperson in Canada, in a December 13, 2002, speech to the Federation of Saskatchewan Indian Nations (FSIN). Ahenakew, a former chief of the Assembly of First Nations (1982–5) and a recipient of the Order of Canada distinction (1978), was asked following the speech by a reporter for the *Saskatoon*

Star Phoenix to clarify a remark about "goddamn immigrants." In the explanation that followed, Ahenakew referred to Jews as a "disease." He elaborated the point, defending Hitler's determination "to make damn sure that the Jews didn't take over Germany, or even Europe."[4] This is a unique and extreme case of distance between an Indigenous leader and the Jewish community. However, the coupling of redress for anti-Semitic ideas with advocacy for and linkages with the state of Israel is central to the hegemonic Zionist narrative and is supported by pro-Israel political advocates.[5] It is a coupling that is elemental to the Israel/Palestine racial contract. The linkage between a particularized expression of Zionism and the Israeli state project and Indigenous peoples internationally has, for example, also been claimed at events commemorating Indigenous activist William Cooper in Australia and Israel.[6]

Importantly, the association of the state of Israel with Jewish "Indigeneity" has been widely contested, including among members of both the Indigenous and Jewish communities in Canada and the United States.[7] More recently, visits of Indigenous women and women of color feminists to Israel/Palestine (It Starts With Us 2018) have resulted in challenges to the Zionist narrative and have demonstrated unequivocal support for Palestinian rights, including calls for boycott, divestment, and sanctions against Israel. In an important statement, leading feminists including Rabab Abdulhadi, Angela Y. Davis, Chandra Mohanty, Barbara Ransby, and Waziyatawin publicly endorsed the BDS call and invited others to join them.[8] Palestinians have extended their solidarity with movements such as Idle No More and Indigenous rights internationally (USPCN 2012), and Indigenous movements have in turn supported Palestinian resistance to colonialism (Bhandar 2014; Lee 2014; Razack 2010).

The claim of Jewish origins in the "land of Israel" remains hegemonic in the Israel/Palestine racial contract and is traceable, of course, to biblical discourse, and this has served as a reference point in Israeli state narratives since the establishment of the state in 1948, and in earlier Zionist claims to Palestinian territory (Freeman-Maloy 2016; Salaita 2006). It has also served to justify political Zionism since its founding in the work of Theodor Herzl (see Slabodsky 2014), and in the colonial discourse of *terra nullius*, or empty land (Pateman 2007). This hegemonic narrative rests uncomfortably, however, with other narratives associated with claims to Israel's unique position of modernity, normally linked to secularism and rationality. While the origin story has resonance in historic Zionist interpretations of the ancient "land of Israel," the specific link to Indigeneity—associated with Indigenous peoples in colonial and white settler societies such as Canada, the United States, and Australia—marks an unlikely departure and ideological positioning. Zionism has more commonly been rooted in millennial Jewish diaspora, where the seeking of a connection with land is posed from the perspective of dispersed wandering. Rather than a close association with an historic landed location, Jewish diaspora is associated with the yearning of "a people without a land." This has served precisely as the background to the Zionist claim to seek, find, and settle "a land without a people" (see Boyarin and Boyarin 2002; Said 1979b; Zangwill 1901).

As indicated in earlier chapters, the history of modern Zionism centers on the search for land that could serve as the geopolitical ground for an exclusively Jewish state. This is a search that has been closely connected with European and US empire building. The discourse of "colonization" has been frequently adopted, with the European Jewish migratory trajectory on the side of the imperial state (Sacher 2005, 2007). By turning to the use of the "Indigeneity" discourse, Zionist framings seem to be, rather curiously, forwarding identity claims that represent both, and simultaneously, the colonized and the colonizer. The association of Jewishness—as a civil and social identity and as distinguishable from adherence to Judaism as a religious belief system—in the twenty-first century with Indigeneity in historic Palestine is therefore troubling. This can be addressed in both historical and normative terms. The narrative constructing a single, continuous lineage from modern Jewish identity to the prenational, unbordered region of the Middle East has been amply dislodged by extensive archeological and historical research. Joan Peters' *From Time Immemorial* (1984) claimed to demonstrate that historic Palestine was empty land, devoid of population on the eve of Zionist colonization; Palestinians asserting refugee status were claimed in fact to be recent immigrants from surrounding Middle Eastern states. Soon after its publication, this work was discovered to be based on falsified demographic evidence, following the research of a young Norman Finkelstein (at the time a doctoral student at Princeton University) (Finkelstein and Paul 1985).

Further evidence based on available archival material in Israel has confirmed not only the existence of Palestinian society prior to the establishment of the state of Israel in 1948 but also the militarized occupation and ethnic-cleansing operations that accompanied that establishment. The 1948 *Nakba*, as noted earlier, has been recognized as a pivotal moment. This is evidenced in extensive Palestinian reportage as well as among a movement of Israeli historical scholars collectively referred to as "revisionists." Their work compels a challenge to the historical accuracy of the biblical story of Israeli origins and includes research grounded in Israeli state documentation and extensive archeological evidence. In terms of the former, Benny Morris, a revisionist historian, recognizes the impact of the release of new documents, though he has continued to defend the Zionist project politically. As Morris states: "How one perceives 1948 bears heavily on how one perceives the whole Zionist/Israeli experience" (2008: 34). Adopting a very different normative position in challenging the legitimacy of the Zionist settlement project, Israeli historian Ilan Pappe, also part of the revisionist school, recognizes this evidence in his detailed accounting of the 1945–9 period in the region (2006b).

Normally, Indigenous claims to land are grounded in the history and experiences of those victimized by military and racialized assault and removal from established communities and homelands, as expressed in the notion of "pre-invasion" and "pre-colonial" in the UN definition (also see de la Cadena and Starn 2002). The origin story of the Israeli state, however, is clearly associated with the victimization and forced removal of resident Palestinian communities through the activities of the occupiers and settlers. The formation of the state of Israel emerged in opposition—militarily, physically, and morally—to the extant and Indigenous rights of the occupied.

Another Israeli historian, Shlomo Sand (2009), has synthesized historical and archeological findings to conclude that the very notion of a geopolitically bounded "Jewish people" is an example of Hobsbawm's concept of the "invention of tradition." Sand contests historical interpretations that ascribe national boundaries and identities to premodern and prenational state conditions. Moreover, Sand goes beyond Hobsbawm to identify a diversity of national projects even in the European enlightenment moment. Drawing on a Gramscian notion of the construction of hegemony, Sand sees the consistent thread in the construction of national belonging over a sustained period of time to be the result of a self-identified elite project, associated with both an intellectual and material basis of power (2009: 23–63). Sand has unpacked the myth of the historic, unified "Jewish people" through an extensive survey of extant empirical findings. He notes how various biblical myths that were incorporated into Israeli state policy and Israeli Jewish educational and cultural practices have been proven to be historically false. Paralleling the work of the revisionist historians, "the new Israeli archeologists and scholars concerned themselves less with event-oriented political exploration and more with socio-anthropological investigation" (Sand 2009: 119). The curious interface between biblical storytelling and scientific evidence-based history, the latter including extensive archeological findings, poses a dilemma for the Zionist narrative of millennial Indigeneity. Particularly disrupted was the origin story of a once-mighty Hebraic empire, memorialized as the "ancient land of Israel." Sand writes of this biblical story:

> The united Kingdom of David and Solomon was the glorious golden age in Jewish history. All the future political models fed on this paragon of the biblical past and drew from its imagery, thinking and intellectual exhilaration.... Then came the post-1967 archeologists and Bible scholars, who began to cast doubt on the very existence of this mighty kingdom, which, according to the Bible, grew rapidly after the period of the Judges. Excavations in Jerusalem in the 1970s—that is, after the city had been "reunified forever" by the Israeli government—undermined the fantasies about the glorious past ... No vestige was ever found of monumental structures, walls or grand palaces, and the pottery found there was scanty and quite simple. (2009: 120)

To be clear, the existence of an Indigenous Jewish population, among other peoples in the region of historic Palestine, is certainly not in doubt. However, followers of Jewish faith and practices also existed in many other corners of the ancient world. Moreover, in a long period where Judaism, from which Christianity emerged, was one of many complex cultural, ideological, and religious faith systems, divisions among the beliefs and among the believers were unfixed and fluid. Consequently, even as various religious sects cohered, or were compelled into coherence by elites competing for power, conversion into and out of religious faith was common (Sand 2009). Consistent with Sand's historical documentation is the interpretive work of Daniel Boyarin (1994), a US scholar of Jewish Talmudic history. He contextualizes the history of religious expressions as works of allegory, to be understood as part of premodern conversations and ideological positionings. According to Boyarin, many contemporary interpretations have exaggerated divisions between Old and New Testament biblical stories and social contexts. The notion of a single, original "nation" of the "Ancient Hebrews" is not supported, even in the context of the biblical presentations as they are written. Rather, Jews and Christians were often the same people. Notable in this connection is Boyarin's hermeneutic reading of Paul's letters, which he understands to be "the spiritual autobiography of a first-century Jew" (1994: 2), and the accompanying transformative movement of the Jewish Saul to the Christian Paul. As both Jew and follower of Christ, Paul represents more accurately the lived experiences of ancient theological and cultural practices than the ascribed interpretations of Jewish "Indigeneity." According to Boyarin:

> In his very extremity and marginality, Paul is in a sense paradigmatic of the "Jew".... When Galatians wish to take on Jewish cultural practice, Paul cries out to them with real pathos: Remain as I am, for I have become as you are.... When Paul says, There is no Jew or Greek, no male or female in Christ, he is raising an issue with which we still struggle. (1994: 3)

Daniel Boyarin, in other writings with coauthor and legal expert Jonathon Boyarin, extends this analytical frame regarding the notion of diaspora in contemporary and historic Jewish cultural identity. While "diaspora" is commonly ascribed to the experiences of refugee populations, including post-1948 Palestinian experiences, the term itself finds original usage in reference to the dispersal of global Judaism. In the latter context, Boyarin and Boyarin insist that it is precisely the absence of a geopolitical homeland, in the sense of a unified identity with a single national state, that has enriched the Jewish cultural reality. Such an understanding is both historically accurate and a counter to hegemonic Zionist discourse. Perhaps more profoundly, it promises to contribute to and participate with other diasporic experiences, advancing comparative diasporic studies and a normative position of solidarity across difference. In this view, the "homeland" is understood as an idea grounded in Jewish contemplative tradition rather than a national state. Such a perspective suggests

> an alternative "ground" to that of the territorial state for the intricate and always contentious linkage between cultural identity and political organization. Such an alternative ground could avoid the necessarily

> violent ways in which states resist their own impermanence.... Jewish diasporic relation to *the homeland* (rather than the relation of its various branches to each other) is primarily commemorative, rather than kin-based or economic. (Boyarin and Boyarin 2002: 10; emphasis original)

To summarize to this point, Zionist assertions of a particular and singular Jewish claim to Indigeneity in the "ancient land" that is Palestine can be most accurately understood as an ideological construction necessary to Israeli state hegemony in the Middle East. As Sand notes, the "distilled biblical 'truth' was not a universal narrative about the history of humanity, but the story of a sacred people whom a secularized modern reading turned into the first nation in human history" (2009: 65). This has proven to be a powerful and convincing narrative in the post–Second World War period and has been reinvigorated in the post-9/11 era, coinciding particularly with constructions of identity as Judeo-Christian in the United States and Western European contexts (see Feldman 2015). This ideological construction of a biblical origin story fits neatly into the Israel/Palestine racial contract.

Widely accepted claims that the territory of Palestine is "the promised land" and that this promise belongs particularly to the constructed dispersed nation of the "Jews" who are "the chosen people" (Abu-Laban 1975) have proven useful to the Zionist political project. The late David Noble aptly summarizes the post–Second World War ideological context, which saw the development of a close relationship between political Zionism and the Western reconstruction project in a new world order.

> The proposition of establishing a renascent state of Israel in Palestine in the twentieth century would have been unthinkable, indeed preposterous—imperial intrigue and nationalist stirrings notwithstanding—were it not for the enduring resonance of the Hebrew mythology that both inspired the Zionists and ideologically inclined their British and US patrons, who had long ago rooted their own empires in the same stories.... The Zionist vision, as in the biblical text itself, all were variations on the same theme: the longing for the promised land. (2005: 39–40)

The extent of this vision in Zionist ideology within Israel is well documented. It involves constructing Israeli Jews as "Jewish" nationals, while Palestinians are rendered invisible under the constructed identity of "Israeli Arabs" (Jamal 2009), consistent with the Israel/Palestine racial contract. Such a framing elides, however, Palestinian claims to Indigeneity that are grounded in historical reality and that challenge Israeli state hegemony.

Palestinian claims to Indigeneity in historic Palestine and the Diaspora

In keeping with global studies of neglected Indigenous peoples, Palestinian history and identity need to be brought front and center to establish what a claim to Indigeneity may consider. The reality of the colonization of Palestine and the concomitant denial of this reality in the hegemonic discourse of post–Second World War ideology associated with Zionism and the state of Israel are elemental to the Israel/Palestine racial contract. Adopting a claim of native Palestinian or Indigenous status, however, does not rest on rejecting other forms of oppression, particularly anti-Jewish racism or anti-Semitism. Rather, at the most immediate level, the claim relates to the implications and outcome of a conflict dating back to the late nineteenth century between the majority native, non-Jewish inhabitants of Palestine (in particular, Palestinian Arabs) and the Zionist political movement, which originated outside the region in the continent of Europe (Said 1988: 1). The 1968 Palestine Liberation Organization (PLO) Charter, far from denying a Jewish presence in historic Palestine, held that "Jews who were normally resident in Palestine prior to the Zionist invasion will be considered Palestinian." Moreover, Palestinian political discourse still holds that "Palestinians" may be Jews and any others prepared to accept citizenship in a Palestinian state (Tilley 2005b: 145).

Opposition to Zionism as a political movement aimed at establishing an exclusively Jewish state in historic Palestine is premised on the fact that in its European roots, this was a settler-colonial project. Hence, as noted earlier, the early-twentieth-century slogan of the Zionist movement, "a land without a people for a people without a land," was highly significant. Though many European supporters of the movement may have actually believed Palestine to be empty land, and while Zionism itself extended its influence significantly in response to the racism targeting Jews in Europe, at the point when Zionists confronted the reality of the Indigenous Palestinian population, racialized Orientalist discourses came to the fore. It is useful to be reminded that, as noted in Chapter 2, the founder of political Zionism, Theodore Herzl, spoke negatively about Palestine's "dirty Arabs" and "blackened Arab villages" (Massad 1993: 101–2). It is thus understandable that, by 1908, the Arabic-language press registered a growing concern over the implications of Zionism and Zionist colonization for the Indigenous population of Palestine (Khalidi 2010: 121). Moreover, on the ground, from the latter half of the nineteenth century, Zionist agricultural colonization resulted in clashes with the local Palestinian rural population (Khalidi 2010: 96–111). As Donald Harman Akenson notes, much of the discourse of Zionists in the early twentieth century was familiar in relation to other settler-colonial projects, encompassing,

> the same arguments employed in previous centuries (when tailoring for local circumstances) by the Australian colonists concerning the aborigine; the Canadian settlers about native Canadians; the American frontier expansionists about the Amerindians; the Afrikaners concerning the Xhosa and Zulu; the British, French, German, Portuguese, and Belgians about black Africans. The same canonical justifications were used by all European imperialists when explaining why it was all right for the colonists to bash the indigene. (1991: 170)

Yet, by the early years of the twentieth century, as noted previously, there was also a sense of common identity among Arab inhabitants of Palestine, and there was an emerging demand for self-rule in the form of a nation-state (Khalidi 2010). This emergent movement for self-determination was evident in discussions between Arab leaders under Ottoman rule and French and British authorities during the First World War, during the period of the British Mandate, and in responses to the Balfour Declaration (MacMillan 2001: 336–426). As Margaret MacMillan notes of Palestinian Arabs, "the Balfour Declaration in 1917 and the arrival of the Zionist commission in 1918, the waving of the blue and white Zionist flag throughout Palestine, the tactless demand of a Zionist conference in Jaffa that the name of the area immediately be changed to Eretz Israel ('the Land of Israel'), all worried them exceedingly" (2001: 421). This worry stemmed from the fact that, from 1917, Zionist settlers produced "literally thousands of documents and public statements in which the words 'settler' and 'colonist' were not meant in any obscure or technical or metaphorical or archaic sense" (Akenson 1991: 166).

Undoubtedly, Palestinian identity was further solidified by the shared trauma of the destruction in 1948 of Arab Palestine (Khalidi 2010; Khalidi 2006: 182). Indeed, the 1948 war and the subsequent creation of the state of Israel as a colonial-settler state annihilated Palestinian society; some 80 percent of the Palestinians who had lived in the area where Israel was established became refugees (Abu-Lughod and Sa'di 2007a: 3). At the same time, the *Nakba* of 1948 made it difficult to effectively challenge key elements of Zionist discourse and historical narrative. This discourse emphasized that Palestinians were not really a people; Palestinians were backward, and since they were not productive, they were never really dispossessed (Akenson 1991: 170–2). To the extent that Israeli discourses of "making the desert bloom" carried popular purchase within and beyond the region, the constructed image of the empty and infertile land may be seen as part of the hegemonic narrative necessary to Israeli claims to state power.

The history of the Palestinians encompasses further discursive challenges, including those that stem from religious ideology. As Nur Masalha (2007) notes, there are complex linkages between the Hebrew Bible (Old Testament), the Christian tradition in the West, and the ideology that Palestine has always been "the land of Israel." The naming of the new Zionist state according to biblical testament therefore serves to suggest historic continuity. The biblical legacy embedded in Zionist ideology works to render a constructed stability to the occupation and dispossession of Palestinians.

> The inevitable outcome of the obsession with the Hebrew Bible in the West—an obsession illustrated by description of the land as "biblical" and by an exclusive interest in a small section of the history of the land—has resulted in a focus on the Israelite identity of a land that has actually been non-Jewish in terms of its Indigenous population for the larger part of its recorded history.... The biblical academia in Israel and the West has been deeply complicit in Israeli occupation and its apartheid policies on several counts, including its view of Indigenous Palestinians as trespassers or "resident aliens" in someone else's territory and its obsession with a short period of ancient history. (Masalha 2007: 310–11)

A longstanding history of claims for self-determination is also indicated by a movement among Palestinians holding Israeli citizenship for collective rights and autonomy. These claims are inspired by "the voice of Indigenous populations in different countries in the world and their assertion of their rights as original inhabitants of the land" (Jamal 2007: 274). Additionally, however, it is important to note that this self-consciousness connection to land resonates for Palestinians living under occupation and in the diaspora. As Abu-Lughod and Sa'di note, "For Palestinians, the places of the pre-Nakba past and the land of Palestine itself... are not simply sites of memory but symbols of all that has been lost and sites of longing to which return is barred" (2007a: 13). This shows up in the preservation of deeds to formerly owned land and the careful protection of keys to houses that were fled (Abu-Lughod and Sa'di 2007a: 13). It is also demonstrable in strong attachments to a city, village, and region among dwellers and nomads alike, and among Palestinian refugees who have been in exile for several generations (Khalidi 2010: 153).

In conclusion: On articulating contentious origin stories

It is against these larger challenges of racialization and invisibility and of state ideology and hegemonic religious justification that claims to Indigeneity on the part of Palestinians and Palestinian solidarity activists may be cast. Establishing constructive discursive space regarding claims to Indigeneity necessarily demands recognition of these realities. It is by attending to this contested terrain and framing dialogical impasses in the context of narratives grounded in unequal power relations that a new type of effective solidarity can be forwarded.

This necessitates, however, attention to the interests of various great powers historically (Britain) and contemporaneously (the United States and Canada) in the region, which have worked to perpetuate the racialization, repression, and statelessness of Palestinians. There is a need, then, to extend the work of comparative analytical scholarship to encompass Palestinian Indigeneity claims. In a context of growing attention within political science and other disciplines in the social sciences to issues of race, ethnicity, and Indigeneity, it is notable that attention to origin stories and related claims in Israel/Palestine have commonly been overlooked.

For example, in a paper specifically devoted to self-determination in Israel/Palestine, the late Iris Marion Young took great pains to explain that while "it is useful to take the claims of Indigenous people for self-determination as paradigmatic rather than exceptional" (2005: 141), she did not "wish to take a position on whether Palestinians qualify as Indigenous under the current definition of international law" (2005: 143). Similarly, Will Kymlicka raises critical questions about possible "long-term risk" in an internationalization and expansion of the category of "Indigenous people," which he suggests are not adequately considered "within the policy networks that are affiliated with the UN Indigenous track" (2007: 289–90). While he observes, notably in a footnote, that Palestinians might be seen to be an Indigenous people as "some commentators argue that Israel should be included as a European settler state" (2007: 278, n. 33), he also suggests that this move would involve a form of relabeling, "from a national minority to an Indigenous people" (2007: 284–5).

This lacuna, we suggest, stems from the Israel/Palestine racial contract. The state of Israel is treated as exceptional and unique, outside the bounds of much comparative scholarly critique and discussion. This is consistent, as we have noted, with its ideologically constructed origin story—one challenged by the historical reality of Israeli settler colonialism and the occupation and dispossession of the Palestinian people. By way of contrast, although the history and basis of Palestinian claims have been obscured in much political and scholarly discussion, especially in the West, explicit attention to this history opens up space to better understand a major conflict in the region and in the world over the course of the twentieth and twenty-first centuries. This approach moves Israel/Palestine from a marginalized case study considered unsuitable for comparison to other regions to the center of contemporary discussions of regions with experiences of colonization. Multidisciplinary questions of racialization, citizenship, and decolonization are enriched by, and in turn shed light on, the racial contract as it relates to Israel/Palestine. Significantly, the state of Israel has been uniquely supported by an international racial contract that has allowed for the ideology of Zionism to become a form of elite hegemony in a contemporary context of settler colonialism. Following from this, explicitly considering Palestinian identity and history opens the way for thinking about consistent anti-racist and anti-colonial practices. Such consistency grows in importance as the influence of the 2007 United Nations Declaration on the Rights of Indigenous Peoples advances internationally.

Notes

1 The United Nations Declaration on the Rights of Indigenous Peoples was adopted by the UN General Assembly on September 13, 2007. Voting in favor were 143 states, while 11 abstained and 4 (Australia, Canada, New Zealand, and the United States) voted against. Israel was one of the thirty-four states that were absent from the vote (UN News 2007). On November 12, 2010, Canada signed on, indicating: "Although the Declaration is a non-legally binding document that does not reflect customary international law nor change Canadian laws, our endorsement gives us the opportunity to reiterate our commitment to continue working in partnership with Aboriginal peoples in creating a better Canada" (INAC 2010). The United States, Australia, and New Zealand also later endorsed, reversing their 2007 positions.

2 The CJC concluded its activities in 2011 and was renamed the Centre for Israel and Jewish Affairs (CIJA). This was, and remains, a contentious organization in Canada and internationally. See, for example, Dan Freeman-Maloy (2006).

3 Irwin Cotler, "Statement by Irwin Cotler on the Issue of Yom HaAtxma'ut—Israel's Independence Day," *The Jerusalem Post*, May 14, 2008, https://www.jpost.com/Opinion/Op-Ed-Contributors/The-gathering-storm-and-beyond.

4 *CBC News*, "Ahenakew Charged with Spreading Hate," June 11, 2003, https://www.cbc.ca/news/canada/ahenakew-charged-with-spreading-hate-1.390644.

5 For example, see Barbara Kay, "Barbara Kay: The Indigenous Tribes of Israel," *National Post*, June 28, 2016, https://nationalpost.com/opinion/barbara-kay-the-Indigenous-tribes-of-israel.

6 Nadav Shemer, "Israel Honors Aboriginal Australian Who Protested Against Nazis," *Haaretz.com*, May 1, 2009, https://www.haaretz.com/1.5045984.

7 See, for example, Hannah Kawas, "Open Letter to the Assembly of First Nations," *CPA.org*, March 6, 2006, http://www.cpavancouver.org/index.php/2006/03/06/an-open-letter-by-cpa-to-the-assembly-of-first-nations; and Rhonda Spivak, "Editorial: Response to Aboriginal Speaker Who Mocked Irwin Cotler During Israeli Apartheid Week," *WinnipegJewishReview.com*, May 12, 2010, http://www.winnipegjewishreview.com/article_detail.cfm?id=115&sec=1.

8 Ali Abunimah, "After Witnessing Palestine's Apartheid, Indigenous and Women of Color Feminists Endorse BDS," *The Electronic Intifada*, July 12, 2011, https://electronicintifada.net/blogs/ali-abunimah/after-witnessing-palestines-apartheid-Indigenous-and-women-color-feminists.

6 GLOBAL CIVIL SOCIETY AND A "UNITED NATIONS FROM BELOW": THE BDS MOVEMENT

The racial contract and Palestine solidarity

Israel's twenty-two-day war on Gaza (December 2008–January 2009) provoked a wave of international solidarity with the people of occupied Palestine. The violence of this event, while tragically consistent with Israeli military assaults on Palestine, was unique in marking a decisive shift in global public opinion regarding the ongoing crisis in the Middle East. The BDS movement gained considerable legitimacy among a broad coalition of progressive scholars and activists, including many sectors that had previously not engaged in Palestine solidarity. While there have continued to be many other important moments in advancing global attention, the 2008–9 war on Gaza can be seen as a historic turning point. Canadian journalist and author Naomi Klein, for example, was provoked by the war on Gaza to extend her strong endorsement of the ongoing social movement to target Israel's violations of international law and human rights. Her position echoed similar voices internationally, not least in North America and Europe. Following the war on Lebanon in 2006 and the ongoing siege of Gaza, the 2008–9 war on Gaza marked what Palestinian human rights activist and scholar Omar Barghouti has termed "a real transformation in world public opinion against Israel's policies" (2011: 9).

The immediate conditions of the military incursion resulted in recorded estimates of 1,285 Palestinian deaths, 4,336 wounded, and 2,400 destroyed houses (Palestinian Centre for Human Rights 2009). In the aftermath, Gaza has remained under siege. Moreover, the extent of the damage to the lives of the survivors continues to the present, exacerbated by conditions of global isolation and renewed Israeli attacks in 2012 ("Operation Pillar of Defense") and 2014 ("Operation Protective Edge"). The impact of the 2008–9 war remains unmeasured, particularly as there is evidence of the use of exceptionally violent weaponry, including white phosphorus explosives (Ageel 2016).[1]

Since the 2008–9 war on Gaza, new governments have been elected both in the United States—the most powerful and consistent ally of Israel—and in Israel itself. While there was originally much hope associated with the departure of former President George W. Bush from the White House, the impact of President Barack Obama's agenda for "change" on the lives of Palestinians proved to be disappointing. The outcome of the election in Israel indicated no change at all regarding the goals and actions associated with Operation Cast Lead.[2] The administration of US President Donald Trump has brought even closer ties between the United States and Israel, even if the initial press conference revealed a remarkably confusing orientation on the part of the new US administration.[3]

The conditions that led to the war on Gaza and the circumstances of Israeli aggression and Palestinian occupation have worsened in the years since, with Gaza facing renewed attacks and international siege (Ageel 2016). But there is also hope that a global movement for social change from below that offers considerable promise is rising. Over the same time, support for the BDS movement has substantially expanded, deepening within and across civil society and finding resonance among multiple communities as sites of education and solidarity.

This chapter addresses the history, context, and strategic significance of the organized transnational movement of civil society actors calling for a campaign of boycott, divestment, and sanctions (BDS) aimed at protesting the Israeli state's illegal military occupation of Palestine and refusal to adhere to international law. We argue that such an effective civil society initiative as a strategy of resistance and cross-border solidarity can be usefully framed as an anti-racist movement that contests the Israel/Palestine racial contract. This post–Second World War hegemonic construction of state ideology serves, in a neo-Gramscian sense and where Zionism plays a central role, to enforce a racial contract that hides the apartheid-like character of the state of Israel.

Following the 2008–9 war on Gaza, the BDS call was reiterated (Palestinian BNC 2008). New actors and new voices joined the call and have continued to join this movement in rapid response (Barghouti 2011; Palestinian BNC 2018; Shapiro 2016; Ziadah 2016). The war on Gaza attracted attention from the international community, exposing Israel's blatant violation of international law and denial of basic principles of human rights. However, for Palestinians living within the 1948 borders of Israel, in the Occupied Territories, or as refugees in the diaspora, Operation Cast Lead was unfortunately familiar. Significantly, a new movement of Palestinian civil society was organized to respond, calling for meaningful and ongoing solidarity. Launched three years prior to the 2008–9 war on Gaza, the BDS movement inspired new layers of civil society actors in countries of the global North as well as the global South to challenge the hegemonic idea of Israel as a victim state in the face of Palestinian "terrorism." The BDS movement has served to expose and challenge a series of corresponding repressive policies, including denial of the right of return of Palestinian refugees; militarized violence directed against Palestinian men, women, and children; the confiscation of land from Palestinians; the demolition of Palestinian homes; and the daily racism invoked by a series of policies directed at Palestinians that encumber their freedom of mobility, access to education, ability to earn a living, and access to environmental necessities including land, water, and clean air.

The BDS campaign has been, however, highly controversial and met by a concerted counter-response. This challenge includes opposition to the call for an academic boycott of Israeli universities, included in the broad BDS call (Dawson and Mullen 2015; Mullen 2013; Rose and Rose 2008). Opposition to the BDS call has been associated with claims that the campaign is destined to be ineffective; that it is counterproductive to peace and/or security; that it is contrary to norms of academic freedom; and that it is, in fact, motivated not by progressive but reactionary sentiment tied to anti-Semitism (meaning anti-Jewish racism). The movement has reached such significant proportions that it has also attracted a defensive response from the Israeli government and various state allies, including Canada and the United States (Abu-Laban and Bakan 2012b; Bakan and Abu Laban 2016; Barghouti 2011).

In light of the fact that serious debate about Israel's violent and illegal practices is frequently hampered by challenges about the motivations of analysts and the legitimacy of voice, there are barriers to simply beginning with analytical assumptions as is standard in a consideration of solidarity movements (see Carroll 1992; Drummond 2013; Masri 2011). Some analyses have attempted to discredit recent scholarly contributions that suggest the legitimacy of the BDS movement from the perspective of social movements, anti-oppression politics, and global solidarity with claims of ostensible neutrality, suggesting that BDS is a divisive or "moralistic" approach (see Fishman 2012; Yi and Phillips 2015). Such responses are reminiscent of arguments used to dismiss earlier movements that redressed privilege and power, such as feminist and anti-racist movements, or the movement against apartheid in South Africa (see Freeman 1997). Others have viewed the BDS movement as part of a wider delegitimization campaign comparable to a military security threat (Cohen and Freilich 2018). Importantly, the BDS movement is explicitly inspired by the anti-apartheid movement that contributed to the successful demise of state practices of legalized racism in South Africa and by the nonviolent civil rights movement in the United States (Barghouti 2011).[4] As we have indicated, however, the Israel/Palestine racial contract is grounded on unequal power relations that insist upon a rhetoric of neutrality in order to absent the experiences of Palestinian colonization.

Our analytical framework considers the call for a comprehensive campaign of boycott, divestment, and sanctions against Israel from the perspective of international solidarity. The approach posits the campaign as a positive and progressive step in coalition-building and the advance of social movements that can challenge the hegemony of the Israel/Palestine racial contract. Further, we argue that support for this campaign can serve as a challenge to a particular element of Western, elite hegemony in the form of the ideology of Zionism. We consider the origins and history of the BDS campaign and the debates it has engendered in the context of the Israel/Palestine racial contract, and consider the implications for global human rights and the role of the United Nations.

The BDS movement serves as an example of an alternative to what has been perceived as the false promise of the United Nations, following from experiences highlighted in previous chapters. In a sense, the BDS movement represents a movement symbolic of a different UN—a kind of United Nations from below based in civil society. An internationally recognized coordinating body for the BDS movement, the Boycott, Divestment and Sanctions National Committee (BNC) has indicated such an orientation.

> Since its inception in 2005, the global, Palestinian-led BDS movement has been anchored in the Universal Declaration of Human Rights. It is an inclusive human rights movement that categorically rejects all forms of racism and discrimination.... This key anti-racism statement reiterates this long-held principle at a time when the racist and xenophobic far-right is rising in Washington, DC, Tel Aviv and many places in between. (Abunimah 2017)

Indeed, the paradox of the UN regarding human rights and the Israel/Palestine racial contract is indicated by varied, and sometimes contradictory, responses to the Palestinian civil society call for BDS. For example, a 2017 report from the UN Economic and Social Commission for Western Asia, titled *Israeli Practices towards the Palestinian People and the Question of Apartheid*, recommends that "efforts should be made to broaden support for boycott, divestment and sanctions initiatives among civil society actors" (UN ESCWA 2017: 56). However, the implementation of such a general appeal and the related mechanisms necessary for enforcement from the UN remains an elusive challenge.

In what follows, we present a brief overview of the practical and theoretical significance of international solidarity and coalition-building in the context of the Israel/Palestine racial contract. We then consider a more detailed historical overview of calls for the boycott of Israel, followed by an elaboration of the recent movement for boycott, divestment, and sanctions, including a contextualization of the call for an academic institutional boycott and related responses in the West. The chapter concludes with a consideration of some of the tasks and challenges of solidarity activists in navigating the terrain of this emergent and expanding movement.

Boycotting Israel: History and context

The importance of the BDS campaign as a strategy of international solidarity is particularly significant in the current context of frustrations in peace-building initiatives in the Middle East, and in Israel/Palestine in particular. For example, former US President Jimmy Carter, already established as a critic of Israel's intransigence in his provocatively titled book *Palestine: Peace Not Apartheid* (2006), also published a sequel. In *We Can Have Peace in the Holy Land: A Plan*

That Will Work, Carter expressed a near-desperate plea for Israel to adhere to international law through a negotiated settlement and a deep faith "that God, with our help, will bring peace to the Holy Land" (2009: vii). Israel's interest in compliance with such a plea remains, however, demonstrably lacking. The BDS call addresses the need for a more overarching, coordinated campaign to focus attention on Israel's violation of international law and to impose consequences for noncompliance. Rather than turning to other state actors or military aggression, the BDS movement is based on a strategy of education and nonviolent civil disobedience, comparable to the international movement that challenged apartheid South Africa. Discussions on a comprehensive boycott of Israel are a recent phenomenon within civil society in Europe and North America. However, similar discussions have taken place in the Middle East since Israel's inception in 1948. In situating the resonance of the current BDS movement in the West, it is useful to consider the changed historical context and the distinctive elements that place the current debates as an expression of international solidarity against racism, colonialism, and occupation, and as part of this wider counterhegemonic discourse.

In 1948, a call for the boycott of the state of Israel was initiated by the League of Arab States (hereafter the Arab League). Three main interdependent features characterized the Arab League boycott and indicated some limitations to its wider resonance: its continued inability to effectively publicize the human (and human rights) dimension of the Palestinian plight after 1948, particularly in countries of the industrialized West; its statist, rather than popular, dimension, which obscured how boycotts may be a form of peaceful resistance to colonialism and racism; and its regional, rather than international, dimension. The year 1948 signals a relevant starting point for illustrating these features, through the reconsideration of the contested historiography of Israel/Palestine, as well as the contested character of international boycotts in response to this conflict zone.

In the Israeli national narrative, the events of 1948 leading up to the formation of the state of Israel are referred to as a war of independence from the British or a liberation from the Diaspora. As Ilan Pappe notes, neither of these terms give any explicit reference to the Indigenous Arab population. It is precisely the experiences of this population that, since the 1980s, have formed the backbone of the revisionist "post-Zionist" history that has challenged the assumptions underlying the dominant

Israeli national narrative (2006b: 256–7). This revisionist history is relevant in considering how the human face of the Palestinian population is central to the contemporary BDS movement. It should be noted, however, that the core elements of the revisionist history correspond with a longstanding Palestinian national narrative. This more accurate nomenclature views the year 1948 as the *Nakba*, characterized by over half of the Arab population losing homes and property and becoming stateless refugees outside and inside historic Palestine.

Ronit Lentin identifies this contested terrain of memory in the context of a challenge to the Israeli state's "active memoricide of both the Nakba and the ethnically cleansed Palestinians" (2008b: 209). Abu-Lughod and Sa'di note of the *Nakba*: "It is the focal point for what might be called Palestinian time. The Nakba is the point of reference for other events, past and future" (2007a: 5). An additional feature of the Palestinian narrative is the understanding that in its European roots, and in its simultaneous erasure and racialization of the Indigenous Arab population, the Israeli state was an outgrowth of settler colonization. As we have demonstrated, the Israel/Palestine racial contract has served to render the state of Israel as exceptional in its relationship to international law, while absenting Palestinians as simultaneously nonwhite, the subjects of extreme repression, and stateless. Prior to 1948, when Palestine was under the British Mandate, Palestinian Arabs expressed a form of resistance to growing numbers of settlers by boycotting Zionist businesses and goods (Chill 1976: 1).

This kind of consumer-driven boycott may be seen to have contemporary parallels. For example, anticonsumerist activism, particularly in advanced capitalist countries, was a component of the transnational popular opposition to neoliberal globalization and the quest for global justice that marked the first period of the new millennium (see Littler 2005: 227–52). Links with the Palestinian resistance to occupation and war have been a central component of theorizations of the movement for global justice since the Seattle protests against the neoliberal policies of the World Trade Organization marked the opening of the 2000s (Alexander and Rose 2001: 185–95; see also Bakan 2000a: 19–36; Bakan 2000b; Danaher and Burbach 2000: 85–93). Not surprisingly, antiglobalization theorists such as Naomi Klein, noted above, have readily challenged Israel's links with corporate capitalism and have supported movements for boycott that seek alternative economic outlets (Klein 2000, 2008).

Also important to consider, however, are boycotts initiated by states and the context in which these are done. Modern proponents of boycotts have drawn on an understanding of political action that blends aspects of Western and Eastern political and religious beliefs (Spector 2004). Significantly, the current movement combines calls for boycott and divestment as well as sanctions against Israel—the latter suggesting calls for state action in combination with those at the level of civil society. The role of the United States (and allies in the UN) in imposing extensive sanctions on Saddam Hussein's Iraq after the 1990 invasion of Kuwait is a case in point. While Iraq experienced one of the most comprehensive boycotts in history, other countries (such as Cuba, Iran, Libya, and Sudan) have also been a focus for the United States (O'Sullivan 2003: 6–7). Beginning in 1948, a central way in which opposition continued to be registered regarding the violent origins of the Israeli state—and the consequent condition of the Palestinians—was through the Arab League's boycott against Israeli companies and Israeli-made goods.

From its 1945 foundation with six members to its twenty-two members in 2018, the Arab League has been a regional organization. The Arab League has not, however, achieved a high level of economic and political integration. In contrast, whereas there is now a European Union citizenship, even if a highly contested one post-Brexit, the Arab League does not directly link with citizens of member states. As such, and notwithstanding longstanding and continuing provisions made for representing the stateless Palestinians, the Arab League boycott needs to be seen as having a heavily statist dimension. As it developed, the Arab League boycott came to focus on three tiers:

> The primary boycott prohibits the importation of Israeli-origin goods and services into the boycotting countries. The secondary boycott prohibits individuals, as well as private and public sector firms and organizations, in member countries from engaging in business with any entity that does business in Israel. The Arab League maintains a blacklist of such firms. The tertiary boycott prohibits any entity in a member country from doing business with a company or individual that has business dealings with U.S. or other firms on the Arab League blacklist. (Weiss 2006: 2)

The Arab League boycott, still formally in effect today, represents the longest-standing case of economic sanctions being applied against a state

(Feiler 1998: 1). By 2006, however, this boycott had largely waned and was eventually described as no more than "lip service" (Halpern 2006, as quoted in Weiss 2006: 3). Regulations are not binding on member states, and moreover, not all participated. For instance, some members of the Arab League signed other agreements with Israel that effectively ended the boycott (e.g., Egypt since 1979, and Jordan since 1994) (Weiss 2006: 2–3). It appears clear that the boycott's tenacity is shaped by the intensity of Israel's efforts to occupy and absent the Palestinian experience and by the tenacity of the Israeli/Palestine racial contract. Therefore, in the wake of the Oslo Accords and the subsequent 1990s discussions of Arab–Israeli regional economic cooperation (Clawson 1994), some were led to describe the boycott of Israel as "disintegrating" (Feiler 1998: 1).

More broadly, the impacts of both neoliberal globalization and pressures by third countries are also relevant. Some analysts have noted the difficulty of even applying the boycott at the secondary and tertiary levels given contemporary production processes, where a finished product from one state may in fact be made up of a number of unmarked component parts from other states (Raphaeli 2006: 3). Regardless, the impact of third countries in challenging the Arab League boycott is apparent. For Arab League members, abandoning the boycott was a requirement for entering into free-trade agreements with the United States (such as Bahrain in 2005 and Oman in 2006); similarly, Saudi Arabia officially dropped the boycott to meet a condition of joining the World Trade Organization (Weiss 2006: 4). And further, the United States in particular has actively worked to oppose this boycott, especially after the 1973 Arab–Israeli War.

A full account of the US response to the Arab League boycott of Israel goes beyond the scope of this discussion. However, some relevant factors may be noted. These include the historic Israel/Palestine racial contract, and the related absenting of Palestine and Palestinian rights in global relations. More specifically, the blunt interests of US capital and Israeli business activities deserve mention, as these were early targets of the boycott. For example, in 1960, the number of US companies on the Arab League boycott list was only 53, but by 1970, it had soared to over 1,500 (Schaefer 1996: 168–9). The boycott allowed for the disclosure of US companies that endorsed or complied with the Arab League boycott, leading to a backlash against these businesses and the loss of government contracts and tax benefits (Schaefer 1996: 169–70). Significantly, by 1975–6, the anti-boycott movement was supported by various US-based, pro-Israel, Zionist organizations, such as the

Anti-Defamation League of B'nai Brith, the American-Israeli Public Affairs Committee, and the American Jewish Congress. This movement had gained enough momentum for then US President Gerald Ford to agree to sign into law anti-boycott legislation (Schaefer 1996: 169). The language of preventing "discrimination" against Americans on the basis of race, color, religion, national origin, gender, etc. peppered the justification of these measures (Malholtra 1964; Schaefer 1996: 168–70). Other Western states, including France, Germany, and the Benelux countries, also subsequently passed anti-boycott legislation; trade between Israel and Britain, Japan, the EU countries, Canada, and Australia subsequently accelerated (Feiler 1998: 4–5).

The statist element of the Arab League boycott coupled with the shifting commitment of states in the boycott over time coincided with the Arab League's inability to present the boycott as a means of peaceful resistance to colonialism and/or racism. Relatedly, this statist character inhibited the extension of the boycott beyond the regional level, despite attempts to have it taken up in the UN. A contrasting case of the transformative impact of an international boycott is the 1950s challenge to South Africa's apartheid system. This movement ultimately involved a combination of popular, state-supported, and UN sanctions (Gurney 2000: 123–44; Schwartzman 2001: 115–46), which were embraced by a host of Western states, ultimately including, significantly, the United States and Canada (Freeman 1997; Hoile 1988: 14–16).

The South African example therefore forms an interesting point of comparison, as numerous analysts have pointed out, not least because there are relevant similarities between apartheid South Africa and Israel/Palestine, including the West Bank and Gaza (see Abu-Lughod and Abu-Laban 1974a; Ageel 2016; Farsoun 1976: 13–21; Will and Ryan 1990). These relate to the manner in which apartheid and the political orientation of Zionism, which serves to deny the realities of Israeli apartheid, have served to undermine liberty (especially the mobility of persons), equality (especially the economic equality between identifiable groups), and democracy (especially the franchise) (Glaser 2003: 403–21). Moreover, Israel stood out among states internationally for continuing to cooperate with apartheid South Africa, including in the nuclear and military spheres (Adams 1984; Joseph 1988; Newsome 1991: 19–48). In sum, the Arab League's boycott did not win over others outside the region in the manner that accompanied the boycott of South Africa. As Will states:

Apartheid South Africa was overwhelmingly regarded as a pariah state by the international community. By contrast, Israel, which in the eyes of its critics shared a legacy of settler colonialism, was staunchly embraced by the United States and abetted the regime in South Africa. Despite the opprobrium of the majority of the United Nations General Assembly, Israel was not subject to international pressure for change comparable to that exerted on South Africa. (2007: 412)

It is perhaps an indication of the inability of the Arab League boycott to effectively publicize the human rights dimensions of the Palestinians in the industrialized West, or to present the boycott as a form of resistance to colonialism and racism, that it has been rendered a limited point of reference in the current BDS movement. In contrast, since the 2000s, the BDS movement has included South African spokespersons such as Archbishop Desmond Tutu,[5] and an extensive conversation regarding comparative apartheid has emerged (see UN ESCWA 2017, and Chapter 9 this volume).

In contrast with the Arab League boycott, the contemporary BDS movement is nonhierarchical and has made use of new forms of communication—including international websites and social media networks, blogs, and Web-based journalism—to provide information that translates readily from Arabic to English and other languages and to facilitate coordinated mobilization (Aouragh 2011). For example, the expanding influence of the online publication *Electronic Intifada*, established in 2001, has been immeasurable in providing information and analyses from a Palestinian perspective.[6] Whatever the challenges of defining the reach of global civil society, this type of communication has supported and facilitated changes in strategies of resistance and solidarity (Aouragh 2011; Kiely 2005: 138–53).

The BDS movement has been advanced to affect public perceptions, challenging the hegemony of the Israel/Palestine racial contract. This hegemonic view remains one that has continued to position Israel ahistorically and without global comparators, as an exceptional state grounded in a mythologized anti-racist narrative of rescue of Jews from the Holocaust—but it is, significantly, now faced with an effective counternarrative. After decades of ongoing resistance by the Palestinian people, a new counterhegemonic discourse is emerging and finding resonance in international solidarity campaigns in the West. This climate has created new space for discussions of history, including the *Nakba* and the shared history of Jews, Christians, and Muslims in the region of Israel/Palestine. It is therefore perhaps no coincidence that there is also a growing number of voices challenging a two-state solution in the aftermath of the Oslo period and calling for a secular democratic state that looks to postapartheid South Africa as a comparative model (see Chapter 9) (Sussman 2004: 37–42; Tilley 2005b). Of course, the BDS movement continues to face significant opposition and repression, but there is little question that it has forged a new space for public education, discussion, and solidarity.

Palestinian civil society and the BDS call

The BDS movement includes a number of initiating moments, but the most comprehensive call for a global campaign for boycott, divestment, and sanctions was launched in July 2005 by 170 civil society organizations within Palestine itself. Civil society here refers to nonstate organizations, including trade unions, faith-based communities, student organizations, social movement organizations, academic professional associations, and political parties. The achievement of a unified response among Palestinian organizations challenged divisions that had developed particularly since Oslo and pointed to a strategy of nonviolence and international solidarity inspired by the successful transition from apartheid South Africa (Barghouti 2011; Ziadah 2016).

> The BDS Call, with unprecedented near-consensus support among Palestinians inside historic Palestine as well as in exile, reminded the world that the Indigenous Palestinian people include the refugees forcibly displaced from their homeland—by Zionist militias and later the state of Israel—during the 1948 Nakba and ever since, as well as Palestinian citizens of Israel who remained on their land and now live under a regime of legalized discrimination. (Barghouti 2011: 7)

The call-out is in direct response to Israel's persistent violation of international law as described by the UN. The call is structured to provide a basis of unity that can combine broadly diffuse organizations and forces. The unified call embraces three demands grounded in basic principles of human rights widely recognized in international human rights practices and discourse. To quote:

In light of Israel's persistent violations of international law, and given that, since 1948, hundreds of UN resolutions have condemned Israel's colonial and discriminatory policies as illegal and called for immediate, adequate and effective remedies, and given that all forms of international intervention and peace-making have until now failed to convince or force Israel to comply with humanitarian law, to respect fundamental human rights and to end its occupation and oppression of the people of Palestine, and

In view of the fact that people of conscience in the international community have historically shouldered the moral responsibility to fight injustice, as exemplified in the struggle to abolish apartheid in South Africa through diverse forms of boycott, divestment and sanctions;

Inspired by the struggle of South Africans against apartheid and in the spirit of international solidarity, moral consistency and resistance to injustice and oppression,

We, representatives of Palestinian civil society, call upon international civil society organizations and people of conscience all over the world to impose broad boycotts and implement divestment initiatives against Israel similar to those applied to South Africa in the apartheid era. We appeal to you to pressure your respective states to impose embargoes and sanctions against Israel. We also invite conscientious Israelis to support this Call, for the sake of justice and genuine peace.

These non-violent punitive measures should be maintained until Israel meets its obligation to recognize the Palestinian people's inalienable right to self-determination and fully complies with the precepts of international law by:

1. Ending its occupation and colonization of all Arab lands and dismantling the Wall;
2. Recognizing the fundamental rights of the Arab-Palestinian citizens of Israel to full equality; and
3. Respecting, protecting and promoting the rights of Palestinian refugees to return to their homes and properties as stipulated in UN resolution 194. (Palestinian BNC 2005)

This initiative followed the ruling of the International Court of Justice (ICJ) regarding the legality of the construction of Israel's separation wall through the West Bank and East Jerusalem. The unified BDS statement opens with this recognition and was released on the one-year anniversary date of the ICJ ruling. The appeal is expressed in terms that indicate the failure of and frustration with existing international channels, speaking directly from a coalition from Palestinian civil society to international civil society organizations:

> One year after the historic Advisory Opinion of the International Court of Justice (ICJ) which found Israel's Wall built on occupied Palestinian territory to be illegal, Israel continues its construction of the colonial Wall with total disregard to the Court's decision. Thirty-eight years into Israel's occupation of the Palestinian West Bank (including East Jerusalem), Gaza Strip and the Syrian Golan Heights, Israel continues to expand Jewish colonies. It has unilaterally annexed occupied East Jerusalem and the Golan Heights and is now de facto annexing large parts of the West Bank by means of the Wall. Israel is also preparing—in the shadow of its planned redeployment from the Gaza Strip—to build and expand colonies in the West Bank. Fifty-seven years after the state of Israel was built mainly on land ethnically cleansed of its Palestinian owners, a majority of Palestinians are refugees, most of whom are stateless. Moreover, Israel's entrenched system of racial discrimination against its own Arab-Palestinian citizens remains intact. (Palestinian BNC 2005)

The ongoing construction of the "Apartheid Wall" served as a turning point. Construction began on June 16, 2002; upon completion, it was expected to extend over 810 kilometers, consisting of a series of twenty-five-foot-high concrete walls, barbed wire and electric fences, trenches, electronic sensors, thermal imaging and video cameras, and unmanned aerial vehicles. The building of the wall also included a series of new roads for patrol vehicles and towers equipped for armed Israeli snipers.

According to a study completed by the Palestinian Grassroots Anti-Apartheid Wall Campaign (2010), estimates are that by completion, 46 percent of the West Bank population will be affected by the construction of the wall through loss of land and de facto isolation in ghettoes encircled by the snake-like wall. As noted within Israel as well as occupied Palestine, the construction and enforcement of the boundaries of the wall have provoked comparisons with South African apartheid.

> Comparisons between white rule in South Africa and Israel's system of control over the Arab peoples it governs are increasingly heard. Opponents of the vast steel and concrete barrier under construction through the West Bank and Jerusalem dubbed it the "apartheid wall" because it forces communities apart and grabs land. Critics of Ariel Sharon's plan to carve up the West Bank, apportioning blobs of territory to the Palestinians, draw comparisons with South Africa's "bantustans"—the nominally independent homelands into which millions of black men and women were herded. An Israeli human rights organisation has described segregation of West Bank roads by the military as apartheid. Arab Israeli lawyers argue antidiscrimination cases before the supreme court by drawing out similarities between some Israeli legislation and white South Africa's oppressive laws.[7]

The wall's boundaries go beyond previous borders between Israel and the occupied territory of the West Bank, with only 20 percent of the wall coinciding with the green line that marked Israel's borders prior to the 1967 Six-Day War. Construction companies contracted to blast, dig, and build sections of the wall are commonly surrounded by armed forces, often supplemented by private mercenaries who stand with their fingers on the triggers of handguns as the armed units seize Palestinian lands (Bakan 2005a; Palestinian Anti-Apartheid Wall Campaign 2010). The wall's construction has been identified as a method of land confiscation, extending Israeli colonial occupation and forcing Indigenous Palestinians into further poverty, isolation, and threat of persecution. This view is shared even by those not normally associated with radical activism, such as former US President Jimmy Carter:

> Especially troublesome is the huge dividing wall in the populated areas and an impassable fence in rural areas. The status of this barrier is key to the future of peace in the Middle East.... The governments of Ariel Sharon and Ehud Olmert have built the fence and the wall entirely within Palestinian territory, intruding deeply in the West Bank to encompass Israeli settlement blocs and large areas of other Palestinian land.... The area between the segregation barrier and the Israeli border has been designated a closed military region for an indefinite period of time. Israeli directives state that every Palestinian over the age of twelve living in the closed area has to obtain a "permanent resident permit" from the civil administration to enable them to live in their

own homes. They are considered to be aliens, without the rights of Israeli citizens. (2006: 190–2)

Unusually, even former US President George W. Bush stated his discomfort with Israel's insistence on constructing the wall. Bush commented in 2003 at a joint White House press conference with then Palestinian Prime Minister Mahmoud Abbas, "I think the wall is a problem. It is very difficult to develop confidence between Palestinians and the Israelis with a wall snaking through the West Bank" (as quoted in Mearsheimer and Walt 2007: 215–16; see also Carter 2006: 193).

The comprehensive call for boycott, divestment, and sanctions was launched one year after the ICJ ruling of July 9, 2004, that found the construction of the wall to be in violation of international law (ICJ Reports 2004). This finding was subsequently endorsed by the UN General Assembly. Israel overtly refused to comply and, further, did not face any consequences regarding its international stature, which has been noted in subsequent UN reviews that confirm Israel's apartheid policies (UN ESCWA 2017). These events served as a unifying moment among BDS founding organizations (Usher 2006: 9–30).

The BDS call is distinct in its clarity and broad base of support within Palestinian society. It was preceded by the longstanding calls for boycott from Arab states referred to above, as well as a call for an economic, cultural, and academic boycott of Israel in 2004 (PACBI 2004). It has been followed in turn by parallel calls from: Palestinian filmmakers, artists, and cultural workers; a broad coalition of Palestinian labor federations, vocational and professional trade unions; and endorsements from major organizations, federations, professional associations, and celebrities spreading across the United States, Canada, France, Italy, Spain, and elsewhere (Barghouti 2011: 21). The BDS call is also distinct in the responses it has met among civil society groups in the global North, notably Europe and North America. For example, award-winning British filmmaker Ken Loach was an early supporter, declining an invitation to present one of his films at the Haifa Film Festival and issuing a public statement in August 2006.

> I support the call by Palestinian film-makers, artists and others to boycott state sponsored Israeli cultural institutions and urge others to join their campaign. Palestinians are driven to call for this boycott after forty years of the occupation of their land, destruction of their

homes and the kidnapping and murder of their civilians. They have no immediate hope that this oppression will end. As British citizens we have to acknowledge our own responsibility. We must condemn the British and US governments for supporting and arming Israel. We must also oppose the terrorist activities of the British and US governments in pursuing their illegal wars and occupations. However, it is impossible to ignore the appeals of Palestinian comrades. Consequently, I would decline any invitation to the Haifa Film Festival or other such occasions.

In Canada, a small but significant political party in the province of Quebec, Québec Solidaire (QS), has endorsed the BDS call (QS 2010),[8] and the call has been actively debated, though not adopted, by Canada's Green Party (Green Party of Canada 2016). As an indication of the reach of the BDS call for academic and cultural boycott, in 2013 the late internationally acclaimed physicist Stephen Hawking cancelled an Israeli government invitation to speak at a conference after appeals from Palestinian academics.[9]

Associating the conditions of Palestinians directly with churches, student organizations, trade unions, municipalities, professional associations, and social movements, the BDS strategy is designed not only to promote economic consequences for Israel's economy but also, and often deemed more importantly, to disrupt the hegemonic discourse that Israel is a progressive, democratic state. The stated goals of the campaign are specifically grounded in education and in building an international culture that supports Palestinian human rights:

> The main goals of this call are: To reveal to the world the nature of Israel's occupation and apartheid regime; To give human rights a real value by making Israel accountable and forcing it to pay a price for its crimes; To reveal and highlight the responsibility of the international community in supporting Israeli crimes and violations of human rights and international law; [and] Above all, to end international support for Israeli occupation and apartheid since these cannot survive without external assistance. (Coalition Against Israeli Apartheid 2008: 83)

The campaign is designed to be flexible in its application and subject to adaptation to specific conditions in various international, regional, and local contexts. Consistently, however, the place of Zionism as a hegemonic element in Western ideology has been challenged, and debates regarding the nature of racism and anti-racism have inevitably ensued. Despite facing intense lobbying and opposition to varying degrees among organized Zionist interests, the BDS campaign has continued to grow, drawing wider circles of support from multiple communities internationally. The movement for academic boycott acquired heightened attention as a result of an initiative from British university and college lecturers to extend an educational campaign. This was met with considerable backlash, resonating among Canadian universities, but not in a manner that served to stall momentum for discussions of the implications of academic boycott in either the UK or Canada.[10]

The reach of the BDS call has been, however, much wider. Other examples indicate the impact. Following the precedent of the American Studies Association, a wave of academic professional associations in the United States has seen positions in support of academic boycott (Dawson and Mullen 2015). University students in the UK, in protests considered comparable to the events of the 1960s, were galvanized to demand among other issues, and often successfully, that their universities divest funds from Israeli institutions.[11] In the United States, the prestigious Hampshire College in Amherst, Massachusetts, became the first of any postsecondary institution in that country "to divest from companies on the grounds of their involvement in the Israeli occupation of Palestine."[12] Labor actions have included historic acts of solidarity. Dockworkers who were members of the South African Transport and Allied Workers Union (SATAWU) in Durban, South Africa, for example, refused to offload an Israeli ship in anticipation of its arrival on February 8, 2009 (Palestinian BNC 2009a). In Norway, the Locomotive Drivers Union on 8 January of the same year saw all trains, trams and subways come to a halt in a two-minute protest, during which time a statement demanding "the immediate withdrawal of all Israeli troops from Palestinian territory" was read to all passengers (Green Party Peace Network 2009). Voices in support of boycotting Israel also include significant challenges to the mainstream Zionist organizations among the international Jewish community (Bakan 2014a).[13] The close identification of this campaign with the global movement for social justice was indicated at the 100,000 strong meeting of the World Social Forum (WSF) in Belém, Brazil, in 2009. The WSF issued a statement in support of the BDS campaign and, further, called for an international day of action (Becker 2009; Palestinian

BNC 2009b). Support for the BDS campaign has advanced even in the face of considerable opposition. In October 2018, the Nobel Prize in Chemistry was awarded to Dr. George P. Smith, a US-based professor at the University of Missouri, Columbia, who has been a longstanding supporter of the BDS campaign (Palestinian BNC 2018).

Even before the Gaza events, the call was extending its adherents. For example, in a November 2008 statement, the president of the United Nations General Assembly, Father Miguel D'Escoto Brockman, urged the use by the UN of the term "apartheid" to describe Israeli policies in the Occupied Palestinian Territories. He noted the effectiveness of the sanction campaign against South Africa in the UN historically and suggested, "perhaps we in the United Nations should consider following the lead of a new generation of civil society, who are calling for a similar non-violent campaign of boycott, divestment and sanctions to pressure Israel to end its violations" (2008). The civil society organizations endorsing the BDS initiative in Europe included: the Dutch ASN Bank, which became the first bank to divest from companies benefiting from Israeli occupation in November 2006; the Norwegian Civil Service Union, which in the same month voted in favor of a boycott of Israel though an arms embargo; and Connex Ireland, operator of railway lines in Ireland, which cancelled plans to train Israeli engineers and drivers in Ireland in August 2006. The Irish Joint Committee on Foreign Affairs also called for the Irish government to push for sanctions against Israel in the EU due to Israel's human rights abuses; also in the same month, organizers for the Edinburgh Film Festival cancelled sponsorship of the festival by the Israeli embassy and returned all funds received from the Israeli government. And, also in August 2006, the administrative council of the Greek Cinematography Centre withdrew all Greek films from participation in the Haifa Cinema Festival scheduled for October 2006 (Coalition Against Israeli Apartheid 2008: 82). Previously, in December 2005, the local council of the region of Sør-Trøndelag in Norway passed a motion calling for a comprehensive boycott of Israeli goods, to be followed up with an awareness-raising campaign across the region. In a statement reporting on the motion, it was noted that:

> Sør-Trøndelag has a population of 270,000 out of Norway's 4.6 million. Trondheim, Norway's third largest city, forms part of the region and will participate in the boycott initiative. The council committed itself to this motion as a result of intensive work by Norwegian activists

> that had launched a national Boycott Israel campaign this June [2005]. (Stop the Wall Campaign 2005)

This motion followed a similar one passed by a municipality in the Basque country, Arbizu (Stop the Wall Campaign 2005).

In South Africa, the campaign for boycott, divestment, and sanctions against Israel, modeled on the international movement that supported the anti-apartheid struggle, met the 2008–9 attacks on Gaza with an already-established history of support from the major trade union federations, student organizations, and leading representatives of postapartheid governments (Vally 2008). Archbishop Desmond Tutu's open comparison of Israel's treatment of the Palestinians to that of Blacks in apartheid South Africa generated considerable support.[14] This support has, in turn, fueled the appeal of the BDS campaign in other countries where memories of solidarity actions against apartheid South Africa continue to resonate.

The 2008 statement of the UN General Assembly president reflects the aim of the BDS movement to adopt the analogy between Israel and apartheid South Africa as an educational tool. This analogy has acted as a means of breaking down the ideological framing of Israel as an exceptional state on the grounds of its self-described "Jewish" character, presuming an identity between Judaism, Jewish culture, and Zionism. The direct association between South African activists and Palestinian solidarity organizing on university campuses has been important in expanding civil society support for the BDS movement. One indication of this is the growth of a movement for internationally coordinated educational conferences under the banner of "Israeli Apartheid Week." By 2008, it was noted:

> Israeli Apartheid Week (IAW), which began in Toronto four years ago, took place in 25 places across the world including, for the first time, Palestine and South Africa. In a symbolic gesture, exiled Palestinian member of the Israeli Knesset, Azmi Bishara, gave the opening address of IAW in Soweto, South Africa. Bishara said, "Reconciliation happened in South Africa after apartheid was dismantled, not instead. The message sent to the Palestinians is that you have to make peace and reconcile. We can reconcile after racism and occupation is dismantled." Dr. Bishara's lecture was screened during IAW in participating cities around the world, a sign of the new level of coordination between anti-

apartheid activists on a global level. The 2008 IAW was held under the banner "60 Years of Nakba: End Israeli Apartheid." The analysis of apartheid put forward during IAW in previous years has played an important role in raising awareness and disseminating information about Zionism, the Palestinian liberation struggle, and its similarities with the Indigenous sovereignty struggle in North America and the South African anti-Apartheid movement. (Ziadah 2008)

IAW events have gone on to spread to over 200 cities in more than 20 countries, and BDS campaigns have been launched among student unions in Canada, the United States, and Europe (Ageel 2016; Palestinian BNC 2012).

Other examples in the global South can also be noted, and these trace the emergence of the BDS movement over the 2000s. In Indonesia, for example, a women's tennis team scheduled to play in a major playoff in Israel in July 2006 withdrew from a tie as an act of solidarity with Palestinians. The Indonesian Tennis Federation and government representatives from the ministries of sport and foreign affairs also announced a boycott of the games in response to Israeli aggression against Palestinians in the Gaza Strip (Coalition Against Israeli Apartheid 2008: 82).

In an important indication of state sanctions allying with civil society initiatives in Latin America, in August 2006 then Venezuelan President Hugo Chavez withdrew the country's ambassador from Israel in response to Israel's war on Lebanon (Mather 2006). The war on Gaza saw an extension of Venezuela's show of solidarity with the Palestinian cause. On January 6, 2009, Chavez expelled Israel's ambassador to Venezuela in protest of the attacks on Gaza.[15] Days later, Bolivia's President Evo Morales similarly severed the country's diplomatic ties with Israel.

In North America, the US Green Party adopted a position in support of divestment and boycott of the state of Israel in May 2006. In Canada, the Canadian Union of Public Employees (CUPE) Ontario regional convention passed a resolution in May 2006 supporting the comprehensive call for BDS. Despite a concerted and organized campaign to compel union delegates to reverse the decision, the union leadership responded with a mass educational campaign in defense of "Resolution 50." The resolution is now policy, entrenched in union educational, research, and policy documents. However, Sid Ryan, former president of CUPE Ontario, reflected on his experience:

> I've fought as a trade union leader and I'm from the Republic of Ireland. I've seen racism and reactionaries. But never have I experienced the type of attacks we faced after our own rank and file delegates unanimously adopted Resolution 50 responding to the people of Palestine. These attacks were not from our own members. In CUPE, of 225,000 members, only two locals, five e-mails and two phone calls objected. From outside the union there were more than 30,000 e-mails, death threats, attacks on my family, and on the memory of my father and mother. But we stood firm and we are standing firm. (2008)

The United Church of Canada's Toronto Conference supported the position for boycott, divestment, and sanctions adopted by CUPE Ontario in a public press conference in June 2006. This followed a proposal supported by a United Church task force committee to boycott products from the Occupied Palestinian Territories (United Church 2006). By 2012, support among faith-based communities had expanded considerably (see United Church 2012), following the call for concrete solidarity from an alliance of Palestinian Christians. This is also evident in the United States where:

> [T]he Quaker Friends Fiduciary Corporation (FFC) divested $900,000 in shares of Caterpillar, targeted over its sale of bulldozers to Israel that are used to violate Palestinian rights. The worldwide United Methodist Church and the Presbyterian Church in the US have both called on their members to boycott produce from illegal Israeli settlements. (Palestinian BNC 2012)

In April 2008, the Canadian Union of Postal Workers (CUPW) was the first national union in North America to pass a motion modeled directly on the BDS resolution adopted by CUPE at the provincial level (CUPW 2008). Both unions committed considerable resources to membership education and debate among rank and file trade union members, extending the reach of discussion and support for Palestinian rights. Significantly, a number of Jewish civil society organizations and prominent individuals have also endorsed the BDS campaign (see Butler 2014; Independent Jewish Voices 2017).

The links established between civil society organizations internationally and within Palestine itself have also been significant. One Canadian journalist reported on a BDS conference in Palestine taking place in November 2007, noting the sense of unity and optimism that the campaign inspired, even in the face of relentless military aggression.

> The BDS strategy is powerful precisely because it defies the political fragmentation that has been the consequence of Israel's expulsion, settlement, and bantustanization policies.... It contributes to building a united framework for a struggle for self-determination that Palestinians living in the Diaspora, Arab countries, Gaza, the West Bank, and Israel can all participate in. BDS avoids creating a situation in which solidarity activists undermine that unity by funding or grooming the Palestinian counterpart that reflect their own sense of a just solution, or of what "self-determination" should look like. Islah Jahad, a professor of Women's Studies at Birzeit University, referred to BDS as a way of developing "joint ownership" over a political process, and contrasts it with the divisive "clientelism" that has characterized the vast majority of international support for Palestinian non-governmental organizations since the first Intifada. (Schmidt 2008)

These early initiatives have swelled dramatically over the twenty-first century, resonating with and linking movements against racism and colonialism to the call for Palestinian rights and challenging the hegemonic mythologized exceptionalism of the Israel/Palestine racial contract.

In conclusion: Counterhegemony and the Israel/Palestine racial contract

The continued development of the BDS movement demands widening dialogues, and as such, it has helped to establish the prospect of a more open atmosphere of reasoned debate regarding the Israel/Palestine reality. However, considerable backlash continues. Despite the ways in which the BDS movement may peacefully challenge the Zionist settler project as carried out by Israel and supported by allies, repression of the rights of Palestinians has increased, as have efforts to repress and silence solidarity campaigns internationally. The charged atmosphere that has surrounded the calls for an academic boycott in the UK, Canada, and the United States is a case in point. The claim has been widely made, not least by a concerted movement of university and college presidents across

Canada and the United States, that calls to boycott Israeli universities abrogate principles of free speech and academic freedom. By way of contrast, in the name of defending Israel from Hamas rocket fire, the Islamic University in Gaza was leveled during Operation Cast Lead. As Israeli professors Neve Gordon and Jeff Halper stated during the attacks, writing on December 31, 2008:

> Not one of the nearly 450 presidents of American colleges and universities who prominently denounced an effort by British academics to boycott Israeli universities in September 2007 have raised their voice in opposition to Israel's bombardment of the Islamic University of Gaza earlier this week.... Most others who signed similar petitions, like the 11,000 professors from nearly 1,000 universities around the world, have also refrained from expressing their outrage at Israel's attack on the leading university in Gaza.[16]

Notably, during the height of South African apartheid, the African National Congress called for an academic boycott as a way to further pressure the apartheid regime. Inspired by this movement, in 2002 an academic boycott of Israel was first advanced by two British-based academics, Hilary and Steven Rose, who viewed the academic, cultural, and sports boycotts imposed on apartheid South Africa as a model for resisting Israeli policies.[17] They subsequently replied to claims suggesting that Steven Rose was a "self-hating Jew":

> The charge is intellectually absurd, personally disgusting—especially when leveled against those whose own families died in the death camps and who have spent their active public lives opposing racism and Fascism—and politically hazardous, in that it suggests any criticism of Israel is equivalent to attacking Jews. (as quoted in Jakubowicz 2003)

Indeed, for those advocating an academic boycott of Israeli institutions, this is advanced precisely because it is a peaceful, nonviolent tactic. It is a way to apply international pressure in the hopes that the structural racism experienced by Palestinians at the hands of the Israeli state will be dismantled, following the example of South Africa, where apartheid was dismantled (see, for example, Pappe 2003). The academic boycott of Israeli institutions, which is geared to institutions and not individuals, is only one component of the broader boycott, divestment, and sanctions movement aimed at delivering a just and lasting peace (Rose and Rose 2008: 1–20).

The BDS movement can therefore most effectively be understood as a counterhegemonic movement aimed at challenging an entrenched but weakening Israel/Palestine racial contract. The increasing influence of the movement among students and labor and human rights activists since the pivotal moment of the 2008–9 war on Gaza is indicative of its combined strategic and educational capacity. In framing Israel as an apartheid state, the BDS call has contributed to an anti-racist challenge to the Orientalist and Islamophobic messaging associated with the post-9/11 war on terror. It has brought back "the question of Palestine" in a way that resonates across multiple divisions fueled by state actors domestically and internationally (see Massad 2006; Said 1992).

However, at the core of the effectiveness of the BDS movement is the unity of purpose that it reflects within Palestine itself. This indicates the centrality of subaltern forces in Palestine and is key to the BDS movement's effectiveness as a counterhegemonic force. After decades of disappointment and fragmentation in the aftermath of the failed Oslo Accords, the BDS movement has united Palestinians across borders, political factions, and generations. It has renewed attention to Israel's persistent violations of international law, including the construction of the Apartheid Wall, the denial of civil rights of Palestinian Israelis, and the denial of the right of return of Palestinian refugees.

The current conjuncture, then, is one in which a historic hegemony where Zionism has been incorporated in an international racial contract is under intense challenge through the resistance from Palestinian civil society. There is, in this context, a deepening resonance to the counterhegemonic argument that views Israel as a state that should be isolated internationally through boycott, divestment, and sanctions until it reverses its violations of international law and human rights. In contrast to the failure of the UN to effectively sanction the Israeli state's defiance of international law, what could be seen as a United Nations from below has shouldered the responsibility. The BDS movement is one that international solidarity activists and anti-racist social theorists can constructively embrace and advance, regardless of the fraught atmosphere of debate and challenges. In fact, these challenges can be understood as an inevitable feature of an ongoing dislodgement of a historic hegemonic discourse. The next part of our discussion turns to focus on key elements of this dislodgement, including Israel's efforts to "rebrand" its public image in the face of increasingly effective resistance.

Notes

1 See also, Sheera Frankel, "Amnesty International: Gaza White Phosphorus Shells Were US Made," *The Times*, February 24, 2009, https://www.thetimes.co.uk/article/amnesty-international-gaza-white-phosphorus-shells-were-us-made-gqqrj6p0cf7; James Hider and Sheera Frankel, "Israel Admits Using White Phosphorous in Attacks on Gaza," *The Times*, January 24, 2009, https://www.thetimes.co.uk/article/israel-admits-using-white-phosphorous-in-attacks-on-gaza-3jngp502vh0.

2 Dorit Naaman, "Israel's Elections Are Nothing to Celebrate," *rabble.ca*, February 11, 2009, http://rabble.ca/news/israels-elections-why-we-should-not-celebrate-only-democracy-middle-east.

3 *CNN*, "Fast Facts on Benjamin Netanyahu," *cnn.com*, February 18, 2017, http://www.cnn.com/2013/01/01/world/meast/benjamin-netanyahu—fast-facts/.

4 Noura Erakat, "Roundtable on Anti-Blackness and Black-Palestinian Solidarity," moderated by Noura Erakat, *Jadaliyya*, June 3, 2013, http://www.jadaliyya.com/pages/index/21764/roundtable-on-anti-blackness-and-black-palestinian.

5 Desmond Tutu, "Apartheid and the Holy Land," *The Guardian*, April 29, 2002, https://www.theguardian.com/world/2002/apr/29/comment; Desmond Tutu, "Of Occupation and Apartheid: Do I Divest?," *CounterPunch*, October 17, 2002, https://www.counterpunch.org/2002/10/17/do-i-divest/.

6 Available at http://www.electronicintifada.net/.

7 Chris McGreal, "Worlds Apart," *The Guardian*, February 6, 2006, https://www.theguardian.com/world/2006/feb/06/southafrica.israel.

8 See also Richard Fidler, "Québec Solidaire Supports Pro-Palestine BDS Campaign," *Socialist Voice: Marxist Perspectives for the 21st Century*, November 30, 2009, http://www.socialistvoice.ca/?p=798%5D.

9 *Al Jazeera*, "Stephen Hawking Backs Israeli Boycott," May 8, 2013, http://www.aljazeera.com/news/europe/2013/05/2013589372057682.

10 Margaret Aziza Pappano, "The Ivory Tower Behind the Apartheid Wall," *Electronic Intifida*, July 25, 2007, https://electronicintifada.net/content/ivory-tower-behind-apartheid-wall/7073; Zac Smith, "Countering Palestine Solidarity Work in Canada," *ZSpace*, 2009, www.zmag.org. Link no longer working.

11 Emily Dugan, "Students Are Revolting: The Spirit of '68 Is Reawakening," *The Independent*, February 8, 2009, www.independent.co.uk/news/

education/education-news/students-are-revolting-the-spirit-of-68-is-reawakening-1604043.html.

12 *Electronic Intifada*, "Hampshire College First in US to Divest from Israel," February 12, 2009, https://electronicintifada.net/content/hampshire-college-first-us-divest-israel/932.

13 Adrienne Rich, "Why Support the US Campaign for Academic and Cultural Boycott of Israel?," *MRZine*, February 3, 2009, http://mrzine.monthlyreview.org/rich080209.html.

14 *BBC News*, "Tutu Condemns Israeli 'Apartheid,'" April 29, 2002, http://news.bbc.co.uk/2/hi/africa/1957644.stm.

15 *Reuters*, "Venezuela Expels Israel Envoy over Gaza Attacks," January 6, 2009, http://www.reuters.com/article/middleeastCrisis/idUSN06444577.

16 Neve Gordon and Jeff Halper, "Where's the Academic Outrage over the Bombing of a University in Gaza?," *Counterpunch*, December 31, 2008, https://www.counterpunch.org/2008/12/31/where-s-the-academic-outrage-over-the-bombing-of-a-university-in-gaza/.

17 Hilary Rose and Steven Rose, "The Choice Is to Do Nothing or to Try to Bring About Change: Why We Launched the Boycott of Israeli Institutions," *The Guardian*, July 15, 2002, http://www.guardian.co.uk/world/2002/jul/15/comment.stevenrose.

PART THREE

THE ISRAEL/ PALESTINE RACIAL CONTRACT: REBRANDING AND RESISTANCE

7 ISRAEL'S REBRANDING CAMPAIGN AND THE POLITICS OF GENDER

Introduction

Images of gender and governance are critical to understanding the evolution of "brand Israel" in the Western popular imaginary, and, since the 2000s, in Israel's "rebranding campaign." In this chapter, we argue that rebranding Israel is a state-led process of reframing apartheid-like policies to be read as democratic, modern, and inclusive of gender and sexual diversity. This process depends significantly on absenting Palestinians, and, relatedly, on Israeli colonial subjugation and the ongoing dispossession of Palestinians. It also relies on presenting alternative, and racialized, images of Palestinians as "culturally" undemocratic, violent, and sexist/patriarchal. These stereotypes belie the rich, diverse, and varied histories and experiences of Palestinians, while serving to advance the Israel/Palestine racial contract.

In what follows, we take a fourfold approach. First, we pick up a theme advanced earlier, namely the way in which the idea of "Israel" resonates in Western hegemony, but also show the relevance of gender and sexuality in theorizing this evolving national and global construction. While in its first two decades, Israel's relevance in relation to the Christian Bible may have been critically important, in recent years, this marketing pitch has perhaps reached its best before date. Certainly, since September 11, 2001, there has been a greater shift toward what Jasbir K. Puar refers to as "homonationalism," a process that is deeply implicated in Orientalist constructions of a mythical ascribed Muslim sexuality (2007: 4). Second, the chapter turns to consider Israel's historic branding and rebranding around issues related to gender, specifically constructions of masculinity and femininity in relation to national discourses. Third, we address in greater detail a more recent feature in rebranding efforts that focus on gay rights, a development that critics have referred to as "pinkwashing" Israel's apartheid policies. Using the specific example of attempts to ban the organization Queers Against Israeli Apartheid (QUAIA) from a major North American pride parade held annually in Toronto, Canada, we consider the contradictions of pinkwashing from the vantage point of LGBTQ (lesbian, gay, bisexual, transgender/transsexual, and queer/questioning) rights and human rights. Fourth, we conclude this chapter by turning attention specifically to the Palestinians as "Brand Israel's" implicit other. While the Palestinian narrative is absented within Brand Israel, we consider the gendered dimensions of how Palestinians are imagined—both in Israel and in the West. We also consider the gendered impact of colonialism and occupation on the Palestinian population.

Gender, nation, and homonationalism after 9/11

As noted throughout this volume, there is an inherent contradiction in a polity that claims to be simultaneously open and inclusive, or democratic, while positing an exclusive core mission—insisting on Israel's national identity as a distinctly "Jewish" state rather than a state of all its citizens. This contradiction, though perhaps more blatant on the international scene in recent years, has characterized Israel since its foundation in 1948 and lies at the heart of the Israel/Palestine racial contract. It is expressed through a collection of policies designed to eradicate the physical presence of the Indigenous Palestinian population through repression and also in public and historical discourse. It is expressed also through the ongoing erosion and erasure of Palestinian substantive and symbolic power. The process has drawn support from political allies in various ways, particularly the United States, Canada, and other Western states, thereby forming an international Israel/Palestine racial contract.

Although there are many examples of state officials and citizens protecting power and privilege through the mobilization of domestic and international discourses, what is notable about the Israeli case is the degree to which these have gone largely unchallenged in an era of what is commonly termed the "human rights revolution" (Iriye, Goedde, and Hitchcock 2012). This differs from the mobilization of the international community, for example, that took place regarding South Africa during the apartheid era through the United Nations and international civil society. More recently, Canada, the United States, Australia, and New Zealand were eventually compelled to sign on to the 2007 United Nations Declaration of the Rights of Indigenous Peoples (UNDRIP), itself a reflection of the historic and increasing demands of Indigenous peoples globally (Beier 2007). In contrast, Israel has been much more successful in mitigating and resisting the impact of criticisms of its racialized practices and related policies.

Relevant to this discussion is the way that the idea of Israel has absented the Palestinians, especially in the popular imaginaries of the industrialized West and, Israel's close and powerful partner, the United States. As discussed earlier in relation to Israel's contested origin stories and Indigeneity, scholars of the biblical tradition—associated with both the Hebrew and Christian Bibles—have similarly presented a particular interpretation consistent with political Zionism. In this view, "the land of Palestine" is seen as identical to Israel (Masalha 2007: 310–11). In the context of Canada, Prime Minister Lester B. Pearson was instrumental in forging Canadian support for the 1947 Partition Plan prior to becoming one of Canada's most notable and leading politicians. He credited his own Christian Sunday school lessons for learning that "the Jews belonged in Palestine" (Engler 2010: 25). This also helps to explain the support evident among contemporary American evangelical Christians for Zionism and the state of Israel (Lewis 2010). Indeed, organized visits of American Christians to see the "Holy Land" and the "land of the Bible" have been an important part of Israeli tourism, and hence a version of "Brand Israel."

However, the conflation of Israel and Zionism with the (Christian) Bible does not refer to the only source contributing to the idea of Israel and the absenting of the Palestinians. For Western, and particularly American, audiences, bestselling writer Leon Uris' 1958 novel *Exodus* was a critical cultural contribution to the popular imaginary. The book blurs the reader's understanding of reality and fiction through the author's misleading suggestion that "most of the events in *Exodus* are a matter of history and public record" even if "all the characters in *Exodus* are the complete creation of the author, and entirely fictional" (Uris 1958: ii). In the words of literary critic Ira Nadel, the book and the subsequent 1960 movie starring Paul Newman and Eva Marie Saint were important for fostering American support for both Zionism and the Israeli state:

> The impact of *Exodus* on the psyche of Americans, Jew and non-Jew alike, was incalculable. Not only did travel and contributions to Israel increase, but the perception of the country, and by extension the perception of Jews, changed. They were no longer victims but heroes. The sheer number of copies sold meant that many experienced Jewish history and heroism dramatically and romantically.... Popular culture soon reconstructed public memory as the value of the Holocaust and Zionism altered from despair to triumph. (2010: 115)

An American-born Jew, Uris is described as having been angered at "the image of the 'soft' Jew" (Nadel 2010: 96). Indeed, Uris once claimed to have been inspired to write the novel *Exodus* because of his admiration of the Israeli army: "Jews in the field kicking the hell out of somebody" (as quoted in Nadel 2010: 97). In this way, the novel *Exodus*, which traces the activities of protagonist Ari Ben Canaan in transporting Jewish refugees to Mandate Palestine and culminates in the birth of the Israeli state, is in essence a valorization of the masculinized imagery associated with the "new Jew," discussed below.

As literary critic Edward Said noted early in the twenty-first century, the ignorance of many Americans about the Palestinian narrative and experience of 1948 may be attributed in part to the fact that Uris' book *Exodus* was a sustaining part of "the main narrative model that dominates American thinking" (2004b: 101). This could well be why former Israeli Prime Minister David Ben-Gurion observed of *Exodus* that, "as a literary work it isn't much. But as a piece of propaganda, it's the greatest thing ever written about Israel" (as quoted in Nadel 2010: 116). In addition to biblical and modern literary and cinematic imagery associated with Israel, its connections with ideals of modernity, democracy, and equality—including gender equality—are of relevance. Indeed, as contemporary feminist scholarship has made clear, constructions of masculinity and femininity are highly relevant in nationalist movements and national expressions in colonial and postcolonial contexts (Abdo 2011; Abu-Laban 2008a; Bannerji 2000; McClintock 1995; Yuval-Davis 1997). In the post-9/11 period, such gendered constructions have taken on renewed and cross-national significance. This period has been marked by a context in which Islam is considered to be in conflict with the ideals associated with Western democracy and equality, and states with Muslim majorities and Muslims have widely come to be treated as premodern and traditional. In particular, civilizational discourses relating to Islam and gender equality have emerged in a new way, particularly since 9/11, in the spheres of both international and domestic (Western) politics, providing a form of justification for the US-led war on terror and anti-Muslim racism (Razack 2008; Razack et al. 2010).

Civilizational discourses pertaining to Islam and LGBTQ rights have advanced in the spheres of both international and domestic politics in Western states. The mobilization of what Puar (2007) has termed "homonationalism" marks a state project of the appropriation of gay rights discourse to the cause of US imperialism and the war on terror abroad, while also intensifying the subordination of racialized minorities within Western polities. It is of interest to note, for example, that in the Netherlands, the rights of sexual minorities have become a new discursive dividing line between local, modern, and democratic values, considered to be synonymous with "Dutch" identity; values purported to be consistent with foreign, traditional, and undemocratic states are associated with immigrants, particularly those from the global South (Mepschen, Duyvendak, and Tonkens 2010). This is reflective of a parallel trend in which the rights of women have been posited as a line of division between non-Muslims and Muslim immigrants and minorities across Western polities in Europe and North America (Razack 2008).

It is in this context that Israel's explicit rebranding campaign is of special note. It necessitates close critical and analytical attention to women's equality, LGBTQ rights, and essentialized constructions of modernity versus tradition. Such constructions collectively serve to advance and reproduce ostensibly immutable boundaries between groups and societies. Zionist narratives have long treated Arabs as "backward" others, lacking the capacity to "make the desert bloom." Hence, notions of "modern" Israel and "traditional" but unnamed Palestine have formed an integral part of Israeli settler colonization. Such distinctions are by no means confined to the Israeli project, finding parallels in other settler-colonial state settings, including Canada (Abu-Laban and Couture 2010). As we address below, however, when applied to Israel/Palestine, such constructions demand complex analysis, because the racial contract intersects with gendered relations in specific ways.

Women's equality, brand Israel, and rebranding

The idea of Israel has historically intersected gendered narratives that are simultaneously racialized. The Zionist framing of an exclusively "Jewish" state rests, rather curiously, beside another narrative where the colonial project is understood as an act of heroic male conquest, challenging the simultaneously threatening and weakened Indigenous Palestinian population. As Ghada Karmi (2007) reminds us, the first Zionist Congress of 1897, in Basel, Switzerland, entertained the idea of establishing a "Jewish state" in Palestine in such terms. Those in attendance heard the result of the explorations of two representatives to the region who had gone to consider the suitability of the project site for construction of a Zionist state. They reported to the conference by cable: "The bride is beautiful, but she is married to another man" (Karmi 2007: v). The land was not in fact a "land without a people," but inhabited by an Indigenous Palestinian Arab population. The effeminized land was framed in this brief statement as a married woman, and the Palestinian population was constructed as a competitor in the form of a masculinized threat, as "another" man. The contest for the land was, therefore, symbolized at the outset as one of patriarchal male competition for the previously betrothed, and objectified, bride.

Other gendered narratives have continued, adapted to various moments in the making of both the state and idea of Israel. These are associated particularly with the masculinized military conquest that defined the Zionist project in the formative moment of the *Nakba* of 1948 and also with the construction of identity as a "Jewish state" with implications for maternal birth. The contemporary symbolisms are counterpoised and related to the gendered framing of the Holocaust, or *Shoa*, memorialized as indicative of Jewish effeminate weakness. As Ronit Lentin describes it:

> I was a member of "the (Israeli) first generation to redemption", coached to despise those "dia-spora Jews", for having allegedly gone passively to their death during the Shoah, "like lambs to the slaughter". Israel was the place where Jews would be proud again, would take up arms to fight their "enemies", would never again "go to their death like lambs to the slaughter". I was also a member of a family of

> Shoah survivors. An act of naming I was only able to engage in while researching this book.... [I]n constructing itself as a "new Jewish entity" ... Israel construct[ed] itself as masculine thereby "feminising" diaspora Jewry and the Shoah. (Lentin 2000: xiii)

The Israeli military has become symbolic of a Zionist ideal of conquest as a form of overcoming perceived weakness. This weakness has been widely seen in Zionist interpretations to rest within the European Jewish population itself (Herzl 1988). The tradition of Jewish resistance to war and fascism is absented, replaced by the construction of a particular type of Zionist masculinity (see Reiter 2016). This construction, which is opposed to but also imitative of the anti-Jewish masculinity that is simultaneously despised and admired, has been identified by Joseph Massad as endemic to the Israeli colonial settlement project (2006). Massad's analysis views the construction of the Zionist male identity as part of Orientalist racialized notions of the Palestinian Other. Daniel Boyarin (1997) analyzes the construction of the idealized Zionist "New Jew" as aggressively heterosexual, at least in part in response to a certain purported queerness characteristic of the rabbinic, diasporic, Jewish male scholar. In a traditional anti-Semitic trope, Western Christian thought identified Jewish males as supposedly bearing an extreme sexual appetite, while simultaneously depicting them as inherently effeminate. Boyarin further maintains that Zionism can be understood as a profound "straightening" effort, meant to heterosexualize the new Jewish man. Building on Boyarin's observation of the gendered masculinization of the Zionist project, Yaron Peleg, however, objects to the claim that all early Zionists categorically rejected the homosexual image. Peleg identifies a series of gay male subjects as heroic models in Zionist literature, in accordance with the "healthy simplicity of the Greek male nudes" who represented "physical rigor, ascetic lifestyle, morality, discipline, and a proximity to nature that all national movements in Europe extolled" (2006: 33). Regardless of the historical and cultural roots, Peleg returns to Boyarin's premises in seeing a linkage between aggressive male heterosexuality and contemporary Israeli identities (2006: 44).

The Zionist ideal is further complicated as it has not been entirely linear in its sexualized and sexist imagination. Rooted in both the military settler project and associations with "progressive" labor politics, an ethos of gender equality has also been embedded in the settler project. This has generated a contradictory and complex framing of women's role in the construction of the Israeli "nation." Ruth Halperin-Kaddari and Yaacov Yadgar, in a detailed study of politics and gender among Israeli Jews, indicate the contradictory legacy.

> The movement professed a completely egalitarian ideology, according to which women were to have full and equal participation at all levels of the nation-building enterprise. Thus, for example, women had equal voting rights in since [*sic*] the second Zionist Congress as early as 1898, and most Zionist utopian writings, including Herzl's visionary *Altnoiland,* depicted women as having equal rights to those of men. However ... reality was very different. Ultimately, what the Zionist movement's egalitarian ideology formed was not an egalitarian society, but rather a powerful and long-lasting myth of equality which consistently suppressed much of the criticism and mobilization efforts in the direction of women's advancement. (2010a: 17–18; emphasis original)

This pattern of gender inequality, albeit discursively blurred by equality rhetoric, is well documented (Abdo 2011; Halperin-Kaddari and Yadgar 2010a; Moore 2011; Razack 2010). And, "of all the various explanations offered, the main ones are religion, and male-centered militarism" (Halperin-Kaddari and Yadgar 2010a: 18). Regarding the first of these explanations, "religion" in a "Jewish" state is necessarily imbricated with the politics of the state. Moreover, "religion, as an institution rather than a spiritual relationship between the individual and her God, is not an essentialist or stagnant force. It is not an ahistorical notion fixed in time and space" (Abdo 2011: 27). Israel has enshrined specific power relations in a series of laws—including the Law of Return favoring Jewish immigration and citizenship claims—relying on a rabbinical definition of Jewish identity based on maternal genealogy. In the sphere of personal relations, Rabbinical Courts remain legally and culturally decisive, including in marriage, intermarriage, children's rights, and divorce (Abdo 2011: 26; Halperin-Kaddari and Yadgar 2010a: 18). The tension between Israel's projection as simultaneously modern and religious generates ongoing contradictions and also renders the nation's "branding" efforts inherently gendered. As noted:

> According to secular law, all persons are equal, while religious law accepts inequality as a basic concept. Inferiority of women is a basic

> premise of religious laws: Men divorce women, but not vice versa; a man can marry another woman if his wife refuses a divorce, but a woman cannot do the same. A woman who has a sexual relationship with another man while married may be divorced by her husband without her consent and without alimony or her share of the mutual property. She may even lose custody over her children. No such laws apply to men.... Religious law has always been accorded supremacy, so that whenever there has been a clash between secular and religious laws, religious law has been upheld. (Moore 2011: 61)

Recurring arguments for the institutionalization of civil marriage are challenged by multiple interests in Israeli society, not least those that oppose opening the door to marriage across religious and racial/ethnic lines (Halperin-Kaddari and Yadgar 2010b: 911–13; Masri 2017). In the context of a state project perceived to be threatened by the existence and advancement of the Indigenous Palestinian population relative to the settler Jewish population—a condition referred to in common racialized terminology as the "demographic threat"—nationhood and reproduction are deeply interconnected.

> Motherhood was established as a path to civil status for women, marking them as "bearers of the collective". In the context of the Jewish national collective this carries not only the actual biological reproductive function of women, but also the determination of the boundaries of national identity. (Halperin-Kaddari and Yadgar 2010b: 911)

The military and colonial framing of Israeli statehood intersects with the religiously sanctioned rights of Jewish settlement, enshrined in Israeli law, where Jewish identity is associated with maternal birth. These discussions define not only the Israeli nation domestically but stretch well beyond Israel/Palestine. As Susan Martha Kahn notes:

> These philosophical debates take place alongside certain irrefutable Jewish kinship beliefs: anyone born to a Jewish mother is a Jew, suggesting that there is something intrinsically physical about Jewish identity. And yet Jewishness can be acquired by conversion—suggesting that however embodied Jewish identity may be, it is an identity that can be willfully assumed by a non-Jewish body. In short,

> opposing concepts of Jewishness, as a product of kinship versus a product of commitment, have always existed in dynamic tension. (2010: 12)

As the Israeli state makes efforts to rebrand as more modern, and therefore more sexually egalitarian, sections of Israeli society have proven resistant. Indeed, the contradiction between "Jewish" and "democratic" state identities inherent in the settler state project has intensified, exemplified by a notable backlash among a section of Orthodox Israelis. In a 2012 article in the *New York Times*, Moshe Halbertal, a professor of Jewish philosophy at Hebrew University, is quoted as saying, "Just as secular nationalism and socialism posed challenges to the religious establishment a century ago, today the issue is feminism." The article goes on to note:

> The list of controversies grows weekly: Organizers of a conference last week on women's health and Jewish law barred women from speaking from the podium, leading at least eight speakers to cancel; ultra-Orthodox men spit on an 8-year-old girl whom they deemed immodestly dressed; the chief rabbi of the air force resigned his post because the army declined to excuse ultra-Orthodox soldiers from attending events where female singers perform; protesters depicted the Jerusalem police commander as Hitler on posters because he instructed public bus lines with mixed-sex seating to drive through ultra-Orthodox neighborhoods; vandals blacked out women's faces on Jerusalem billboards.[1]

If religion provides the ground for one common explanation for persistent gender inequality in Israel, another is rooted in military culture. The military is deeply entrenched in Israeli national identity, influencing political leadership, social status in education, and access to employment. As Israel is a settler society founded and maintained through permanent war against the Indigenous Palestinian population, "the link between military service and citizenship takes on special meaning" (Sasson-Levy 2002: 359). The Israeli Defence Force (IDF) has served as a key institutional mechanism in reproducing and articulating Israeli state practices in terms of the material and ideological oppression of the Palestinian population, as well as in the gendered racialization of Israeli society.

> The Zionist vision of a "people's army" has turned Israel into the only state in the West that maintains compulsory conscription for both men and women.... Thus, although recruitment and promotion in the army are purportedly based on universal and achievement-based criteria, the Israeli army is male-dominated territory where masculinity is the norm. Women in Israel are enlisted according to mandatory conscription law but are easily exempted from military service on the grounds of marriage, pregnancy, or religious belief.... Women comprise only 32 percent of the regular army; they serve a shorter term than men; and for the most part they are excluded from combat roles. (Sasson-Levy 2002: 369)

The Israeli military is a central element of the Israeli state, constructed and maintained to defend that state, and can only be understood in the context of this relationship. While challenges to women's exclusion from combat duties have been taken up by liberal feminist activists, "Israeli women's efforts to integrate into combat are still a long way from completion" (Levy 2010: 189). Challenges to ongoing sexual harassment and aims to achieve equitable officer training continue, while institutionalized hierarchy and sexism remain (Levy 2010: 193–4; Sasson-Levy 2003). Women are "often portrayed in military culture as irresponsible, potentially disloyal, and when unaccompanied by partners, easily seduced by men" (Sion and Ben-Ari 2009: 35).

In sum, neither the continued linkages between the state and Jewish traditional religious practices nor the institution of the Israeli state military can be understood in isolation from the Israel/Palestine racial contract or the associated racialized and colonial structures that define the Israeli nation-building project. The specific contexts of global and regional politics have impacted the voices of resistance to women's oppression, in that there are contested relations to what is often termed the "peace project" or the "conflict." Only a minority of feminist currents in Israel have, significantly, linked Jewish women's oppression to the wider context of Palestinian occupation, such as the Women in Black movement (Abdo 2011; Blumen and Halevi 2009; Byrne 2009).

Clearly, not all women in Israel/Palestine experience gender oppression in the same ways. This is obviously relevant to considering Palestinian women's rights. Women with "Jewish nationality" are entitled to a range of rights inaccessible to Palestinian women but are denied other rights accessible only to Israeli men. Further, the hierarchical status of Ashkenazi (European) Jewish women relative to those who are Mizrahi (Oriental) has generated a diversity of feminisms, with some having greater status and attention than others. As Smadar Lavie explains:

> When Israeli Ashkenazi feminism arose in the 1970s, many of its members were middle-class Ashkenazim who had immigrated to Israel from English-speaking countries. Their activism included founding a system of shelters for battered women, rape crisis lines, courage-to-heal groups for incest survivors, and a prostitute rehabilitation movement and fighting against the commodification of women's bodies in commercials. From the mid-1980s on, the space that middle class Ashkenazi feminists had created for feminism in the public sphere was usurped by the gvarot (ladies) of the liberal Ashkenazi elite. The upper-class Ashkenazi feminists had the wealth, leisure, and Zionist pedigree to conduct full-time feminist advocacy through their fathers, husbands and other kinship ties. (2011: 58–9)

Mizrahi feminism, alternatively, while similarly retaining an adherence to the Zionist project, was "inspired by the distinct voice of US feminists of color who had emerged in the 1970s arguing white feminism could not transcend the racism, ethnocentrism, and privilege that typified the Western public sphere and liberal feminist movements" (Lavie 2011: 59). In recent years, the increasing role of nongovernmental organizations (NGOs) in all aspects of feminist organization in Israel/Palestine has indicated further fragmentation (Herzog 2008).

The various Zionist narratives, collectively, overwhelmingly define a strictly binary gendered model, but one that is complex in that it both asserts and denies male dominance and female subordination. On a global level, recurrent Israeli governments have been keenly aware of the significance of Israel's public image, dependent not only on Western military and economic support but also on an ideological framing as both a "Jewish state" and a "democratic state." Israel is claimed to serve as a safe haven from anti-Semitism for Jews across the globe. Yet, not only Ashkenazi but also African Jewish and non-Jewish refugees, as well as Palestinians, remain excluded from the purported inclusiveness of the Israeli state (see Sheen 2015). It is in this context that Israel's rebranding campaign of the 2000s, where significant effort and resources have been devoted to projecting Israel as not only multicultural and green but also women- and queer-friendly, has been particularly advanced.

Rebranding, pinkwashing, and silencing expression: Queers against Israeli apartheid

In the twenty-first century, the politics of recognition and sexual equality rights have increasingly moved to address the citizenship rights of gays and lesbians, while wider issues of gender identity, including queer and transgender/transsexual rights, have challenged the limits of liberal inclusion models (B. Noble 2012: 277–92). In the post-9/11 context, the mythologized image of Israel as a socially, and sexually, progressive state has come into conflict with the reality of its violent aggression against Palestine and Palestinians in a region catapulted to the center of global politics. While women's rights had long been contested and the Israeli women's movement had been challenged to address the overarching reality of Palestinian women's oppression, in the twenty-first century, gay rights moved from the local to the global scale.

As in other countries internationally, the rights of gay parents to adopt is a contested issue in Israel. In December 2018, the Israeli High Court of Justice ruled in favor of two gay men who jointly adopted a child but were denied the child's birth certificate. The High Court ruling found that Israel's Interior Ministry cannot refuse to write the name of a parent on a birth certificate because of the parent's sex.[2] These contested norms have also affected the Israeli military. A study of the iconic and all-male Israeli reserve forces indicated that male homosexuality among soldiers is considered "potentially more dangerous than women because gay men can join military groups, threatening the friendship and intimacy of the (heterosexual) men" (Sion and Ben-Ari 2009: 34). While the IDF abolished all formal restrictions to the service of openly gay soldiers in 1993—regarding recruitment, assignment of duties, and promotion—these changes have "only partly percolated into practice" (Kaplan and Ben-Ari 2000: 401). In wider Israeli society, current trends in popular literature are seen by Peleg to indicate tendencies to legitimate gay characters by releasing them "from their negative stigma as weak and effeminate," but in turn constructing them to be masculinized "New Jews as well, which often means soldiers and officers" (2006: 44).

Reforms in the 1990s were sufficient, however, for the period to come to be known as "Israel's gay decade" (Puar 2011: 135). During this time, there was an unprecedented series of reforms associated with increasing recognition of same-sex partner benefits and protection from workplace discrimination, as well as changes in the military. This was also, and arguably not coincidentally, a period of post-Oslo intensification of surveillance and repression of the Palestinian population (Puar 2011: 135; Stein 2010: 521). Israel's nominal acceptance of sexual minorities attracted global attention when Jerusalem became the chosen site for the 2006 World Pride event. As Jasbir Puar (2007) notes, a queer coalition in New York City responded with a campaign to move World Pride to a different location, adopting as its name "No Pride Without Palestinians." The coalition maintained that Palestinian queers, and many from neighboring Arab countries, would be excluded from the global celebrations, while those present would risk increased surveillance, harassment, and deportation for attendance (Puar 2007: 16). However, the event took place despite intensified international debate.

> Israel's decision to host World Pride was irritatingly strategic, as the event would showcase Israel as a tolerant, diverse, and democratic society, further submerging its dismal human rights record.... From the circuits of "transnational queerdom," this decision covertly impelled collusion with the oppressive Israeli state policy toward Palestinians while also encouraging and sanctioning overt anti-Palestinian sentiments. (Puar 2007: 16)

This move to "pinkwash" Israeli state practices emerged as part of a systematic state policy to rebrand Israel as sexually modernist, emphasizing its claimed cultural distance from an ascribed sexually conservative Arab and Palestinian population (Gillespie 2015). One of the cities specifically identified in an influential Israeli think tank report as a global site of threatened "delegitimization" of Israel's progressive "brand" is Toronto, Canada's largest urban center in the country's largest province of Ontario (Reut Institute 2010; Ziadah 2010). It is significant therefore that the issue of exposing Israel's pinkwashing became a central issue in Toronto's Pride events in 2010, and in the process, it encountered unprecedented repression when the group Queers Against Israeli Apartheid (QuAIA) was banned from participation.

A brief summary of these events indicates graphically how the Israel/Palestine racial contract moved to issues of LGBTQ politics in Canada (see also Bakan and Y. Abu-Laban 2016). In early May 2010, Toronto City Council under the leadership of Mayor David Miller (who would participate in the Pride Parade in July of that year and decline to run for reelection in the October 25, 2010, city election) became a locus of contested regulation of public space. At issue was the application of the apartheid analysis to the state of Israel, targeting QuAIA specifically. This was despite the fact that QuAIA's participation was clearly consistent with Pride Toronto's mandate and history.

> Queers Against Israeli Apartheid formed to work in solidarity with queers in Palestine and Palestine solidarity movements around the world. Today, in response to increasing criticism of its occupation of Palestine, Israel is cultivating an image of itself as an oasis of gay tolerance in the Middle East, a practice that is called pinkwashing. As queers, we recognize that homophobia exists in Israel, Palestine, and across all borders. However, the struggle for sexual rights cannot come at the price of other rights. Queer Palestinians continue to face the challenge of living under occupation and apartheid, subject to Israeli state violence and control, regardless of liberal laws within Israel that allow gays to serve in the military, or recognize same sex marriage and adoption for Israeli citizens. QuAIA works to fight homophobia, transphobia and gender oppression wherever they exist. (QuAIA 2011)

The council entertained a motion to withdraw city funding from Pride Toronto if QuAIA was allowed to participate. Pride Toronto's board voted to ban the use of the phrase "Israeli apartheid" at all Pride events in the same month.[3] As news of the ban was made public, opposition within and beyond the LGBTQ community surged, expressed as a counter-response to the decision of the Pride board of directors. In a groundswell considered comparable only to events dating back to the 1970s, when gay bathhouses were subject to surveillance and police raids, pressure for reversal of the ban on grounds of freedom of expression mounted.[4]

The decision was ultimately reversed. QuAIA was permitted to march in the July 4, 2010, parade along with a newly constituted ally, the Pride Coalition for Free Speech (McLean 2010).[5] However, the challenge continued after the October 2010 municipal election, which saw the late ultra-conservative Rob Ford win the mayoral office. Once again, motions to ban QuAIA's participation came to the Toronto City Council. An effort to render funding for the annual Pride Toronto event—a space for LGBTQ public expression known to be contrary to the socially conservative views of the Ford administration—was again placed in the context of purported humanitarian grounds.

The emergent hegemony, giving license to every state level to view the allegation of apartheid when applied to Israel as anti-Semitic hate speech, continued to embolden new voices. The council waited for the findings of a report from the office of the independent city manager, Joseph Pennachetti, "to review Pride Toronto's compliance with the City's Anti-Discrimination Policy and whether the participation of Queers Against Israeli Apartheid (QuAIA) including carrying banners in the Pride Parade constitutes a violation under the City's Anti-Discrimination Policy" (Pennachetti 2011: 1). The conclusion of this review was definitively in favor of QuAIA's right to participate in Pride (Pennachetti 2011: 1). However, a debate regarding acceptance of the report followed, including the presentation of public deputations for and against the findings.

Contestation of QuAIA's right to participate in the annual Pride march continued in 2012. In June 2012, Toronto City Council voted to renew annual funding to Pride Toronto, but also voted to condemn the term "Israeli apartheid," noting the role of QuAIA in the funding debate.[6] The Toronto Pride organization, under its recognized dispute resolution process, held a formal arbitration hearing to consider a complaint presented by the League for Human Rights of B'nai Brith Canada against QuAIA's right to participate in the annual Pride events. The panel ruled, on June 29, 2012, just before the annual Pride Parade scheduled for the 1st of July, that:

> the activities of QUAIA, described in the Complaint and at the hearing, are not likely to present images or messages that promote, condone or may promote or condone violence, hatred, degradation or negative stereotypes of a person or group, contrary to the City of Toronto's Anti-Discrimination Policy. (Pride Toronto 2012)

Though this particular moment of contested public space occurred through the local Toronto state in relation to the Pride events, the banning of QuAIA received wider attention (Gillespie 2015) and was largely shaped by the federal and provincial Ontario contexts. This Toronto/Ontario/Canadian example forms an important instance of the international context in which the term "apartheid" in relation to Israel has come under intensive scrutiny. As such, it indicates the global reach and context of the Israel/Palestine racial contract. Events, organizations, and individuals seen to use this language have been subject to particularly intense surveillance and repression (Abu-Laban and Bakan 2012a). The use of the term "apartheid" is also identified as a cause for concern, motivating Israel's rebranding efforts, as the application of the term to Israel is interpreted as a feature of "delegitimization" (Dugard 2009; Reut Institute 2010; Soske and Jacobs 2015b).

Rebranding Israel as a nation that is far different from reality is nonetheless proving to be a challenge. In a period when Israel's appeal for Jewish immigration from the West has waned, the internationally directed rebranding campaign has extended to target Israeli expatriates who have moved away, principally to the United States. These appeals to "come home" to Israel have been notably gendered. A campaign organized by the Israeli state's Ministry for Immigrant Absorption (recently named the Ministry of Aliya—from the Hebrew term for "ascent" or "going up"—and Integration) is a case in point. The campaign included a series of pictures and short videos portraying various family settings where intimate relationships are strained by cultural tensions associated with Israeli national symbols—symbols themselves rendered coterminous with Jewish identity.

> One video advertisement shows a Jewish elderly couple distraught that their Israeli granddaughter in the United States thinks Hanukkah is Christmas. Another shows a clueless American boyfriend who does not get why his Israeli expatriate girlfriend is saddened on Israel's memorial day. A third shows a toddler calling "Daddy! Daddy!" to his napping Israeli expatriate father, who finally awakens when the child switches to Hebrew: "Abba!"[7]

This promotional campaign was aggressively heteronormative, presenting various family images according to traditional ideals, norms, and practices associated with heterosexual couples across generations.

This imaging runs curiously parallel to the homonationalism of the "new Israel." The new, apparently gay-friendly Israel posits a selectively cultivated image—not with the advancement of human rights inclusive of gay and lesbian rights in mind, but rather to pinkwash the Israel/Palestine racial contract domestically and internationally. The campaign to lure back Israeli expatriates was sufficiently offensive to American Jewish viewers, including organizations not normally critical of Israel, such as the Jewish Federations of North America and the Anti-Defamation

League, that Israel was compelled to withdraw the billboards and video promotional material.[8] However, the ministry's website continued for some months to showcase these advertisements to expatriate Israelis abroad, later replacing them with a campaign to target entrepreneurs (Israel Ministry of Aliyah and Immigration 2017).

At stake in the establishment of this pinkwashed, inclusive, and modernized image of Israel is the continuing and further absenting of the reality of Palestinian oppression.

Gendered stereotypes and the impact of settler colonialism and occupation on Palestinians

Palestinians, and their rootedness to historic Palestine, have been absented by the branding and rebranding of Israel, a particularly intentional feature of the Israel/Palestine racial contract. At the same time, however, Orientalist and Islamophobic stereotypes also play out in distinctive ways. Thus, whereas the Palestinian male has been constructed as a "violent terrorist" and as "uncivilized" and "premodern," the Palestinian woman, if considered at all, is frequently treated as his oppressed victim. In this way, if the modern Israeli state is mythologized in relation to women's, and more recently gay, equality, the Palestinians are essentialized as oppressive to women, and by extension to all members of the LGBTQ community.

Rebranding, while recent, also relies on historical contexts of colonialism. The image of the oppressed "Oriental" woman pre-dates the foundation of the state of Israel and was reflected in Europe's colonial encounters in the Middle East. It is also part of an important and still evident branch of feminist thought that has been aptly dubbed Eurocentric/Orientalist feminism (Abdo 2002). An 1898 passage from the work of University of Chicago professor of pedagogy Julia E. Bulkley is instructive in this regard:

> Women in Palestine are under somewhat similar social conditions as in Turkey or Egypt. Their Moslem [*sic*] conquerors have imposed upon them the veil, the seclusion, and many other limitations. (1898: 69)

Evident in Bulkley's description are certain enduring tropes that find parallels in many contemporary Western and Israeli feminist writings, which present Muslim and Palestinian women as variously oppressed by Islam, Muslim men, nationalism, culture, and familial relations (Abdo 2011; Razack 2007). For her part, Bulkley went on to ask, rather bluntly, how to "lift these women" from "degraded conditions of living" and thereby save them from the "dirt and ignorance and enslavement in which they exist" (1898: 78).

Bulkley's explicit emphasis on the promise of Christian spirit and teachings to "lift" Palestinian women may not find much resonance with many feminist scholars today. However, Western stereotypes and myths about Arab and Palestinian women continue, including an emphasis on familial violence at the expense of the violence of the colonial present for Palestinians, and the silence in many Ashkenazi and Western feminist writings about Zionism as a settler-colonial project (see Abdo 2011: 76–144; Hasso 1998: 457–8; Holt 2010: 414). Indeed, it is such contemporary discussions of commission, or omission, that may be seen to be complicit in the making of Palestinian women as the "other Other." In short, an emphasis on culture (e.g., Islam) and fixation on women's bodies (e.g., the hijab) is problematic and has particular implications for the Israel/Palestine racial contract when carried out in the context of Western/Ashkenazi feminists critiquing the culture of the "other Other." Indeed, when non-Western (including Muslim) feminists attempt to reclaim cultural identities (Abdo 2002), the context of the racial contract and its attendant hierarchies remains significant, as new cultural identities threaten to challenge prior hegemonic patterns. This is because attention to the historical conditions imposed by colonialism and the material realities of occupation and dispossession are critical to analysis that accurately sees the intersections of gender, race, class, colonialism, and political economy (see Bakan and Y. Abu-Laban 2017).

Attention to the impact of settler colonialism, stereotypes, and occupation should therefore be treated as fundamental in understanding shifting constructions of masculinity, femininity, and gender relations for Palestinians. For example, as Joseph Massad (1995) has noted, early articulations of Palestinian nationality fostered a situation in which Palestinian identity was masculinized. But to understand this, it is important to recognize that it was after the *Nakba* that fathers came to be explicitly upheld as "reproducing" the nation. For example, in the 1964 Palestinian National Charter, one was deemed to be an Arab

Palestinian if born in or living in Palestine before 1947,[9] but since the Palestinian diaspora and the establishment of Israel, Palestinian identity is also conferred by being born to a Palestinian father (Massad 1995: 472). According to Massad (1995), the historic shifts in national identity construction by Palestinians followed from the partition plan and the events of 1948. This new construction allowed for the replacement of residence with paternal lineage. The replacement of "territory" with "paternity" in the reproduction of the Palestinian nation was significant (Massad 1995: 472). This change in the definition of Palestinian identity was paralleled by increasingly standardized metaphoric references to the "land of Palestine" as feminized and "Zionists" as masculinized. Not incidentally, as noted in our earlier discussion, this also meshed with the gendered referents in early Zionist discourse and hegemonic discourse concerning Israel as masculinized. Massad notes:

> In the introduction to the Palestinian Nationalist [*sic*] Charter, the Zionist conquest of Palestine is presented as a rape of the land. It views Palestinians as the children of Palestine, portrayed as the mother. The Zionist enemy is clearly seen as masculine, and the wrong committed by this enemy against the Palestinians is considered metaphorically to be of a violent sexual nature. This view is in full concert with early Zionist discourse that viewed the role of Zionists as fertilizing the virgin land.... The Israeli Sabra, like the American Adam, but unlike the "feminine" diaspora Jews, was a new masculine power impregnating the virgin/motherland with new life. This pregnancy was to result in the birth of the "New Jew." (1995: 470–1)

In the current context of the Israel/Palestine racial contract, the colonial violence and racism expressed through Israeli state actions interact in complex ways with gender norms and constructions of masculinity and femininity within Palestinian society. For instance, as Sherene Razack observes of the checkpoints and the wall, which express colonial power through space and impeded mobility, Palestinian women and girls confront unique obstacles to more traditional expressions of femininity:

> At checkpoints, girls learn that their own communities are limited in their capacity to prevent them from all kinds of violence—the violence of the Israeli soldiers but also the patriarchal violence of their own

communities as they rush home to avoid curfew. Parents also impose restrictions on girls' activities, fearing that they will be harassed by soldiers. In effect, the wall teaches girls and women in an embodied way that they are under surveillance and condemned to a lesser life.... Girls who are forced to climb over hills, ditches, and walls, to take clandestine routes and to risk search and seizure, are denied the bodily integrity of full citizens but also the modesty that under patriarchy would otherwise mark them as the sex to be protected. (2010: 96)

There is a growing emphasis on understanding constructions of masculinity and "crises" of masculinity in feminist scholarship (Faludi 2000; Giese 2018). This perhaps explains a certain contemporary currency in examining Palestinian masculinity, and particularly that of Palestinians holding Israeli citizenship. However, studies on Palestinian masculinity commonly avoid attention to settler-colonial processes and racialized violence (see, e.g., Gvion 201; Sa'ar and Yahia-Younis 2008). As Rubenberg broadly notes, the politics of dispossession, occupation, and poverty have impacted the ability of many Palestinian men to achieve the ideals associated with a more traditional male honor code (2001: 42). As she relates in regard to the West Bank specifically:

> Given the poverty and powerlessness of individuals in West Bank camps and villages, most men are no longer materially able to prove their honor through demonstration of their autonomy, independence, hospitality, adequate family maintenance, and generosity.... Female honor, in turn, has become the primary, sometimes the only, vehicle through which men can affirm their honor or moral worth. (42)

In other words, such ideals associated with female honor as virginity, chastity, and motherhood need to be understood not merely as features of "culture" but rather in the historical and material context in which Palestinians find themselves. That Palestinian "womanhood" has been shaped by such images as a good activist/homemaker, fertile mother, and signifier of the nation's honor (Abdulhadi 1998: 655) has particular resonance and import given the demolition of the homes of Palestinians, and their collective experience of ethnic cleansing, dispossession, and forced diasporic presence outside of historic Palestine.

Gendered norms and expressions of honor may take on considerable variation through reasons of class, region, and diverse experiences among individual families. They may also shift in recognition of political exigencies, as contained in the idea of "land before honor"—a slogan developed to counter the targeted sexualized torture experienced by female Palestinian prisoners who engage in military confrontation (Abdulhadi 1998: 655; see also Abdo 2008). Further, the experience of Palestinian women in refugee camps and rural areas of the West Bank detailed by Rubenberg (2001) stands in sharp contrast to the experience of single Palestinian women living in Jerusalem detailed by Abowd (2007). In both cases, however, the continued appropriation of Palestinian land by Israel and other features of the Israel/Palestine racial contract shape many negative aspects of these experiences.

Despite the fact that Palestinian women are caught between colonial repression and patriarchal control, their agency remains central and challenges the hegemony of the Israel/Palestine racial contract. Palestinian women not merely have been used by nationalist interests as implied in some accounts (see, for example, those critiqued in Abdo 2011: 78) but have constructed a movement for self-determination on their own terms (Hasso 1998: 442). Significantly, Palestinian women have been active in challenging and re-envisioning the basis of national identity along patrilineal lines. As one example, following the Oslo process, in 1994 the Women's Affairs Technical Committee (an outgrowth of demands by the women's movement in the West Bank and Gaza), in concert with the General Union of Palestinian Women (GUPW) (established in 1965 as a mass-based organization as part of the newly formed PLO), developed a Palestinian Women's Charter. Among other points, the 1994 Charter insisted on the right of the Palestinian woman "to acquire, preserve or change her nationality"; that "marriage to a non-Palestinian or a change of her husband's nationality while married will not necessarily change the citizenship of the wife"; and that a woman be "granted the right to give citizenship to her husband and children" (Jad, Johnson, and Giacaman 2000: 146).

The momentum for the 1994 Palestinian Women's Charter drew upon a long history of women's activism both before and after the *Nakba*. This activism was frequently tied to national aspirations. For example, Palestinian women led demonstrations against the Balfour Declaration and founded the Palestinian Women's Union in 1921. And, during the Palestinian Revolt of 1936–9 under the British Mandate, Palestinian women cared for the injured and defended land with arms; after 1948, many assumed new roles of responsibility in their families and in building political and social organizations in Gaza, the West Bank, Israel, and in the diaspora to advance Palestinian welfare and rights (Abdulhadi 1998: 654). Women's organizing was also tied to women's rights and gender-related justice. Thus, the GUPW in the 1960s emphasized the role of both mothers and fathers in defining the "Palestinianness" of offspring (Abdulhadi 1998: 654).

The combination of the first Intifada and the growing and active participation of women and their leadership in the national project indicated the central role of Palestinian women in the international community. Moreover, given Orientalist tropes that portray Palestinian/Arab men as barbaric and women as passive, women's participation "appeared to symbolize the modernity and civilized nature of Palestinian society to the international community" (Hasso 1998: 455). Certainly, the first Intifada made it harder to sustain the traditional (Palestinian) and modern (Israeli) dichotomy. Accordingly, there is, in fact, a substantive literature detailing women's mass mobilization and active role in the first Intifada, challenging the presumed expectation of women's inequality or absence consistent with the hegemony of the Israel/Palestine racial contract. This involvement was made more obvious in contrast to their decreasing visibility in the apartheid logic produced post-Oslo, and, relatedly, in the second Palestinian Intifada (Johnson and Kuttab 2001).

During the first Intifada, women's presence was manifested by the very public role played by former Palestinian spokesperson and legislator Hanan Ashrawi, particularly in relation to the United States. Speaking before the 1992 Global Feminist Conference organized by the National Organization for Women in Washington, DC, Ashrawi held that:

> My participation in the peace process is not because of an accident of history and not as a result of tokenism or symbolic women's presence. It is rather a part of the cumulative achievements of Palestinian women who have struggled for so long to make themselves heard, to make their achievements felt, and to forge a place for themselves, a place of equality with the men, regardless of all the different types of oppression we suffer from. (as quoted in Abdulhadi 1998: 662)

The post-Oslo period was to feature a kind of demobilization brought on by the "NGO-ization" of Palestinian women's organizations that spoke more to the desires of donors than the lived context of diverse women (Jad 2010; see also Jamal 2001: 25 and Kuttab 2008: 108). In addition, the rise of

Hamas in Gaza introduced a new complexity in women's organizing and discourses that belied binary constructions of tradition versus modernity (Jad 2011; see also Holt 2010). In Western and Israeli popular discourses, the associations between Islam and tradition, now accompanied by a fetishization of the female suicide bomber/martyr (Holt 2010: 398), were reinforced in the post-9/11 period. Such developments and discourses need to be addressed with an understanding that the post-Oslo period is one in which the hope of "peace" has been increasingly betrayed by growing forms of apartheid, surveillance, and violence (Gordon 2008b), as manifest expressions of the Israel/Palestine racial contract.

It is against this backdrop that the rise of Israel's rebranding and pinkwashing are particularly striking. As Jasbir Puar has put it, "in the colonial period, the question of 'how do you treat your women?' as a determining factor of a nation's capacity for sovereignty has now been appended with the barometer of 'how well do you treat your homosexuals'?" (2011: 139). However, the attempts made to establish a new "Brand Israel" as "gay friendly" (read democratic and progressive) in contrast to "homophobic" Islamic states and Palestinians (read undemocratic, regressive, and exclusive of Christian Palestinians) are presented as justification for a deeply entrenched Israel/Palestine racial contract (see Puar 2011: 135; Hochberg, Maikey, Rima, and Saraya 2010: 608).

Conclusion

As with issues of women's and gender rights, issues of LGBTQ rights in Palestinian society cannot be separated from settler colonialism and the denial of Palestinian self-determination. The idea of Israel as a mythologized neutral space of equality is not new, but it continues to be altered in light of new global and regional conditions. The politics of rebranding also impacts international state relations. A selective association of the production of the "homophobic" other was advanced, for example, by the Conservative Canadian administrations of Prime Minister Stephen Harper (prime minister from 2006 to 2015) and has not abated under the administration of Liberal Prime Minister Justin Trudeau (elected in 2015). A September 2011 address to the United Nations by then Minister of Foreign Affairs John Baird not only asserted Canada's close relationship with Israel, but challenged the treatment of women, gays, and lesbians in a number of states variously associated with human rights violations and security threats associated with Al Qaeda. All were states in the global South (DFAIT 2011).

The various "brands" of Israel have also influenced international feminist framings. The historically collective agricultural cooperatives, or *kibbutzim*, for example, have become idealized symbols of gendered equality, abstracted from the colonial context of Israel/Palestine. British activist and scholar Nina Power, author of *One Dimensional Woman* (2009), in an otherwise radical call for renewed visions of feminism, identifies the ideal model of the kibbutz as an inspiring alternative to capitalism. In an earlier feminist generation, Canadian socialist feminist Margaret Benston, in her classic and foundational article "Political Economy of Women's Liberation," similarly posed the kibbutz as an inspirational alternative to women's oppression (Benston 1969; rpt. 2000). However, women's equality on the kibbutzim is more myth than reality (Moore 2011: 60). And research indicates kibbutz life for gay adolescents compels a choice between suppression and exclusion (Ben-Ari 2001: 112). In fact, even the heteronormative space of the Israeli military has been found to be less repressive of gay male identity than the kibbutz (Ben-Ari 2001: 115). More profoundly, however, the kibbutzim were established as part of the early European-style settlement and land occupation goals of Zionist settlement. As Padnan-Eisenstark explained (with a disturbingly misplaced enthusiasm given its consequences for Indigenous Palestinians):

> Women, especially in the Kibbutzim, have shared many of the strenuous and dangerous tasks of colonization and underground defense activities before the founding of the State. (1973: 538)

In contrast to the purported equality between Israeli men and women that has been at the heart of Israel's branding and rebranding efforts, more careful attention to lived reality suggests ongoing inequality. Gender relations among Israeli Jews in all their diversity, like issues of LGBTQ rights, need to be understood in relation to a common and shared relationship to the settler-colonial foundation of Israel and the state's ongoing repression and violence toward Indigenous Palestinians. The dispossession of the Palestinian population, consistent with the Israel/Palestine racial contract, has rendered their voices and history variously unheard or distorted. This has been all the more the case for Palestinian women, who can be understood to be "the subaltern of the subaltern" (Holt 2010).

There is a risk, then, as we have suggested, of replicating Orientalist and racialized assumptions and stereotypes in feminist readings of Israel/Palestine. Alternatively, the history of Palestinian women suggests that their experiences, while varied and diverse, have been shaped in important ways by settler colonialism, occupation, and dispossession. In addition, and contrary to the image presented in feminist Orientalist accounts, Palestinian women have also expressed both agency and solidarity in demanding gender equality as part of the struggle of the Palestinian people for self-determination and freedom.

The lessons from this overview are instructive for thinking about the ways in which themes of governance and gender play out in relation to Brand Israel. These lessons are also instructive for a more holistic account of LGBTQ issues, which have come to the fore in discussions of Israel/Palestine. While rebranding efforts may seek to "pinkwash" Israel's still unresolved "question of Palestine," the Israel/Palestine racial contract also faces sustained resistance. A realistic assessment of LGBTQ rights in Israel/Palestine cannot be divorced from the Israel/Palestine racial contract that has rendered Palestinians nonwhite and the subjects of state repression.

As this chapter has suggested, the racial contract works in multiple ways, including through the politics of patriarchy and heteronormativity. In the next chapter, we consider how the Israel/Palestine racial contract also shapes relationships with the environment in contested territory, including land, water, and air, and how this is a further example of Israel's rebranding efforts.

Notes

1 Ethan Bronner and Isabel Kershner, "Israelis Facing a Seismic Rift over Role of Women," *The New York Times*, January 14, 2012, https://www.nytimes.com/2012/01/15/world/middleeast/israel-faces-crisis-over-role-of-ultra-orthodox-in-society.html?_r=1&hp.

2 "Top Court Rules for Gay Parents in Birth Certificate Fight," *The Times of Israel*, December 13, 2018, https://www.timesofisrael.com/top-court-rules-for-gay-parents-in-birth-certificate-fight/.

3 Daniel Dale, "Pride Prohibits Phrase 'Israeli Apartheid'" *TheStar.com*, May 21, 2010, https://www.thestar.com/news/gta/2010/05/21/pride_prohibits_phrase_israeli_apartheid.html.

4 Jesse McLean, "Backlash Grows Against Pride's 'Israeli Apartheid' Ban," *TheStar.com*, June 6, 2010, https://www.thestar.com/news/gta/2010/06/06/backlash_grows_against_prides_israeli_apartheid_ban.html.

5 Ibid.

6 Robyn Doolittle, "Pride Toronto Gets City Funding–With a Warning About 'Israeli Apartheid' Activists," *Toronto Star*, June 8, 2012, https://www.thestar.com/news/gta/2012/06/08/pride_toronto_gets_city_funding_with_a_warning_about_israeli_apartheid_activists.html.

7 Isabel Kershner and Joseph Berger, "After American Jewish Outcry, Israel Ends Ad Campaign Aimed at Expatriates," *The New York Times*, December 2, 2011, https://www.nytimes.com/2011/12/03/world/middleeast/after-american-outcry-israel-ends-ad-campaign-aimed-at-expatriates.html.

8 Ibid.

9 Article 7 of the original charter held that "Jews of Palestinian origin are considered Palestinians if they are willing to live peacefully and loyally in Palestine." See *The Palestinian National Charter* (1964), http://www.pac-usa.org/the_palestinian_charter.htm.

8 ENVIRONMENTAL RACISM AND CONTESTED TERRITORY

Land, water, and air in Israel/Palestine

Palestine and UNDRIP

In this chapter, we extend the analytical lens of the Israel/Palestine racial contract to consider environmental racism. We also consider its obverse, namely environmental justice, in the Israel/Palestine context. As argued earlier, Palestinians living in the diaspora, within the Occupied Territories, and within the borders of 1948 Israel have recurrently sought support from various United Nations policies and bodies, often experiencing considerable frustration. The paradox of human rights in the context of the UN indicates a pattern of both promise and frustration. This is consistent with the orientations of other Indigenous, occupied, stateless, and diasporic groups that have turned to international arenas in their efforts to circumvent repressive practices from national states (de Costa 2006; de la Cadena and Starn 2002).

There is an expanding literature that considers the implications of racialization in the context of environmental politics (see Bullard 1993; Mirpuri, Feldman, and Roberts 2009; Jaber 2018) and the relationship between imperialism and environmental degradation (Davis 2003; Foster 2009). This literature is largely grounded in specific contexts. For example, the impact and legacy of Hurricane Katrina on the Black population of New Orleans has starkly exposed these connections in the United States, the richest and most powerful country in the world (Bullard and Wright 2009).

> What Katrina uncovered was a truth that those of us fighting for environmental justice already knew. That truth is that minorities and the poor are more likely than all other groups to be underprepared and underserved, and to be living in unsafe, substandard housing. The impact is also cumulative. After a disaster, minorities and the poor suffer a much slower recovery. (Bullard and Wright 2009: xx)

If we move to consider the case of Palestine and Palestinians, prolonged deprivation of resources and services has been exacerbated by recurrent wars and attendant restrictions on basic rights to land and water access. Further, airspace and air quality have become arenas of Israeli military regulation, extending environmental destruction through the use of white phosphorous and other chemical weapons.

Despite the extensive documented evidence of the environmental racism suffered by the Palestinian population, this dimension of the region has received limited attention. This is not, arguably, accidental or merely the product of a lack of information. As we have demonstrated, the specific Israel/Palestine racial contract that identifies Israel with Western states has resulted in an epistemology of ignorance (Mills 1997; Sullivan and Tuana 2007) that absents the realities of Palestine and Palestinians. Racialization, statelessness, and ascribed stereotypes associated with the Arab/Muslim "terrorist" have challenged critical understandings of the impact of environmental racism on the Indigenous Palestinian population.

In particular, Israel's foundational myth as a state that has "made the desert bloom" contrasts sharply with the racialized effects of colonization, occupation, and settlement. In what follows, we consider the Israel/Palestine racial contract in terms of the implications of environmental racism. This in turn suggests there is a case to be made for legitimate redress claims for environmental justice as suggested in the United Nations Declaration on the Rights of Indigenous Peoples (UNDRIP 2007). We consider some specificities associated with the regional and historical context, followed by attention to environmental racism associated with access to land, water, and air. The chapter concludes with a consideration of serious justice claims counterpoised to the Israeli state's efforts to "greenwash" its public image as part of its rebranding campaign aimed to offset criticism on the global stage.

Environmental racism in historical and regional context

The impact and consequences of environmental racism for Indigenous peoples are inseparable from the history of colonialism and dispossession. These consequences include the destruction of established relationships between humans and surrounding wildlife, land, and natural resources, as well as the ongoing and continuing destructive impact of market-driven, and imperialist, exploitation. Environmental racism can be understood to be a process of hegemonic policies and practices, including state participation and/or complicity, where discrimination based on physical or cultural characteristics ascribed to a specific group results in disproportionate damage to people and the environment. Analyzing environmental racism therefore demands understanding of and attention to specific historical and geopolitical contexts; concomitantly, environmental justice claims involve naming such processes and legitimating claims for redress for the effects of colonial dispossession and other harms.

The contemporary realities of environmental racism in Israel/Palestine are therefore inseparable from the history of settlement and occupation of Indigenous Palestinian land. Ilan Pappe summarizes these linkages in regard to Gaza:

> The Gaza Strip is a little bit more than 2 percent of Palestine. This small detail is never mentioned whenever the Strip is in the news nor has it been mentioned during the Israeli onslaught on Gaza in January 2009.... Gaza's history before the Zionization of Palestine was not unique and it was always connected administratively and politically to the rest of Palestine. It was until 1948 an integral and natural part of the rest of the country. As one of Palestine's principal land and sea gates to the rest of the world it tended to develop a more flexible and cosmopolitan way of life, not dissimilar to other gateways [*sic*] societies in the eastern Mediterranean in the modern era ... until this life was disrupted and nearly destroyed by the Israeli ethnic cleansing of Palestine in 1948. Between 1948 and 1967, Gaza became a huge refugee camp restricted severely by the respective Israeli and Egyptian policies: both states disallowed any movement out of the Strip.... This once pastoral coastal part of southern Palestine became within two decades one of the world's densest areas of habitation, without any adequate economic infrastructure to support it. (2010: 171–2)

A further complication is presented in addressing Palestinian Indigenous experiences of environmental racism, due to the specific nature of the occupying state. Recurrent Israeli governments and global allies have understood Israel as a site of humanitarian rescue for Jewish victims of anti-Semitism. This is in fact, as we have demonstrated, a contested analysis of Israel's relationship to Jewish experience and suffering. Further, this claim elides the fact that Israel, and the attendant Zionist state ideology, has played a very different role in the lived geopolitical conditions of the Middle East, and specifically in its encounters with Indigenous Palestinians (Zureik 2011). The compatibility of Zionism with Euro-American expansion into the oil-rich region of the Middle East coincided with a claimed attentiveness to the previously unheard appeals of Jewish refugees and survivors. The notion that Indigenous Palestinian land was uninhabited desert has been demonstrated to be a constructed myth, disproved by historical fact evidenced both by Palestinian documentation and by the more recent body of Israeli revisionist historical scholarship.

The relationship of Palestinians to the "land" is even further complicated by associations quite distant from normalized political analysis, particularly biblical scriptures with attendant ideas of a "promised" or "holy" land that are often used as moral justifications for the Israeli state (Noble 2005). As Nur Masalha summarizes:

> In terms of Palestine, the Zionist idea of a "Jewish homeland", which saw, eventually, the destruction of Palestine and the establishment of Israel in 1948, was prepared for in advance by knowledge accumulated by British biblical scholars and theologians, biblical archeologists, colonial administrators, and experts who had been surveying the area and exploring the "Bible lands" since the mid-nineteenth century. It was this knowledge that enabled the Zionists to maintain arguments similar to those of the British imperial project. (2007: 281)

As the declining imperial interests of British empire in the region were replaced by ascending US imperialism, even in the midst of the "human rights era," the role of Israel as a pro-Western state in the Middle East met a series of geopolitical goals. The myth of empty land, resonant of the early European colonial concept of "terra nullius," is consistent with the Israel/Palestine racial contract (Pateman 2007).

From the perspective of the international political economy, Israel has developed as an expansionist, capitalist, and highly militarized state, bordering other states that have the richest oil reserves in the world. The transformation of the region in the wake of the Arab Spring, notably the fall of Israel's longstanding ally, Hosni Mubarak, in Egypt, highlights the instability of this delicate balance.[1] However, the capitalist drive for accumulation of resources and markets in both domestic and international spheres has proven to advance the most environmentally destructive system in human history (Foster 2009). The historical and regional context in the case of Israel/Palestine is therefore intimately linked with the most basic issues of environmental politics, indicating an important element in the Israel/Palestine racial contract.

In every regard, the specific differentiation between those who have rights of entitlement based on Israeli citizenship—and more specifically a state-designated category of "Jewish nationality"—and those who do not, principally Indigenous Arab Palestinians (Muslim or Christian), has contributed to a situation of environmental inequality and injustice. This is evidenced in a number of ways, including unequal access to land, water, and clean air. While the Israel/Palestine racial contract is very specific in a number of ways, it is not, as we have argued, beyond comparison. The regulation of the right of return, for example, has affected generations of Palestinians, but it is also a feature of the environmental racism experienced by evacuated residents of New Orleans following the 2005 devastation of Hurricane Katrina. In advancing claims to rebuild their lives in post-Katrina conditions, the community and advocates developed a "Katrina Bill of Rights," noting "the right to return" as a central demand (Morial 2009: xvii). The fact that the vast majority of those displaced by Katrina's devastation were poor African Americans highlights the linkages between race and environmental impacts and compensatory justice claims. As Mtangulizi Sanyika notes:

> Those who suffered through and survived Katrina and its aftermath have been referred to by many names—survivors, evacuees, refugees, the dislocated, the dispersed, exiles, new immigrants, and the diaspora. Under international covenants and law, the most appropriate term might be "internally displaced persons" … All displaced persons should retain the right of return to New Orleans as an international human right.... The city should not be depopulated of its majority African-American and lower-income citizens, and must be rebuilt to economically include all those who were displaced. (2009: 96–7)

This brings us to a more specific discussion of environmental racism and justice claims in a consideration of land, water, and air in the Israel/ Palestine context.

Land

The initial refusal of key settler-colonial states (Canada, the United States, Australia, and New Zealand) to endorse the 2007 UNDRIP was related to its implications for control over resources. This is a feature that might also help explain why the Canadian government, then led by Stephen Harper and the Conservative Party, only finally endorsed UNDRIP in 2010, noting that the declaration was not legally binding. Specifically, the UN has identified Palestine's poor performance in meeting international development goals as the result of a lack of access to water, undernourishment, and maternal mortality—all factors seen as "heavily affected by occupation and blockades" (UN and LAS 2013: 51).

Consistent with the Israel/Palestine racial contract, occupation limits the mobility of Indigenous Palestinians on the land; even access to "public" land takes racialized forms, whereby the Palestinian population faces perpetual regulation through expropriation, annexation, partition, and dispossession. Historically, land has featured highly in the conflict generated by the Zionist colonial project from the late nineteenth century. In particular, the Palestinian society that Jewish immigrants from Europe settled in during the late nineteenth and early twentieth centuries involved the expansion of agricultural colonies. These were especially pivotal in the settlement projects, even if it involved small numbers of the overall settler population. These settlers tended to be strongly committed Zionists with clear political objectives, and the location of the newly established agricultural colonies favored the most fertile lands (Khalidi 2010: 96–7). From its inception, the process of Zionist agricultural colonization involved confrontation with the Indigenous Arab Palestinian population:

> The process would begin with the purchase of land, generally from an absentee landlord, followed by the imposition of a new order on the existing Arab cultivators—sometimes involving their transformation into tenant-farmers or agricultural laborers, and sometimes their expulsion—and finally the settlement of new Jewish immigrants. (Khalidi 2010: 98)

Prior to the establishment of Israel in 1948, Zionists concentrated on purchasing land from Arabs, but by 1948, Jewish land ownership still only amounted to 6 percent of the total area of mandatory Palestine (Khamaisi 2011: 336). Tactics and outcomes were to change dramatically after the 1948 war, when purchasing land was dwarfed by the Israeli state's confiscation, dispossession, and occupation of Palestinian land, as well as subverting of traditional legal norms around inheritance (Khamaisi 2011: 335). These conditions regarding land and environmental racism, as part of the Israel/Palestine racial contract, are also relevant to Israel and the Occupied Palestinian Territories. These areas are considered in more detail in the following sections.

Israel

An early and graphic example of confiscation relates to the lands of the refugees who had fled Palestine during and after the war of 1948. This confiscation was aided by colonial and Zionist data collection during the period of the British mandate over Palestine. From the 1920s to the 1940s, the use of survey maps and records on land registration and ownership reached heightened status, but it was the collection of land records by Zionist agencies and the related usage of mandatory data that decisively led to major changes in the demographic and spatial nature of Arab Palestinian society after 1948 (Fischbach 2010: 311). As Fischbach explains, in this process during the period following the 1948 war:

> Israel seized a huge amount of land vacated by the 750,000 Palestinian refugees who fled or were expelled by Jewish forces during and after the war. Over 6 million dunums [1 dunum equals approximately 0.25 acres] were confiscated by the Israeli authorities. In January 1949, and again in September 1950, the Israeli government sold a large portion of this refugee land to the Jewish National Fund. Yet the JNF insisted upon the transfer of these properties' legal titles to it from the Israeli government's Custodian or Absentee Property on behalf of the Development Authority. Israeli authorities were therefore anxious to reconstruct missing British land registers [concerning Palestinian rather than Jewish-owned property since the latter had been left to the Jewish Agency after Britain vacated Palestine] to assist them in the task of transferring title to the now vacant lands to the JNF so it could settle them with Jewish immigrants.... Britain turned over the films in stages during the first months of 1952. Thereafter, the Israeli Directorate of Land Registration worked with staff members seconded by the JNF to recreate land registers for the refugees' property from the state to the JNF ... As a result, title to most of the 2,372,576 dunums of refugee land that the JNF purchased in 1949 and 1950 had been transferred to the Fund by 1958. (2010: 310)

In addition to confiscating the "absentee land" of Palestinian refugees, the state took other measures that facilitated the diminution of Palestinian territory in Israel. Significantly, Palestinian refugees were prohibited from returning to their lands and homes by the military government in place from 1948 to 1966. By 1960, fully 93 percent of land came under Israeli state ownership (Khamaisi 2011: 342). While Indigenous Palestinians represent some 17 percent of Israeli citizens, they own a scant 3.5 percent of the land (Khamaisi 2011: 342). Moreover, the strategy of "Judaization" of the land should be seen as one connected to racialized power, reliant upon militarized and repressive means to deny Palestinian refugees a right of return. These include spatial relocation, or transfer, of the remaining Palestinian minority population in Israel and establishing control over Palestinians in Israel through segregation (Sa'di 2011: 86). A further segmentation is also seen in the labor market, with Palestinians in Israel having significantly lower incomes and working in such areas as construction or carpentry, while Israeli Jews dominate in technical positions and highly skilled positions in military industries and related high-tech and surveillance industries (Gordon 2011: 100; Said et al. 1988: 278–87). As Oren Yiftachel observes of Israel/Palestine, social relations have been "fundamentally shaped by the material, territorial, political, and cultural aspects of the Judaization dynamic and by the various forms of resistance to that project" (2006: 3).

Such resistance is indicated, for example, by "Land Day," which since 1976 has been marked every March 30th by Palestinians both inside Israel proper and in the diaspora. Land Day commemorates the 1976 general strike and demonstrations led by Palestinians who held citizenship in Israel when they challenged Israel's plans for expropriating more land for the purposes of "security" and "settlement." Revealingly, the Palestinians faced violent repercussions from the Israeli military and police during that period.

The West Bank and Gaza

The racialized power relations around land are also evident, in ways that are both similar and distinct, in the Occupied Palestinian Territories. In the West Bank and Gaza, the procedures for acquiring land differed. Because much land in Gaza had been declared "state land" under Egyptian rule (1948–67), following the 1967 War, Israel appropriated this same land (and, until the 2005 withdrawal, made use of it for settlements) (Gordon 2008b: 120). In the case of the West Bank, which had been under Jordanian rule between 1948 and 1967, Israel largely constructed legal rationales and mechanisms to seize land, including the following:

> 1) declaring land to be absentee property; 2) declaring land to be the property of a hostile state or agent; 3) confiscating land for public needs; 4) declaring land to be part of nature reserves; 5) requisitioning land for military needs; 6) declaring land to be state property; 7) helping Jewish citizens to purchase land on the free market. (Gordon 2008b: 120)

The ongoing occupation has been heavily shaped by the issues of land confiscation and the building of Israeli Jewish settlements (or what Palestinians often refer to less euphemistically as "colonies"). As early as September of 1967, the Israeli government and military offered support to Israeli Jews to move to the West Bank and establish settlements (Gordon 2008b: 116). Since that period, the number of settlements has grown rapidly. By 2015, there were 127 government-approved settlements in the West Bank (not including East Jerusalem and settlements in Hebron) and another 100 settlement "outposts" that, although not formally approved by the government, operate with government assistance, comprised of 588,000 Israeli settlers (B'Tselem 2017). Importantly, since 1967 successive Israeli governments (including both Likud and Labour) have supported settlements financially, justified in terms of security and imagery taken from a particular biblical reading. The support and exponential growth of settlements contravenes several major statutes of international law.

> The UN Charter clearly prohibits the acquisition of territory by force. IHL [International Humanitarian Law] reinforces this protection during occupation by strictly prohibiting the transfer of an occupying power's population into occupied territory. The United Nations Security Council has affirmed that the Fourth Geneva Convention is applicable to the OPT [Occupied Palestinian Territories] and called upon Israel not to transfer its own civilian population, or take any other action that would result in changing its legal status, geographical nature or demographic composition into the occupied territory. Finally, transfer by the occupying power of parts of its own civilian population into the occupied territory is also listed as a war crime under Article 8 of the Rome Statute of the International Criminal Court. (Palestine Monitor 2015: 63)

Indicating a particular symbolic form of "Judaization" of the land, it is relevant to note that within six months of the 1967 War, the Israeli state began to refer to the West Bank as "Judea and Samaria" (Gordon 2008b: 6–7). This language feeds into a particular biblical interpretation of an "Eretz Israel" (Hebrew for the land of Israel)—that is, a Greater Israel far beyond the 1949 Green Line—ordained exclusively for Jewish nationals. The ability of the Israeli state to establish colonies in the West Bank, and until 2005 in Gaza, with relative impunity is indicative of the Israel/Palestine racial contract. Further, settlements and the growing numbers of settlers have served as agents of the Israeli state and military, enforcing overtly racialized repression against Palestinians. A United Nations report refers to settlements as "the most important factor" driving the restrictions imposed on the free movement of Palestinians in the West Bank and East Jerusalem (UN OCHA 2012). These restrictions take the form of physical barriers on the land, such as militarized checkpoints and roadblocks as well as the separation barrier (or apartheid wall). These restrictions also include legal and administrative barriers, such as prohibitions from moving in particular areas or the annexation of land (see Masri 2017: 76–125).

The Israeli state has accorded settlements the status of border communities in the Occupied Palestinian Territories, and therefore settlers use weapons considered necessary for self-defense, often issued by the military. As Neve Gordon notes, however, the "borders" of settlements have extended to fields, roads, and Palestinian villages, contributing to clear and sustained examples of settler violence directed at Palestinians.

> In the fourteen-year period between 1987–2001, 124 Palestinians, among them 23 minors, were killed by Jewish settlers and other Israeli civilians. In addition, the settlers have injured hundreds of Palestinians, burnt mosques, harmed medical teams, attacked journalists, and damaged property in scores of villages. They have stolen Palestinian herds, uprooted thousands of olive trees, and destroyed greenhouses as well as agricultural crops, thus depriving many Palestinians of their source of livelihood. They have entered Palestinian residential areas, shot at homes, damaged property, and committed other acts of vandalism, such as burning cars, breaking windows, and shooting solar heating devices. The objective of many of the attacks is to intimidate and terrorize the Palestinians in order to deter them from resisting acts of dispossession and at times to "persuade" them to abandon their lands and homes. (2008b: 142)

Finally, and relevant for a consideration of the environmental racism relating to land, settlements have directly and indirectly contributed to the dispossession of the Palestinian people. The settlements have challenged Palestinian rights to mobility, assembly, and expression, as well as access to education, services, and work. Significantly, while the settlements themselves take only a small portion of land, they have tended to engulf the most arable agricultural land as well as land built over precious water resources (Palestine Monitor 2015). To function, settlements need further access to arable land and trees, contributing to agricultural degradation (Isaac and Powell 2007: 151). These expansions have included the construction of military bases and of "Jewish-only" bypass roads[2] with large buffers on either side that snake into Palestinian land, impacting both agriculture and construction. Since 2002, the construction of the separation barrier has encroached still further into Palestinian territory. The settlements are home to over half a million settlers, and the annual growth rate for the settler population (excluding East Jerusalem) is over three times the rate of growth of the Israeli population as a whole (Palestine Monitor 2015; 62; B'Tselem 2017). For Palestinians, access to agriculture—a traditional source of livelihood reliant upon arable land and water—has been severely disrupted. Indeed, the clear decline in the numbers of Palestinians working in the agricultural sector was evident within the decade following 1967 (see Graham-Brown 1983).

Gaza itself, since 2005 absented of some twenty-one Israeli settlements, has been subject to a still more stark logic since the 2007 international imposition of the land, air, and sea blockade. It is referred to as an open-air prison or a cage precisely because the population has been cut off from the world by Israel, with the support of Egypt. As the 2008–9 war on Gaza by Israel revealed, the impoverished population, comprising mostly of refugees uprooted by various wars in the region—crowded into one of the most densely populated areas of the world—is a tragically easy target for aerial bombing. This is a population that suffers from being locked into a very small portion of land—for many years and over generations—and has been denied access to basic necessities, including medicine, food, and water (Ageel 2016).

By June 2009, 46 percent of the Gaza Strip's agricultural land was judged to be inaccessible or out of production, with 17 percent of cultivated land destroyed as a result of the chemical contamination and bulldozing that directly followed from "Operation Cast Lead" (FAO 2010: 1–2). This, of course, has severely and further impacted livelihoods from agriculture, already diminished through the blockade that serves to restrict both agricultural imports, such as seeds, and exports, such as strawberries or carnation flowers. Moreover, environmental experts have predicted that the damages wrought by "Operation Cast Lead" will cause long-term changes in agricultural biodiversity, and therefore hamper the agricultural economy well into the future (FAO 2010: 2). In 2014, another fifty-one-day Israeli-led military assault, "Operation Protective Edge," left over 2,100 dead and tens of thousands wounded (Chomsky and Pappe 2010; Palestine Monitor 2015: 2), greatly exacerbating the conditions left by the blockade and previous assault. According to the UN Food and Agricultural Organization (UN FAO), the consequences of the 2014 assault were devastating, leaving "24,000 families of farmers, herders and fishers [suffering] debilitating damage and losses. This includes virtually all types of assets needed to make a living from agriculture and supply markets with local food" (FAO 2015).

Water

Water is tied very clearly to issues pertaining to the environment, and Israel/Palestine is challenged by a lack of availability of fresh water due to desertification, limited arable land, and drought. Added to these challenges are those emerging from contamination of water and soil, whether from industry or war. Water is critically important for human health and for agriculture as well as for industrial use. In the case of Israel/Palestine, control over access to water is a major issue, and the impact of the Israel/Palestine racial contract is clearly evident.

Following the 1967 war, Israel took full control over the water resources of both the West Bank and Gaza. It is important to note that 80 percent of the mountain aquifers that hold the largest reservoirs are under the West Bank, while only 20 percent are within Green Line Israel (Gordon 2008b: 127). As Neve Gordon (2008b) has identified, Israel's control over water resources came in two stages: originally through the military authorities, and then through Israel's water commissioner and Ministry of Agriculture. The net result has been that the water resources of both the West Bank and the Gaza Strip were integrated with those of Israel into a single centralized system, virtually as if the Green Line did not exist (Gordon 2008b: 127). The resulting asymmetric power relations between Israeli Jews and the Palestinian Arabs living under occupation have ensured that the Israeli state has been able to appropriate resources, including water, according to its own interests as Palestinians lack environmental sovereignty (Isaac and Powell 2007: 144–64).

The inequities suffered by Palestinians as a collectivity in relation to water are numerous and cumulative. On an annual per capita basis, Israelis consume more than four times the volume of water as Palestinians, a figure that reflects how Israel allocates water in a highly differentiated manner for purposes of agriculture, industry, and personal consumption (Isaac and Powell 2007: 149).

The Israel/Palestine racial contract around water, therefore, also has implications for sustainable agricultural, industrial, and social development. Both surface and groundwater resources in the Occupied Palestinian Territories have deteriorated in quality over time. In Gaza, with its dense population, overpumping has lowered the water table below sea level, leading to the intrusion of salt water. Moreover, perennially inadequate sewage networks—further damaged by repeated wars—have contaminated groundwater (Issac and Powell 2007: 150; UN FAO 2010). In the case of the West Bank, settlements have exacerbated water quality because large amounts of untreated waste water are regularly dumped onto Palestinian land. Consider that 80 percent of the roughly 471 tons of solid waste produced daily by Israeli settlers living in the West Bank and East Jerusalem finds its way directly onto Palestinian land or into dumps (Isaac and Powell 2007: 150). Water resources are also being depleted in the West Bank, mostly due to Israeli consumption patterns, which target more than 80 percent of the available water resources in the Occupied Territories (Isaac and Powell 2007: 149).

In Gaza, UN agencies and the Coastal Municipal Water Utility estimate that the water suitable for human consumption supplied by the coastal aquifer—the only water source—could disappear (UNICEF and PHG 2010: 1). Palestinians in Gaza, two-thirds of whom are political refugees, may face the additional burden of becoming "environmental refugees" due to water conditions.

Water affects human health. The World Health Organization holds that there should be a minimum of 100 liters of water a day per person (World Bank 2009: 17). In the case of the West Bank, Palestinians have, on average, access to 86 liters a day, of which only 60 is drinkable, whereas Israeli settlers have access to 280 liters a day (Palestine Monitor 2015). Further, the rates vary considerably, with some Palestinians having access to as little as 10 to 15 liters a day—a level considered by humanitarian agencies to be at or below the threshold to avoid epidemics (World Bank 2009: v). The World Bank notes that not only is the supply of water variable and discontinuous, there have been few improvements made for Palestinians since the Oslo II Accord of 1995 (2009: v). It should also be noted that while Oslo II featured a discussion of Palestinian water rights, albeit undefined, only half of what Oslo II posited to be "immediate needs" relating to water was met (World Bank 2009: vii).

The situation is far worse in the Gaza Strip, where an estimated 97 percent of the population is not connected to water networks and 90 to 95 percent of the water is not fit for human consumption (UNICEF and PHG 2010: 1). This kind of situation forces a deeply impoverished population to have to purchase desalinated water at rates considered unaffordable for most households (World Bank 2016). Gaza's children are particularly at risk in relation to health. In fact, it is significant that in the four weeks prior to one survey, one-quarter of the children under five years of age in Gaza were reported to have had diarrhea, a major cause of childhood death in impoverished countries (UNICEF and PHG 2010: 2).

Water access is a key component in the Israel/Palestine racial contract, impacting Palestinian children and adults. For dispossessed Palestinians, access to water is tied to social planning and sustainable development (Isaac and Powell 2007: 158). Environmental sovereignty and control over natural resources is therefore a key area of justice claims for Palestinians.

Air

Neve Gordon, citing Eyal Weisman, notes that Israel displays a "politics of verticality" based on "Israel's simultaneous attempt to control three spatial levels—the ground, the air, and the subterranean level—in order to manage the Palestinian population" in the Occupied Territories (2008b: 127–8). Palestinian air space is a locus of Israel's exercise of occupation. The regulation of air space has been a central feature of Israel's relationship to the West Bank and the Gaza Strip, maintained and continued even in ostensible peace agreements from the Oslo Accords to the Roadmap for Peace (Karmi 2007: 121–59). This regulation allows for extensive Israeli aerial mapping, used to divide Palestinian land and regulate the development of Israeli settlements. Aerial maps are also used to manage scarce water access and to build and enforce a dual-road system that denies Palestinians access to major highways (Gordon 2008a, 2008b; Zureik 2011). Air space is also, as noted earlier, a locus of extensive twenty-four-hour surveillance.

> Israeli companies are among the world leaders [in] electro-optical and laser applications which help overcome the impediments caused by darkness or distance. A range of optronics technologies developed in Israel such as thermal imaging, lasers, and infra-red optics are used by fighter aircrafts to carry out reconnaissance missions and strikes as well as in unmanned air vehicles (UAVs). They are also deployed in special cameras used in small satellites or industry automated optical inspection systems and binoculars as well as in a range of personal night vision devices for combat. Elop, a subsidiary of the Israeli military giant Elbit, manufactures an array of electro-optics products including thermal imaging devices which aim to "deliver a 24/7 observation and surveillance advantage" and a threat detection and countermeasure device for airborne platforms. (Gordon 2009b: 35)

Air is an arena for the assertion of Israeli military control. For example, Israel has developed a weapon for dispersing protesters referred to as the "Scream" (*Tze'aka* in Hebrew).[3] The minute-long blast, based on a combination of low-frequency sound waves at high intensities, forces protesters to their knees with profound headaches, nausea, and loss of balance. According to a source in the Israeli Defence Force (IDF):

> The intention is to disperse crowds with sound pulses that create nausea and dizziness.... It is probably the cleanest device we have ever had, when you compare it to rubber bullets or tear gas. It is completely non-lethal.[4]

The weapon was apparently under development for some years prior to its appearance, when it was used to repress protests opposing the building of the security barrier (apartheid wall) on Palestinian land in the West Bank village of Bil'in. The technology is considered similar to the Long Range Acoustic Device (LRAD) used by the US military forces in Iraq.[5] Military defense and expansion in Israel are heavily linked to aerospace technology that is integrated with US and Canadian state agreements, private capital, surveillance, and weapons development (Kilibarda 2008; Zureik 2011).

The impact of the Israel/Palestine racial contract in terms of environmental degradation is continuous and largely unmeasured. However, there are also more acute moments of environmental injustice articulated through the occupation of Palestinian airspace. An extreme example is the use of white phosphorous as a central weapon in the Israeli arsenal during the December 2008–January 2009 military assault on Gaza. As Desmond Tutu noted:

> Every so often, the world witnesses events of such naked brutality that concerned observers must recoil in outrage and demand an end to the madness. We saw this in my own country [South Africa] after the Sharpeville Massacre, a bloodletting that finally awakened the world to the evils of Apartheid.... In the waning days of 2008, we saw it once again in the Middle East. Israel had launched a bloody assault on the Gaza Strip, what its military called Operation Cast Lead, and for three weeks one of the world's most sophisticated armies pummeled a captive Palestinian population. (2011: vii)

The publication of the United Nations Fact-Finding Mission on the Gaza Conflict, referred to as the *Goldstone Report*, offers, in the words of Naomi Klein, "a serious, fair-minded, and extremely disturbing" (2011: xiii) consideration of the impact of the Israeli assault, not least in relation to the environmental impact. Regarding environmental justice, and specifically the implications of occupied airspace, the widespread use of white phosphorous as a weapon against Palestinian civilians is notable in the report and is supported by other findings. A study on the impact of white phosphorus on patients in Gaza, reported in leading medical journal *The Lancet*, explains the effect of the weapon.

> White phosphorus is a smoke-producing, waxy, yellow transparent combustible solid, which is used mainly in military and industrial settings. In the presence of oxygen, it spontaneously ignites with a yellow flame and produces dense smoke; it extinguishes only when deprived of oxygen or totally consumed. (Al Barqouni et al. 2010: 68)

The use of white phosphorus by the Israeli military was only discovered after patients with treated burns returned with further wounds.

> In January, 2009, an 18-year-old man presented to the emergency department after suffering an attack with an incendiary shell. He had

many painful patches of full-thickness burns, which were surrounded by sloughed tissue. His wounds covered 30% of his body surface area, and were distributed on both upper and lower limbs, and his right shoulder. There were no signs of inhalation burns. After a clinical diagnosis of white phosphorus burns was made, the airway was secured, resuscitation fluid was initiated, and wounds were irrigated with diluted sodium bicarbonate solution before wet dressing. 1 day after admission to the burns unit, white smoke was noticed emanating from the wounds, which now contained extensive necrotic tissue and had extended into the underlying tissue… He was urgently transferred to the operating room. (Al Barqouni et al. 2010: 68)

According to the *Goldstone Report*, white phosphorous was widely deployed as a weapon during the attack on Gaza, and its use was defended by the Israeli government because it was "not a proscribed weapon under international law" and it was "deployed with a high degree of success." The report further noted the high risk of the chemical weapon to civilian health and safety and the risk to medical practitioners. It suggested that "serious consideration should be given to banning the use of white phosphorous as an obscurant" (Goldstone 2011a: 142–3).

Other weapons deployed through air attacks were flechettes, dart-like pieces of composite metal usually fired from canister projectiles. Notably, "on impact the darts will hit whatever is within a certain zone. They are incapable of discriminating between objectives after detonation" (Goldstone 2011a: 143). Moreover, two Norwegian doctors, Dr. Mads Gilbert and Dr. Eric Fosse, who carried out medical surgeries in al-Shifa hospital in Gaza from December 31, 2008, to January 10, 2009, reported to the UN Fact-Finding Mission a demonstrably high number of amputations resulting from burns and injuries during that period. The mission found that such injuries were compatible with those from DIME weapons, which "consist of a carbon-fibre casing filled with a homogenous mixture of an explosive material and small particles, basically a powder, of a heavy metal, for instance, a tungsten alloy." The alloy particles are suspected of being "highly carcinogenic and so small that they cannot be extracted from a patient's body" (Goldstone 2011a: 144–5). The long-term impact of these types of explosive and chemical weapons on survivors and the environment is unknown.

The response of the Israeli state and Israel's advocates focused public attention on the motives of its author, Richard Goldstone, the South

African former judge responsible for the UN Mission, rather than on the findings of the UN-sponsored investigation. In April 2011, Goldstone published a statement in *The Washington Post*, indicating that on the basis of more recent knowledge, he was no longer prepared to sustain the previous findings of "allegations of intentionality by Israel" in the conducting of war crimes during the Gaza war.[6] Regardless of his own motivations, stated or otherwise, Goldstone was the subject of exceptional and unusual pressure from the Israeli state, and from Zionist defenders in the United States and internationally, following the publication of the report (Slater 2011). Irrespective of Goldstone's personal stance, the findings of the report remain unambiguous.

Conclusion: Greenwashing

The Israel/Palestine racial contract includes systemic environmental racism, affecting sustainability of and access to land, water, and air for Palestinians. It is worth returning to the question of why these themes have not been more prominently featured in growing discussions of environmental racism. Consistent with Israel's rebranding efforts discussed earlier, there has been an active public relations campaign to imagine a very different idea of Israel, a process referred to as "greenwashing."

The concept of "greenwashing" has been primarily used in relation to corporate marketing strategies.[7] However, it is also befitting for Israel in light of its strong efforts to present its image in the face of growing criticism within Western countries and accompanying support for the boycott, divestment, and sanctions movement. Israel's greenwashing delinks environmental issues from the ethnic cleansing of Palestine in 1948, and from the full consequences of its land occupation, dispossession, and regulation of access to resources including water and air. Thus, it is claimed on Israel's Ministry of Environmental Protection website that the office supports "an integrated, inclusive policy for the protection of the environment" (2018). Israel's Ministry of Environmental Protection website specifically indicates advocacy of environmental justice, advanced in a new plan in 2014. It posits that the ministry has "taken steps towards integrating environmental justice principals in its programs, policies and actions" (2018). However, the rights of Palestinians are not named in the plan.

Meanwhile, the effects of environmental racism continue. Ali Abunimah has highlighted the marketing surrounding Better Place, an Israeli company that developed charging stations for automobiles along Jewish-only roads in the West Bank. Indeed, Better Place won the support and investment of former World Bank President and Middle East Quartet envoy James D. Wolfensohn.[8] State-led greenwashing efforts have thus joined forces with business-marketing initiatives in ways consistent with the Israel/Palestine racial contract, enforcing the case for a comprehensive campaign for boycott, divestment, and sanctions. This also exposes the apartheid nature of the Israeli state and brings to light the importance of discussions of alternatives, which is the focus of the next chapter.

Notes

1 Ali Abunimah, "Egypt's Uprising and Its Implications for Palestine," *Electronic Intifada*, January 29, 2011, http://electronicintifada.net/v2/article11762.shtml.

2 These bypass roads allow Jewish Israeli settlers access to and from different settlements, as well to and from (Green Line) Israel.

3 Mitch Potter, "Israelis Unleash Scream at Protest: New Weapon Knocks Crowds off Feet, Sound Blast Triggers Nausea, Dizziness," *The Toronto Star*, July 8, 2005, https://www.indymedia.org.uk/en/2005/06/315129.html.

4 Quoted in Ibid.

5 Ibid.

6 Richard Goldstone, "Reconsidering the Goldstone Report on Israel and War Crimes," *The Washington Post*, April 1, 2011, http://www.washingtonpost.com/opinions/reconsidering-the-goldstone-report-on-israel-and-war-crimes/2011/04/01/AFg111JC_print.html.

7 Bruce Watson, "The Troubling Evolution of Corporate Greenwashing," *The Guardian.com*, August 20, 2016, https://www.theguardian.com/sustainable-business/2016/aug/20/greenwashing-environmentalism-lies-companies.

8 Ali Abumimah, "Quartet Ex Envoy's Investment Helps Israel Greenwash Settlements." *Electronic Intifada*, May 6, 2010, http://electronicintifada.net/content/quartet-ex-envoys-investment-helps-israel-greenwash-settlements/8805.

9 ISRAEL/PALESTINE AND THE APARTHEID ANALYSIS: TOWARD A ONE-STATE SOLUTION?

Apartheid—What's in a name?

The application of the term "apartheid" to the policies and practices of the Israeli state forms a flashpoint in contemporary politics, far outside the geographic context of Israel/Palestine. The apartheid analysis of Israel/Palestine has often been seen as unusual, removed from normalized comparative and analytical discourse. In the words of one author published in the journal *Israel Studies*, it is claimed to be part of "official Palestinian propaganda" (Inbar 2006: 827). However, clearly comparisons between South Africa and Israel have been made not only by Palestinians but by many analysts of varying identities, including Jewish critics and others whose identities fall between and/or outside these groupings. More significantly, the dismissal of this analysis as "propaganda" omits the fact that there is an established tradition of scholarship that places Israel in a context comparable to other settler societies, including South Africa (Cliff 2000: 9; Pollak 2009; Rodinson 1973; Will 2007: 412). Further, South Africa has provided a point of comparison for many state formations and policies, including those of the United States and Brazil (Marx 1998).

The analysis of state practices and policies as grounded in "apartheid" is increasingly part of the standard terminology adopted in comparative political analysis. The term has been frequently used—notably without major controversy or charges—in relation to a range of states and systems other than Israel, as is discussed in more detail below. The application of the term "apartheid"—meaning state-sponsored "separateness" of "races"—is also consistent with the racial contract framework, as it draws attention to the exclusionary character of the Israeli Zionist state project regarding the Indigenous Palestinian population. Because of the transformation evident in South Africa since 1994, the reference to the apartheid experience also draws attention to the possibility of change, even in the face of continuity. Many of those who advocate the need for profound and structural transformation in order to address the ongoing conflict in Israel/Palestine—most notably a one-state solution—frame their arguments with reference to or in the context of a challenge to an apartheid-like system (Abunimah 2006; Ageel 2016; Barghouti 2011; Cook 2006; Davis 2003; Farsakh 2002, 2005, 2011; Karmi 2007; Tilley 2005b; Soske and Jacobs 2015b).

In considering the broad range of transformative moments in the recent history of global governance, one of the most significant would be the transition from apartheid to representative government in South Africa. The practice of "apartheid," an Afrikaans word literally meaning "apartness," was overt in its embrace of white supremacy and privilege and in its concomitant denigration and limitation of the rights of the majority Indigenous African Black population. Color and class were closely linked, and those of various mixed race, Indian origin, or "colored" status experienced sharply differentiated access to a hierarchy of rights and freedoms. David Theo Goldberg aptly dubs the ideological framings that justified these differential power relations "racial Southafricanization" (2009: 245–326). Regardless of the actual and discriminatory record of state policies internationally since the end of the Second World War, apartheid South Africa's overt acceptance of racism as a foundational state practice stood in contrast to the liberal notion of formal equality espoused in the United Nations Universal Declaration of Human Rights adopted in 1948.

In this chapter, we seek to advance discussions of the Israel/Palestine racial contract by considering the implications of the apartheid analysis in the context of a social justice framing, including considerations of a one-state solution. We suggest that from the perspective of comparative political science, the notion of apartheid serves as a useful categorization of the Israeli state, applicable not only after 1967 but since the state's establishment in 1948. Indeed, common experiences in the United States, South Africa, and Israel/Palestine have long been identified internationally among social movements challenging racism, colonialism, and, notably, apartheid (Davis 2016; Salaita 2016). The one-state perspective can be usefully linked to the apartheid analysis in that it not only suggests a framework for understanding the racialized and ethnically exclusive character of the Israeli state but also presents a conceptualization that can point to its opposite—a postapartheid reality. Therefore, the apartheid framework offers a transformative positioning, an alternative to ethnic particularism, and a challenge to the discourse of Israeli exceptionalism. The institutionalized system of racial separation—apartheid—was embraced by the ruling National Party of South Africa, which formed the government from June 4, 1948, until May 9, 1994. It would have been difficult in the late 1940s, or even in the late 1980s, to predict the election of a Black head of state, Nelson Mandela (1918–2013), as president of South Africa (serving from 1994 to 1999), the leader of the formerly banned African National Congress (ANC). However, there is now an extensive literature addressing the complexities of the transition from apartheid. A considerable body of work indicates extreme disappointment, identification of continuities of economic inequality along racial lines, often labeled "economic apartheid," and dashed hopes in the transition to democracy. Sometimes considered part of the discourse representing "Afropessimism" (de B'béri and Louw 2011; Saul 2002), the legacy of entrenched racism and the continued restraints of capitalistic social relations (Bond 2000) have no doubt weighed heavily in the postapartheid era. The unmet expectations in the wake of democratic advances since the fall of apartheid are significant, and questions continue regarding the implications for policy and practice in contemporary South Africa (McDonald 2009; McDonald and Smith 2004).

However, in the wider historical and global context, the impact of a successful transition from a legalized system of racialized inequality in citizenship rights (apartheid) to universal electoral rights and formally egalitarian legal structures (postapartheid) has been substantial. This has also impacted the wider regional context where South Africa has been a dominant economic and military power. Further, the global impact of this transition is also apparent, as witnessed in the outpouring of grief and commentary by leaders and anti-racist activists from across different world regions upon hearing that Nelson Mandela died in December 2013. The global impact of the transition in South Africa is related to the role of the United Nations in both reflecting and shaping state and civil society discourse and movements in the decades since 1948.

The analysis of Israel as an apartheid state does not, however, assume or rely upon an exact correlation with apartheid South Africa. Adopting an approach consistent with the comparative method in political science, we see comparison as a means through which to highlight both similarities and differences. In fact, comparative studies that place Israel in the context of "strong states," or that assume unproblematized similarities with Western liberal democracies, blur characteristics that the apartheid framework serves to bring into focus (Migdal 2001). Both similarities and differences between Israel and apartheid South Africa can be usefully brought into relief, allowing for a more nuanced understanding of the realities under study, including patterns of racialization.

We suggest that in light of state practices of systemic differential treatment based on racialized and ethnicized characteristics that affect citizenship and rights, the apartheid analysis has significant empirical validity in the case of Israel/Palestine. Moreover, it supports an increasingly effective international mobilizing strategy. Providing a contextualization for comparative apartheid studies allows unique characteristics of both Israel and South Africa to be valuably analyzed. The apartheid framing of Israel/Palestine thus helps to open new discursive ground, challenging the silencing that inhibits comparative political analysis of those aspects claimed to be entirely *sui generis* in the Israel/Palestine racial contract. And, taking into account the situation of postapartheid South Africa offers both the promise of transformation within a democratic unified state model, and also warns us of the limitations. Equality in the form of a state that recognizes "one person/one vote" can be understood as a starting point, rather than as a final step, in a transformational project.

To illustrate the dimensions of our argument, we proceed from several points of entry to consider the relationship between the one-state solution and the apartheid analysis. We first review the manner in which the notion of "apartheid" has been a point of reference in comparative scholarship and international law, and how it has been taken up by authors who have adopted the one-state perspective for transformation. Next, we provide a selected literature review, indicating the various ways in which the apartheid framework has been considered useful for understanding both the origins and evolution of the Israeli state. We then analyze the ways in which the context of Israel/Palestine is similar to, and different from, that of apartheid South Africa from the perspective of how a postapartheid South Africa might serve as a model for social change. We conclude by considering the value of the apartheid analysis of Israel/Palestine from the perspective of its strategic significance, advancing a framework of social solidarity with the Palestinian call for boycott, divestment, and sanctions.

Apartheid considered: Comparative scholarship, law, and one-state advocates

Many scholars and political analysts who adopt the one-state perspective as a solution to the crisis in the Middle East accept the assignment of apartheid as applicable to the state of Israel. This idea, if marginal between the 1940s and the 1970s, was largely circumvented by the expectation of a two-state model associated with the Oslo process in the 1990s; more recently, however, discussions of the one-state model have reemerged. Edward Said's pivotal 1999 commentary in *The New York Times*, titled "The One State Solution," was indicative of an emerging new common sense. He stated:

> It is time to question whether the entire process begun in Oslo in 1993 is the right instrument for bringing peace between Palestinians and Israelis.... The alternatives are unpleasantly simple: either the war continues (along with the onerous cost of the current peace process) or a way out, based on peace and equality (as in South Africa after apartheid) is actively sought, despite the many obstacles.[1]

There is now an expansive literature on the subject, matched by a proliferation of scholarly conferences specifically dedicated to assessing the one-state strategy in terms of its policy implications for the Middle East conflict.[2] Ghada Karmi gives a useful summation of the debates: "The two-state solution, whatever its merits or drawbacks, stood little chance of being realized in practice. The obvious alternative to it and to the variety of Israeli unilateralist proposals was the one-state solution" (2007: 229).

The notion of "apartheid" has tended to bridge discussions of the one- and two-state approaches. It has found resonance within Israel and Palestine, associated with, rather than mitigated by, two-state transitional policies and processes. Jonathon Cook indicates the inherent limitations of the two-state model, emphasizing that to the extent that it is accepted within Israeli civil society, it presumes the negation of inclusion of Palestinians, or "Arab Israelis," in an even more exclusive, Jewish-only, Israeli state (2006: 161). In particular, the continued construction of the "security fence," referred to locally as the "Apartheid Wall," indicates that recurrent Israeli governments have envisioned a deepening divide. The comparison with apartheid South Africa has therefore been raised within Israel. This includes the comments of former Prime Minister Ehud Olmert, who has used the term in the context of assessing the risk to Israel if the two-state model fails.[3] In July 2008, the editor of the Israeli daily *Ha'aretz* insisted on the accuracy of labeling Israel as an apartheid state in comments addressing the United Nations. The editor refused to retract the comment when challenged by a local synagogue hosting his visit in Britain, sponsored by the World Zionist Organization.[4] Further, in February 2010, Ehud Barak, then Israel's defense minister, was reported to have delivered "an usually blunt warning to his country that a failure to make peace with the Palestinians would leave either a state with no Jewish majority or an 'apartheid' regime."[5]

In the context of this emerging discourse, the notion of apartheid is arguably gaining a specific meaning in the context of Israel/Palestine, where explicit comparisons with South Africa, while relevant, are neither asserted as reductive nor considered as decisive (Soske and Jacobs 2015b). The adoption of "apartheid" as a systemic framework for state practice and policy is certainly rooted in the South African reality. The policy of legal racial separation was a self-identified ideology of the South African state associated with the National Party (Arrighi and Saul 1973; Callinicos 1992; Van den Berghe 1965) and was a product of colonialism for centuries prior to this (Soske and Jacobs 2015a). However, the applicability of the apartheid analysis is not dependent upon a search for exact similitude. Our argument maintains its applicability in the case of Israel/Palestine in the context of a more general comparative discussion, where apartheid South Africa and Israel are taken as case studies of a more generalized phenomenon in the construction of capitalist state power relations and racial contracts.

This contextualization is, moreover, consistent with trends in current comparative scholarship. "Apartheid" has been the term of choice to describe a number of phenomena marked by sharp inequalities associated with racialized barriers legitimated in state projects. The notion of "global apartheid," for example, has become a common reference point to address the developmental gap and related policies that mark the divide between the global North and global South (Bond 2001, 2004; Ginsburg 2004: 160). The close correlation between racialized division and class in Canada has been identified as a system of "economic apartheid" (Galabuzi 2006), a term also applied to consider the continued class and race divisions in South Africa in a post-political apartheid context (Bond 2001, 2004). Apartheid has been used to explain increasing immigration controls during the post–Cold War period over migrants from the developing world in the wealthy countries of North America, Europe, and Australasia (Richmond 2004); the post–Second World War urban segregation and poverty of African Americans (Massey and Denton 1993); and the underrecognized discrimination toward Korean minorities by the Japanese state (Hicks 1997).

Such an approach is also consistent with international law, where apartheid is identified as a crime (MacAllister 2008; White 2009).[6] The UN's International Convention on the Suppression and Punishment of the Crime of Apartheid (ICSPCA; referred to as the Apartheid Convention) entered into force in 1976 to challenge South African policy specifically. Significantly, it identified South Africa as being in violation of extant international law and applied this generically to the crime of apartheid regardless of country-specific context. The extension of international law based on a specific phenomenon is standard, in that the crime of "slavery" followed the Atlantic slave trade and "genocide" followed the actions of the Nazis in Germany against the Jewish population.[7] Rather than suggesting such crimes are unique to the national contexts from which they derive, an international legal framework indicates the crime; as such, state actions can be committed, resisted, or halted in relation to this crime. It was on the basis of this approach that South Africa's apartheid system became a focus of United Nations policy, ultimately including support for boycott, divestment, and sanctions against South Africa.

The 1960s were to prove to be a turning point in UN policy and discourse regarding South Africa's commitment to apartheid policies and practices. While not without considerable controversy, the global coordination across borders and regional boundaries that challenged apartheid in the South African context was facilitated pivotally through various UN institutions. The General Assembly and a series of conferences related to South African apartheid provided an arena for policy formulation that ultimately saw the emergence of a body of international law. Collectively, these challenge apartheid as a crime against humanity, reaching beyond the specific example of the South African case (see Brits 2005; Dubow 2008; Malhotra 1964; Narang 2001; Reddy 1974).

Much the same conclusion was reached by the Human Sciences Research Council of South Africa (in June 2009) when it released a 300-page report concluding that Israel practiced both colonialism and apartheid, as defined by international law, in the Occupied Palestinian Territories. A summary of the international context by John Dugard, legal expert and former Special Rapporteur to the UN Commission on Human Rights and International Humanitarian Law in the Occupied Palestinian Territory, is apt.

> The Convention on the Suppression and Punishment of the Crime of Apartheid … has its roots in the opposition of the United Nations to the discriminatory racial policies of the South African Government—known as apartheid—which lasted from 1948 to 1990…. In 1966, the General Assembly labeled apartheid as a crime against humanity (resolution 2202 A (XXI) of 16 December 1966) and in 1984 the Security Council endorsed this determination (resolution 556 (1984) of 23 October 1984). The Apartheid Convention was the ultimate step in the condemnation of apartheid as it not only declared that apartheid was unlawful because it violated the Charter of the United Nations, but in addition it declared apartheid to be criminal. The Apartheid Convention was adopted by the General Assembly on 30 November 1973, by 91 votes in favour, four against (Portugal, South Africa, the United Kingdom and the United States) and 26 abstentions. It came into force on 18 July 1976. As of August 2008, it has been ratified by 107 States. (Dugard 2008)[8]

Further, the Rome Statute of the International Criminal Court established apartheid as one of a number of crimes against humanity. Such crimes include acts of murder, extermination, enslavement, deportation, or forcible transfer of population, imprisonment, or severe deprivation, or other inhumane acts "committed as part of a widespread or systematic attack directed against any civilian population, with knowledge of the attack" (Rome Statute 1998). According to Article 7, section 2 (h): "'the crime of apartheid' means inhumane acts … committed in the context of an institutionalized regime of systematic oppression and domination by one racial group over any other racial group or groups and committed with the intention of maintaining that regime" (Rome Statute 1998).

The applicability of the apartheid analysis in the Israel/Palestine context has considerable resonance and has attracted the attention of scholars for many years, and in a variety of ways. Some suggest direct parallels with the South African context; however, more commonly apartheid is addressed as a generic policy associated with colonial-settler states. Apartheid can therefore be seen as a policy framework consistent with racialized and/or ethnic exclusivity, one that can be legitimately challenged, debated, and also, importantly, superseded. The analysis is consistent with a perspective that sees the Israel/Palestine racial contract as part of a hegemonic global project of capitalism and colonialism, persistent but also subject to challenge and resistance. Understanding apartheid in this more generic sense is, we maintain, not only useful analytically in the Israel/Palestine case but also incorporates variation and local differences within its basic defining parameters. It disrupts the Zionist ideological framework, which posits the characteristics of the state of Israel as exceptional, rather than those of a state that can be understood as one particular manifestation of apartheid.

Apartheid compared: South Africa, Israel and the one-state literature

A comprehensive review of the extensive interdisciplinary and international literature addressing the one-state solution based on drawing connections between Israeli and South African apartheid systems goes beyond the scope of this chapter. However, a brief consideration of selected texts is useful in indicating the value of the apartheid analysis from the vantage point of transformation.

Many of those who adopt a one-state vision of social change in Israel/Palestine incorporate the notion of apartheid as an analytical and comparative tool. Virginia Tilley, for example, in *The One-State Solution: A Breakthrough for Peace in the Israeli-Palestinian Deadlock* (2005b), recurrently points to the contradictory realities of pre-1994 South Africa to highlight similar tensions in post-1967 Israel. A central point in her case for the one-state option is the deep integration of the Occupied Territories in the infrastructure of the Israeli state, rendering moot the Oslo model of an effective Palestinian state. Her emphasis is that Israel is in effect already so deeply entrenched in the infrastructure of occupation in the Occupied Territories that a move to a single democratic state is the only possible next step toward a peaceful solution to the conflict. Her analysis is more empirical than analytical in that it focuses on the realities of the Israel/Palestine case study. The case is made that Israel/Palestine is currently, in a sense, a single state, unstable in its apartheid framing, and that a democratic single state is a necessary corrective.

Leila Farsakh (2002, 2005, 2012) also advocates explicitly for the one-state model. Her argument draws a close comparison with apartheid South Africa. However, she maintains that the positive correlations are not universal, but specifically associated with labor recruitment policies. She holds that since the 1967 occupation, and even more so since the enactment of the economic and labor policies associated with the Oslo Accords in the 1990s, Israel/Palestine has been moving closer to the South African apartheid model. The analogy with apartheid South Africa is, therefore, in this view, on a trajectory of increasing similarity, even as South Africa itself, and international public opinion, move in the opposite direction. Specifically, Farsakh argues that negotiations ostensibly toward the creation of a viable Palestinian state have in fact mimicked South African "Bantustanization." The fragmentation and isolation of Palestinian communities that have been separated by militarized checkpoints, labor restrictions, and the construction of the Apartheid Wall have in fact ensured the failure of a viable Palestinian state.

From the perspective of a critical race analysis rooted in history, it is also important to consider the ethnically exclusive character of Israel within the 1948 boundaries. The 1948 context is addressed by a number of scholars who convincingly trace apartheid to the origins of the Israeli state. In his classic study, Uri Davis (2003) emphasizes the applicability of the apartheid analysis to Israel since 1948, rooted in the notion of an exclusively "Jewish" state. Explicitly addressing the comparison with South Africa, Davis sees Israel and South Africa as two examples of apartheid as defined in international law. While recognizing differences, Davis maintains that to reject the applicability of the apartheid analysis on the basis of differences alone serves to absent or distort the significant similarities. The specific, and contradictory, character of Israeli apartheid is indicated in part by the state's historic rhetorical identification with liberal democracy (Davis 2003: 87).

Ali Abunimah (2006), also an advocate of a one-state solution, similarly traces the apartheid character of Israel to the period of the original conquest of Palestinian land. He approaches the discussion from the entry point of the 1967 occupation and the failure of the two-state model. What Abunimah terms the "impossible partition" of Israel/Palestine not only is a feature of the current crisis but has a history dating back to 1930s colonialism (2006: 19–54). The two-state model, popularized through the Oslo process, has been rendered increasingly less feasible as recent Israeli policy has strived to alter the "demographic dilemma"—a racialized expression, common in Israeli discourse, of the fact of the rising Palestinian population relative to the Jewish population. Since 2005, Jews in Israel have no longer constituted an absolute majority within the territory controlled by the state, and demographic projections point to a Palestinian majority in the future. Israel's approach to a two-state model, rather than making an accommodation to demands for Palestinian self-determination, is in fact, according to Abunimah, "an effort to define boundaries for the state that assure a Jewish majority, but [this] doesn't involve genuinely giving up control of the occupied territories" (2006: 57–8).

Abunimah's approach to the South Africa comparison specifically addresses distinctions, not least between the Afrikaner and Zionist self-images and historical narratives. He traces the foundational roots of both settler projects in the realities of colonialism but indicates distinct local expressions. Noting Israeli professor of political geography Oren Yiftachel in his critique of the "exclusively Jewish discourse" that relegates Palestinians as a kind of "silent backdrop or incidental stage setting," Abunimah addresses similarities in Zionist and Afrikaner founding ideologies (2006: 138–9; see also Yiftachel 2005). Abunimah's analysis leads him to an optimistic projection of the future, anticipating that, overall, "[t]he Palestinians are winning" (2014: xi).

Heribert Adam and Kogila Moodley's (2005) comprehensive comparison of peacemaking in Israel/Palestine and South Africa focuses on a wide range of issues, from the political contexts of South African pre- and postapartheid negotiations and the two-state model in the Middle East to the roles of leadership, religion, and political economy. Their emphasis in this comparison is to identify differences as more significant than similarities (2005: 19). Adam and Moodley also consider seriously the one-state model in the context of recognition that "currently, the very physical possibility of a Palestinian state is being destroyed" (175). However, the political context for a realistic one-state system is treated with skepticism in Israel/Palestine on the grounds that entrenched "bicommunalism" could not be readily accommodated and that security consciousness is likely the most salient factor (Adam and Moodley 2005: 179–80). The suggestion is that a viable two-state model might serve as an interim solution until greater trust is built and a unified state is possible (180).

From the perspective of comparative political science, the significant point is not, however, merely that there are differences to weigh against similarities but that a comparative context is found when Israel/Palestine is considered in relation to apartheid South Africa. The fact of the comparison challenges the claimed exceptionalism of the Israeli state and compels a focus on racialized ethnic divisions. Further, these recent examples of applications of the apartheid analysis to Israel/Palestine relevant to contemporary global events in fact build on earlier accounts. For example, Ibrahim Abu-Lughod and Baha Abu-Laban (1974b) offer foundational arguments in the current apartheid literature (Will 2007: 412). They identify particularly "the role of belief in racial superiority and manifest destiny in the colonialist position" in both Israel and apartheid South Africa (Abu-Lughod and Abu-Laban 1974a: viii). Achille Mbembe has maintained that the comparison regarding apartheid stretches the bounds of South African experience. The extent of institutionalized racism endured by Palestinians in Israel, he argues, "is not apartheid, South African style. It is far more lethal. It looks like high-tech Jim Crow-cum-apartheid" (Mbembe 2015: vii–viii).

Comparisons with South African apartheid have not always been rejected by Zionist advocates. The link is in fact traceable to the foundational roots of Israeli state ideology. Theodor Herzl, the Austro-Hungarian journalist and founder of modern Zionism in the late 1800s, compared his project to that of Cecil Rhodes, the British colonialist who spearheaded industrial settlement in South Africa and Rhodesia (the colonial predecessor of Zimbabwe) (Halbrook 1972: 86; Herzl 1960). The leader of the South African Defence Force during the First World War, Jan Smuts, was an early advocate of the 1917 Balfour Declaration that established British colonial support for the Zionist settlement of Palestine (Weinstock 1989). At the other end of the political spectrum, the comparison between Israel and South Africa has been raised by Marxist critics of Zionism to indicate the settler-colonial character of the Israeli state (Rodinson 1973). In his autobiography, the late British-Israeli Marxist Tony Cliff recalls how, as an anti-Zionist Jew, he drew the comparison regarding the apartheid system in his early years in

Israel/Palestine along with his partner Charnie Rosenberg, a South African who originally came to Palestine as a socialist-Zionist but soon moved to an anti-Zionist position (2000: 9).

This brief and selective review indicates that the apartheid analysis, including references that compare Israel/Palestine and apartheid South Africa, has both historic and contemporary relevance. It draws attention to a pattern of entrenched racism in Israel as well as the potential for radical transformation, particularly in terms of the one-state solution. At the same time, differences in the specific forms of apartheid are brought into relief. In the next section, we consider the nature of these similarities and differences between Israel and apartheid South Africa from the perspective of visioning a postapartheid model.

Apartheid Israel in a postapartheid era: Challenge and transformation

Part of the value of framing Israel as an apartheid state is the vision it offers in an era marked by a postapartheid reality in the aftermath of the transition in South Africa. The complexities associated with the democratic project in postapartheid South Africa—regarding critical issues such as institutional structures and continuing and new configurations of racialized politics (see Peberdy and Crush 2007; Shepherd 2009)—certainly merit concerted attention. Our focus here, however, is the transition from apartheid to formal democracy as a significant event and how this has compelled comparative attention that disrupts the Israel/Palestine racial contract. We suggest that the transition from apartheid to a postapartheid state in South Africa has altered the frame of consideration of Israel/Palestine in relation to other states. The continuing realities of deep inequality in South Africa, commonly referred to as economic apartheid, notwithstanding, the transition on this scale in a major country of the global South has served as an inspiration to those who identify with the particularized oppression experienced by the Black South African population. It is also an indication that postapartheid society is not a utopia, but merely a necessary first step in expanding democratic rights to those who have been victims of colonial settlement. Nelson Mandela, once imprisoned for life and labeled a "terrorist," now stands as a moral icon of inspiration, even if he also symbolizes an era of high expectations that were not fulfilled by outcomes. While there are obvious limitations in efforts to directly imitate the search for a "new" Mandela (Adam and Moodley 2005), the potential for transformation has significantly inspired attention to the one-state solution in the Middle East. Arguably, debates in the twenty-first century have taken place in the context of this postapartheid era, including attention to processes of "truth and reconciliation," ongoing systemic racism and colonialism, even in an age of a politics of recognition (Coulthard 2014; Salaita 2016; Soske and Jacobs 2015b). George Bisharat (2008) has emphasized the importance of a rights-based approach to the Israel/Palestine conflict, not as an abstract goal, but as a necessary, though not sufficient, strategic orientation.

The sense of accomplishment in achieving a state transition to a postapartheid South Africa has been expressed in part by United Nations representatives attentive to Israel/Palestine. For example, in the UN *Report of the Special Rapporteur on the Situation of Human Rights in the Palestinian Territories Occupied Since 1967*, Richard Falk took "particular note of the fact that the military occupation of the Palestinian territory has gone on for more than 40 years and that it possesses characteristics of colonialism and apartheid" (2008). A similar analysis is reported in the UN Economic and Social Commission for Western Asia report titled *Israeli Practices towards the Palestinian People and the Question of Apartheid* (UN ESCWA 2017) and in the 2018 UN report from the Special Rapporteur on the Palestinian Territories (UNHRC 2018).

According to Virginia Tilley, Israel's model of "ethnic democracy" is, beyond other objectionable features, problematically outdated in light of an emerging postapartheid global pattern in terms of legal state structures. It marks an increasingly "intolerable embarrassment, as the model is long obsolete elsewhere.... The shift rose to catch South Africa and quickly discredited apartheid" (Tilley 2005b: 181). Tilley also lists Milosovic's "Greater Serbia," the "White Australia" project, and the official and unofficial policies of racial exclusion associated with pre-1960s southern US states as similarly outdated models. Israel suffers, according to Tilley, from exceptionally poor timing; international trends since the Second World War have indicated, albeit at a slow pace, a move away from ethnically exclusive principles in democratic states (2005b: 182).

Seen through a postapartheid lens, both apartheid South Africa and contemporary Israel can be understood to violate a basic human rights principle of the equal moral worth of human beings. For instance, Daryl Glaser acknowledges not only the empirical similarities between apartheid South Africa and Israel but moral ones relating to such ideals as individual liberty, substantive equality, and democracy (2003: 405–6). For Glaser, the comparison between apartheid South Africa and Israel is at its strongest in the West Bank and Gaza, noting that "Israeli Zionism is as bad as apartheid morally, and that it is as bad in similar ways" (2003: 404). Raef Zreik (2004) suggests that an emphasis on the South African experience tends to privilege a focus on law and rights, and that this may come at the expense of historical specificity and complexity regarding the Palestinian experience because of Palestinians' distinct, and continuing, post-1948 fragmentation. He acknowledges that apartheid is especially obvious regarding the situation of the Palestinians in the West Bank and Gaza in light of the Apartheid Wall, parallel laws, the pass system, the separate roads for Jewish Israelis only, and so on (Zriek 2004: 72). However, he notes that the national context is different.

> Whereas in South Africa the blacks, whites, and "coloreds" all considered themselves South Africans.... in Israel ... even in the best of times the civic "we" that had tentatively begun to emerge was always permeated and even overridden on both sides by a national "we." (2004: 76)

The apartheid framework can be, however, aptly applied regarding the experiences of Palestinians from the period of Israel's establishment in 1948. Hence, as established above, a major point of similarity relates to the European settler-colonial foundation of South Africa and the Israeli Zionist project and how each came to include both the expropriation of resources from the Indigenous population as well as legal differentiation between identifiable groups (Farsakh 2005: 232). However, the Zionist narrative highlights unique traits associated specifically with Israeli apartheid. As Gabriel Piterberg notes, Israel, in its original ethnic cleansing and forced exile of Indigenous Palestinians as well as in its foundational myths, offers an example of settler colonialism, where "the Zionist superstructure, even though it has its distinguishing features, is nonetheless typical of a settler society and comparable to those of other settler societies" (2008: 54).

As Mark Marshall suggests, legal differences promoting separateness can be seen to operate in the way the Absentee Property Law of 1950 served to prevent the return of *Nakba* refugees (referring to the original inhabitants of mandate Palestine in 1948), as well as to exclude Palestinians in the West Bank and Gaza over generations (1995: 19). Marshall likens Palestinians with Israeli citizenship and voting rights to "the privileged minority of Blacks who were allowed to live in White areas" while being denied power in South Africa (1995: 19). Ben White, who advocates the applicability of the apartheid analysis in the case of Israel/Palestine, sees the "main difference" with the South African case as being that "Israel has not practiced so-called 'petty apartheid'—in other words, there are no public toilets marked 'Jews' and 'Non-Jews'" (2009: 7). White further maintains that this is less a reflection of dissimilar practice than an indication of avoidance of overtly discriminatory discourse that would jeopardize Israel's "outside support" (2009: 8).

Despite this difference from the South African context, continued violations of the civil rights of Arab Israelis or Palestinians with Israeli citizenship status are sharply exposed and can be challenged from the vantage point of the apartheid framework. In a postapartheid era, denial of basic civil rights of Palestinians inside the Green Line comes into explicit focus, despite formal recognition of the rights of Arab Israelis. As noted by Jonathon Cook, the founding document of the Israeli state, the "Declaration of Independence," promises to "uphold the full social and political equality of all its citizens, without distinction of religion, race or sex."[9] However, since 1948, Israel has maintained its "emergency status" inherited from the British Mandate government. In a condition of martial law, Palestinians are treated as suspected terrorists and apartheid conditions are normalized despite the rhetoric of legal democracy. A series of laws and practices instituted in the name of "security" apply specifically to those suspected of "terrorism." These laws include administrative detention, where imprisonment of Palestinians without charges is common, creating a political climate of constant threat of incarceration, wiretapping, and censorship. Apartheid is also manifest in an absence of law in some areas of civil life. For example, Israel has not enshrined freedom of speech into law. Instead, under an emergency regulation, the Press Ordinance of 1933, also inherited from the British Mandate period, the government can arbitrarily close down news media, a measure used repeatedly against Arabic media.[10]

Regarding education—on the grounds that Arabs and Jews speak two different languages, have distinct cultures, and are largely geographically segregated—Israel has two educational systems in place up to university entry. There are also two systems in terms of educational resources, and Arab students face documented discrimination in terms of access in Israeli higher education (Arar and Mustafa 2011). The formally segregated system nominally ends with integration among Arab and Jewish students at the college and university level. However, Palestinian students in the postsecondary age group constitute about 25 percent of Israelis, but comprise less than 10 percent of the university student population. Academic testing favors the Hebrew language over Arabic, using a point system that offers a higher value to Hebrew. Psychometric tests are also used for university admission, which have been demonstrated to include cultural references that bias them toward awarding higher scores among Jewish students. There are also admissions interviews, which are conducted in Hebrew. Notably, these inherent biases against Arabic-speaking students were identified and corrected in 2003; this was later changed again, however, on the grounds that the change was "seen to be at the expense of Jewish children," who are expected to be the overwhelming majority in the postsecondary education system (Cook 2004a). The tenacity of bias was again confirmed by a 2018 international report from the Global Coalition to Protect Education from Attack (GCPEA), which found that systematic discrimination in education occurred in Israel against Palestinian children (GCPEA 2018: 145–56).

More profound distinctions between Israel/Palestine and the South African context, however, are suggested by the Zionist project that attempted to exclude the Indigenous Palestinian population entirely from the exclusively "Jewish state." Zionism, as a political strategy to address Western anti-Semitism (or anti-Jewish racism), saw no place for an Arab working class in the establishment of an ethnically exclusive national capitalist state. As Leila Farsakh points out, Palestinian labor after 1948 was a minority of the workforce, in contrast to Black South African labor, which constituted the majority of the labor force between 1913 and 1948 (2005: 232–3). Consequently, Labor Zionists excluded Palestinian labor and constructed the collectivist tradition of *kibbutzim* on occupied land (Piterberg 2008; Shafir and Peled 2002). Through the specific nature of Israeli apartheid, therefore, Palestinians were rendered a demographic minority in post-1948 Israel; in contrast, Black South Africans were the majority (Farsakh 2005: 233). The role of the Black working class in challenging South African apartheid, including the role of labor unions and strike action (Callinicos 1992), is different in the Israel/Palestine context.

These unique features combine with the fact that Zionism claims to be a progressive ideology in the West, even though it serves to advance a colonialist settler exclusivist practice, to render the apartheid analysis particularly challenging. In addition to its collectivist presentation through labor Zionism, the post–Second World War positioning of Zionist ideology in the West presents within a framework of claimed "anti-racism" as part of the specific Israel/Palestine racial contract. This is clearly different from the more widely recognized racist position presented by proponents of apartheid in South Africa. Israeli Zionism specifically is underpinned by a network in the West, particularly in the United States, and in both civil society and state organizations, that asserts an uninterrupted position of victimhood, typically claiming that any challenge to the Israeli state and its policies is tantamount to anti-Semitism (Finkelstein 2003a; Mearsheimer and Walt 2007). The centrality of education, debate, and a normalized atmosphere of discussion in assessing the apartheid nature of Israel/Palestine is therefore heightened relative to the South African example.

The role of the United Nations in relation to South Africa has tended to be positioned differently than its role related to Israel when it comes to the apartheid analysis. In particular, common challenges to movements in solidarity with Palestine, and specifically with calls for boycott, divestment, and sanctions against Israel, have objected to what is presented as a singular (and by extension, unfair) focus on Israel's violations of human rights. Certainly, there are many other states with established records of extreme and violent racism and human rights abuses. But the strategy adopted by the UN to focus on one specific state in a concerted global effort to challenge legal apartheid has as a precedent its successful opposition to apartheid in South Africa. This background is traced explicitly in South Africa's Truth and Reconciliation Commission process (South Africa Department of Justice 1998: vol. 3) and in the proceedings of the 1978 and 1983 World Conferences to Combat Racism and Racial Discrimination (UN Archives, S-0913–0019-04, 1978: 1; UN Archives, S-1028–0007-02, 1983, *Press Release*: 1). It is also evident in the establishment in 1966 of March 21st as the annual international Day for the Elimination of Racial Discrimination, as this date was adopted to commemorate the victims of the Sharpeville massacre in the Transvaal region of South Africa on that date in 1960 that brutally exposed the realities of apartheid. The "attempt to shift the comparison from Israel/South Africa" (Soske and Jacobs 2015a: 7) can therefore be understood as consistent with efforts to maintain the hegemony of the Israel/Palestine racial contract, rather than as a sincere effort to seek appropriate comparative analysis.

In conclusion: Strategic implications of the apartheid analysis

The preceding discussion underlines both the empirical relevance and normative significance of the apartheid analysis regarding the Israel/Palestine racial contract. A focus on the entrenched discriminatory treatment of Palestinians—within the Occupied Territories, inside the Green Line, and in the global diaspora—indicates the commonalities of a population dispersed by decades of colonial occupation.

Moreover, framing Israel as a specifically apartheid state suggests a challenge not only to Israel's racialized policies and practices but also to the mythologized idea of "Israel" presented in the dominant Zionist narrative in post-Second World War Western ideology. This highlights a major difference in the degree of support in the international community for challenging the South African apartheid system (including, ultimately, through sanctions and via the United Nations) in contrast to Israel (Farsakh 2005: 237; Will 2007: 420). In order to advance a strategic anti-apartheid movement in the case of Israel/Palestine, a progressive, anti-racist deconstruction of the hegemonic role of Zionism is called for, one which simultaneously opposes genuine anti-Semitism. Challenging Israeli apartheid is a necessary condition for extending solidarity with the Palestinian movement for self-determination and equal rights, expressed most clearly, as noted earlier, in the BDS movement.

The vision of a single democratic state grounded in principles of democratic inclusion and equality in the land of Israel/Palestine can offer some hope and optimism amid conditions that appear to be otherwise mired in violent conflict. Omar Barghouti, a founding scholar in the BDS movement and also an advocate of the one-state solution, has advanced the strategic inspiration of boycott, divestment, and sanctions, not least as an alternative to the response of the NGO community.

> Only by ending the occupation and apartheid can we get there. And, experience tells us, the most reliable, morally justifiable way to do that

> is by treating Israel as apartheid South Africa was, by applying various, context-sensitive and evolving measures of BDS against it.[11]

As George Bisharat notes, attention to such themes as the right of return and equality for Palestinian citizens of Israel addresses "rights that are not easily accommodated within a two-state framework" (2008: 29). The issues being framed by many of those using the apartheid analogy are also difficult to meet through the two-state solution (Bisharat 2008: 34). Indeed, these are reasons that have led some to ask "is the two-state solution dead?" (Sussman 2004).

The significance of the apartheid analysis, therefore, is grounded not only in sound comparative political science as a methodology but also in the potential it offers for advancing a movement of global solidarity. It can inspire support for a movement for equality, peace, and justice in the Middle East that resonates with all those opposing organized state racism and violence. The apartheid analysis suggests the value of both adopting the comparative method in relation to real-world states as well as expanding our collective political imagination when it comes to thinking about change in Israel/Palestine. Antonio Gramsci approached hegemonic exploitation and oppression with such a commitment to clear analysis, but also recalled that hope is possible, when he said, on December 19, 1929: "I'm a pessimist because of intelligence, but an optimist because of will" (as quoted in Rosengarten 2011).

A postapartheid Israel/Palestine in the Middle East is associated with a transformative vision that imagines a single democratic state for all its citizens. This offers a normative stance that is both critical and optimistic and has the potential to move from being marginal to one that is attractive to a wide layer of civil society advocates internationally. Angela Davis suggests such an approach is consistent with intersectional feminism and points to a new moment in global solidarity, referring to those who have died at the hands of racist state violence in the United States and in Palestine:

> I think we constantly have to make connections. So that when we are engaged in the struggle against racist violence, in relation to Ferguson, Michael Brown, and New York, Eric Garner, we can't forget the connections with Palestine. So in many ways I think we have to engage in an exercise of intersectionality. Of always foregrounding those connections so that people remember that nothing happens in

isolation. That when we see the police repressing protests in Ferguson we also have to think about the Israeli police and the Israeli army repressing protests in occupied Palestine. (2016: 47)[12]

Notes

1 Edward Said, "The One State Solution," *The New York Times*, January 10, 1999, http://www.nytimes.com/1999/01/10/magazine/the-one-state-solution.html.

2 These conferences include: "Israel/Palestine: Mapping Models of Statehood and Paths to Peace," York University, Toronto, Ontario, Canada (June 22–24, 2009), www.yorku.ca/ipconf; "One State for Palestine/Israel: A Country for All Its Citizens?," University of Massachusetts, Boston, Massachusetts, US (March 28–29, 2009), http://onestateforpalestineisrael.tari.org/index.php?option=com_content&view=article&id=3&Itemid=3; "Re-Envisioning Israel/Palestine," an international conference organized by the Middle East Project of the Democracy and Governance Programme, Human Sciences and Research Council, Cape Town, South Africa (June 12–14, 2009), http://www.hsrc.ac.za/en/events/events/international-conference-re-envisioning-israel-palestine; and "Challenging the Boundaries: A Single State in Palestine/Israel" (November 17–18, 2007), SOAS, London, UK, https://electronicintifada.net/content/palestinian-israeli-scholars-advance-one-state-solution-london/7212.

3 Aluf Benn, David Landau, Barak Ravid, and Shmuel Rosner, "Olmert to Haaretz: Two-State Solution or Israel Done For," November 11, 2007, https://www.haaretz.com/1.4961269; *Haaretz*, "Olmert Blasts Netanyahu's Foreign Policy, Warns of Risk of Apartheid in Israel," October 2, 2015, https://www.haaretz.com/olmert-warns-of-risk-of-apartheid-in-israel-1.5404995; Lizzie Dearden, "Israel's Former Prime Minister Says Country Faces 'Slippery Slope' to Apartheid," *Independent*, June 21, 2017, https://www.independent.co.uk/news/world/middle-east/israel-palestine-apartheid-slippery-slope-ehud-barak-former-prime-minister-comments-netanyahu-a7801466.html.

4 Ezra HaLevi, "Haaretz Editor Refuses to Retract Israel Apartheid Statements," *Arutz Sheva*, July 31, 2008, http://www.israelnationalnews.com/News/News.aspx/123596.

5 Rory McCarthy, "Barak: Make Peace with Palestinians or Face Apartheid," *Guardian.co.uk*, February 3, 2010, https://www.theguardian.com/world/2010/feb/03/barak-apartheid-palestine-peace.

6 Hazem Jamjoum, "Not an Analogy: Israel and the Crime of Apartheid," *Common Dreams*, March 31, 2009, https://www.commondreams.org/views/2009/03/31/not-analogy-israel-and-crime-apartheid.

7 Ibid.

8 In some accounts, apartheid is seen to have ended in South Africa in 1994, with the first general election utilizing a universal franchise; in others, the ending is rooted in developments from 1990 (including lifting the ban on the African National Congress and the release of Nelson Mandela from prison).

9 Jonathan Cook, "'Democratic' Racism (I)," *Al-Ahram Weekly On-line*, July 8–14, 2004, http://weekly.ahram.org.eg/Archive/2004/698/op11.htm.

10 Jonathan Cook, "'Democratic' Racism (II)," *Al-Haram Weekly On-line*, July 15–21, 2004, http://weekly.ahram.org.eg/Archive/2004/699/op11.htm.

11 Omar Barghouti, "Countering the Critics: The Boycott and Palestinian Groups," *Counterpunch*, October 21, 2008, http://www.counterpunch.org/barghouti10212008.html.

12 Michael Brown was an eighteen-year-old Black man who was shot and killed on August 9, 2014, by Darren Wilson, a police officer in Ferguson, Missouri, the United States. On March 4, 2015, in a federal investigation, Wilson was cleared of all charges related to the incident. Eric Garner was a forty-three-year-old Black man who died in Staten Island, New York, on July 17, 2014, after a New York police officer held him in a prolonged chokehold. Following an independent investigation by the US Department of Justice, an out-of-court settlement was reached involving a payment to the Garners. In both Ferguson and New York, the deaths provoked mass movements led by the Black community, demanding justice.

CONCLUSION

GLOBAL RESPONSE TO THE ISRAEL/PALESTINE RACIAL CONTRACT: BDS FROM SOUTH AFRICA TO PALESTINE

Summarizing the Israel/Palestine racial contract in context

In this book, our argument began with the understanding that racism takes multiple forms and is supported by states and sections of civil society, but is also continually resisted. The challenge in narrating, analyzing, and naming racism in its various forms is endemic to the racial contract. We draw upon this as a heuristic theoretical tool advanced by Charles Mills (1997), to frame our discussion specifically in the context of the politics of race in Israel/Palestine. We adapted the racial contract approach to consider a specific context and to forward the concept of the Israel/Palestine racial contract. This is not only about a contested state formation in a pivotal region in global geopolitics; the Israel/Palestine racial contract is also an ideological construct. Because of this ideological element, we view Gramsci's (1971) concept of hegemony as consistent with Mills' (1997) notion of non-ideal theory. We, therefore, see hegemony as useful to explaining how the Israel/Palestine racial contract emerged in the post–Second World War era of human rights, simultaneously asserting a dominant mythologized idea about Israel and a conceptual and political absenting of Palestine and Palestinians. We consider this to be a global racial contract, expressed not only within and among states but also through the United Nations in various and contradictory ways. Our study has analyzed this in relationship to Canada in particular, as an example of one state that has maintained a notably close relationship with Israel in the twenty-first century and is commonly overlooked. In the first part of this discussion, we addressed the Israel/Palestine racial contract in the context of scholarship and the social sciences; in the second part, we considered the global political context; and in the third and final part, we focused on rebranding and resistance.

In keeping with Gramsci's theory of hegemony, the Israel/Palestine racial contract has been sustained through both coercion, or force, as well as consent, or ideological negotiation. These elements are not static, but dynamic. In the current period, even in the face of massively increased surveillance and anti-Muslim racism in the name of security, the Palestinian population, as a subaltern force, has been at the center of contesting the Israel/Palestine racial contract. They have done so within Israel, in the Occupied Palestinian Territories, and in the diaspora. The hegemony of the Israel/Palestine racial contract has been considerably challenged, we maintain, by the Palestinian call for boycott, divestment, and sanctions (BDS), which has served as a kind of United Nations from below, calling on other actors in global civil society to bring Israel to account and adhere to international law. The analysis of Israel as an apartheid state, consistent with international law as developed by the United Nations, is compatible with this analysis of the Israel/Palestine racial contract.

Resistance under the broad call for BDS has continued to expand, and to both unify and motivate wider networks of solidarity. Various creative and inspiring forms of nonviolent resistance continue among Palestinians within Israel/Palestine (Ageel 2016; Barghouti 2011). Some progressive Jewish supporters in Israel have advanced solidarity actions within and beyond the Israeli military,[1] including a movement to "boycott from within" (BoycottIsrael.info 2019). The network of expanding support includes international artists and cultural workers who adhere to the boycott and refuse invitations or cancel performances. The movement has also opened space for a wider scope for critical intellectual scholarship in the social sciences related to Israel/Palestine (Ageel 2016; Aouragh 2011; Feldman 2015; Freeman-Maloy 2011; Hanieh 2003; Salaita 2016; Ziadah 2016), even in the face of considerable repression

(Dawson and Mullen 2015; Desai 2015; Drummond 2013; Masri 2011, 2017; Salaita 2015; Thompson 2011).

A number of scholars have highlighted a major difference in the degree of support in the international community for challenging the South African apartheid system, including through sanctions and support from the United Nations, in contrast to that of Israel (Farsakh 2005: 237; Will 2007: 420). This is significant in terms of the specific nature of the Israel/Palestine racial contract. Israeli representatives and advocates claim that the state is democratic and inclusive, distinct from apartheid South Africa, where the ruling National Party (1948–94) proudly asserted its commitment to legalized racial inequity (Malhotra 1964). However, it is also important to recall that UN support for boycotting South Africa was itself the product of decades of contentious debate, led by the actions of Black workers and students within the country, and supported by a movement that faced massive and violent state repression in South Africa and internationally. This movement was also expressed within the UN, dating back to the earliest meetings of the General Assembly in 1945 (Brits 2005).

The history of the BDS movement against apartheid South Africa is notable in terms of contemporary arguments. In particular, there is a common claim that those who support the BDS movement against Israel's racist policies toward the Palestinian population are unfairly "singling out" this state, targeting a distinctly Jewish state, and therefore the movement is reflective of anti-Semitism rather than a defense of universal human rights. This idea was, for example, explicitly used in a US State Department press release concerning the Durbin Review Conference held in Geneva in 2009 to assess the progress since the 2001 World Conference Against Racism; the press release expressed concerns over a draft document that "singles out Israel for criticism" and contains "efforts to brand Israel as racist."[2] Israel's purported mistreatment was further captured in the words of Anne Bayefsky, author and legal analyst, who asserted that "Israel is the Rosa Parks of the United Nations system."[3] After personifying the state of Israel and cynically attempting to appropriate the legacy of a major leader of the Black civil rights movement in the United States, Bayefsky continued:

> How else to explain the hate fests that are held year after year, the second-class treatment, the resolutions targeting Israel for alleged human rights abuses but letting gross violators like China and Zimbabwe off the hook?[4]

Our research indicates, however, that the idea that no state has ever been singled out for its policies and racism is inconsistent with actual UN history. This was precisely the strategy adopted and resonating among at first only a small minority of state delegates in the UN General Assembly, which ultimately was expressed in support for a global movement to isolate South Africa until it adhered to international law. In terms of the United Nations regarding Israel/Palestine, by way of conclusion, it is useful to recall the contested scholarship associated with the World Conference Against Racism that took place at the turn of the millennium in Durban, notably a city in postapartheid South Africa. What follows is a brief summary of UN policies and debates regarding South African apartheid and a revisiting of these debates in the UN World Conferences Against Racism that preceded the Durban world conference in 2001. This context demonstrates, we suggest, that the UN has a history of serving as an arena for debates challenging apartheid. The unique situation of Israel is not, therefore, that it has been "singled out." Rather, this discourse demonstrates the extent to which the Israel/Palestine racial contract has allowed Israel to avoid the consequences or ramifications of its consistent violations of international law.

The United Nations and apartheid South Africa

The Universal Declaration of Human Rights, adopted in 1948, maintained that "[a]ll human beings are born free and equal in dignity and rights" (Article 1). From the first meetings of the United Nations, India initiated a concerted campaign to challenge the treatment of people of Indian origin in South Africa. This was part of a historic series of racialized restrictions on Indian immigrants and indentured laborers in South Africa, dating from 1860. The position of Indian delegates to the UN represented the extension of a state-led movement that included Indian trade sanctions against South Africa.

> In the United Nations, a stalemate had developed since 1945. India, which each year put the item on the General Assembly's agenda, repeatedly pressed for a commission of inquiry into South Africa's racial policies, but failed to obtain the two-thirds' majority of votes

required to enforce such a resolution. South Africa, on the other hand, consistently refused to acknowledge UN competence to deal with the issue, arguing that even a mere discussion of its racial policies in the General Assembly involved condemnation ... Moreover, the Universal Declaration of Human Rights, adopted by the General Assembly in 1948, was not supported or acknowledged by the South African government. (Brits 2005: 757)

The United States was an important player in the emerging UN context for debate regarding apartheid South Africa. This was not a consistent role. US policy supported the legitimacy of the UN's competence to discuss the domestic policies of South African apartheid, but avoided commitment to or opposed resolutions that specifically challenged apartheid (Brits 2005: 771). The United States was attempting to position itself as a UN supporter and was aggressive in advancing human rights as an essential element of post–Second World War and Cold War geopolitics. This was symbolized by the speeches of President Franklin D. Roosevelt and the work of Eleanor Roosevelt on the Universal Declaration and in chairing the Commission on Human Rights. But the United States also had no interest in drawing attention to its own racially discriminatory domestic politics and policies. In this period, the United States supported national origin quotas in immigration, the internment of Japanese Americans, and the enforced segregation of African Americans. Further, the United States maintained significant economic ties to resource-rich South Africa and embraced the regime's regional interests. As a consequence, and reflecting the paradoxes that attend to human rights in the UN, by the early 1950s, the United States had articulated a policy that basically stayed in place until the mid-1980s, despite mass civil society movements calling for a consistent policy to isolate South Africa until it adhered to international law.

Beginning in the 1960s, growing opposition to South Africa's intransigence emerged in the global arena. A variety of factors came together, including successful resistance to colonial practices and the rise of states in the global South as representatives of anticolonial strategies, and, pivotally, the rise of the US civil rights movement. The Sharpeville Massacre in South Africa proved to be a turning point in attracting international attention to the violence and racism of the apartheid regime. Black South African demonstrators, peacefully challenging the racist pass laws in the township of Sharpeville in the Transvaal region, marched to the local police station on March 21, 1960. The police opened fire on the demonstrators, with the official figure indicating 69 fatalities and over 300 injuries (South Africa TRC, 1998: vol. 3, ch. 6, paras. 24–42). Though the facts of the massacre were not accepted by the South African ruling elite at the time, the findings of the postapartheid South African government's Truth and Reconciliation Commission (TRC) confirm the convictions maintained through an international outcry:

> The Commission finds that the police deliberately opened fire on an unarmed crowd that had gathered peacefully at Sharpville [*sic*] on 21 March 1960 to protest against the pass laws. The Commission finds further that the SAP [South African Police] failed to give the crowd an order to disperse before they began firing and that they continued to fire upon the fleeing crowd, resulting in hundreds of people being shot in the back ... The Commission finds further that the police failed to facilitate access to medical and/or other assistance to those who were wounded immediately after the march. The Commission finds that many of the participants in the march were apolitical, women and unarmed, and had attended the march because they were opposed to the pass laws ... The Commission finds the former state and the Minister of Police directly responsible for the commission of gross human rights violations in that excessive force was unnecessarily used to stop a gathering of unarmed people. (South Africa TRC, 1998: vol. 3, ch. 6, para. 42)

In 1961, the UN General Assembly passed a resolution on "The Question of Race Conflict in South Africa Resulting from the Politics of Apartheid of the Government of the Republic of South Africa." The resolution summarized prior commitments, identified South Africa's continual refusal to adhere to international appeals and obligations, and urged,

> all States to take such separate and collective action as is open to them in conformity with the Charter to bring about an abandonment of those policies. (Article 5)

The UN General Assembly, in 1963, adopted the "Declaration on the Elimination of All Forms of Racial Discrimination." This declaration named "apartheid" specifically in the preamble, noting that the UN representatives were *alarmed* by the manifestations of racial discrimination still in evidence in some areas of the world, some of which are imposed by certain Governments by means of legislative, administrative or other measures, in the form, inter alia, of apartheid, segregation and separation, as well as by the promotion and dissemination of doctrines of racial superiority and expansionism in certain areas. (Preamble)

And, further, the declaration stated in Article 1 that,

> Discrimination between human beings on the ground of race, colour or ethnic origin is an offence to human dignity and shall be condemned as a denial of the principles of the Charter of the United Nations, as a violation of the human rights and fundamental freedoms proclaimed in the Universal Declaration of Human Rights, as an obstacle to friendly and peaceful relations among nations and as a fact capable of disturbing peace and security among peoples.

However, while it was important in marking the growing opposition to apartheid among delegates in the General Assembly, this was not a legally binding document. This is the background to the institution of the "International Convention on the Elimination of All Forms of Racial Discrimination," which is legally binding on signatory countries. It was adopted in 1965 and came into force in 1968. The convention also established the Committee on the Elimination of Racial Discrimination (CERD), which serves as "the first such human rights treaty body [and] oversees implementation of the Convention by reviewing reports of the States Parties to the Convention" (Narang 2001: 2495).

Opposition to South Africa's apartheid policies started to gain support in the General Assembly. As noted earlier, in the aftermath of the Sharpeville Massacre, March 21st was declared to be the International Day for the Elimination of Racial Discrimination (UN 2014). The more powerful UN Security Council, however, was reluctant to address the issue of apartheid in South Africa. As the TRC notes, it took an event on the scale of Sharpeville to even provoke discussion. Following the Sharpeville massacre,

> [t]he policy of apartheid came under the spotlight and was debated for the first time by the United Nations Security Council. (South Africa TRC, 1998: vol. 3, ch. 6, para. 27)

Still, South Africa's traditional Western trading partners continued to use their veto as permanent members of the Security Council to reject "proposals to isolate the country or impose sanctions: apartheid was objectionable, but South Africa remained an important supplier of strategic minerals in the West" (Brits 2005: 775). By the twenty-ninth session of the General Assembly, in 1974, a majority of the delegates of the General Assembly rejected the membership credentials of South Africa on the grounds of violation of the principles of the Charter and Universal Declaration of Human Rights and called on the Security Council to review the relationship of the UN with South Africa.

Even when the majority of the permanent and nonpermanent members of the Security Council supported the expulsion of South Africa from the UN, no decision was taken due to the exercise of vetoes by France, the UK, and the United States (Reddy 1974: 19). The veto capacity of states in the Security Council ensured that other UN venues operated largely through the "weapons of the weak" (Scott 1985), including educational and civil society campaigns. This brings us to a more detailed discussion of the role of the United Nations' world conferences against racial discrimination, the precursors to the 2001 WCAR in Durban, South Africa.

World conferences to combat racism and racial discrimination, 1978 and 1983

In 1968, the first International Conference on Human Rights was held in Tehran, where there was a call for the criminalization of racist organizations internationally. This conference took place shortly before the enactment of the International Convention on the Elimination of All Forms of Discrimination. In 1969, the General Assembly designated 1971 to be the International Year for Action to Combat Racism and Racial Discrimination. In 1972, the General Assembly designated the ten-year period starting from December 10, 1973, to be the first Decade of Action to Combat Racism and Racial Discrimination. The aim was to carry out a global educational campaign to advance public knowledge and the profile of the new UN instruments for the elimination of racism and racial discrimination (Narang 2001: 2495). This was to be the first of three consecutive decades of this kind over the period 1973–2003. In the resolution to advance the third decade, it was noted that the context demanded ongoing attention, including "the outcome of the two World Conferences to Combat Racism and Racial Discrimination, held at Geneva in 1978 and 1983" (UN General Assembly 1993).

Parallel with these developments was a perceived "great urgency" given to addressing South Africa over the course of 1976 (United Nations Archives, S-1003–0006-06, 1977: p. 1). This was in response to the student protests in the South African township of Soweto, which served as another turning point. The events are summarized by the TRC:

> On 16 June, the Soweto uprising begins. Police open fire on approximately 10 000 pupils protesting against the use of Afrikaans as a medium of instruction. Resistance spreads nationwide and continues for several months. There are 575 official deaths, including 390 in the Transvaal and 137 in the Western Cape. Over 2 000 people are injured. Arrests, deaths in detention and trials follow the revolt. (South Africa TRC, 1998: vol. 3, ch. 1: 18)

The response of the South African state is notable. The police shot and killed a young Black student, and photographer Sam Nzima captured the tragic moment.

> If ever there has been an image, a document from the South African past, that is both memorial and symbolic, it is this photograph, which came to epitomize the Soweto uprising of June 16, 1976.... Zollie Hector Pieterson was 13 when he was shot and killed by the South African police. There is little doubt that a chill wind blew through South Africa's heart when this photograph appeared on the front pages of the world's newspapers. (Pohlandt-McCormick 2006: 4–5)

In relation to the UN General Assembly, the response to the developments of 1976 took the form of sponsoring a world conference entirely devoted to apartheid South Africa.

In August of 1977, South Africa was specifically "singled out" at the meetings of the UN-sponsored World Conference for Action Against Apartheid, which met in Lagos, Nigeria, over the period of 22–26 August. As stated in the first volume of the report from this conference:

> Throughout the years, the United Nations, within the letter and spirit of the Charter, attempted to deal with the situation [of South Africa]

> in many ways. In the early stages it had been hoped that wise counsel, coupled with a sense of justice and respect for human rights and human dignity, would prevail in South Africa. To that end, appeals were directed to the South African Government to put an end to its practice of racial discrimination and to accord all of its citizens equal rights and opportunities. South Africa's refusal to respond to those appeals led to demands by many States for political and diplomatic pressures. Subsequently with the continued entrenchment of apartheid, demands for international action included the application of economic sanction and an arms embargo. (United Nations Archives S-1003–0006-06 *Report* p. 3)

Following the conference against apartheid, the chair of the Anti-Apartheid Committee stated to the 1978 World Conference to Combat Racism and Racial Discrimination that the United Nations

> recognized that utmost priority should be given to the eradication of apartheid, the institutionalized system of racist domination and exploitation of millions of people, which constitutes a grave threat to international peace and security. It [the UN] has also proclaimed the year beginning 21 March 1978 as the International anti-Apartheid Year. (United Nations Archives, S-1003–0014-02, 1978, *Press Release* p. 1)

The 1978 World Conference to Combat Racism and Racial Discrimination featured a strong and explicit focus on South Africa. Moreover, building on the 1978 conference, the 1983 conference agreed that "the apartheid system in South Africa represented 'the most extreme form of institutionalized racism in the world' and a 'crime against humanity'" (United Nations Archives, S-1028-0007-02, 1983, *Press Release*, p. 2). It was, however, noted that the "Conference divided sharply on provisions in its Declaration and Programme of Action relating to South Africa and Israel" (United Nations Archives, S-1028-0007-02, 1983, *Press Release*, p. 1). In particular, there were divisions over the legitimacy of armed struggle in the context of liberation in South Africa and over whether to characterize the practices of Israel toward Palestinians as racist. For example, the Canadian delegation insisted that the Middle East conflict represented "a political situation rather than a racial one" (United Nations Archives, S-1028-0007-02, 1983, *Press Release*, p. 10–11). It was nonetheless the case that the conference was able to support a request that the Security Council "urgently consider the imposition of mandatory sanctions against the South African Government, including the prohibition of technological assistance or the provision of arms supplies to South Africa" (United Nations Archives, S-1028-0007-02, 1983, *Press Release*, p. 1).

Reflecting the growing international sentiment, by 1989, then UN secretary general Javier Pèrez de Cuèllar insisted in remarks on March 21st, the Day for the Elimination of Racial Discrimination, that the UN had always stood against apartheid. In his words:

> The United Nations cannot tolerate apartheid. It is a legalized system of racial discrimination violating the most basic human rights in South Africa. It contravenes the letter and spirit of the United Nations Charter. This is why over the last forty years my predecessors and I have urged the Government of South Africa to dismantle it. (United Nations Archives, S-1055-0009-0002, 1989, Statement, p. 1)

Notably, de Cuèllar also "paid tribute to the Special Committee Against Apartheid which has carried out its mandate successfully for more than twenty-five years" (United Nations Archives, 2-1055-0009-0002, 1989 S, Statement, p. 3).

Apartheid then and now: Israel/ Palestine and the politics of race

The global movement against apartheid in South Africa has directly impacted contemporary politics regarding Israel/Palestine. Arguably, the politics of race internationally have been qualitatively changed in light of the transformative movement against apartheid in South Africa. The South African case serves as a reminder that it is the combined impact of state and social actors that reciprocally shapes major transitions, such as the move from apartheid to postapartheid. Notably, Israel and apartheid South Africa retained close ties, and there was significant affinity among the regimes (White 2009: 8–11). In relation to the 2001 WCAR, it is important to note that the Durban Declaration and Programme of Action (DDPA) was the final statement of the WCAR conference agreed upon by consensus of the states present, including Canada and other Western countries. The DDPA notes, in the document's preamble, the particular role of the event's host state, South Africa, under a postapartheid elected government. It is significant enough to quote at length:

> Having met in Durban, South Africa, from 31 August to 8 September 2001,
>
> Expressing deep appreciation to the Government of South Africa for hosting this World Conference,
>
> Drawing inspiration from the heroic struggle of the people of South Africa against the institutionalized system of apartheid, as well as for equality and justice under democracy, development, the rule of law and respect for human rights, recalling in this context the important contribution to that struggle of the international community and, in particular, the pivotal role of the people and Governments of Africa, and noting the important role that different actors of civil society, including non-governmental organizations, played in that struggle and in ongoing efforts to combat racism, racial discrimination, xenophobia and related intolerance …
>
> Fully aware that, despite efforts undertaken by the international community, Governments and local authorities, the scourge of racism, racial discrimination, xenophobia and related intolerance persists and continues to result in violations of human rights, suffering, disadvantage and violence, which must be combated by all available and appropriate means and as a matter of the highest priority, preferably in cooperation with affected communities …
>
> Joining together in a spirit of renewed political will and commitment to universal equality, justice and dignity, we salute the memory of all victims of racism, racial discrimination, xenophobia and related intolerance all over the world and solemnly adopt the Durban Declaration and Programme of Action. (UN 2001)

This preamble also indicates awareness of the impact of the UN's strategic focus on South African apartheid (Thorn 2009).

This awareness helps in understanding why the 2001 WCAR process was a site for attempting to advance claims on behalf of stateless peoples such as the Palestinians living under occupation and in the diaspora. It also helps to explain why Israel's defenders would attempt to challenge these claims, including by charging that Israel was being uniquely singled out. However, the case of Israel/Palestine was, in fact, one of many central global issues that found voice through the WCAR process. And further, the strategic focus for a period of time on a single state where there are notable violations of human rights and consistent state intransigence is not a new feature of UN discourse. There are significant lessons when international law and the role of the United Nations are taken up as part of movements for transformation. While the Israel/Palestine racial contract is deeply systemic and hegemonic, the BDS call to international civil society draws upon international law. The call asks that we educate and act to isolate Israel until it is compliant with such international law. This call is grounded in the experience of the South African movement and continues to find resonance. Indeed, it has inspired hope that such transformation, while difficult, is certainly possible. It is within this wider global and historical context that the chapters in the preceding discussion have advanced the notion of a specific Israel/Palestine racial contract, an approach that identifies the unique features of the region while continually placing these specificities in wider contexts and comparisons.

Race, racialization, and racism, we suggest, permeate the challenges of understanding the politics of Israel/Palestine. In Part One of this volume, "Social Sciences and the Israel/Palestine Racial Contract," three chapters framed the argument to follow. In Chapter 1, "The Idea of Israel and the Absence of Palestine: Limits and Possibilities for Scholarship in North America," we indicated the scope of the challenge of simply advancing a secular scholarly discourse that accurately captures the experiences of Palestinians, a people who are systemically absented. This is complicated not only by anti-Muslim racism and Orientalism but also by the hegemonic, or dominant, idea of Israel as an unproblematized state that is *sui generis* and cannot be compared because it is uniquely democratic and the only "Jewish state" in the Middle East. We further consider the politics of anti-Semitism, or anti-Jewish racism, in both its misplaced relationship to criticisms of Israel's policies and regarding the historic and lasting realities. In Chapter 2, "The Racial Contract and Israel/ Palestine," we introduced, expanded upon, and adapted Charles Mills' concept of the "racial contract" to explain these persistent absences and the mythologized realities associated with both the region and hegemonic Western liberal political thought. We drew on the contributions of Antonio Gramsci to consider how some ideas become hegemonic in the interests of global imperialism and colonialism and considered the Canadian and Israeli states in particular. In Chapter 3, we concluded Part One with a close look at Israel/Palestine in the context of the post-9/11 era. Here, we highlighted issues of surveillance and considered how a process of "social sorting" has led to a certain "Palestinianization" that has occurred in liberal democracies in this period. As such, this approach challenges the claimed exceptionalism of the Israel/Palestine racial contract.

Part Two of the volume, "Global Politics and the Israel/Palestine Racial Contract" focused on various issues related to the international arena in general, and the United Nations in particular. In Chapter 4, "The Paradox of the United Nations: Human Rights, Israel, and Palestine," we argued that the Jewish Holocaust and the Second World War, the *Nakba* and the UN Declaration of Human Rights need to be considered relationally and figure centrally in the construction of the Israel/Palestine racial contract. In fact, the idea of Israel and the absenting of Palestine are grounded in the contradictory inclusions and exclusions that shaped the modern United Nations. In Chapter 5, "Indigenous Palestine: Contested Origin Stories and the UN Declaration for the Rights of Indigenous Peoples," our argument broadened to consider the complex claims associated with Israel/Palestine. We suggested that dominant Zionist claims to Indigeneity in the region challenge the lived realities of Indigeneity associated with Palestine and Palestinian experiences. We examined these contested claims in relation to the United Nations and recent debates regarding Indigenous rights. We also attempted to unpack the Jewish diasporic experience and considered alternative framings of Jewish and Palestinian identity, attending to contributions from revisionist historians and cultural studies scholars. In Chapter 6, we concluded Part Two with a focus on "Global Civil Society and a 'United Nations from Below': The BDS Movement." Here, the emergence, controversies, and growing resonance of the BDS movement internationally were considered in the context of the Israel/Palestine racial contract. We addressed the pivotal turning point of Israel's 2008–9 war on Gaza and the significance of the demands of the movement in challenging hegemonic ideas and absences.

Part Three of the volume turned to specific arenas of contestation, with a focus on "The Israel/Palestine Racial Contract: Rebranding and Resistance." Chapter 7, "Israel's Rebranding Campaign and the Politics of Gender," attended to the complex intersection of the racial contract with gender, citizenship, and power in the context of Israel/Palestine. We considered the ideological construction of Israel's specific "branding" and "rebranding," both domestically and internationally, and associated images of gender inclusion, femininity, and masculinity in relation to national discourses and modes of resistance. This was followed by a close look at "Environmental Justice and the Politics of Contested Territory: Land, Water, and Air in Israel/Palestine" in Chapter 8. Here, we considered the politics of environmental racism, counterpoising the harsh reality of the experience of Palestinians to the foundational myth of empty land where Zionist settlement was presumed to "make the desert bloom." The rebranding theme was continued with a consideration of "greenwashing" and its implications. Part Three concluded with Chapter 9, "Israel/Palestine and the Apartheid Analysis: Toward a One-State Solution?" Bringing the narrative back to the scholarly disciplinary approach forwarded in comparative political science, we considered the meaning of apartheid broadly. We argued that there are grounds for the applicability of the apartheid analysis, understood not as a direct analogy with the South African experience but rather in the context of wider policy and literature reviews.

We have concluded the volume with a more in-depth review of global responses to the Israel/Palestine racial contract, considering the impact of BDS movements from South Africa to Palestine. Our hope is that this conversation will advance further effective analyses and inspire ongoing resistance to the Israel/Palestine racial contract. With this aim in mind, we move to an epilogue gesturing to a politics of solidarity across difference.

Notes

1 Ryan Roderick Beiler, "I Was 'Part of a Terror Organization,' Says Israel Pilot Turned Activist," *Electronic Intifada*, February 10, 2015, https://electronicintifada.net/content/i-was-part-terror-organization-says-israeli-pilot-turned-activist/14253; Miko Peled, "Why Israelis Must Disrupt the Occupation," *Electronic Intifada*, June 12, 2017, https://electronicintifada.net/content/why-israelis-must-disrupt-occupation/20731.

2 Anne Bayefsky, "The Obama Administration Sacrifices Israel," *Forbes*, February 22, 2009, http://www.forbes.com/2009/02/22/obama-israel-holocaust-durban-opinions-contributors_united_nations.html (see also Bayefsky 2002).

3 Pranay Gupte, "For Bayefsky, Keeping Eye on U.N. is a Crucial Mission," *New York Sun*, November 17, 2005, http://www.nysun.com/national/for-bayefsky-keeping-eye-on-un-is-a-crucial/23167/.

4 Quoted in Ibid.

EPILOGUE: TOWARD A POLITICS OF SOLIDARITY

We know too well our freedom is incomplete without the freedom of the Palestinians.

—NELSON MANDELA[1]

In the many years that we have worked together on Israel/Palestine from an anti-racist feminist perspective, we have experienced a roller coaster of emotions concerning the prospects for a more egalitarian future both within and outside of this region of conflict. We have been continually reminded both of the hope inspired by the BDS movement as an effective, mass nonviolent movement for change and of the tremendous forces of repression that try to dislodge its successes and shut down debate. These ups and downs are related. We have been inspired by new voices in civil society that consciously aim to counter the Israel/Palestine racial contract by giving space to the understandings and experiences of Palestinians, including Jewish activists in North America and in Israel who speak out against the oppression of Palestinians. In the 2018 US Congressional election, two newly elected representatives who publicly support BDS—Ilhan Omar, Minnesota Democrat, and Rashida Tlaib, Michigan Democrat—took seats. This represented a first for elected officials in the House of Representatives.

Yet, as the BDS movement grows and becomes more threatening to what we term the hegemonic Israel/Palestine racial contract, efforts to punish and silence supporters also advance. The latter has included proposed legislation to criminalize BDS advocacy. Such legislation has been successfully passed in Canada, under Liberal Party leadership,[2] and in the United States under Obama's administration,[3] while further

US legislation remains under debate (Roskam 2017).[4] There has also been escalated repression in Israel, with legislation aimed at stopping BDS proponents from entering the country.[5] The Israel/Palestine racial contract is tenacious and depends heavily on constraining academic freedom, free speech, and student and civil society activism in order to maintain the dominant idea of Israel and the absence of Palestine and Palestinians, even as Palestinians remain one of the largest groups of refugees in the world.

A notable example of such constraint occurred in 2018, when Angela Davis was selected to be the winner of the Fred Shuttlesworth Human Rights Award by the Birmingham Civil Rights Institute (BCRI) in Alabama, the United States. Then, in early January 2019, the institute suddenly voted to withdraw the award and cancel the public event. The institute withdrew the award after receiving a letter from the Birmingham Holocaust Education Center, which noted Davis' support for the BDS movement. But a mass show of support for Davis, including a letter from Jewish Voice for Peace, saw this reprisal resisted, and the Birmingham City Council unanimously approved a resolution recognizing the life work and contributions of Angela Davis (JVP 2019).[6] Then, in another sudden return to its initial decision, the Birmingham Civil Rights Institute issued a statement on January 25, 2019, indicating that it would reoffer Davis the award "in keeping with its commitment to learning from its mistakes and in order to stay true to the BCRI's founding mission."[7] US Black author and civil rights advocate Michelle Alexander—citing the moment when the award was rescinded from Angela Davis, as well as the stance of Martin Luther King on Vietnam—summarized the challenging climate, noting that "those who speak publicly in support of the liberation of the Palestinian people still risk condemnation and backlash" and pledged to add her voice in solidarity with Palestinian rights.[8] It is notable that Alexander's intervention was featured in the Sunday edition of *The New York Times* in advance of the 2019 US federal holiday, Martin Luther King Jr. Day.

The emotional roller coaster we experience similarly applies to the international arena. We have been cognizant of the value and potential of the United Nations in providing an arena for expanding our knowledge about racialized discrimination directed against various collectivities, while also dismayed and frustrated by the limits of UN rhetoric. We are well versed in how the efforts to counter the racism of civil society, states, and even the most committed of UN actors are easily derailed or marginalized when it comes to issues of international law and human rights regarding Israel/Palestine. The World Conference Against Racism process between 2001 and 2011 is a notable case in point.

While there are clearly some distinct features to the Israel/Palestine racial contract, the roller coaster we describe is not unique. It is really about ongoing struggles and the dynamism of power as captured in Gramsci's concept of hegemony, including contestation and resistance. Despite the promise of the Universal Declaration of Human Rights, and the advances portended in the UN refugee convention, which emerged out of the tragedy of the Second World War and swelling numbers of European refugees, by the end of 2015, the number of refugees and displaced persons worldwide had surpassed that produced at the end of the Second World War (UNHCR 2016). Many of today's refugees come from Africa and also the Middle East, with the ongoing conflicts in Iraq, Afghanistan, and Syria propelling people to seek safety elsewhere. Supportive responses to refugees have mainly come from countries of the global South; in fact, countries of the global North have been increasingly reluctant to open their doors since the end of the Cold War. US President Trump's campaign to build a wall across the US/Mexico border is fueled by racist sentiment against refugees and the UK campaign to leave the European Union, dubbed "Brexit," is similarly driven by anti-immigrant popular sentiment.[9] Former UN Secretary General Ban Ki Moon has observed that current refugee displacement levels—the largest the world has ever seen—are not merely just about numbers but that this "is also a crisis of solidarity" (UNHCR 2016: 5).

The horrific image of a lifeless three-year-old Syrian boy, Aylan Kurdi, who drowned trying to reach the shores of the Greek island of Kos with his family in September 2015, resonated with many, drawing international attention to the inadequacy of the responses of global North states.[10] The boy's Canadian aunt, Tima Kurdi, spoke of failed attempts to bring family members to Canada. Her voice helped to expose the tragic failure to support refugees of the incumbent Conservative government of then Prime Minister Stephen Harper and to forward refugee protection into a key election issue during the 2015 campaign.[11] In winning the election of 2015, the Liberal government of Justin Trudeau was compelled to pledge a more responsive approach to Syrian refugees. By the start of 2017, Canada had resettled more than 40,000 Syrian refugees through a combination of government and private sponsorships (Canada, Citizenship and Immigration 2017).

In light of the solidarity crisis with respect to refugees, the Trudeau government's response to refugees has been significant, as was the response of Germany under Chancellor Angela Merkel. But Canada's, like Germany's, responses are still limited relative to the ongoing needs of refugees globally. It should also be noted that Canada has done more historically than in the present. For example, in 1979–80 alone, some 60,000 Indo-Chinese refugees were welcomed into Canada. And Canada's official commitment to multiculturalism has long coincided with systemic racism and ongoing forms of colonialism, particularly regarding Indigenous peoples (Bakan 2016). Canada is also only one state in North America and is heavily affected by the more populous United States under the Republican presidency of Donald Trump. The opening act of this administration following the presidential inauguration in January 2017 was to institute a travel ban that included blocking Syrian refugees, as well as the travel and immigration of citizens from selected Muslim majority countries in general.[12]

More broadly, the turn to "post-truth" politics and forms of authoritarian governance signaled in the United States and elsewhere brings new potential threats to immigrants, refugees, and racialized Black and Indigenous peoples generally, as well as growing anti-Jewish racism. Here, we can recall the targeting of immigrants following the 2016 Brexit vote in the UK;[13] the shooting of Muslims in a mosque in Quebec City in Canada in 2017;[14] the 2017 overt outpouring of anti-Black, anti-Semitic (anti-Jewish), and anti-Muslim racism by white supremacists in Charlottesville, Virginia;[15] and the 2018 shooting of Jews in a synagogue in Pittsburgh in the United States.[16] These are but a few reminders that the politics of race is central to how states and civil societies work, and that challenging hegemonic racism globally demands solidarity.

Our focus on the politics of race in Israel/Palestine is a response to a particularly notable lacuna in the scholarly literature and in popular understanding, which has led to a dominant, or hegemonic, absenting of discussions of race, racism, and racialization in Israel/Palestine. We suggest that identifying and naming the structures and processes that allow for a politics of race in this conflict zone, as elsewhere in the world, is important and potentially productive. This can better enable a politics of anti-racism, and in global terms, it can support a way of thinking about anti-racism that is consistent. Naming and framing Israel, Palestine, and the politics of race is a necessary element in challenging the Israel/

Palestine racial contract and thereby taking a consistent stand against racism in its multiple and divisive forms.

We have found that an anti-racist feminist response carries considerable promise in this work. Such a perspective advances understanding about interconnections and intersections, and new possibilities for solidarity. Cornel West has described Angela Y. Davis as "one of the few great long-distance intellectuals and freedom fighters in the world," noting her enduring focus over many decades on "the wretched of the Earth" (West 2016: vii). It is significant that Davis explicitly linked the 2014 protests following from the shooting of African American Michael Brown in Ferguson, the United States, by a white police officer, and the experiences of Palestinians in resisting racist colonial oppression and violence. Moreover, Davis emphasizes the value of an intersectional response to violence and oppression. As she puts it:

> Just as the struggle to end South African apartheid was embraced by people all over the world and was incorporated into many social justice agendas, solidarity with Palestine must likewise be taken up by organizations and movements involved in progressive causes all over the world. The tendency has been to consider Palestine a separate—and unfortunately too often marginal—issue. This is precisely the moment to encourage everyone who believes in equality and justice to join the call for a free Palestine. (2016: 10–11)

Further exemplifying the intersections, Davis notes the direct links in practices of repression and resistance. It was Palestinian activists who tweeted "advice for protesters in Ferguson, on how to deal with the tear gas" (Davis 2016: 42), as the canisters used against activists in Ferguson were produced by the same US company (Combined Systems Incorporated) as those used against the Palestinian activists (Davis 2016: 140). Davis further observes that the struggles for justice in Ferguson revealed a "political kinship" with justice struggles in Palestine, not least because the British multinational security services company G4S has—until divestments in Israel in December 2016[17]—played a key role, "from the Palestinian experience of incarceration and torture to racist technologies of separation and apartheid" (Davis 2016: 55–6). Further, G4S plays a role in "prison-like schools in the US and the wall along the US-Mexico border" (Davis 2016: 55–6). Based on all this, Davis concludes:

> I think it's important to insist on the intersectionality of movements. In the abolition movement, we've been trying to find ways to talk about Palestine so that people who are attracted to a campaign to dismantle prisons in the US will also think about the need to end the occupation in Palestine. It can't be an afterthought. It has to be part of the ongoing analysis. (2016: 21)

Clearly, the local and the global are intricately linked in the politics of race. In 2001, and again in 2009 and in 2011, the United Nations World Conference Against Racism fractured on issues relating to Israel and Palestine. As we have demonstrated, however, the issues that animated a global response to racism remain and issues related to Israel/Palestine need to be addressed. It is our hope that this volume can contribute to more comprehensive emerging global conversations, commitments, and actions that will bring this small part of the planet into wider contexts in challenging racism, imperialism, colonialism, and apartheid.

Such a response needs to challenge the hegemonic power structure and the systematic nature of racism. This demands going beyond liberal multiculturalism and the global racial contract. It means seeking a civil society movement that crosses difference within and beyond borders. The Israel/Palestine racial contract is, as we have argued, in many ways the outgrowth of the inability of Western states to deeply and seriously address difference—including in the violence directed against Jewish populations in Europe and North America historically. The refusal of Western countries to welcome Jewish refugees during and after the Second World War is a case in point. While Israel was built on the ashes of the profound failure of states to address Jewish oppression, it was also and simultaneously built upon the dispossession of another people, Palestinians, enforcing rather than eliminating the relationship of racism and state power.

In light of Israel's founding, Judith Butler presents a cogent critique of the Zionist project from the standpoint of Jewish philosophical traditions, also incorporating the works of such Palestinian writers as Edward Said and Mahmoud Darwish. As Butler puts it:

> Rather than a bid for an easy multiculturalism, my proposal is that the vast and violent hegemonic structure of political Zionism must cede its hold on those lands and populations and that what must take its place is a new polity that would presuppose the end to settler colonialism

> and that would imply complex and antagonistic modes of living together, an amelioration of the wretched forms of binationalism that already exist. (2014: 4)

Butler's proposal resonates with other settler-colonial contexts (Coulthard 2014). Her proposal can rest only on forms of ethical solidarity. In the case of Israel and Palestine, such solidarity may only emerge from a new and more robust politics of anti-racism that is fully attuned to the politics of race. As anti-racist feminists committed to such an emergent solidarity, we have strived in this volume, and in our own collaboration, to imagine that another world is possible—a world where the Israel/Palestine racial contract and all forms of hegemonic racism are things of the past.

Notes

1 Nelson Mandela, "Address by President Nelson Mandela at the International Day of Solidarity with the Palestinian People," *South African History Online, Pretoria*, December 4, 1997, http://www.sahistory.org.za/archive/address-president-nelson-mandela-international-day-solidarity-palestinian-people-pretoria-4-.

2 Patrick Martin, "Parliament Votes to Reject Israel Boycott Campaign," *The Globe and Mail*, February 23, 2016, https://www.theglobeandmail.com/news/world/parliament-votes-to-reject-campaign-to-boycott-israel/article28863810/.

3 Rebecca Shimoni Stoil, "Obama Signs Anti-BDS Bill into Law," *The Times of Israel*, June 30, 2015, https://www.timesofisrael.com/obama-signs-anti-bds-bill-into-law/.

4 Editorial Board, "Curbing Speech in the Name of Helping Israel," *The New York Times*, December 18, 2018, https://www.nytimes.com/2018/12/18/opinion/editorials/israel-bds.html.

5 Lizzie Dearden, "Israel Parliament Approves Travel Ban for Foreign Supporters of BDS Movement," *Independent*, March 7, 2017, http://www.independent.co.uk/news/world/middle-east/israel-travel-ban-boycott-supporters-bds-movement-banned-knesset-vote-settlements-visas-residency-a7616701.html.

6 Amy Goodman, "Exclusive: Angela Davis Speaks out on Palestine, BDS and More After Civil Rights Award Is Revoked," *Democracy Now*, January 11, 2019, https://www.democracynow.org/2019/1/11/exclusive_angela_davis_speaks_out_on; Howard Koblowitz, "Birmingham City

Council Passes Resolution 'Recognizing Life Work' of Angela Davis," *Birmingham Real-Time News*, January 8, 2019, https://www.al.com/news/birmingham/2019/01/birmingham-city-council-passes-resolution-recognizing-life-work-of-angela-davis.html.

7 Kimberley Richards, "Angela Davis Reoffered Award by Birmingham Civil Rights Institute," *HuffPost US*, January 25, 2019, https://www.huffingtonpost.ca/entry/angela-davis-birmingham-civil-rights-award_us_5c4b50fbe4b0287e5b8a59f8?ec_carp=1826608858893581029.

8 Michelle Alexander, "Time to Break the Silence on Palestine," *The New York Times*, January 19, 2019, https://www.nytimes.com/2019/01/19/opinion/sunday/martin-luther-king-palestine-israel.html.

9 Julio Ricardo Varela, "Trump's Border Wall Was Never Just About Security. It's Meant to Remind All Latinos We're Unwelcome," *NBCNEWS Think*, December 28, 2018, https://www.nbcnews.com/think/opinion/trump-s-border-wall-was-never-just-about-security-it-ncna952011; Martin Shaw, "Vote Leave Relied on Racism. Brexit: The Uncivil War Disguised the Ugly Truth," *The Guardian, International Edition*, January 8, 2019, https://www.theguardian.com/commentisfree/2019/jan/08/vote-leave-racism-brexit-uncivil-war-channel-4.

10 Peter Edwards and Robin Levinson King, "'I Want to Tell the Rest of the World, at This Point, to Step in and Help the Refugees,' Says Aunt of Drowned Syrian Boys," *TheStar*.com, September 3, 2015, https://www.thestar.com/news/canada/2015/09/03/father-of-aylan-kurdi-describes-how-his-family-drowned.html.

11 Ibid.

12 Steve Almasy and Darran Simon, "A Timeline of President Trump's Travel Bans," *CNN.com*, March 30, 2017, http://www.cnn.com/2017/02/10/us/trump-travel-ban-timeline/index.html.

13 Fiyaz Mughal, "A UK Mosque Is Targeted Once a Week—We Need to Deal with Anti-Muslim Hatred," *New Statesman*, July 14, 2017, http://www.newstatesman.com/politics/uk/2017/07/uk-mosque-targeted-once-week-we-need-deal-anti-muslim-hatred.

14 Rachel Lau, Jesse Ferreras and Rebecca Joseph, "Quebec City Terrorist Attack on Mosque Kills 6, Injures 8," *Globalnews.ca*, January 29, 2017, http://globalnews.ca/news/3213042/shooting-quebec-city-centre-culturel-islamique-mosque/.

15 Meg Wagner, "'Blood and Soil': Protesters Chant Nazi Slogan in Charlottesville," *CNN.com*, August 12, 2017, http://www.cnn.com/2017/08/12/us/charlottesville-unite-the-right-rally/index.html; Jason Wilson, "Charlottesville: Far-Right Crowd with Torches Encircle Counter-Protest Group," *The Guardian*, August 12, 2017, https://www.theguardian.com/

world/2017/aug/12/charlottesville-far-right-crowd-with-torches-encircles-counter-protest-group.

16 Benjamin Wallace-Wells, "The Pittsburgh Synagogue Shooting and the Escalating Crisis of Hate-Fuelled Violence in the Trump-Era," *The New Yorker*, October 27, 2018, https://www.newyorker.com/news/current/the-pittsburgh-synagogue-shooting-and-the-escalating-crisis-of-hate-fuelled-violence-in-the-trump-era.

17 *Haaretz* (2016). "G4S Sells Israel Operation for $110 Million, Denies BDS Pressure" (2 December). Available at http://www.haaretz.com/israel-news/business/1.756666.

REFERENCES

Abdo, Nahla. (2002). "Eurocentrism, Orientalism and Essentialism: Some Reflections on September 11 and Beyond." In Susan Hawthorne and Bronwyn Winter (eds.), *September 11, 2001: Feminist Perspectives*, pp. 372–92. North Melbourne: Spinifex Press.

Abdo, Nahla. (2008). "Palestinian *Munadelat*: Between Western Representation and Lived Reality." In Ronit Lentin (ed.), *Thinking Palestine*, pp. 173–88. London: Zed Books.

Abdo, Nahla. (2011). *Women in Israel: Race, Gender and Citizenship*. London and New York: Zed Books.

Abdulhadi, Rabab. (1998). "The Palestinian Women's Autonomous Movement: Emergence, Dynamics and Challenges." *Gender and Society* 12, 6 (December): 649–73.

Abele, Francis, and Daiva Stasiulis. (1989). "Canada as a 'White Settler Colony': What About Natives and Immigrants?" In Wallace Clement and Glen Williams (eds.), *New Canadian Political Economy*, pp. 240–77. Montreal: McGill-Queen's University Press.

Abella, Irving, and Harold Troper. (2012 [1983]). *None Is Too Many: Canada and the Jews of Europe, 1933–1948*. Toronto: Lester and Orpen Dennys Ltd.

Abowd, Thomas. (2007). "National Boundaries, Colonized Spaces: The Gendered Politics of Residential Life in Contemporary Jerusalem." *Anthropological Quarterly* 80, 4 (Fall): 997–1034.

Abu-Laban, Sharon McIrvin. (1975). "Stereotypes of Middle East Peoples: An Analysis of Church School Curricula." In Baha Abu-Laban and Faith T. Zeadey (eds.), *Arabs in America: Myths and Realities*, pp. 149–69. Wilmette, IL: Medina University Press.

Abu-Laban, Yasmeen. (1998). "Keeping 'em Out: Gender, Race and Class Biases in Canadian Immigration Policy." In Joan Anderson, Avigail Eisenberg, Sherrill Grace, and Veronica Strong-Boag (eds.), *Painting the Maple: Essays on Race, Gender and the Construction of Canada*, pp. 69–82. Vancouver: University of British Columbia Press.

Abu-Laban, Yasmeen. (2000). "Reconstructing an Inclusive Citizenship for a New Millennium." *International Politics* 37, 4 (December): 509–26.

Abu-Laban, Yasmeen. (2001). "Humanizing the Oriental: Edward Said and Western Scholarly Discourse." In Naseer Aruri and Muhammad A. Shuraydi (eds.), *Revising Culture, Reinventing Peace: The Influence of Edward Said*, pp. 74–85. New York and Northampton: Interlink Publishing.

Abu-Laban, Yasmeen. (2004). "The New North America and the Segmentation of Canadian Citizenship." *International Journal of Canadian Studies* 29, 1: 17–40.

Abu-Laban, Yasmeen. (2005). "Regionalism, Migration and (Fortress) North America." *Review of Constitutional Studies* 10, 1 and 2: 135–62.

Abu-Laban, Yasmeen. (2007). "Political Science, Race, Ethnicity and Public Policy." In Michael Orsini and Miriam Smith (eds.), *Critical Public Policy Studies*, pp. 136–57. Vancouver: University of British Columbia Press.

Abu-Laban, Yasmeen., ed. (2008a). *Gendering the Nation-State: Canadian and Comparative Perspectives*. Vancouver: University of British Columbia Press.

Abu-Laban, Yasmeen. (2008b). "Introduction: Gendering the Nation-State: An Introduction." In Yasmeen Abu-Laban (ed.), *Gendering the Nation-State: Canadian and Comparative Perspectives*, pp. 1–18. Vancouver: University of British Columbia Press.

Abu-Laban, Yasmeen. (2014). "The Politics of History Under Harper." *Labour/Le Travail* 73 (Spring): 215–17.

Abu-Laban, Yasmeen. (2015). "Gendering Surveillance Studies: The Empirical and Normative Promise of Feminist Methodology." *Surveillance and Society* 13, 1: 44–56.

Abu-Laban, Yasmeen, and Abigail B. Bakan. (2008). "The Racial Contract: Israel/Palestine and Canada." *Social Identities* 14, 5 (September): 637–60.

Abu-Laban, Yasmeen and Abigail B. Bakan (2010). "The 'Israelization' of Social Sorting and the 'Palestinianization' of the Racial Contract: Reframing Israel/Palestine and the War on Terror." In Elia Zureik, David Lyon, and Yasmeen Abu-Laban (eds.), *Surveillance and Control in Israel/Palestine*, pp. 276–94. London: Routledge.

Abu-Laban, Yasmeen and Abigail B. Bakan (2012a). "After 9/11: Canada, the Israel/Palestine Conflict and the Surveillance of Public Discourse." *Canadian Journal of Law and Society* 27, 3: 319–40.

Abu-Laban, Yasmeen and Abigail B. Bakan (2012b). "Contested Origin Stories and the Case of Israel/Palestine: 'Dialogue' in the Context of Unequal Power." In Mojtaba Mahdavi and W. Andy Knight (eds.), *Towards the Dignity of Difference?: Neither "End of History" nor "Clash of Civilizations,"* pp. 400–27. London: Ashgate.

Abu-Laban, Yasmeen, and Christina Gabriel. (2002). *Selling Diversity: Immigration, Multiculturalism, Employment Equity and Globalization*. Canada: Broadview Press.

Abu-Laban, Yasmeen, and Claude Couture. (2010). "Multiple Minorities and Deceptive Dichotomies: The Theoretical and Political Implications of the Struggle for a Public French Education System in Alberta." *Canadian Journal of Political Science* 43, 2: 433–56.

Abu-Laban, Yasmeen, and Judith Garber. (2005). "The Construction of the Geography of Immigration as a Policy Problem: The United States and Canada Compared," *Urban Affairs Review* 40, 4 (March): 520–61.

Abu-Laban, Yasmeen, Radha Jhappan, and François Rocher, eds. (2008). *Politics in North America: Re-Defining Continental Relations*. Peterborough: Broadview Press and University of Toronto Press.

Abu-Laban, Yasmeen, and Victoria Lamont. (1997). "Crossing Borders: Interdisciplinarity, Immigration and the Melting Pot in the American Cultural Imaginary." *Canadian Review of American Studies* 27, 2 (September–October): 23–43.

Abu-Laban, Yasmeen, and Nisha Nath. (2007). "From Deportation to Apology: Maher Arar and the Canadian State." *Canadian Ethnic Studies* 39, 3: 71–98.

Abu-Lughod, Ibrahim. (1975). "Comment: Ibrahim Abu-Lughod." *Christianity and Crisis*: 311–14.

Abu-Lughod, Ibrahim, and Baha Abu-Laban. (1974a). "Foreword." In Ibrahim Abu-Lughod and Baha Abu-Laban (eds.), *Settler Regimes in Africa and the Arab World: The Illusion of Endurance*, pp. vii–x. Wilmette: Medina University Press International.

Abu-Lughod, Ibrahim, and Baha Abu-Laban. (1974b). *Settler Regimes in Africa and the Arab World: The Illusion of Endurance*. Wilmette: Medina University Press International.

Abu-Lughod, Lila, and Ahmad H. Sa'di. (2007a). "Introduction: The Claims of Memory." In Lila Abu-Lughod and Ahmad H. Sa'di (eds.), *Nakba: Palestine, 1948, and the Claims of Memory*, pp. 1–24. New York: Columbia University Press.

Abu-Lughod, Lila, and Ahmad H. Sa'di, eds. (2007b). *Nakba: Palestine, 1948 and the Claims of Memory*. New York: Columbia University Press.

Abunimah, Ali. (2006 [2005]). *One Country: A Bold Proposal to End the Israeli-Palestinian Impasse*. New York: Metropolitan Books.

Abunimah, Ali. (2010). "Quartet Ex Envoy's Investment Helps Israel Greenwash Settlements." *Electronic Intifada* (6 May). Available at http://electronicintifada.net/content/quartet-ex-envoys-investment-helps-israel-greenwash-settlements/8805 (accessed May 11, 2011).

Abunimah, Ali. (2011a). "After Witnessing Palestine's Apartheid, Indigenous and Women of Color Feminists Endorse BDS." *The Electronic Intifada* (12 July). Available at https://electronicintifada.net/blogs/ali-abunimah/after-witnessing-palestines-apartheid-Indigenous-and-women-color-feminists (accessed May 4, 2019).

Abunimah, Ali. (2011b). "Egypt's Uprising and Its Implications for Palestine." *Electronic Intifada* (29 January). Available at http://electronicintifada.net/v2/article11762.shtml (accessed March 16, 2017).

Abunimah, Ali. (2014). *The Battle for Justice in Palestine*. Chicago: Haymarket Books.

Abunimah, Ali. (2017). "BDS Movement is Part of Global Anti-Racist Struggle." *Electronic Intifada* (9 March). Available at https://electronicintifada.net/blogs/ali-abunimah/israel-boycott-part-global-anti-racist-struggle (accessed March 16, 2017).

Abu-Saad, Ismael. (2004). "Introduction: Special Focus on Racism in Israeli Society." *Social Identities* 10, 1: 7–8.

Achcar, Gilbert. (2009). *The Arabs and the Holocaust: The Arab-Israeli War of Narratives*. Translated by G. M. Goshgarian. New York: Metropolitan Books.

Adam, Heribert, and Kogila Moodley. (2005). *Seeking Mandela: Peacemaking Between Israelis and Palestinians*. Philadelphia: Temple University Press.

Adams, James. (1984). *The Unnatural Alliance*. London: Quartet Books.

Adams, Michael. (1977). "Israel's Treatment of the Arabs in the Occupied Territories." *Journal of Palestine Studies* 6, 2 (Winter): 19–40.

Adcock, Robert, and Mark Bevir. (2005). "The History of Political Science." *Political Studies Review* 3, 1 (February): 1–16.

Adkin, Laurie. (2002). "The Rise and Fall of New Social Movement Theory?" In Abigail B. Bakan and Eleanor MacDonald (eds.), *Critical Political Studies: Debates and Dialogues from the Left*, pp. 281–318. Montreal and Kingston: McGill-Queen's University Press.

African Canadian Legal Clinic et al. (2009). "Find Out the Real Reason Canada Skipped Out on UN Anti-Racism Gathering." *rabble.ca* (27 April). Available at http://www.rabble.ca/news/2009/04/find-out-real-reason-canada-skipped-out-un-anti-racism-gathering (accessed September 10, 2018).

Agamben, Giorgio. (2005). *State of Exception*. Translated by Kevin Attell. Chicago: University of Chicago Press.

Ageel, Ghada, ed. (2016). *Apartheid in Palestine: Hard Laws and Harder Experiences*. Edmonton: University of Alberta Press.

Ahmed, Sarah. (2004). *The Cultural Politics of Emotion*. New York and London: Routledge.

Akenson, Donald Harman. (1991). *God's Peoples: Covenant and Land in South Africa, Israel and Ulster*. Montreal and Kingston: McGill-Queen's University Press.

Al Barqouni, Loai, Sobhi Skaik, Nafiz R. Abu Shaban, and Nabil Barqouni. (2010). "Case Report: White Phosphorus Burn." *Lancet* 376 (3 July): 68.

Al Jazeera. (2013). "Stephen Hawking Backs Israeli Boycott" (8 May). Available at http://www.aljazeera.com/news/europe/2013/05/2013589372057682 (accessed July 17, 2017).

Alexander, Anne, and John Rose. (2001). "Middle East." In Emma Bircham and John Charlton (eds.), *Anti-Capitalism: A Guide to the Movement*, pp. 185–95. London: Bookmarks.

Alexander, Michelle. (2012). *The New Jim Crow: Mass Incarceration in the Age of Colorblindness*, rev. ed. New York: New Press.

Alexander, Michelle. (2019). "Time to Break the Silence on Palestine." *The New York Times* (19 January). Available at https://www.nytimes.com/2019/01/19/opinion/sunday/martin-luther-king-palestine-israel.html (accessed May 5, 2019).

Allen, Theodore W. (1994). *The Invention of the White Race: Racial Oppression and Social Control*. Vol. 1. London: Verso.

Allen, Theodore W. (1997). *The Invention of the White Race: The Origin of Racial Oppression in Anglo-America*. Vol. 2. London: Verso.

Almasy, Steve, and Darran Simon. (2017). "A Timeline of President Trump's Travel Bans." *CNN.com* (30 March). Available at http://www.cnn.com/2017/02/10/us/trump-travel-ban-timeline/index.html (accessed September 4, 2017).

Amazon.com. (2007). "An Interview with President Jimmy Carter" (18 January). Available at http://www.amazon.com/Palestine-Peace-Apartheid-Jimmy-Carter/dp/0743285034 (accessed May 8, 2009).

Aouragh, Miriyam. (2011). *Palestine Online: Transnationalism, the Internet and the Construction of Identity*. London: I.B. Tauris.

Arafat, Yasser. (1975). "Speech of Yasser Arafat." From the United Nations Official English Text and Compared with the Arabic text. *Journal of Palestine Studies* 4, 2 (Winter): 181–94.

Arar, Khalid, and Mohanned Mustafa. (2011). "Access to Higher Education for Palestinians in Israel." *Education, Business and Society: Contemporary Middle Eastern Issues* 4, 3: 207–28.

Arat-Koç, Sedef. (2014). "Rethinking Whiteness, 'Culturalism', and the Bourgeoisie in the Age of Neoliberalis." In Abigail B. Bakan and Enakshi Dua (eds.), *Theorizing Anti-Racism: Linkages in Marxism and Critical Race Theories*, pp. 311–39. Toronto: University of Toronto Press.

Arendt, Hannah. (2006 [1963]). *Eichmann in Jerusalem: A Report on the Banality of Evil*. Introduction by Amos Elon. New York: Penguin Books.

Arrighi, Giovanni, and John S. Saul. (1973). *Essays on the Political Economy of Africa*. New York: Monthly Review Press.

Aruri, Naseer H., ed. (1983). *Occupation: Israel over Palestine*. Belmont: Association of Arab American University Graduates.

Aruri, Naseer H., ed. (1989). *Occupation: Israel over Palestine*. 2nd ed. Belmont: Association of Arab American University Graduates.

Ashrawi, Mikha'il Hanan. (1988). "From the Diary of an Almost-Four-Year-Old." In Salma Khadra Jayyusi (ed.), *An Anthology of Modern Palestinian Literature*, pp. 340–42. New York: Columbia University Press.

Assembly of First Nations (AFN) & Canadian Jewish Congress (CJC). (2006). "Canadian Jewish Congress, Assembly of First Nations Travel to Israel for Educational Mission" (17 February). Available at http://www.afn.ca/article.asp?id=2276 (accessed May 19, 2010).

Avnery, Uri. (2003). "The Prisoner of Ramallah." *Counterpunch* (5 August): 1–13.

Awad, Monica. 2011. *UNICEF Helps Make Safe, Reliable Water Possible in the oPt Marking World Water Day 2011*. UNICEF (22 March). Available at https://www.un.org/unispal/document/unicef-helps-make-safe-reliable-water-possible-in-the-opt-unicef-article/ (accessed May 5, 2019).

BADIL Resource Center. (2004). *Survey of Palestinian Refugees and Internally Displaced Persons*. Bethlehem: BADIL Resource Center for Palestinian Residency and Refugee Rights.

BADIL Resource Center. (2015). *Survey of Palestinian Refugees and Internally Displaced Persons, Vol. viii (2013–15)*. Bethlehem: BADIL Resource Center for Palestinian Residency and Refugee Rights. Available at http://www.badil.org/en/publication/survey-of-refugees.html.

Bakan, Abigail. (1987). "Plantation Slavery and the Capitalist Mode of Production: An Analysis of the Development of the Jamaican Labour Force." *Studies in Political Economy* 22 (Spring): 73–99.

Bakan, Abigail. (2000a). "After Seattle: The Politics of the World Trade Organisation." *International Socialism Journal* 2, 86 (Spring): 19–36.

Bakan, Abigail. (2000b). "From Seattle to Washington: The Making of a Movement." *International Socialism Journal* 2, 87 (Summer): 85–93.

Bakan, Abigail. (2005a). "Observers' Notes, West Bank, OT." March 2005.
Bakan, Abigail. (2005b). "Imperialism and Its Discontents." *Labour/Le Travail* 56 (Fall): 269–82.
Bakan, Abigail. (2008a). "Reconsidering the Underground Railroad: Slavery and Racialization in the Making of the Canadian State." *Socialist Studies* (Spring): 3–29.
Bakan, Abigail. (2008b). "Marxism and Anti-Racism: Rethinking the Politics of Difference." *Rethinking Marxism* 20, 2 (April): 238–56.
Bakan, Abigail. (2012). "The Jewish Question in the 21st Century." Paper presented at the Socialism 2012 Annual Conference: Center for Economic Research and Social Change, Chicago, 2 July.
Bakan, Abigail. (2014a). "Race, Class and Colonialism: Reconsidering the 'Jewish Question.'" In Abigail B. Bakan and Enakshi Dua (eds.), *Theorizing Anti-Racism: Linkages in Marxism and Critical Race Theories*, pp. 252–79. Toronto: University of Toronto Press.
Bakan, Abigail. (2014b). "Permanent Patriots and Temporary Predators?: Post 9/11 Institutionalization of the Arab/Orientalized 'Other' in the United States and the Contributions of Arendt and Said." In Leah F. Vosko, Valerie Preston, and Robert Latham (eds.), *Liberating Temporariness?: Migration, Work, and Citizenship in an Age of Insecurity*, pp. 60–75. Montreal and Kingston: McGill-Queen's University Press.
Bakan, Abigail. (2016). "Multiculturalism and Its Contradictions: Education for Citizenship and Social Justice in Canada." In Andrew Peterson, Robert Hattam, Michalinos Zembylas, and James Arthur (eds.), *The Palgrave International Handbook of Education for Citizenship and Social Justice*, pp. 347–68. London: Palgrave Macmillan.
Bakan, Abigail, and Yasmeen Abu-Laban. (2009). "Palestinian Resistance and International Solidarity: The BDS Campaign." *Race and Class* 51, 1: 29–54.
Bakan, Abigail, and Yasmeen Abu-Laban. (2010). "Israel/Palestine, South Africa and the 'One-State Solution': The Case for an Apartheid Analysis." *Politikon: South African Journal of Political Studies* 37, 2–3 (December): 331–51.
Bakan, Abigail, and Yasmeen Abu-Laban. (2011). "The Idea of Israel and the Absence of Palestine: Conceptual Limits and Possibilities of 'Ethnic Studies' in North America." Paper presented to Settler Colonialism/Heteropatriarchy/ White Supremacy: A Major Conference, University of California (Riverside), Riverside, California, 10–12 March.
Bakan, Abigail, and Yasmeen Abu-Laban. (2015). "History, Reparations and the United Nations." Paper presented to American Studies Association Conference, Toronto, Ontario, Canada (11 October).
Bakan, Abigail, and Yasmeen Abu-Laban. (2016). "Canada, Israeli Apartheid and Freedom of Expression." In Ghada Ageel (ed.), *Apartheid in Palestine: Hard Laws and Harder Experiences*, pp. 163–80. Alberta: The University of Alberta Press.
Bakan, Abigail, and Yasmeen Abu-Laban. (2017). "Intersectionality and the United Nations World Conference Against Racism." *Atlantis: Critical Studies in Gender, Culture and Social Justice* 38, 1: 220–35.

Bakan, Abigail, and Enakshi Dua. (2014). *Theorizing Anti-Racism: Linkages in Marxism and Critical Race Theories*. Toronto: University of Toronto Press.

Bakan, Abigail, and Audrey Kobayashi. (2000). *Employment Equity Policy in Canada: An Interprovincial Comparison*. Ottawa: Status of Women Canada.

Bakan, Abigail, and Eleanor MacDonald, eds. (2002). *Critical Political Studies: Debates and Dialogues from the Left*. Montreal and Kingston: McGill-Queen's University Press.

Bakan, Abigail, and Daiva Stasiulis, eds. (1997). *Not One of the Family: Foreign Domestic Workers in Canada*. Toronto: University of Toronto Press.

Bankoff, Greg. (2003). "Regions of Risk: Western Discourses on Terrorism and the Significance of Islam." *Studies in Conflict and Terrorism* 26: 413–28.

Bannerji, Himani. (1993). *Returning the Gaze: Essays on Racism, Feminism and Politics*. Toronto: Sister Vision Press.

Bannerji, Himani. (1995). *Thinking Through: Essays on Feminism, Marxism and Anti-Racism*. Toronto: Women's Press.

Bannerji, Himani. (2000). *The Dark Side of Nation: Essays on Multiculturalism, Nationalism and Gender*. Toronto: Canadian Scholars' Press.

Barghouti, Omar. (2004). "Boycott as an Act of Moral Resistance: The Case for Boycotting Israel." *Counterpunch* (22 December). Available at https://www.indybay.org/newsitems/2004/12/25/17113381.php (accessed January 15, 2019).

Barghouti, Omar. (2008). "Countering the Critics: The Boycott and Palestinian Groups." *Counterpunch* (21 October). Available at http://www.counterpunch.org/barghouti10212008.html (accessed May 18, 2009). Link no longer working.

Barghouti, Omar. (2011). *Boycott Divestment Sanctions: The Global Struggle for Palestinian Rights*. Chicago: Haymarket Books.

Barkat, Amiran. (2009). "Dig Backs Biblical Account of Philistine City of Gat" (5 August). Available at http://www.haaretz.com/culture/arts-leisure/dig-backs-biblical-account-of-philistine-city-of-gat-1.166315 (accessed March 7, 2011).

Bar-Tal, Daniel, and Yona Teichman. (2005). *Stereotypes and Prejudice in Conflict: Representations of Arabs in Israeli Jewish Society*. Cambridge: Cambridge University Press.

Basic Law. (2018). "Basic Law: Israel—The Nation State of the Jewish People" (unofficial translation Dr. Susan Hattis Rolef). Available at http://knesset.gov.il/laws/special/eng/BasicLawNationState.pdf (accessed May 5, 2019).

Bates, Thomas R. (1975). "Gramsci and the Theory of Hegemony." *Journal of the History of Ideas* 36, 2 (April–June): 351–66.

Baum, Bruce. (2006). *The Rise and Fall of the Caucasian Race: A Political History of Racial Identity*. New York and London: New York University Press.

Bayefsky, Anne. (2002). "The UN World Conference Against Racism: A Racist Anti-Racism Conference." *Proceedings of the Annual Meeting (American Society for International Law)*, 96 (13–16 March): 65–74.

Bayefsky, Anne. (2009). "The Obama Administration Sacrifices Israel." *Forbes* (22 February). Available at http://www.forbes.com/2009/02/22/obama-israel-holocaust-durban-opinions-contributors_united_nations.html (accessed August 28, 2017).

BBC News. (2002). "Tutu Condemns Israeli 'Apartheid'" (29 April). Available at http://news.bbc.co.uk/2/hi/africa/1957644.stm.

BBC News. (2005). "Tube Bombs 'Almost Simultaneous'" (9 July). Available at http://news.bbc.co.uk/2/hi/uk_news/4666591.stm (accessed May 5, 2019).

BBC News. (2009). "Anti-Semitism World Summit Begins" (February 21, 2009). Available at http://news.bbc.co.uk/2/hi/uk_news/7892216.stm (accessed May 5, 2019).

Becker, Marc. (2009). "The World Social Forum Returns to Brazil." *Upside Down World*. Available at http://upsidedownworld.org/main/content/view/1701/63/ (accessed February 5, 2009).

Beier, J. Marshall. (2007). "Inter-National Affairs: Indigeneity, Globality and the Canadian State." *Canadian Foreign Policy* 13, 3: 121–31.

Beiler, Ryan Roderick. (2015). "I Was 'Part of a Terror Organization,' Says Israel Pilot Turned Activist." Electronic Intifada (10 February). Available at https://electronicintifada.net/content/i-was-part-terror-organization-says-israeli-pilot-turned-activist/14253 (accessed August 28, 2017).

Bein, Alexander, ed. (1939). *The Mozkin Book*. Jerusalem: World Zionist Publications.

Begley, Louis. (2009). *Why the Dreyfus Affair Matters*. New Haven: Yale University Press.

Ben-Ari, Adital Tarosh. (2001). "Experiences of 'Not Belonging' in Collectivist Communities: Narratives of Gays in Kibbutzes." *Journal of Homosexuality* 42, 2: 101–24.

Ben-Gurion, David. (1963). "Britain's Contribution to Arming the Haganah." Reprinted in Walid Khalidi (ed.), *From Haven to Conquest: Readings in Zionism and the Palestine Problem Until 1948*, pp. 371–74. Washington: Institute for Palestine Studies (1971, 1987).

Benn, Aluf, and Gideon Alon. (2003). "Netanyahu: Israel's Arabs Are the Real Demographic Threat" (18 December). Available at https://www.haaretz.com/1.4802179 (accessed December 12, 2018).

Benn, Aluf, David Landau, Barak Ravid, and Shmuel Rosner. (2007). "Olmert to Haaretz: Two-State Solution or Israel Done For" (11 November). Available at https://www.haaretz.com/1.4961269 (accessed May 5, 2019).

Bennis, Phyllis. (2009). "Israel: Rise of the Right." Washington: Foreign Policy in Focus (12 February). Available at http://www.fpif.org/fpiftxt/5866 (accessed May 18, 2009). Link no longer working.

Ben-Rafael, Eliezer. (2004). "Where Stands Israel: Response to Daryl J. Glaser." *Ethnic and Racial Studies* 27, 2 (March): 310–16.

Benston, Margaret. (2000). "The Political Economy of Women's Liberation." In Rosemary Hennessy and Chrys Ingraham (eds.), *Materialist Feminism: A Reader in Class, Difference, and Women's Lives*, pp. 18–23. London and Toronto: Mayfield Publishing Co. (Reprinted from Benston, Margaret.

(1969). "The Political Economy of Women's Liberation." *Monthly Review* 21, 7 (December)).

Bercuson, David J. (1985). *Canada and the Birth of Israel: A Study in Canadian Foreign Policy*. Toronto: University of Toronto Press.

Berenbaum, Michael, ed. (2008). *Not Your Father's Antisemitism: Hatred of the Jews in the 21st Century*. St. Paul: Paragon House.

Berndston, Erkki. (1987). "The Rise and Fall of American Political Science: Personalities, Quotations, Speculations." *International Political Science Review* 8, 1: 85–100.

Bhandar, Brenna. (2014). "Some Reflections on BDS and Feminist Political Solidarity." *feminsts@law* 4, 1: 1–14.

Bhattacharyya, Gargi. (2008). "Globalizing Racism and the Myths of the Other in the 'War on Terror.'" In Ronit Lentin (ed.), *Thinking Palestine*, pp. 46–61. London: Zed Books.

Bigo, Didier. (2005). "From Foreigners to 'Abnormal Aliens': How the Faces of the Enemy Have Changed Following September the 11th." In Elspeth Guild and Joanne van Selm (eds.), *International Migration and Security: Opportunities and Challenges*, pp. 64–81. London and New York: Routledge.

Bisharat, George. (2008). "Maximizing Rights: The One-State Solution to the Palestinian-Israeli Conflict." *Global Jurist* 8, 2: (Frontiers), Article 1: 1–36.

Black, Edwin (2011 [2008]). *IBM and the Holocaust: The Strategic Alliance Between Nazi Germany and America's Most Powerful Corporation*. Washington: Dialog Press.

Blackburn, Robin. (1997). *The Making of New World Slavery: From the Baroque to the Modern, 1492–1800*. London: Verso.

Blackburn, Robin. (1998). *The Overthrow of Colonial Slavery, 1776–1848*. London: Verso.

Blackwell, Maylie, and Nadine Naber. (2002). "Intersectionality in an Era of Globalization: The Implications of the UN World Conference Against Racism for Transnational Feminist Practices—A Conference Report." *Meridians: Feminism, Race, Transnationalism* 2, 2: 237–48.

Blair, Tony. (2006). "Speech to the Los Angeles World Affairs Council" (1 August). Available at http://news.bbc.co.uk/2/hi/uk_news/politics/5236896.stm (accessed May 5, 2019).

Blumen, Orna, and Sharon Halevi. (2009). "Staging Peace Through a Gendered Demonstration: Women in Black in Haifa, Israel." *Annals of the Association of American Geographers* 99, 5: 977–85.

Bolaria, B. Singh, and Peter S. Li. (1988). *Racial Oppression in Canada*. Toronto: Garamond Press.

Bond, Patrick. (2000). *Elite Transition: From Apartheid to Neoliberalism in South Africa*. London: Pluto Press.

Bond, Patrick. (2001). *Against Global Apartheid: South Africa Meets the World Bank, IMF and International Finance*. Cape Town: University of Cape Town Press.

Bond, Patrick. (2004). *South Africa and Global Apartheid: Continental and International Policies and Politics*. NAI Discussion Papers (No. 25). Uppsala: Nordic Africa Institute.

Bovard, James. (2003). *Terrorism and Tyranny: Trampling Freedom, Justice, and Peace to Rid the World of Evil*. New York: Palgrave Macmillan.

Bowman, Glenn. (2011). "A Place for Palestinians in the Altneuland: Herzl, Anti-Semitism, and the Jewish State." In Elia Zureik, David Lyon, and Yasmeen Abu-Laban (eds.), *Surveillance and Control in Israel/Palestine: Population, Territory, and Power*, pp. 65–79. London and New York: Routledge.

Boyarin, Daniel. (1994). *A Radical Jew: Paul and the Politics of Identity*. Berkeley: University of California Press.

Boyarin, Daniel. (1997). *Unheroic Conduct: The Rise of Heterosexuality and the Invention of the Jewish Man*. Berkeley: University of California Press.

Boyarin, Daniel. (2004). *Border Lines: The Partition of Judeo-Christianity*. Philadelphia: University of Pennsylvania Press.

Boyarin, Jonathan, and Daniel Boyarin. (2002). *Powers of Diaspora: Two Essays on the Relevance of Jewish Culture*. Minneapolis: University of Minnesota Press.

BoycottIsrael.info. (2017). *Boycott! Supporting the Palestinian BDS Call from Within*. Available at http://boycottisrael.info/ (accessed May 5, 2019).

Brezosky, Lynn. (2007). "Another Side to the Border Fence." *The Seattle Times* (25 May). The Associated Press. Available at https://www.seattletimes.com/nation-world/another-side-to-the-border-fence/ (accessed May 5, 2019).

Brinn, David. (2008). "Israel's Rebranding Efforts to Focus on Toronto." *Jerusalem Post* (16 March). Available at https://www.jpost.com/International/Israels-rebranding-efforts-to-focus-on-Toronto (accessed May 5, 2019).

Bristow, Peggy, Dionne Brand, Linda Carty, Afua P. Cooper, Sylvia Hamilton, and Adrienne Shadd. (1994). *We're Rooted Here and They Can't Pull Us Up: Essays in African Canadian Women's History*. Toronto: University of Toronto Press.

Britain. (1939). White Paper of 1939. *The Avalon Project of Yale Law School*. Available at http://avalon.law.yale.edu/20th_century/brwh1939.asp (accessed May 5, 2019).

Brits, J. P. (2005). "Tiptoeing Along the Apartheid Tightrope: The United States, South Africa, and the United Nations in 1952." *The International History Review* 27, 4: 745–79.

Brockman, Father Miguel d'Escoto. (2008). "UN General Assembly President Calls for BDS Against Israeli Apartheid State" (26 November). Available at https://bdsmovement.net/news/un-general-assembly-president-calls-bds-against-israeli-apartheid-state (accessed May 5, 2019).

Brodkin, Karen. (1998). *How the Jews Became White Folks: And What That Says About Race in America*. New Brunswick: Rutgers University Press.

Broeders, Dennis. (2007). "The New Digital Borders of Europe: EU Databases and the Surveillance of Irregular Migrants." *International Sociology* 22, 1: 71–92.

Bronner, Ethan, and Isabel Kershner. (2012). "Israelis Facing a Seismic Rift over Role of Women." *The New York Times* (14 January). Available at https://www.nytimes.com/2012/01/15/world/middleeast/israel-faces-crisis-over-role-of-ultra-orthodox-in-society.html?_r=1&hp (accessed May 5, 2019).

Brown, Wendy (2010). *Walled States, Waning Sovereignty*. Brooklyn, NY: Zone Books.

Brynen, Rex, and Roula El-Rifai. (2007). "Introduction: Refugee Repatriation, Development, and the Challenges of Palestinian State-Building." In Rex Brynen and Roula El-Rifai (eds.), *Palestinian Refugees: Challenges of Repatriation and Development*, pp. 1–13. Ottawa: I.B. Tauris and the International Development Research Centre.

B'Tselem: Israel Information Centre for Human Rights in the Occupied Territories. (2017). "Statistics on Settlers and Settler Population" (updated 11 May). Available at http://www.btselem.org/settlements/statistics.

Bulkley, Julia E. (1898). "Women in Palestine." *The Biblical World* 11, 2 (February): 69–80.

Bullard, Robert D., ed. (1993). *Confronting Environmental Racism: Voices from the Grassroots*. Boston: South End Press.

Bullard, Robert T., and Beverly Wright, eds. (2009). *Race, Place and Environmental Justice After Hurricane Katrina: Struggles to Reclaim, Rebuild and Revitalize New Orleans and the Gulf Coast*. Boulder: Westview Press.

Burg, Avraham. (2008). *The Holocaust Is Over, We Must Rise from Its Ashes*. New York: Palgrave Macmillan.

Burns, Jimmy. (2005). "Met Adopted Secret Shoot-to-Kill Policy in the Face of a New and Deadly Threat." *FT.Com* (25 July). Available at http://archive.li/GCgYa (accessed May 5, 2019).

Bush, George W. (1982). "The US and the Fight Against International Terrorism." In Benjamin Netanyahu (ed.), *International Terrorism: Challenge and Response*, pp. 332–37. New Brunswick: Transaction Books.

Bush, George W. (2007). "President Bush Welcomes Prime Minister Abbas to White House." Transcript of Remarks by President Bush and Prime Minister Abbas, White House, Office of the Press Secretary, July 25, 2003. Cited in John J. Mearsheimer and Stephen M. Walt. *The Israel Lobby*, pp. 215–16. Toronto: Viking Canada.

Butler, Judith. (2006a [1990, 1999]). *Gender Trouble: Feminism and the Subversion of Identity*. New York and London: Routledge.

Butler, Judith. (2006b). "Israel/Palestine and the Paradoxes of Academic Freedom." *Radical Philosophy* January/February 2006: 8–17.

Butler, Judith. (2008). "The Charge of Anti-Semitism: Jews, Israel, and the Risks of Public Critique." In Laurence J. Silberman (ed.), *Postzionism: A Reader*, pp. 369–86. New Brunswick: Rutgers University Press.

Butler, Judith. (2014). *Parting Ways: Jewishness and the Critique of Zionism*. New York: Columbia University Press.

Buzan, Barry, and Ole Waever. (2003). *Regions and Powers: The Structure of International Security*. Cambridge: Cambridge University Press.

Buzan, Barry, Ole Waever, and Jaap de Wilde. (1998). *Security: A New Framework for Analysis*. Boulder and London: Lynne Reiner Publishers.

Byrne, Siobhan. (2009). "Beyond the Ethnonational Divide: Identity Politics and Women in Northern Ireland and Israel/Palestine." PhD dissertation, Department of Political Studies, Queen's University (January).

Cairns, Alan C. (1999). "Empire, Globalization, and the Rise and Fall of Diversity." In Alan Cairns et al. (eds.) *Citizenship, Diversity and Pluralism: Canadian and Comparative Perspectives*, pp. 23–57. Montreal and Kingston: McGill-Queen's University Press.

Cairns, James, and Susan Ferguson. (2011). "Human Rights Revisionism and the Canadian Parliamentary Coalition to Combat Antisemitism." *Canadian Journal of Communication* 36: 415–34.

Callinicos, Alex, ed. (1992). *Between Apartheid and Capitalism: Conversations with South African Socialists*. London: Bookmarks.

Canada, Citizenship and Immigration Canada. (2009). "Minister Kenney Issues Statement on 'Israeli Apartheid Week'" (3 March). Available at https://www.canada.ca/en/news/archive/2012/03/minister-kenney-issues-statement-israeli-apartheid-week-.html (accessed May 5, 2019).

Canada, Citizenship and Immigration Canada (2017). "#Welcome Refugees: Canada Resettled Syrian Refugees." Available at http://www.cic.gc.ca/english/refugees/welcome/index.asp (accessed May 5, 2019).

Canadian Parliamentary Coalition to Combat Antisemitism (CPCCA). (2009). "Scott Reid and Mario Silva Announce Launch of All-party Canadian Parliamentary Coalition to Combat Antisemitism." Press release. Ottawa (2 June). Available at http://www.cpcca.ca/home.htm (accessed May 5, 2019).

Canadian Union of Postal Workers. (2008). "CUPW Delegates Take Firm Stand to Support Palestinian Workers." Convention 2008 Bulletin (April 24, 2008). Available at www.cupw.ca (accessed February 21, 2009).

Carens, Joseph H. (2000). *Culture, Citizenship and Community: A Contextual Exploration of Justice as Evenhandedness*. New York: Oxford University Press.

Carens, Joseph H. (2013). *The Ethics of Immigration*. Oxford and New York: Oxford University Press.

Carroll, William K., ed. (1992). *Organizing Dissent: Contemporary Social Movements in Theory and Practice*. Toronto: Garamond Press.

Carter, Jimmy. (2006). *Palestine: Peace Not Apartheid*. New York: Simon and Schuster.

Carter, Jimmy. (2009). *We Can Have Peace in the Holy Land: A Plan That Will Work*. New York: Simon and Schuster.

CBC News. (2003). "Ahenakew Charged with Spreading Hate" (11 June). Available at https://www.cbc.ca/news/canada/ahenakew-charged-with-spreading-hate-1.390644 (accessed May 5, 2019).

CBC News. (2008). "PM Cites 'Sad Chapter' in Apology for Residential Schools" (11 June). Available at https://www.cbc.ca/news/canada/pm-cites-sad-chapter-in-apology-for-residential-schools-1.699389 (accessed May 5, 2019).

CBC News. (2010). "Canada to Boycott Durban Conference" (25 November). Available at http://www.cbc.ca/news/politics/story/2010/11/25/kenney-durban.html (accessed May 5, 2019).

Chesler, Phyllis. (2003). *The New Anti-Semitism: The Current Crisis and What We Must Do About It*. San Francisco: Jossey-Bass.

Childers, Erskine B. (1961). "The Other Exodus." Reprinted in Walid Khalidi (ed.), *From Haven to Conquest: Readings in Zionism and the Palestine Problem Until 1948*, pp. 795–803. Washington: Institute for Palestine Studies: 1971/1987.

Chill, Dan S. (1976). *The Arab Boycott of Israel: Economic Aggression and World Reaction*. New York: Praeger.

Chomsky, Noam. (1982). *Toward a New Cold War*. New York: Pantheon Books.

Chomsky, Noam. (1986). *Pirates and Emperors: International Terrorism in the Real World*. New York: Claremont.

Chomsky, Noam, and Ilan Pappe. (2010). *Gaza in Crisis: Reflections on Israel's War Against the Palestinians*. Chicago: Haymarket Press.

Choudry, Aziz. (2010). "What's Left? Canada's 'Global Justice' Movement and Colonial Amnesia." *Race and Class* 52, 1: 97–102.

Chowdhry, Geeta, and Sheila Nair. (2013 [2002]). "Introduction." In Geeta Chowdhury and Sheila Nair (eds.), *Power, Postcolonialism and International Relations: Reading Race, Gender and Class*, pp. 1–32. New York: Routledge.

Clark, Campbell. (2016). "Trump's Victory Shifts Political Ground for Trudeau." *The Globe and Mail* (11 November). Available at http://www.theglobeandmail.com/news/politics/trumps-victory-shifts-political-ground-for-trudeau/article32831003/ (accessed May 5, 2019).

Clarke, Anthony. (1977). "Ethnic Studies: Reflection and Re-Examination." *Journal of Negro Education* 46, 2 (Spring): 124–32.

Clarke, George Elliott. (2006). "Foreword." In Afua Cooper (ed.), *The Hanging of Angélique: The Untold Story of Canadian Slavery and the Burning of Old Montreal*, pp. xi–xviii. Toronto: HarperCollins.

Clawson, Patrick. "Mideast Economies After the Israel-PLO Handshake." *Journal of International Affairs* 48, 1 (1994): 141–64.

Cliff, Tony. (2000). *A World to Win: Life of a Revolutionary*. London: Bookmarks.

CNN. (2008). "Australia Apologizes to Aborigines" (12 January). Available at http://www.cnn.com/2008/WORLD/asiapcf/02/12/australia.aborgines/index.html#cnnSTCText (accessed May 5, 2019).

CNN. (2017). "Fast Facts on Benjamin Netanyahu" (18 February). Available at http://www.cnn.com/2013/01/01/world/meast/benjamin-netanyahu—fast-facts/ (accessed March 16, 2017).

Coalition Against Israeli Apartheid. (2008). "FAQ About Boycott, Divestment and Sanctions." In *Labour for Palestine*, 83–4. Coalition Against Israeli Apartheid. Available at https://www.badil.org/en/resources/documents/human-rights-organizations.html?download=36:labour-for-palestine-2nd-ed&start=60i (accessed December 10, 2018).

Cohen, Matthew S., and Chuck D. Freilich. (2018). "War by Other Means: The Delegitimisation Campaign Against Israel." *Israel Affairs* 24, 1: 1–25.
Cole, David. (2002–2003). "Their Liberties, Our Security: Democracy and Double Standards." *Boston Review* (December–January): 1–17.
Connolly, William E. (2008). *Capitalism and Christianity, American Style.* Durham: Duke University Press.
Cook, Jonathan. (2004a). "'Democratic' Racism I." *Al-Ahram Weekly On-Line* (8–14 July), issue 698. Available at http://weekly.ahram.org.eg/Archive/2004/698/op11.htm (accessed December 13, 2018).
Cook, Jonathan. (2004b). "Democratic Racism (II)." *Al-Haram Weekly On-Line* (15–21 July), issue 699. Available at http://weekly.ahram.org.eg/Archive/2004/699/op11.htm (accessed December 13, 2018).
Cook, Jonathan. (2006). *Blood and Religion: The Unmasking of the Jewish and Democratic State.* London: Pluto Press.
Cooper, Afua. (2005). *The Hanging of Angélique: The Untold Story of Canadian Slavery and the Burning of Old Montreal.* Toronto: HarperCollins.
Cotler, Irwin. (2008). "Statement by Irwin Cotler on the Issue of Yom HaAtxma'ut -Israel's Independence Day." *The Jerusalem Post* (14 May). Reprinted by CJPAC. Available at https://www.jpost.com/Opinion/Op-Ed-Contributors/The-gathering-storm-and-beyond (accessed November 13, 2018).
Coulthard, Glen Sean. (2014). *Red Skin, White Masks: Rejecting the Colonial Politics of Recognition.* Minneapolis: University of Minnesota Press.
Cox, Robert. (1983). "Gramsci, Hegemony and International Relations." *Millenium* 12, 2: 162–75.
Croucher, Sheila L. (1997). "Constructing the Image of Ethnic Harmony in Toronto, Canada: The Politics of Problem Definition and Nondefinition." *Urban Affairs Review* 32, 3: 319–27.
Csillag, Ron. (2015). "Trudeau Government Votes Against UN Anti-Israel Resolutions." *Canadian Jewish News* (26 November). Available at http://www.cjnews.com/news/canada/trudeau-government-opposes-annual-un-onslaught-against-israel (accessed May 5, 2019).
CTV.ca News Staff. (2008). "Canada Pulls Support for UN Anti-Racism Conference" (23 January). Available at https://www.ctvnews.ca/canada-pulls-support-for-un-anti-racism-conference-1.272485 (accessed May 5, 2019).
Daes, Erica-Irene A. (2008). "An Overview of the History of Indigenous Peoples: Self Determination and the United Nations." *Cambridge Review of International Affairs* 21, 1 (March): 7–26.
Dagostina, Scott. (2010). "Toronto City Council Dodges Responsibility for Pride Censorship." *Xtra.ca* (14 June). Available at https://www.dailyxtra.com/toronto-city-council-dodges-responsibility-for-pride-censorship-34916 (accessed May 5, 2019).
Dale, Daniel. (2010). "Pride Prohibits Phrase 'Israeli Apartheid'" (21 May). *TheStar.com*. Available at https://www.thestar.com/news/gta/2010/05/21/pride_prohibits_phrase_israeli_apartheid.html (accessed May 5, 2019).

Danaher, Kevin, and Roger Burbach, eds. (2000). *Globalize This! The Battle Against the World Trade Organization and Corporate Rule*. Monroe: Common Courage Press.

Darwish, Mahmoud. (2011 [1964]). "Identity Card." Available at http://qumsiyeh.org/mahmouddarwish/ (accessed February 21, 2011).

Davidson, Lawrence. (2010). "Israel Classifies Its Past as Top Secret: Analysis." Dissident Voice (31 July). Available at http://dissidentvoice.org/2010/07/israel-classifies-its-past-as-top-secret-an-analysis/#more-20195 (accessed May 5, 2019).

Davis, Angela Y. (1981). *Women, Race and Class*. New York: Random House.

Davis, Angela Y. (2016). *Freedom Is a Constant Struggle: Ferguson, Palestine, and the Foundations of a Movement*. Foreword by Cornell West. Chicago: Haymarket Books.

Davis, Megan. (2008). "Indigenous Struggles in Standard-Setting: The United Nations Declaration on the Rights of Indigenous Peoples." *Melbourne Journal of International Law* 9, 2: 439–71.

Davis, Mike. (2002). *Late Victorian Holocausts: El Nino Famines and the Making of the Third World*. London: Verso.

Davis, Uri. (1977). *Utopia Incorporated: A Study of Class, State and Corporate Kin Control*. London: Zed Press.

Davis, Uri. (2003). *Apartheid Israel: Possibilities for the Struggle Within*. New York: Zed Books.

Dawson, Ashley, and Bill V. Mullen, eds. (2015). *Against Apartheid: The Case for Boycotting Israeli Universities*. Chicago: Haymarket Books.

Dawson, Michael C., and Cathy J. Cohen. (2002). "Problems in the Study of the Politics of Race." In I. Katznelson and H. V. Milner (eds.), *Political Science: State of the Discipline*, pp. 488–510. New York, London, and Washington: W.W. Norton and American Political Science Association.

Dayan, Arie. (1993). "The Debate over Zionism and Racism: An Israeli View." *Journal of Palestine Studies* XXII, 3 (Spring): 96–105.

Dearden, Lizzie. (2017a). "Israel Parliament Approves Travel Ban for Foreign Supporters of BDS Movement." *Independent* (7 March). Available at http://www.independent.co.uk/news/world/middle-east/israel-travel-ban-boycott-supporters-bds-movement-banned-knesset-vote-settlements-visas-residency-a7616701.html (accessed September 4, 2017).

Dearden, Lizzie. (2017b). "Israel's Former Prime Minister Says Country Faces 'Slippery Slope' to Apartheid." *Independent* (21 June). Available at https://www.independent.co.uk/news/world/middle-east/israel-palestine-apartheid-slippery-slope-ehud-barak-former-prime-minister-comments-netanyahu-a7801466.html (accessed May 5, 2019).

de B'béri, Boulou Ebande, and P. Eric Louw. (2011). "Introduction: Afropessimism: A Genealogy of Discourse." *Critical Arts*, 25, 3: 335–46.

de Costa, Ravi. (2006). *A Higher Authority: Indigenous Transnationalism and Australia*. Sydney: University of New South Wales Press.

de la Cadena, Marisol, and Orin Starn, eds. (2002). *Indigenous Experience Today*. New York: Berg.

Demirovic, Alex. (2003). "NGOs, the State, and Civil Society: The Transformation of Hegemony." *Rethinking Marxism* 15, 2: 213–35.

Department of Foreign Affairs and International Trade (DFAIT) Canada. (2011). "Address by the Honourable John Baird, Minister of Foreign Affairs, to the United Nations General Assembly" (26 September). Available at http://www.marketwired.com/press-release/address-honourable-john-baird-minister-foreign-affairs-united-nations-general-1565547.htm (accessed December 13, 2018).

Desai, Chandni. (2015). "Shooting Back in the Occupied Territories: An Anti-Colonial Participatory Politics." *Curriculum Inquiry* 45, 1: 109–28.

De Young, Karen, Ruth Eglash, and Hazem Balousha. (2018). "US Ends Aid to United Nations Agency Supporting Palestinian Refugees." *The Washington Post* (31 August). Available at https://www.washingtonpost.com/world/middle_east/us-aid-cuts-wont-end-the-right-of-return-palestinians-say/2018/08/31/8e3f25b4-ad0c-11e8-8a0c-70b618c98d3c_story.html?noredirect=on&utm_term=.c127c1112049 (accessed May 5, 2019).

Dhamoon, Rita. (2006). "Shifting from Culture to Cultural: Critical Theorizing of Identity/Difference Politics." *Constellations: An International Journal of Critical and Democratic Theory* 13, 3: 354–73.

Dhamoon, Rita. (2010 [2009]). *Identity/Difference Politics: How Difference Is Produced, and Why It Matters*. Vancouver: University of British Columbia Press.

Dhamoon, Rita, and Yasmeen Abu-Laban. (2009). "Dangerous (Internal) Foreigners and Nation-Building: The Case of Canada." *International Political Science Review* 30, 2 (March): 163–83.

Dolphin, Ray. (2006). *The West Bank Wall: Unmaking Palestine*. London: Pluto Press.

Doolittle, Robyn. (2012). "Pride Toronto Gets City Funding—With a Warning About 'Israeli Apartheid' Activists." *Toronto Star* (8 June). Available at https://www.thestar.com/news/gta/2012/06/08/pride_toronto_gets_city_funding_with_a_warning_about_israeli_apartheid_activists.html (accessed May 5, 2019).

Doucet, Andres, and Natasha S. Mauthner. (2006). "Feminist Methodologies and Epistemology." In Clifton D. Bryant and Dennis L. Peck (eds.), *Handbook of 21st Century Sociology*, pp. 36–42. Thousand Oaks: Sage.

Drummond, Susan. (2013). *Unthinkable Thoughts: Academic Freedom and the One-State Model for Israel and Palestine*. Vancouver: University of British Columbia Press.

Dubow, Saul. (2008). "Smuts, the United Nations and the Rhetoric of Race and Rights." *Journal of Contemporary History* 43, 1: 45–74.

Dugan, Emily. (2009). "Students Are Revolting: The Spirit of '68 Is Reawakening." *The Independent* (February 8, 2009). Available at www.independent.co.uk/news/education/education-news/students-are-revolting-the-spirit-of-68-is-reawakening-1604043.html (accessed May 5, 2019).

Dugard, John. (2008). "Convention on the Suppression and Punishment of the Crime of Apartheid." *United Nations Audiovisual Library of International*

Law. Available at http://legal.un.org/avl/ha/cspca/cspca.html (accessed December 13, 2018).

Dugard, John. (2009). "Foreword." In Ben White (ed.), *Israeli Apartheid: A Beginner's Guide*, pp. xiii–xvii. London: Pluto.

Edwards, Peter, and Robin Levinson King. (2015). "'I Want to Tell the Rest of the World at This Point, to Step in and Help the Refugees,' Says Aunt of Drowned Syrian Boys." *TheStar.com* (3 September). Available at https://www.thestar.com/news/canada/2015/09/03/father-of-aylan-kurdi-describes-how-his-family-drowned.html (accessed May 5, 2019).

El Asmar, Fouzi. (1986). *Through the Hebrew Looking-Glass: Arab Stereotypes in Children's Literature*. London: Zed Books.

Electronic Intifada. (2009). "Hampshire College First in US to Divest from Israel." (12 February). Available from https://electronicintifada.net/content/hampshire-college-first-us-divest-israel/932 (accessed February 8, 2019).

Electronic Intifada. (2017). Available at http://www.electronicintifada.net/ (accessed May 5, 2019).

Ellis, Marc H. (2000). "Indigenous Minority Rights, Citizenship and the New Jerusalem: A Reflection on the Future of Palestinians and Jews in the Expanded State of Israel." *Journal of Church and State* 42, 2: 297–310.

Engler, Yves. (2010). *Canada and Israel: Building Apartheid*. Vancouver and Black Point: RED Publishing and Fernwood Press.

Engler, Yves, and Anthony Fenton. (2005). *Canada in Haiti: Waging War on the Poor Majority*. Vancouver: Fernwood Press.

Erakat, Noura. (2015). "Roundtable on Anti-Blackness and Black-Palestinian Solidarity." Moderated by Noura Erakat. *Jadaliyya* (3 June). Available at http://www.jadaliyya.com/pages/index/21764/roundtable-on-anti-blackness-and-black-palestinian (accessed May 5, 2019).

Erevelles, Nirmala. (2011). *Disability and Difference in Global Contexts: Enabling a Transformative Body Politic*. London: Palgrave.

Estorick, Eric. (1939). "The Evian Conference and the Intergovernmental Committee." *The Annals of the American Academy of Political and Social Science*, 203, 1 (May): 136–41.

Falk, Richard. (2008). *Report of the Special Rapporteur on the Situation of Human Rights in the Palestinian Territories Occupied Since 1967*. Assembly, Sixty-Third Session, Item 67 (C) of the Provisional Agenda. https://www.un.org/unispal/document/report-of-the-special-rapporteur-on-the-situation-of-human-rights-in-the-palestinian-territories-occupied-since-1967-advance-unedited-version/ (accessed May 5, 2019).

Faludi, Susan. (2000). *Stiffed: The Betrayal of the American Man*. New York: Perennial.

Faris, Hani. (1975). "Israel Zangwill's Challenge to Zionism." *Journal of Palestine Studies* 4, 3: 74–90.

Farsakh, Leila. (2002). "Palestinian Labor Flows to the Israeli Economy: A Finished Story?" *Journal of Palestinian Studies* 32, 1(Autumn): 13–27.

Farsakh, Leila. (2005). "Independence, Cantons, or Bantustans: Whither the Palestinian State?" *Middle East Journal* 59, 2 (Spring): 230–45.

Farsakh, Leila. (2011). "The One-State Solution and the Israeli-Palestinian Conflict: Palestinian Challenges and Prospects." *The Middle East Journal* 65, 1 (Winter): 55–71.

Farsakh, Leila. (2012). *Palestinian Labour Migration to Israel: Labour, Land and Occupation*. London and New York: Routledge.

Farsoun, Samih. (1976). "Settler Colonialism and Herrenvolk-Democracy." In Richard P. Stevens and Abdelwahab M. Elmessiri (eds.), *Israel and South Africa: The Progression of a Relationship*, pp. 13–21. New York: New World Press.

Farsoun, Samih K., and Naseer H. Aruri. (2006). *Palestine and the Palestinians: A Social and Political History*. Boulder CO: Westview Press.

Feiler, Gil. (1998). *From Boycott to Economic Cooperation: The Political Economy of the Arab Boycott of Israel*. London: Routledge.

Feldman, Keith P. (2015). *A Shadow over Palestine: Imperial Life of Race in America*. Minneapolis: University of Minnesota Press.

Fekete, Liz. (2004). "Anti-Muslim Racism and the European Security State." *Race and Class* 46, 1: 3–29.

Fekete, Liz. (2012). "The Muslim Conspiracy Theory and the Oslo Massacre." *Race and Class* 53, 3: 30–47.

Ferguson, Sue. (2007). "Tear Down That Wall!" Special issue on "The New Apartheid: Inside the Growing Anti-Israel Boycott." *This Magazine* 41, 2 (September/October): 20–25.

Fidler, Richard. (2009). "Québec Solidaire Supports Pro-Palestine BDS Campaign." *Socialist Voice: Marxist Perspectives for the 21st Century* (30 November). Available at http://www.socialistvoice.ca/?p=798%5D (accessed May 5, 2019).

Finkelstein, Norman. (2000; 2003a). *The Holocaust Industry: Reflections on the Exploitation of Jewish Suffering*. London: Verso.

Finkelstein, Norman. (2003b). *Image and Reality of the Israel-Palestine Conflict*. 2nd ed. London: Verso.

Finkelstein, Norman. (2005). *Beyond Chutzpah: On the Misuse of Anti-Semitism and the Abuse of History*. Berkeley: University of California Press.

Finkelstein, Norman, and Jim Paul. (1985). "The Scope of This Fraud Was Huge." *MERIP Reports* 136/7 (October–December): 38–40. Available at http://www.jstor.org/stable/3012350 (accessed May 5, 2019).

Fischbach, Michael R. (2010). "British and Zionist Data Gathering on Palestinian Arab Landownerhsip and Population During the Mandata." In Elia Zureik, David Lyon, and Yasmeen Abu-Laban (eds.), *Surveillance and Control in Israel/Palestine: Population, Territory and Power*, pp. 297–312. London and New York: Routledge.

Fishman, Joel S. (2012). "The BDS Message of Anti-Zionism, Anti-Semitism, and Incitement to Discrimination." *Israel Affairs* 183, 3: 412–25.

Flood, Allison. (2012). "Alice Walker Declines Request to Publish Israeli Edition of the Color Purple." *The Guardian* (20 June). Available at http://www.guardian.co.uk/books/2012/jun/20/alice-walker-declines-israeli-color-purple?newsfeed=true (accessed May 5, 2019).

Foner, Eric. (1988). *Reconstruction: America's Unfinished Revolution*. New York: Harper and Row.

Food and Agriculture Organization of the United Nations (FAO). 2015. *Gaza Crisis*. FAO. Available at http://www.fao.org/emergencies/crisis/gaza/en/ (accessed May 5, 2019).

Food and Agricultural Organization of the United Nations (FAO) and the United Nations Office for the Coordination of Humanitarian Affairs (OCHA). 2010. *Farming Without Land, Fishing Without Water: Gaza Agriculture Sector Struggles to Survive: Fact Sheet*. FAO and OCHA, 26 May. Available at https://reliefweb.int/sites/reliefweb.int/files/resources/761D3CD5EC5777C3C125772E0049D62F-Full_Report.pdf (accessed May 5, 2019).

Foster, John Bellamy. (2009). *The Ecological Revolution: Making Peace with the Planet*. New York: Monthly Review Press.

Foundation for Middle East Peace. (2011a). "Settlements in Jerusalem." *FMEP.org* (13 January). Available at http://www.fmep.org/settlement_info/settlement-info-and-tables/stats-data/settlements-in-east-jerusalem (accessed May 5, 2019).

Foundation for Middle East Peace. (2011b). "Settlements in the West Bank." *FMEP.org*. Available at http://www.fmep.org/settlement_info/settlement-info-and-tables/stats-data/settlements-in-the-west-bank-1/ (accessed May 9, 2011). Link no longer working.

Frankel, Sheera. (2009). "Amnesty International: Gaza White Phosphorus Shells Were US Made." *The Times* (24 February). Available at https://www.thetimes.co.uk/article/amnesty-international-gaza-white-phosphorus-shells-were-us-made-gqqrj6p0cf7 (accessed May 5, 2019).

Frankenberg, Ruth. (2005). "Cracks in the Façade: Whiteness and the Construction of 9/11." *Social Identities* 11, 6: 553–71.

Freeman-Maloy, Dan. (2006). "AIPAC North." *ZNet* (26 June). Available at https://zcomm.org/znetarticle/aipac-north-by-dan-freeman-maloy-1-2 (accessed May 5, 2019).

Freeman-Maloy, Dan. (2011). "Israeli Power and Its Liberal Alibis." *Race and Class* 52, 3: 61–72.

Freeman-Maloy, Dan. (2016). "Canada and the Palestine Question: On Zionism, Empire and the Colour Line." PhD dissertation, Middle East Politics, University of Exeter.

Freeman, Linda. (1997). *The Ambiguous Champion: Canada and South Africa in the Trudeau and Mulroney Years*. Toronto: University of Toronto Press.

Galabuzi, Grace-Edward. (2005). *Canada's Economic Apartheid: The Social Exclusion of Racialized Groups in the New Century*. Toronto: Canadian Scholars Press.

Galabuzi, Grace-Edward. (2006). *Canada's Economic Apartheid: The Social Exclusion of Racialized Groups in the New Century*. Toronto: Canadian Scholars Press.

Galabuzi, Grace-Edward. (2007). "Marxism and Anti-Racism: Extending the Dialogue on Race and Class." *Marxism: A Socialist Annual, Solidarity, Resistance, Liberation* 5: 47–50.

Galligan, Brian, and Emma Larking. (2009). "Rights Protection: Comparative Perspectives." *Australian Journal of Political Science* 44, 1 (March): 1–11.

Galloway, George. (2009). "Widening the Struggle." *Morning Star* (16 January). Available at https://sudhan.wordpress.com/2009/01/18/galloway-widening-the-struggle/ (accessed December 13, 2018).

Garfield, Leanna. (2016). "Trumps $25 Billion Wall Would Be Nearly Impossible to Build, According to Architects." *Business Insider* (13 November). Available at http://www.businessinsider.com/trump-wall-impossible-build-architects-2016-11 (accessed May 5, 2019).

Garfinkle, Adam M. (1991). "On the Origin, Use and Abuse of a Phrase." *Middle Eastern Studies* 27, 4: 539–50.

Gatehouse, Jonathon. (2002). "The New Solitudes." *Macleans.ca.* (27 May). Available at https://archive.macleans.ca/article/2002/5/27/the-new-solitudes.

Germain, Randall D., and Michael Kenny. (1998). "Engaging Gramsci: International Relations Theory and the New Gramscians." *Review of International Studies* 24, 1: 3–21.

Ghirmire, Kléber. (2011). "The United Nations World Summits and Civil Society Activism: Grasping the Centrality of National Dynamics." *European Journal of International Relations* 17 (March): 75–95.

Giese, Rachel. (2018). *Boys: What It Means to Become a Man.* Toronto: Patrick Crean Editions (imprint of HarperCollinsCanada).

Giles, Frank (1989). "Interview with Golda Meir," *The Sunday Times* (15 June).

Gill, Stephen, ed. (1993). *Gramsci, Historical Materialism and International Relations.* Cambridge: Cambridge University Press.

Gill, Stephen, ed. (2000). "Toward a Postmodern Prince?: The Battle in Seattle as a Moment in the New Politics of Globalisation." *Millennium* 29, 1: 131–40.

Gillespie, Kelly. (2015). "Toward a Queer Palestine." In Jon Soske and Sean Jacobs (eds.), *Apartheid Israel: The Politics of an Analogy*, pp. 105–09. Chicago: Haymarket Books.

Ginsburg, Norman. (2004). "Globalization and Racism." In Vic George and Robert M. Page (eds.), *Global Social Problems*, pp. 160–76. Cambridge: Polity Press.

Glaser, Daryl J. (2003). "Zionism and Apartheid: A Moral Comparison." *Ethnic and Racial Studies* 26, 3 (May 2003): 403–21.

Glazer, Nathan. (1964). "Negroes and Jews: The New Challenge to Pluralism." *Commentary* 38, 6 (December): 29–34.

Global BDS Movement. (2009). Boycott, Divestment and Sanctions for Palestine. Available at http://www.bdsmovement.net/ (accessed May 5, 2019).

Global Coalition to Protect Education from Attack (GCPEA). (2018). *Education Under Attack: 2018.* http://www.protectingeducation.org/sites/default/files/documents/eua_2018_full.pdf (accessed January 20, 2019).

Glover, Danny. (2009). "Race and the Obama Administration." *The Nation* (20 April). Available at http://www.thenation.com/article/race-and-obama-administration (accessed May 5, 2019).

Goldberg, David Howard. (1990). *Foreign Policy and Ethnic Interest Groups: American and Canadian Jews Lobby for Israel.* New York: Greenwood Press.

Goldberg, David Theo. (2009). *The Threat of Race: Reflections on Racial Neoliberalism*. Malden: Wiley Blackwell.

Goldberg, David Theo, and Saree Makdisi. (2009). "The Trial of Israel's Campus Critics." *Tikkum Magazine* (September/October). Available at http://www.tikkun.org/article.php/sept_oct_09_goldberg_makdisi (accessed March 1, 2011).

Goldstein, Eric L. (2006). *The Price of Whiteness: Jews, Race and American Identity*. Oxfordshire: Princeton University Press.

Goldstone, Richard. (2011a). "Report of the United Nations Fact-Finding Mission in the Gaza Conflict (Abridged)." In Adam Horowitz, Lizzy Ratner, and Philip Weiss (eds.), *The Goldstone Report: The Legacy of the Landmark Investigation of the Gaza Conflict*, pp. 1–326. New York: Nation Books.

Goldstone, Richard. (2011b). "Reconsidering the Goldstone Report on Israel and War Crimes." *The Washington Post* (1 April). Available at http://www.washingtonpost.com/opinions/reconsidering-the-goldstone-report-on-israel-and-war-crimes/2011/04/01/AFg111JC_print.html (accessed May 5, 2019).

Goodenough, Patrick. (2008). "'Apartheid' Israel, Islamophobia on the Agenda for the U.N. Racism Meeting." *CNSNews.com* (11 November). Available at http://www.cnsnews.com/public/Content/Article.aspx?rsrcid=39125 (accessed May 9, 2009). Link no longer working.

Goodman, Amy. (2019). "Exclusive: Angela Davis Speaks Out on Palestine, BDS and More After Civil Rights Award Is Revoked." *Democracy Now* (11 January). Available from https://www.democracynow.org/2019/1/11/exclusive_angela_davis_speaks_out_on (accessed May 5, 2019).

Gordon, Neve. (2008a). "From Colonization to Separation: Exploring the Structure of Israel's Occupation." *Third World Quarterly* 29, 1: 25–44.

Gordon, Neve. (2008b). *Israel's Occupation*. Berkeley: University of California Press.

Gordon, Neve. (2009a). "Avigdor Lieberman, Israel's Shame." *Guardian* (25 March). Available at http://www.guardian.co.uk/commentisfree/2009/mar/25/avigdor-lieberman-binyamin-netanyahu-israel (accessed May 5, 2019).

Gordon, Neve. (2009b). "The Political Economy of Israel's Homeland Security/Surveillance Industry." Working Paper III, The New Transparency: Surveillnce and Social Sorting, Queen's University. Available from https://www.sscqueens.org/sites/sscqueens.org/files/The%20Political%20Economy%20of%20Israel's%20Homeland%20Security.pdf (accessed May 4, 2019).

Gordon, Neve. (2011). "Israel's Emergence as a Homeland Security Capital." In Elia Zureik, David Lyon, and Yasmeen Abu-Laban (eds.), *Surveillance and Control in Israel/Palestine: Population, Territory and Power*, pp. 153–70. London and New York: Routledge.

Gordon, Neve, and Jeff Halper. (2008). "Where's the Academic Outrage over the Bombing of a University in Gaza?" *Counterpunch* (31 December). Available at https://www.counterpunch.org/2008/12/31/where-s-the-academic-outrage-over-the-bombing-of-a-university-in-gaza/ (accessed December 14, 2018).

Government of Canada, Ministry of Public Safety. (2008). "Declaration of Intent Between the Department of Public Safety and Emergency Preparedness of Canada and the Ministry of Public Security of the Government of the State of Israel" (23 March). Available at http://www.marketwired.com/press-release/canada-and-israel-sign-declaration-to-cooperate-on-public-safety-835257.htm. Link no longer working.

Graham-Brown, Sara. (1983). "The Economic Consequences of Occupation." In Naseer Aruri (ed.), *Occupation: Israel over Palestine*, pp. 297–360. Belmont: Association of Arab-American University Graduates.

Gramsci, Antonio. (1971). *Selections from the Prison Notebooks*. Edited by Quentin Hoare and translated by Geoffrey Nowell Smith. London: Lawrence and Wishart.

Great Britain. (1971/1987). "The Anglo-American Committee of Enquiry Regarding the Problems of European Jewry and Palestine (1946)." Reprinted in Walid Khalidi (ed.), *From Haven to Conquest: Readings in Zionism and the Palestine Problem Until 1948*, pp. 595–600. Washington: Institute for Palestine Studies.

Green Party of Canada. (2016). "Palestinian Self-Determination and the Movement for Boycott, Divestment and Sanctions." Policy resolution Green Party National Convention 2016, Code: G16-Poo6. Dimitri Lascaris, Justice Critic, Green Party of Canada Shadow Cabinet. Available at https://www.greenparty.ca/en/convention-2016/voting/resolutions/g1. Link no longer working.

Green Party Peace Network. (2009). "Norwegian Train Drivers Strike for Gaza" (11 January). Available at http://greenpartypeacenetwork.wordpress.com/2009/01/11/norwegian-train-drivers-strike-for-gaza/ (accessed February 21, 2009).

Greene, Richard Allen. (2006). "Bush's Language Angers US Muslims." *BBC News* (12 August). Available at http://news.bbc.co.uk/2/hi/4785065.stm (accessed December 14, 2018).

Grossman, Guy, and Rami Kaplan. (2006). "Courage to Refuse." *Peace Review: A Journal of Social Justice* 18: 189–97.

Gunnell, John, G. (2002). "Handbooks and History: Is It Still the American Science of Politics?" *International Political Science Review* 23, 4: 339–54.

Gunnell, John, G. (2006). "The Founding of the American Political Science Association: Discipline, Profession, Political Theory and Politics." *American Political Science Review* 100, 4: 479–86.

Gupte, Pranay. (2005). "For Bayefsky, Keeping Eye on U.N. Is a Crucial Mission." *New York Sun* (17 November). Available at http://www.nysun.com/national/for-bayefsky-keeping-eye-on-un-is-a-crucial/23167/ (accessed May 5, 2019).

Gurney, Christabel. (2000). "'A Great Cause': The Origins of the Anti-Apartheid Movement, June 1959–March 1960." *Journal of Southern African Studies* 26, 1 (March): 123–44.

Gvion, Liora. (2011). "Cooking, Food, and Masculinity: Palestinian Men in Israeli Society." *Men and Masculinities* 14, 4: 408–29.

Haaretz. (2015). "Olmert Blasts Netanyahu's Foreign Policy, Warns of Risk of Apartheid in Israel" (2 October). Available at https://www.haaretz.com/olmert-warns-of-risk-of-apartheid-in-israel-1.5404995 (accessed January 9, 2019).

Haaretz. (2016). "G4S Sells Israel Operation for $110 Million, Denies BDS Pressure" (2 December). Available at http://www.haaretz.com/israel-news/business/1.756666 (accessed May 5, 2019).

Habib, Jasmin. (2004). *Israel, Diaspora, and the Routes of National Belonging*. Toronto: University of Toronto Press.

Hadawi, Sami. (1967). *Bitter Harvest: Palestine Between 1914 and 1967*. New York: New World Press.

Haklai, Oded. (2011). *Palestinian Ethnonationalism in Israel*. Philadelphia: University of Pennsylvania Press.

Halbrook, Stephen. (1972). "The Class Origins of Zionist Ideology." *Journal of Palestine Studies* 2, 1 (Autumn): 86–110.

Hale, Grace Elizabeth. (1998). *Making Whiteness: The Culture and Segregation in the South, 1890–1940*. New York: Vintage Books.

HaLevi, Ezra. (2008). "Haaretz Editor Refuses to Retract Israel Apartheid Statements." *Arutz Sheva* (31 July). Available at http://www.israelnationalnews.com/News/News.aspx/123596 (accessed May 5, 2019).

Hall, Stuart. (1986). "Gramsci's Relevance for the Study of Race and Ethnicity." *Common Inquiry* 10, 2: 5–27.

Halperin-Kaddari, Ruth, and Yaacov Yadgar. (2010a). "Religion, Politics and Gender Equality Among Jews in Israel." *Final Research Report for the Religion, Politics and Gender Equality Project. Geneva: United Nations Research Institute for Social Development and Heinrich-Böll-Stiftung* (June). Available at https://www.researchgate.net/publication/265746489_Religion_Politics_and_Gender_Equality_among_Jews_in_Israel_Religion_Politics_and_Gender_Equality (accessed December 14, 2018).

Halperin-Kaddari, Ruth, and Yaacov Yadgar. (2010b). "Between Universal Feminism and Particular Nationalism: Politics, Religion and Gender (In) Equality in Israel." *Third World Quarterly* 31, 6: 905–20.

Halpern, Orly. (2006). "Arab Boycott Largely 'Lip Service.'" *Jerusalem Post* (28 February), as cited in Weiss, "Arab League Boycott." p. 3.

Hammer, Juliane. (2005). *Palestinians Born in Exile: Diaspora and the Search for a Homeland*. Austin: University of Texas Press.

Hanchard, Michael, and Erin Aeran Chung. (2004). "From Race Relations to Comparative Racial Politics: A Survey of Cross-National Scholarship on Race in the Social Sciences." *Du Bois Review* 1, 2: 319–43.

Hanieh, Adam. (2003). "From State-Led Growth to Globalization: The Evolution of Israeli Capitalism." *Journal of Palestine Studies* XXXII, 4: 5–21.

Hansard, House of Commons Debates. (2016). Government Orders, Business of Supply, "Opposition Motion—Israel," Hon. Tony Clement (Parry Sound-Muskoka, CPC), vol. 148, no. 020, 1st session, 42nd Parliament (18 February). Available at http://www.parl.gc.ca/HousePublications/

Publication.aspx?Pub=hansard&Language=E&Mode=1&Parl=42&Ses=1&DocId=8105393&File=0of (accessed May 5, 2019).
Hare, John B. (2009). "Sacred Texts: The Philistines by R.A.S. Macalister." Available at http://www.sacred-texts.com/ane/phc/index.htm (accessed May 5, 2019).
Harle, Vilho. (2000). *The Enemy with a Thousand Faces: The Tradition of Other in Western Political Thought and History*. Westport and London: Praeger.
Harman, Chris. (2006). "Hizbollah and the War Israel Lost." *International Socialism Journal* 112 (October): 8–41.
Harper, Stephen. (2008). "Prime Minister Stephen Harper's Statement of Apology." *CBC News* (11 June). Available at https://www.cbc.ca/news/canada/prime-minister-stephen-harper-s-statement-of-apology-1.734250 (accessed December 4, 2018).
Harper, Stephen. (2014). "Read the Full Text of Harper's Historic Speech to Israel's Knesset." *The Globe and Mail* (20 January). Available at http://www.theglobeandmail.com/news/politics/read-the-full-text-of-harpers-historic-speech-to-israels-knesset/article16406371/ (accessed 19 July 2019).
Hassan, Nir. (2010). "MKs Seek Ban on East Jerusalem Arabs Guiding the City." *Haaretz.com* (26 October). Available at https://www.haaretz.com/1.5127356 (accessed May 5, 2019).
Hasso, Frances. S. (1998). "The 'Women's Front': Nationalism, Feminism and Modernity in Palestine." *Gender and Society* 12, 4 (August): 441–65.
Henry, Frances, and Carol Tator. (2002). *Discourses of Domination: Racial Bias in the Canadian English-Language Press*. Toronto: University of Toronto Press.
Henry, Frances, Carol Tator, Winston Mattis, and Tim Rees. (1995). *The Colour of Democracy: Racism in Canadian Society*. Toronto: Harcourt Brace.
Herman, Edward, and Noam Chomsky. (1988). *Manufacturing Consent: The Political Economy of the Mass Media*. New York: Pantheon Books.
Hertzberg, Arthur, ed. (1997). *The Zionist Idea: A Historical Analysis and Reader*. Philadelphia: Jewish Publication Society.
Herzl, Theodore. (1960 [circa 1895–1904]) *The Complete Diaries of Theodore Herzl: Vol. 111*. New York: Herzl Press and Thomas Yoseloff. Available at https://archive.org/stream/TheCompleteDiariesOfTheodorHerzl_201606/TheCompleteDiariesOfTheodorHerzlEngVolume1_OCR_djvu.txt (accessed January 20, 2019).
Herzl, Theodore. (1988 [1896, 1944]). *The Jewish Question*. New York: Dover Publications.
Herzog, Hanna. (2004). "Both an Arab and a Woman: Gendered, Racialized Experiences of Female Palestinian Citizens of Israel." *Social Identities* 10, 1: 53–82.
Herzog, Hanna. (2008). "Re/Visioning the Women's Movement in Israel." *Citizenship Studies* 12, 3 (June): 265–82.
Hicks, George. (1997). *Japan's Hidden Apartheid: The Korean Minority and the Japanese*. London: Ashgate.

Hider, James, and Sheera Frankel. (2009). "Israel Admits Using White Phosphorous in Attacks on Gaza." *The Times* (24 January). Available at https://www.thetimes.co.uk/article/israel-admits-using-white-phosphorous-in-attacks-on-gaza-3jngp502vh0 (accessed December 14, 2018).

Hitchens, Christopher. (2007). "Defending Islamofascism: It's a Valid Term and Here's Why." *Slate* (22 October). Available at https://slate.com/news-and-politics/2007/10/defending-the-term-islamofascism.html (accessed May 5, 2019).

Hobsbawm, Eric, and Terence Ranger, eds. (1983). *The Invention of Tradition.* Cambridge: Cambridge University Press.

Hochberg, Gil, Z., Haneen Maikey, Rima, and Samira Saraya. (2010). "No Pride in Occupation: A Roundtable Discussion." *GLQ: A Journal of Gay and Lesbian Studies* 16, 4: 599–610.

Hoile, David. (1988). *Understanding Sanctions*. London: International Freedom Foundation: 14–16.

Holt, Maria. (2010). "Agents of Defiance and Despair: The Impact of Islamic Resistance on Palestinian Women in the West Bank and Gaza Strip." *Totalitarian Movements and Political Religions* 11, 3–4: 397–415.

Homer-Dixon, Thomas F. (1991). "On the Threshold: Environmental Changes as Causes of Acute Conflict." *International Security* 16, 2: 76–116.

Honig-Parnass, Tikva. (2003). "Israel's Colonial Strategies to Destroy Palestinian Nationalism." *Race and Class* 45, 68: 68–75.

Horwitz, Sari. (2005). "Israeli Experts Teach Police on Terrorism: Training Programs Prompt Policy Shifts." *Washington Post* (12 June). Available at http://www.washingtonpost.com/wp-dyn/content/article/2005/06/11/AR2005061100648.html (accessed May 5, 2019).

Houston, Andrea. (2010). "Drawing Battle Lines: Pride, QUAIA and Toronto Council." *Xtra.ca* (20 November). Available at https://www.dailyxtra.com/drawing-battle-lines-pride-quaia-and-toronto-council-8676 (accessed May 5, 2019).

Human Rights Watch. (2001). "Second Class: Discrimination Against Palestinian Arab Children in Israel's Schools." Available at http://www.violencestudy.org/a199 (accessed May 17, 2009).

Human Sciences Research Council of South Africa. (2009). "Occupation, Colonialism, Apartheid?: A Re-Assessment of Israel's Practices in the Occupied Palestinian Territories Under International Law." *South Africa: HSRC* (June). Available at http://www.alhaq.org/attachments/article/236/Occupation_Colonialism_Apartheid-FullStudy.pdf (accessed May 5, 2019).

Huntington, Samuel. (1993). "The Clash of Civilizations?" *Foreign Affairs* 72, 3: 22–49.

Huntington, Samuel. (1996). *The Clash of Civilizations: Remaking of World Order*. New York: Simon and Schuster.

Huntington, Samuel. (2005). *Who Are We?: The Challenges to America's National Identity*. New York: Simon and Schuster.

Huysmans, Jef. (2000). "The European Union and the Securitization of Migration." *Journal of Common Market Studies* 38, 5: 751–77.
Ignatieff, Michael. (2007). *The Rights Revolution*. Toronto: House of Anansi Press.
Ignatieff, Michael. (2009). "Michael Ignatieff: Israel Apartheid Week and CUPE Ontario's anti-Israel Posturing Should Be Condemned" (5 March). Available at http://spme.org/boycotts-divestments-sanctions-bds/boycotts-divestments-and-sanctions-bds-news/michael-ignatieff-israel-apartheid-week-and-cupe-ontarios-anti-israel-posturing-should-be-condemned/6513/ (accessed December 14, 2018).
Inbar, Efraim. (2006). "Israel's Palestinian Challenge." *Israel Studies* 12, 4 (October): 823–42.
Independent Jewish Voices. (2017). "Introducing the BDS Movement." Available at https://ijvcanada.org/what-is-the-bds-campaign/.
Indian and Northern Affairs, Government of Canada. (2010). "Canada's Statement of Support on the United Nations Declaration on the Rights of Indigenous Peoples" (12 November). Available at https://www.aadnc-aandc.gc.ca/eng/1309374239861/1309374546142 (accessed December 14, 2018).
Inglis, Christine. (1996). "Multiculturalism: New Policy Responses to Diversity." Management of Social Transformations (MOST) Policy Paper Number 4/ UNESCO. Available at https://unesdoc.unesco.org/ark:/48223/pf0000105582 (accessed December 12, 2018).
International Court of Justice (IJC). (2004). "Press Release: Legal Consequences of the Construction of a Wall in the Occupied Palestinian Territory, Advisory Opinion" (9 July). Available at https://www.icj-cij.org/files/case-related/131/131-20040709-ADV-01-00-EN.pdf (accessed December 14, 2018).
International Court of Justice (ICJ) Reports. (2004). "Legal Consequences of the Construction of a Wall in the Occupied Palestinian Territory, Advisory Opinion." Available at http://www.icj-cij.org/docket/files/131/1671.pdf (accessed July 17, 2017).
Inter-Parliamentary Coalition for Combating Antisemitism (ICCA). (2009). "The London Declaration for Combating Antisemitism." London: Lancaster House (17 February). Available at http://cjpac.ca/conference-on-combating-antisemitism/ (accessed May 5, 2019).
Iriye, Akira, Petra Goedde, and William I. Hitchkock, eds. (2012). *The Human Rights Revolution: An International History*. Oxford: Oxford University Press.
Isaac, Jad, and Owen Powell. (2007). "The Transformation of the Palestinian Environment." In Jamil Hilal (ed.), *Where Now for Palestine?: The Demise of the Two-State Solution* pp. 144–66. London and New York: Zed Books.
Ismael, Tareq Y. (1994). *Canada and the Middle East: The Foreign Policy of a Client State*. Calgary: Detselig.
Israel Ministry of Aliyah and Immigration. (2017). Available at http://www.moia.gov.il/english/pages/default.aspx (accessed July 24, 2017).

Israel Ministry of Environmental Protection. "About Us." http://www.sviva.gov.il/English/AboutUs/Pages/AboutUs.aspx (accessed January 20, 2018).
Israel Ministry of Foreign Affairs. (2002). "Which Came First—Terrorism or Occupation—Major Arab Terrorist Attacks Against Israelis Prior to the 1967 Six Day War." Available at http://www.mfa.gov.il/MFA/Terrorism-+Obstacle+to+Peace/Palestinian+terror+before+2000/Which+Came+First-+Terrorism+or+Occupation+-+Major.htm (accessed March 5, 2009).
Israel Today. (2006). "Israel to Re-Brand Itself in the World" (12 September). Available at http://www.israeltoday.co.il/default.aspx?tabid=178&nid=9460.
Israeli Apartheid Week (IAW). (2009). Home Page. Available at http://apartheidweek.org/ (accessed May 12, 2009).
It Starts with Us. "Update: Indigenous Land Defence Across Borders: Solidarity Exchange with Palestine." (2018). *ItStartsWithUs—mmiw.com* (26 July). Available at http://itstartswithus-mmiw.com/update-Indigenous-land-defence-across-borders-solidarity-exchange-with-palestine/ (accessed November 24, 2018).
Ives, Peter, and Nicola Short. (2013). "On Gramsci and the International: A Textual Analysis." *Review of International Studies* 39, 3 (July): 621–42.
Jaber, A. D. (2018). "Settler Colonialism and Ecocide: Case Study of Al-Khadar, Palestine." *Setter Colonial Studies* (31 October). Available at https://www.tandfonline.com/doi/full/10.1080/2201473X.2018.1487127 (accessed January 20, 2018).
Jackson, Peter, and Mathieu Faupin. (2008). "The United Nations Role in Fighting Racism and Racial Discrimintion." *The Ardent Review* 1 (April): 1–8. Available at http://www.academia.edu/3717763/The_Ardent_Anti-Racism_and_Decolonization_Review (accessed December 14, 2018).
Jacoby, Tami Amanda. (2000). "Canadian Peacebuilding in the Middle East: Case Study of the Canada Fund in Israel/Palestine and Jordan." *Canadian Foreign Policy* 8, 1 (Fall): 83–91.
Jad, Islah. (2010). "NGOs: Between Buzzwords and Social Movements." *Development in Practice* 17, 4–5: 622–29.
Jad, Islah. (2011). "Islamist Women of Hamas: Between Feminism and Nationalism." *Inter-Asia Cultural Studies* 12, 2 (2011): 176–201.
Jad, Islah, Penny Johnson, and Rita Giacaman. (2000). "Gender and Citizenship Under the Palestinian Authority." In Suad Joseph (ed.), *Gender and Justice in the Middle East* pp. 137–57. Syracuse: Syracuse University Press.
Jakubowicz, Andrew. (2003). "Civility and Terror in Academic Life: The Israeli Academic Boycotts." *Borderlands E-Journal* 2, 3. Available at http://www.borderlands.net.au/vol2no3_2003/jakubowicz.htm (accessed May 5, 2019).
Jamal, Amal. (2001). "Engendering State-Building: The Women's Movement and Gender-Regime in Palestine." *Middle East Journal* 55, 2 (Spring): 256–76.
Jamal, Amal. (2005). "On the Morality of Arab Collective Rights in Israel." *Adalah's* Newsletter 12 (April): 1–7.
Jamal, Amal. (2007). "Strategies of Minority Struggle for Equality in Ethnic States: Arab Politics in Israel." *Citizenship Studies* 11, 3: 253–82.

Jamal, Amal. (2009). "The Contradictions of State-Minority Relations in Israel: The Search for Clarifications." *Constellations* 16, 3: 493–508.

Jamal, Amal. (2011). *Arab Minority Nationalism in Israel: The Politics of Indigeneity*. London and New York: Routledge.

James, Cyril L. R. (1989). *The Black Jacobins: Toussaint L'Ouverture and the San Domingo Revolution*. New York: Vintage.

Jamjoum, Hazem. (2009). "Not an Analogy: Israel and the Crime of Apartheid." *Common Dreams* (31 March). Available at https://www.commondreams.org/views/2009/03/31/not-analogy-israel-and-crime-apartheid (accessed December 4, 2018).

Jewish Voice for Peace (JVP). (2019). "JVP Academic Letter in Support of Angela Davis." Available at https://docs.google.com/forms/d/e/1FAIpQLSfXxqQvu8OzVuZY2ZakFVGe-JTpbzQL7olyt_hEdfpExJAPcw/viewform (accessed January 23, 2019).

John, Robert, and Sami Hadawi. (1970). *The Palestine Diary: Volume One 1914–1945*. Beirut: Palestine Research Center.

Johnson, Genevieve Fuji, and Randy Enomoto, eds. (2007). *Race, Racialization and Antiracism in Canada and Beyond*. Toronto: University of Toronto Press.

Johnson, Penny, and Eileen Kuttab. (2001). "Where Have All the Women (and Men) Gone: Reflections on Gender and the Second Intifada." *Feminist Review* 69 (Winter): 21–43.

Johnston, Richard, Keith Banting, Will Kymlicka, and Stuart Soroka. (2010). "National Identity and Support for the Welfare State." *Canadian Journal of Political Science* 43, 2 (June): 349–78.

Jordan, Michael J. (2009). "Ahmadinejad Polarizes UN Racism Conference." *The Christian Science Monitor* (20 April). Available at https://www.csmonitor.com/World/2009/0420/p06s07-wogn.html (accessed May 5, 2019).

Joseph, Benjamin M. (1988). *Besieged Bedfellows: Israel and the Land of Apartheid*. New York: Greenwood Press.

Juan, E. San. (1991). "Multiculturalism vs. Hegemony: Ethnic Studies, Asian Americans and US Racial Politics." *Massachusetts Review* 32, 3 (Fall): 467–77.

Kahn, Susan Martha. (2010). "Are Genes Jewish?: Conceptual Ambiguities in the New Genetic Age." In Susan A. Glenn and Naomi B. Sokoloff (eds.), *Boundaries of Jewish Identity*, pp. 12–26. Seattle: University of Washington Press.

Kapitan, Tomis, and Erich Schulte. (2003). "The Rhetoric of 'Terrorism' and Its Consequences." *Journal of Political and Military Sociology* 30, 1 (Summer): 172–96.

Kaplan, Danny, and Eyal Ben-Ari. (2000). "Brothers and Others in Arms: Managing Gay Identity in Combat Units in the Israeli Army." *Journal of Contemporary Ethnography* 29, 4 (August): 396–432.

Karmi, Ghada. (2007). *Married to Another Man: Israel's Dilemma in Palestine*. London: Pluto Press.

Katz, Hagai. (2006). "Gramsci, Hegemony and Global Civil Society Networks." *Voluntas: International Journal of Voluntary and Nonprofit Organizations* 17, 4: 332–47.

Kawas, Hanna. (2006). "Open Letter to the Assembly of First Nations" (6 March). Available at http://www.cpavancouver.org/index.php/2006/03/06/an-open-letter-by-cpa-to-the-assembly-of-first-nations/ (accessed December 10, 2018).

Kay, Barbara. (2016). "Barbara Kay: The Indigenous Tribes of Israel." *National Post* (28 June). Available at https://nationalpost.com/opinion/barbara-kay-the-Indigenous-tribes-of-israel (accessed May 5, 2019).

Kay, Zachariah. (1978). *Canada and Palestine: The Politics of Non-Commitment*. Jerusalem: Israel Universities Press.

Kay, Zachariah. (1996). *The Diplomacy of Prudence: Canada and Israel, 1948–1958*. Montreal and Kingston: McGill-Queen's University Press.

Keehn, Jeremy. (2015). "What Justin Trudeau's Victory Means for Canada." *The New Yorker* (20 October). Available at http://www.newyorker.com/news/news-desk/what-justin-trudeaus-victory-means-for-canada (accessed May 5, 2019).

Kellogg, Paul. (2004). "After Left Nationalism: The Future of Canadian Political Economy." *Marxism* 2: 21–31.

Kellogg, Paul. (2005). "Kari Levitt and the Long Detour of Canadian Political Economy." *Studies in Political Economy* 76 (Autumn): 31–60.

Kellogg, Paul. (2015). *Escape from the Staple Trap: Canadian Political Economy After Left Nationalism*. Toronto: University of Toronto Press.

Kernerman, Gerald. (2005). *Multicultural Nationalism: Civilizing Difference, Constituting Community*. Vancouver: University of British Columbia Press.

Kershner, Isabel, and Joseph Berger (2011). "After American Jewish Outcry, Israel Ends Ad Campaign Aimed at Expatriates," *The New York Times* (2 December). https://www.nytimes.com/2011/12/03/world/middleeast/after-american-outcry-israel-ends-ad-campaign-aimed-at-expatriates.html (accessed May 5, 2019).

Kettler, David. (2006). "The Political Theory Question in Political Science." *American Political Science Review* 100, 4: 531–37.

Khalidi, Rashid. (2006). *The Iron Cage: The Story of the Palestinian Struggle for Statehood*. Boston: Beacon Press.

Khalidi, Rashid. (2010 [1997]). *Palestinian Identity: The Construction of Modern National Consciousness*. New York: Columbia University Press.

Khalidi, Walid. (1985). "A Palestinian Perspective on the Arab-Israeli Conflict." *Journal of Palestine Studies* XIV, 4 (Summer 1985): 35–48.

Khalidi, Walid. (1987 [1971]). *From Haven to Conquest: Readings in Zionism and the Palestine Problem Until 1948*. Washington: Institute for Palestine Studies.

Khamaisi, Rassem. (2011). "Territorial Dispossession and Population Control of the Palestinians." In Elia Zureik, David Lyon, and Yasmeen Abu-Laban (eds.), *Surveillance and Control in Israel/Palestine: Population, Territory and Power*, pp. 335–52. London and New York: Routledge.

Kiely, Ray. (2005). "Global Civil Society and Spaces of Resistance." In John Eade and Darren O'Byrne (eds.), *Global Ethics and Civil Society*, pp. 138–53. Aldershot: Ashgate.

Kilibarda, Kole. (2008). "*Canadian and Israeli Defense—Industrial and Homeland Security Ties: An Analysis.*" Report for the New Transparency: Surveillance and Social Sorting. Queen's University (November). Available at https://www.sscqueens.org/sites/sscqueens.org/files/Canadian%20and%20Israeli%20Defense%20Industrial%20and%20Homeland%20Security%20Ties.pdf (accessed May 7, 2019). Link no longer working.

Kimche, Jon, and David Kimche. (1955). "The Mossad Machine—Confounding Military Intelligence 1946–1947." Reprinted in Walid Khalidi, *From Haven to Conquest: Readings in Zionism and the Palestine Problem Until 1948*, pp. 615–23. Washington: Institute for Palestine Studies (1971/1987).

Klein, Naomi. (2000). *No Logo: Taking Aim at the Brand Bullies*. Toronto: Viking Canada.

Klein, Naomi. (2007). *The Shock Doctrine: The Rise of Disaster Capitalism*. Toronto: Alfred A. Knopf Canada.

Klein, Naomi. (2008). "Israel: Don't Act Normal." Paper presented to Independent Jewish Voices Conference, Alliance of Concerned Jewish Canadians, Toronto, Canada (28 May). *Activist Magazine*. Video available at http://activistmagazine.com/index.php?option=content&task=view&id=840&Itemid=1 (accessed May 5, 2019). Link no longer working.

Klein, Naomi. (2009a). "Enough. It's Time for Boycott." *The Guardian* (10 January). Available at http://www.guardian.co.uk/commentisfree/2009/jan/10/naomi-klein-boycott-israel (accessed May 5, 2019).

Klein, Naomi. (2009b). "Israel: Boycott, Divest, Sanction." *The Nation* (7 January). Available at https://www.thenation.com/article/israel-boycott-divest-sanction/ (accessed February 21, 2009).

Klein, Naomi. (2009c). "Minority Death Match: Jews, Blacks and the 'Post-Racial' Presidency." *Harper's Magazine* (September): 53–67.

Klein, Naomi. (2011). "Introduction: The End of Israeli Exceptionalism." In Adam Horowitz, Lizzy Ratner, and Philip Weiss (eds.), *The Goldstone Report: The Legacy of the Landmark Investigation of the Gaza Conflict*, pp. xi–xvii. New York: Nation Books.

Klingemann, Hans-Dieter, ed. (2007). *The State of Political Science in Western Europe*. Orpaden: Budrich.

Koblowitz, Howard. (2019). "Birmingham City Council Passes Resolution 'Recognizing Life Work' of Angela Davis." *Birmingham Real-Time News* (8 January). Available from https://www.al.com/news/birmingham/2019/01/birmingham-city-council-passes-resolution-recognizing-life-work-of-angela-davis.html (accessed May 5, 2019).

Kolodziej, Edward A. (2005). *Security and International Relations*. Cambridge: Cambridge University Press.

Korn, Alina. (2000). "Military Government, Political Control and Crime: The Case of Israeli Arabs." *Crime, Law and Social Change* 34: 159–82.

Krieger, Joel. (2005). *Globalization and State Power: Who Wins When America Rules?* Great Questions in Politics Series. US: Pearson Education, Inc.

Küntzel, Matthias. (2007). *Jihad and Jew Hatred: Islamism, Nazism and the Roots of 9/11*. New York: Telos.

Kushner, Tony, and Alisa Solomon, eds. (2003). *Wresting with Zion: Progressive Jewish-American Responses to the Israeli-Palestinian Conflict*. New York: Grove Press.

Kuttab, Eileen. (2008). "Palestinian Women's Organizations: Global Cooption and Local Contradiction." *Cultural Dynamics* 20: 99–117.

Kymlicka, Will. (1989). *Liberalism, Community and Culture*. Oxford: Oxford University Press.

Kymlicka, Will. (1995). *Multicultural Citizenship*. Oxford: Clarendon Press.

Kymlicka, Will. (1998). *Finding Our Way: Rethinking Ethnocultural Relations in Canada*. Don Mills: Oxford University Press.

Kymlicka, Will. (2007). *Multicultural Odysseys: Navigating the New International Politics of Diversity*. Oxford: Oxford University Press.

Lau, Rachel, Jesse Ferreras, and Rebecca Joseph. (2017). "Quebec City Terrorist Attack on Mosque Kills 6, Injures 8." *Globalnews.ca*. Available at http://globalnews.ca/news/3213042/shooting-quebec-city-centre-culturel-islamique-mosque/ (accessed September 4, 2017).

Lavie, Smadar. (2011). "Mizrahi Feminism and the Question of Palestine." *Journal of Middle East Women's Studies* 7, 2 (Spring): 56–88.

Lawrence, Bonita. (2004). *"Real" Indians and Others: Mixed Blood Urban Native Peoples and Indigenous Nationhood*. Vancouver: University of British Columbia Press.

Leblanc, Daniel, Steven Chase, and Gloria Galloway. (2015). "Trudeau Sets Fresh Tone with Cabinet Ready to Tackle Thorny Issues." *The Globe and Mail* (4 November). Available at http://www.theglobeandmail.com/news/politics/trudeau-sworn-in-at-rideau-hall/article27096353/ (accessed May 5, 2019).

Lee, Erica Violet. (2014). "Our Revolution: First Nations Women in Solidarity with Palestine." *Moontime Warrior* (19 August). Available at https://moontimewarrior.com/2014/08/19/our-revolution-first-nations-women-in-solidarity-with-palestine/ (accessed May 5, 2019).

Lentin, Ronit. (2000). *Israel and the Daughters of the Shoah: Reoccupying the Territories of Silence*. New York: Berghahn Book.

Lentin, Ronit. (2008a). "Introduction: Thinking Palestine." In Ronit Lentin (ed.), *Thinking Palestine*, pp. 1–22. London and New York: Zed Books.

Lentin, Ronit. (2008b). "The Contested Memory of Dispossession: Commemorizing the Palestinian Nakba in Israel. In Ronit Lentin (ed.), *Thinking Palestine*, p. 209. London and New York: Zed Books.

Lentin, Ronit., ed. (2008c). *Thinking Palestine*. London and New York: Zed Books.

Levine-Rasky, Cynthia. (2007). "The Parents of Baywoods: Intersections Between Whiteness and Jewish Ethnicity." In Paul Carr and Darren Lund (eds.), *The Great White North?: Exploring Whiteness, Privilege and Identity in Education in Canada*, pp. 159–173. Rotterdam: Sense Publishers.

Levy, Yagil. (2010). "The Clash Between Feminism and Religion in the Israeli Military: A Multilayered Analysis." *Social Politics* 17, 2: 185–209.

Lewis, Donald M. (2010). *Origins of Christian Zionism and Evangelical Support for Jewish Homeland.* New York: Cambridge University Press.
Lia, Brynjar. (2006). *A Police Force Without a State: A History of the Palestinian Security Forces in the West Bank and Gaza.* Reading, UK: Ithaca Press.
Lilienthal, Alfred M. (1978). *The Zionist Connection: What Price Peace?* New York: Dodd Mead.
Lindsay, James G. (2012). "Reforming UNRWA." *Middle East Quarterly* 19, 4 (Fall): 85–91.
Littler, Jo. (2005) "Beyond the Boycott: Anti-Consumerism, Cultural Change and the Limits of Reflexivity." *Cultural studies* 19, 2 (March): 227–52.
Loach, Ken. (2006). "Press Release: Ken Loach Joins the Cultural Boycott of Israel" (24 August). Available at https://bdsmovement.net/news/press-release-ken-loach-joins-cultural-boycott-israel (accessed May 5, 2019).
Loshitzky, Yosefa. (2009). "Israel's Blonde Bombshells and Real Bombs in Gaza." *Electronic Intifada* (5 January). Available at https://electronicintifada.net/content/israels-blonde-bombshells-and-real-bombs-gaza/7923 (accessed July 17, 2017).
Lourde, Audre. (2007 [1984]). *Sister Outsider: Essays and Speeches.* Foreword by Cheryl Clarke. Berkeley: Crossing Press.
Lyapichev, Semyon. (2010). "The UN Human Rights Council: Its Roots and Evolution." *International Affairs* 6: 138–50.
Lyon, David. (2003). *Surveillance After September 11.* Cambridge: Polity Press.
Lyon, David. (2007). *Surveillance Studies: An Overview.* Cambridge: Polity Press.
Lyon, David, and Elia Zureik. (1996). "Surveillance, Privacy and the New Technology." In David Lyon and Elia Zureik (eds.), *Computers, Surveillance and Privacy*, pp. 1–18. Minneapolis: University of Minnesota Press.
MacAllister, Karine. (2008). "Applicability of the Crime of Apartheid to Israel." *Al-Majdal*, BADIL Resource Center 38 (Summer): 1–14. Available at http://www.badil.org/en/component/k2/item/72-applicability-of-the-crime-of-apartheid-to-israel (accessed December 14, 2018).
MacCharles, Tonda, Les Whittington, and Bruce Campion-Smith. (2015). "Prime Minister Justin Trudeau Unveils Diverse Cabinet in Touching Ceremony." *TheStar.com* (4 November). Available at http://www.thestar.com/news/canada/2015/11/04/trudeaus-cabinet-prospects-found-for-rideau-hall.html (accessed May 5, 2019).
MacDonald, David. (2008). *Identity Politics in the Age of Genocide: The Holocaust and Historical Representation.* London: Routledge.
Mackey, Eva. (2002). *The House of Difference: Cultural Politics and National Identity in Canada.* Toronto: University of Toronto Press.
Macklin, Audrey. (2001). "Borderline Security." In Ronald J. Daniels, Patrick Macklen, and Kent Roach (eds.), *The Security of Freedom: Essays on Canada's Anti-Terrorism Bill*, pp. 383–404. Toronto: University of Toronto Press.
MacMillan, Margaret. (2001). *Paris 1919.* New York: Random House.
Malhotra, Ram C. (1964). "Apartheid and the United Nations: Africa in Motion." *Annals of the Academy of Political and Social Sciences* 354 (July): 135–44.

Mallison, Jr., William T. (1971). "The Balfour Declaration: An Appraisal in International Law." In Ibrahim Abu-Lughod (ed.), *The Transformation of Palestine; Essays on the Origin and Development of the Arab-Israeli Conflict*, pp. 61–111. Evanston: Northwestern University Press.

Maltz, Judy. (2016). "Where Does President-Elect Donald Trump Stand on Israel?" *Haaretz* (11 November). Available at http://www.haaretz.com/israel-news/.premium-1.752467 (accessed November 11, 2016).

Maman, Daniel. (1999). "The Social Organization of the Israeli Economy: A Comparative Analysis." *Israel Affairs* 5, 2: 87–102.

Mamdani, Mahmood. (2004). *Good Muslim, Bad Muslim: America, the Cold War, and the Roots of Terror*. New York: Pantheon Books.

Mandela, Nelson. (1997). "Address by President Nelson Mandela at the International Day of Solidarity with the Palestinian People." *Pretoria South African History Online* (4 December). Available at http://www.sahistory.org.za/archive/address-president-nelson-mandela-international-day-solidarity-palestinian-people-pretoria-4- (accessed September 1, 2017).

Maniquet, Scott. (2010). "Excerpt: Harper's Speech on Israel, Anti-Semitism." *National Post* (8 November). Available at http://news.nationalpost.com/2010/11/08/excerpt-harpers-speech-on-israel-anti-semitism/ (accessed May 5, 2019).

Marshall, Mark. (1995). "Rethinking the Palestine Question: The Apartheid Paradigm." *Journal of Palestine Studies* 25, 1 (Autumn): 15–22.

Martin, Patrick. (2016). "Parliament Votes to Reject Israel Boycott Campaign." *The Globe and Mail* (23 February). Available at https://www.theglobeandmail.com/news/world/parliament-votes-to-reject-campaign-to-boycott-israel/article28863810/ (accessed January 28, 2019).

Marx, Anthony W. (1998). *Making Race and Nation: A Comparison of South Africa, the United States and Brazil*. Cambridge: Cambridge University Press.

Masalha, Nur. (2007). *The Bible and Zionism: Invented Traditions, Archaeology and Post-Colonialism in Israel-Palestine*. London and New York: Zed Books.

Masri, Mazen. (2011). "A Tale of Two Conferences: On Power, Identity and Academic Freedom." *AAUP Journal of Academic Freedom* 2: 1–28.

Masri, Mazen. (2017). *The Dynamics of Exclusionary Constitutionalism: Israel as a Jewish and Democratic State*. Oxford and Portland: Hart Publishing (imprint of Bloomsbury Publishing).

Massad, Joseph. (1993). "Palestinians and the Limits of Racialized Discourse." *Social Text* 34: 94–114.

Massad, Joseph. (1995). "Conceiving the Masculine: Gender and Palestinian Nationalism." *Middle East Journal* 3 (Spring): 467–83.

Massad, Joseph. (2006). *The Persistence of the Palestinian Question: Essays on Zionism and the Palestinians*. London: Routledge.

Massey, Douglas S., and Nancy A. Denton. (1993). *American Apartheid: Segregation and the Making of the Underclass and the Urban Underclass*. Cambridge: Harvard University Press.

Mather, Steven. (2006) "Israel Withdraws Its Ambassador for Venezuela." *Venezuelanalysis.com* (8 August). Available at https://venezuelanalysis.com/news/1875 (accessed December 10, 2018).

May, Stephen, Tariq Modood, and Judith Squires. (2004). "Ethnicity, Nationalism, and Minority Rights: Charting the Disciplinary Debates." In Stephen May, Tariq Modood, and Judith Squires (eds.), *Ethnicity, Nationalism and Minority Rights*, pp. 1–23. Cambridge: Cambridge University Press.

Mbembe, Achille. (2001). *On the Postcolony*. California: University of California Press.

Mbembe, Achille. (2003). "Necropolitics." *Public Culture* 15, 1: 11–40.

Mbembe, Achille. (2015). "On Palestine." In Jon Soske and Sean Jacobs (eds.), *Apartheid Israel: The Politics of an Analogy*, pp. vii–viii. Chicago: Haymarket Books.

McCarthy, Rory. (2010). "Barak: Make Peace with Palestinians or Face Apartheid." *Guardian.co.uk* (3 February). Available at https://www.theguardian.com/world/2010/feb/03/barak-apartheid-palestine-peace (accessed December 14, 2018).

McClintock, Anne. (1995). *Imperial Leather: Race, Gender and Sexuality in the Colonial Context*. New York and London: Routledge.

McCulloch, Jude, and Vicki Sentas. (2006). "The Killing of Jean Charles de Menezes: Hyper-Militarism in the Neoliberal Economic Free-Fire Zone." *Social Justice* 33, 4 (Winter): 1–13.

McDonagh, John. (2004). "The Philistines as Scapegoats: Narratives and Myths in the Invention of Ancient Israel and in Modern Critical Theory." *Holy Land Studies* 3, 1: 93–111.

McDonald, David A. (2009). *Electric Capitalism: Recolonizing Africa on the Power Grid*. London: Earthscan and Cape Town: HSRC Press.

McDonald, David A., and L. Smith. (2004). "Privatizing Cape Town: From Apartheid to Neoliberalism in the Mother City." *Urban Studies* 41, 8: 1461–84.

McGreal, Chris. (2006). "Worlds Apart." *The Guardian* (6 February). Available at https://www.theguardian.com/world/2006/feb/06/southafrica.israel (accessed May 14, 2009).

McGuinness, Margaret E. (2011). "Peace v. Justice: The Universal Declaration of Human Rights and the Modern Origins of the Debate." *Diplomatic History* 35, 5 (November): 749–68.

McKay, Ian. (2005). *Rebels, Reds, Radicals: Rethinking Canada's Left History*. Toronto: Between the Lines Press.

McKay, Ian. (2008). *Reasoning Otherwise: Leftists and the People's Enlightenment in Canada, 1890–1920*. Toronto: Between the Lines Press.

McKittrick, Katherine. (2006). *Demonic Grounds: Black Women and the Cartographies of Struggle*. Minneapolis: University of Minnesota Press.

McKittrick, Katherine, and Clyde Woods, eds. (2007). *Black Geographies and the Politics of Place*. Boston: Between the Lines Press.

McLean, Jesse. (2010). "Backlash Grows Against Pride's 'Israeli Apartheid' Ban." *TheStar.com*. (6 June). Available at https://www.thestar.com/news/

gta/2010/06/06/backlash_grows_against_prides_israeli_apartheid_ban.html (accessed May 5, 2019).
McSweeney, Bill. (1999). *Security, Identity and Interests: A Sociology of International Relations*. Cambridge: Cambridge University Press.
Mearsheimer, John J., and Stephen M. Walt. (2006). "The Israel Lobby." *London Review of Books* 28, 6: 3–12.
Mearsheimer, John J., and Stephen M. Walt. (2007). *The Israel Lobby and US Foreign Policy*. New York: Farrar, Straus and Giroux.
Mepschen, Pual, Jan Willem Duyvendak, and Evelien H. Tonkens. (2010). "Sexual Politics, Orientalism and Multicultural Citizenship in the Netherlands." *Sociology* 44, 5: 962–79.
Merlan, Francesca. (2009). "Indigeneity: Global and Local." *Current Anthropology* 50, 3: 303–33.
Mezvinsky, Norton. (2012). *Christian Zionism: The Promised Land and the Arab-Palestinian Conflict*. Pluto Press.
Migdal, Joel S. (2001). *Through the Lens of Israel: Explorations in State and Society*. Albany: State University of New York Press.
Miki, Roy. (2005). *Redress: Inside the Japanese Canadian Call for Justice*. Vancouver: Raincoast Books.
Mills, Charles. (1997). *The Racial Contract*. Ithaca: Cornell University.
Mirpuri, Anoop, Keith P. Feldman, and Georgia M. Roberts. (2009). "Antiracism and Environmental Justice in an Age of Neoliberalism: An Interview with Van Jones." *Antipode* 41, 3: 401–15.
Monture-Angus, Patricia. (1995). *Thunder in My Soul: A Mohawk Woman Speaks*. Halifax: Fernwood.
Moore, Dahlia. (2011). "Feminist Changes in Israel." In A. Rutherford et al. (eds.), *Handbook of International Feminisms: Perspectives on Psychology, Women, Culture and Rights*, pp. 59–82. New York: Springer.
Morial, Marc H. (2009). "Foreword." In Robert T. Bullard and Beverly Wright (eds.), *Race, Place and Environmental Justice After Hurricane Katrina: Struggles to Reclaim, Rebuild and Revitalize New Orleans and the Gulf Coast*, pp. xv–xviii. Boulder: Westview Press.
Morris, Benny. (2008). "The New Historiography: Israel Confronts Its Past." In Laurence J. Silberstein (ed.), *Postzionism: A Reader*, pp. 31–45. New Brunswick: Rutgers University Press.
Morton, Adam David. (2003). "Historicizing Gramsci: Situating Ideas in and Beyond Their Contexts." *International Political Economy* 10, 1 (February): 118–46.
Morton, Adam David. (2007a). *Unraveling Gramsci: Hegemony and Passive Revolution in the Global Political Economy*. London: Pluto Press.
Morton, Adam David. (2007b). "Waiting for Gramsci: State Formation, Passive Revolution and the International." *Millennium: Journal of International Studies* 35, 3 (September): 597–621.
Morton, Adam David. (2011). *Revolution and State in Modern Mexico: The Political Economy of Uneven Development*. Lanham: Rowman and Littlefield.
Mouammar, Khaled. (2005). "Khaled Mouammar's Complaint Re: Ontario Provincial Police's Trip to Israel." *Address to Professional Standards*

Bureau, Ontario Provincial Police (11 August). Available at http://www.montrealmuslimnews.net/khaled.pdf.

Mughal, Fiyaz. (2017). "A UK Mosque Is Targeted Once a Week—We Need to Deal with Anti-Muslim Hatred." *New Statesman* (14 July). Available at http://www.newstatesman.com/politics/uk/2017/07/uk-mosque-targeted-once-week-we-need-deal-anti-muslim-hatred (accessed September 4, 2017).

Mullen, Bill V. (2013). "Palestine, Boycott, and Academic Freedom: A Reassessment Introduction." *American Association of University Professors (AAUP) Journal of Academic Freedom* 4: 1–5.

Naaman, Dorit. (2006). "The Silenced Outcry: A Feminist Perspective from the Israeli Checkpoints in Palestine." *NWSA Journal* 18, 3 (Fall): 168–80.

Naaman, Dorit. (2007). "Brides of Palestine/Angels of Death: Media, Gender, and Performance in the Case of the Palestinian Female Suicide Bombers." *Signs: Journal of Women in Culture and Society* 32, 4: 933–55.

Naaman, Dorit. (2009). "Israel's Elections Are Nothing to Celebrate." *Rabble.ca* (11 February). Available at http://rabble.ca/news/israels-elections-why-we-should-not-celebrate-only-democracy-middle-east (accessed May 5, 2019).

Nadeau, Mary-Jo, and Alan Sears. (2010). "The Palestine Test: Countering the Silencing Campaign." *Studies in Political Economy* 85 (Spring): 7–33.

Nadeau, Mary-Jo, and Alan Sears. (2011). "This Is What Complicity Looks Like: Palestine and the Silencing Campaign on Campus." *The Bullet* (5 March). Available at http://www.socialistproject.ca/bullet/475.php#continue (accessed May 4, 2019).

Nadel, Ira B. (2010). *Leon Uris: Life of a Best Seller*. Austin: University of Texas Press.

Narang, A. S. (2001). "World Conferences Against Racism: Prospects and Challenges." *Economic and Political Weekly* 36, 27 (7–13 July): 2495–99.

Nath, Nisha, Ethel Tungohan, and Megan Gaucher. (2018). "The Future of Canadian Political Science: Boundary Transgressions, Gender and Anti-Oppression Frameworks." *Canadian Journal of Political Science* 51, 3 (September): 619–42.

Netanyahu, Benjamin. (1982). "Foreword." In Benjamin Netanyahu (ed.), *International Terrorism: Challenge and Response*, pp. 1–2. New Brunswick: Transaction Publishers.

Neumann, Michael. (2005). *The Case Against Israel*. Oakland: Counterpunch.

New York Times. (1975). "UN Resolution on Zionism." (Report). *Journal of Palestine Studies* 5, 1 and 2 (Autumn 1975–Winter 1976): 252–54.

New York Times, Editorial Board. (2018). "Curbing Speech in the Name of Helping Israel." *The New York Times* (18 December). Available at https://www.nytimes.com/2018/12/18/opinion/editorials/israel-bds.html (accessed January 28, 2019).

Newsome, Yvonne D. (1991). "International Issues and Domestic Ethnic Relations: African-Americas, American Jews, and the Israel-South Africa Debate." *International Journal of Politics, Culture and Society* 5, 1: 19–48.

Noble, Bobby. (2012). "Trans-." In Catherine M. Orr, Ann Braithwaite, and Diane Lichtenstein (eds.), *Rethinking Women's and Gender Studies*, pp. 277–292. New York: Routledge.

Noble, David F. (2005). *Beyond the Promised Land: The Movement and the Myth.* Toronto: Between the Lines.

Not in Our Name (NION). (2009). "Jewish Voices Opposing Zionism." Available at www.nion.ca. Link no longer working.

OCHAOPT.org. (2009). "West Bank Movement and Access Update" (25 May). Available at http://www.ochaopt.org/documents/ocha_opt_movement_and_access_2009_05_25_english.pdf. Link no longer working.

Ochman, Patricia. (2008). "Recent Developments in Canadian Aboriginal Law: Overview of Case Law and of Certain Principles of Aboriginal Law." *International Community Law Review* 10: 319–50.

Ong, Aihwa. (2006). *Neoliberalism as Exception: Mutations in Citizenship and Sovereignty.* Durham: Duke University Press.

O'Sullivan, Meghan L. (2003). *Shrewd Sanctions: Statecraft and State Sponsors of Terrorism.* Washington: Brookings Institution Press.

Padnan-Eisenstark, Dorit D. (1973). "Are Israeli Women Really Equal? Trends and Patterns of Israeli Women's Labor Force Participation: A Comparative Analysis." *Journal of Marriage and the Family* 35, 3 (August): 538–45.

Palestine Monitor. (2015). "Factbook 2015." Available at http://www.palestinemonitor.org/details.php?id=pezte3a10667y0cifjtlt9 (accessed November 18, 2016).

Palestinian BNC (Boycott, Divestment and Sanctions National Committee). (2005). "Palestinian Civil Society Calls for Boycott, Divestment and Sanctions Against Israel Until It Complies with International Law and Universal Principles of Human Rights" (9 July). Available at http://www.bdsmovement.net/call (accessed November 11, 2016).

Palestinian BNC (Boycott, Divestment and Sanctions National Committee). (2008). "Boycott Committee: Stop the Massacre in Gaza—Boycott Israel Now!" (27 December). Available at https://electronicintifada.net/content/boycott-committee-stop-massacre-gaza-boycott-israel-now/888 (accessed December 17, 2018).

Palestinian BNC (Boycott, Divestment and Sanctions National Committee). (2009a). "The BNC Salutes South African Dock Workers Action!" (3 February). Available at https://bdsmovement.net/news/bnc-salutes-south-african-dock-workers-action (accessed May 4, 2019).

Palestinian BNC (Boycott, Divestment and Sanctions National Committee). (2009b). "Join the Global BDS Action Day, March 30 (launched at the WSF 2009)" (12 February). Available at http://www.bdsmovement.net/?q=node/303 (accessed February 21, 2009). Link no longer working.

Palestinian BNC (Boycott, Divestment and Sanctions National Committee). (2012). "BDS at 7! Celebrating, Reflecting and Further Mainstreaming." Available at http://www.bdsmovement.net/2012/bds-at-7-9206 (accessed May 5, 2019).

Palestinian BNC (Boycott, Divestment and Sanctions National Committee). (2015). "Palestinian Civil Society Condemns Canadian Government Disinformation and Repression Against Boycott Movement." Statement (5 February). Available at https://bdsmovement.net/2015/palestinian-civil-society-condemns-canadian-government-disinformation-and-repression-against-boycott-movement-13051 (accessed May 5, 2019).

Palestinian BNC (Boycott, Divestment and Sanctions National Committee). (2018). "Nobel Prize Winner Supports BDS Movement for Palestinian Rights, Ending Military Aid to Israel" (5 October). Available at https://bdsmovement.net/news/nobel-prize-winner-supports-bds-movement-palestinian-rights-ending-military-aid-israel (accessed May 5, 2019).

Palestinian Campaign for the Academic and Cultural Boycott of Israel (PACBI). (2004). "Call for an Academic and Cultural Boycott of Israel" (6 July). Available at https://bdsmovement.net/pacbi/pacbi-call (accessed July 17, 2017).

Palestinian Campaign for the Academic and Cultural Boycott of Israel (PACBI). (n.d.). Home Page. Available at https://bdsmovement.net/pacbi/ (accessed November 20, 2018).

Palestinian Campaign for the Academic and Cultural Boycott of Israel (PACBI). (n.d.). "History." Available at https://bdsmovement.net/pacbi/pacbi-call (accessed December 21, 2018).

Palestinian Campaign for the Academic and Cultural Boycott of Israel (PACBI). (2006). "The PACBI Call for Academic Boycott Revised: Adjusting the Parameters of the Debate" (28 January). Available at https://bdsmovement.net/pacbi and at https://bdsmovement.net/news/pacbi-call-academic-boycott-revised-adjusting-parameters-debate (accessed December 19, 2018).

Palestinian Centre for Human Rights. (2009). "IOF Offensive on the Gaza Strip Makes It Like Earthquake Zone and Claims Civilian and Property." Press Release (22 January). Available at https://pchrgaza.org/en/?p=2411 (accessed December 17, 2018).

Palestinian Grassroots Anti-Apartheid Wall Campaign. (2010). *Apartheid Wall: Land Theft and Forced Exile, Factsheet*. Available at www.stopthewall.org (accessed July 17, 2017).

Pappano, Margaret Aziza. (2007). "The Ivory Tower Behind the Apartheid Wall." *Electronic Intifida* (25 July). Available at https://electronicintifada.net/content/ivory-tower-behind-apartheid-wall/7073 (accessed May 5, 2019).

Pappe, Ilan. (2003). "The Case for Boycott." *Borderlands E-Journal* 2, 3. Available at http://www.borderlands.net.au/vol2no3_2003/pappe.htm (accessed February 21, 2009).

Pappe, Ilan. (2006a) *A History of Modern Palestine*. 2nd ed. Cambridge: Cambridge University Press.

Pappe, Ilan. (2006b; 2007). *The Ethnic Cleansing of Palestine*. Oxford: Oneworld Publishing.

Pappe, Ilan. (2008). "The *Mukhabarat* State of Israel: A State of Oppression Is Not a State of Exception." In Ronit Lentin (ed.), *Thinking Palestine*, pp. 148–69. London: Zed Books.

Pappe, Ilan. (2010). "The Killing Fields of Gaza, 2004–2009." In Noam Chomsky and Ilan Pappe (eds.), *Gaza in Crisis—Reflections on Israel's War Against the Palestinians*, pp. 171–194. Chicago: Haymarket Books.

Pappe, Ilan. (2014). *The Idea of Israel: A History of Power and Knowledge*. London: Verso.

Pateman, Carol. (2007). "The Settler Contract." In Carol Pateman and Charles Mills (eds.), *Contract and Domination*, pp. 35–78. Malden, Mass.: Polity Press.

Pateman, Carol, and Charles Mills. (2007). *Contract and Domination*. Malden, Mass.: Polity Press.

Patten, Howard A. (2013). *Israel and the Cold War: Diplomacy, Strategy and the Policy of the Periphery at the United Nations*. London: I.B. Tauris.

Peberdy, Sally, and Jonathan Crush. (2007). "Histories, Realities and Negotiating Free Movement in Southern Africa." In Antoine Pécoud and Paul de Guchteneire (eds.), *Migration Without Borders: Essays on the Free Movement of People*, pp. 175–97. Paris and New York: United Nations Educational, Scientific and Cultural Organization and Berghahn Books.

Peled, Miko. (2017). "Why Israelis Must Disrupt the Occupation." *Electronic Intifada* (12 June). Available at https://electronicintifada.net/content/why-israelis-must-disrupt-occupation/20731 (accessed August 28, 2017).

Peled-Elhanan, Nurit. (2012). *Palestine in Israeli School Books*. London: I.B. Tauris.

Peleg, Yaron. (2006). "Heroic Conduct: Homoeroticism and the Creation of Modern, Jewish Masculinities." *Jewish Social Studies* (new series) 13, 1 (Autumn): 31–58.

Pennachetti, Joseph P. (2011). "Compliance with the City of Toronto's Anti-Discrimination Policy—Pride Toronto." (2 April). Available at https://www.toronto.ca/legdocs/mmis/2011/ex/bgrd/backgroundfile-38160.pdf (accessed May 4, 2019).

Perera, Suvendrini, and Sherene Razack, eds. (2014). *At the Limits of Justice: Women of Colour on Terror*. Toronto: University of Toronto Press.

Perry, Marvin, and Frederick Schweitzer, eds. (2008). *Antisemitic Myths: A Historical and Contemporary Anthology*. Bloomington: Indiana University Press.

Peter, Tom A., and Ilene R. Prusher. (2009). "Israeli Proposal: Make Jordan the Official Palestinian Homeland." *The Christian Science Monitor* (1 June). Available at http://www.csmonitor.com/World/Middle-East/2009/0601/p06s01-wome.html (accessed May 5, 2019).

Peters, Joan. (1984). *From Time Immemorial: The Origins of the Arab-Jewish Conflict over Palestine*. USA: JKAP Publishers.

Peto, Jennifer. (2010). "The Victimhood of the Powerful: White Jews, Zionism and the Racism of Hegemonic Holocaust Education." MA Thesis, Department of Sociology and Equity Studies in Education, University of Toronto.

Pieterse, Jan Nederveen. (1985). "Israel's Role in the Third World: Exporting West Bank Expertise." *Race and Class* XXV1, 3: 9–30.

Piterberg, Gabriel. (2008). *The Returns of Zionism: Myths, Politics and Scholarship in Israel.* London and New York: Verso.

Podur, Justin. (2009). "A Reply to Ignatieff on Israeli Apartheid Week." *Rabble.ca.* (9 March). Available at http://www.rabble.ca/news/reply-ignatieff-israeli-apartheid-week (accessed May 5, 2019).

Pohlandt-McCormick, Helena. (2006). *"I Saw a Nightmare ..." Doing Violence to Memory: The Soweto Uprising, June 16, 1976.* New York: Columbia University Press.

Polakow-Suransky, Sasha. (2010). *The Unspoken Alliance: Israel's Secret Relationship with Apartheid South Africa.* New York: Pantheon Books.

Pollak, Joel B. (2009). *The Kasrils Affair: Jews and Minority Politics in Post-Apartheid South Africa.* Capetown: Juta and Company Ltd.

Potter, Mitch. (2005). "Israelis Unleash Scream at Protest: New Weapon Knocks Crowds off Feet, Sound Blast Triggers Nausea, Dizziness." *The Toronto Star* (8 July). Available at https://www.indymedia.org.uk/en/2005/06/315129.html (accessed May 5, 2015).

Power, Nina. (2009). *One Dimensional Woman.* Hants, UK: Zero Books, John Hunt Publishing Ltd.

Prashad, Vijay. (2006). "Ethnic Studies Inside Out." *Journal of Asian American Studies* 9, 2 (June): 157–76.

Prashad, Vijay. (2012). "Pride Toronto Dispute Resolution Panel Complaint Decision Released." "Pride Toronto Dispute Resolution Process." Statement (29 June). Available at http://www.pridetoronto.com/about/press/news/pride-toronto-dispute-resolution-panel-complaint-decision-released/. Link no longer working.

Pride Toronto. (2011). "About Us." Available at http://www.pridetoronto.com/about-us/.

Pride Toronto. (2012). "Pride Toronto Dispute Resolution Panel Complaint Decision Released." "Pride Toronto Dispute Resolution Process." Statement (29 June). Available at http://www.pridetoronto.com/about/press/news/pride-toronto-dispute-resolution-panel-complaint-decision-released/. Link no longer working.

Puar, Jasbir K. (2007). *Terrorist Assemblages: Homonationalism in Queer Times.* Durham and London: Duke University Press.

Puar, Jasbir K. (2011). "Citation and Censorship: The Politics of Talking About the Sexual Politics of Israel." *Feminist Legal Studies* 19: 133–42.

QuAIA. (2011). "Who We Are: Queers Against Israeli Apartheid (QuAIA)." Available at http://queersagainstapartheid.org/who/ (accessed May 5, 2019).

Québec Solidaire (QS). (2010). "Boycott, Désinvestissement et Sanctions (BDS) Contre l'Apartheid Israélien." *Communiqué de Presse (National)* (18 April). Available at https://quebecsolidaire.net/nouvelle/boycott-desinvestissement-et-sanctions-bds-contre-lapartheid-israelien (accessed May 5, 2019).

Qumsieh, Mazin B. (2004). *Sharing the Land of Canaan: Human Rights and the Israeli-Palestinian Struggle*. London: Pluto Press.

Rabkin, Yakov M. (2006). *A Threat from Within: A Century of Jewish Opposition to Zionism*. New York: Zed Books.

Ralph, Diana. (2006). "Islamophobia and the 'War on Terror': The Continuing Pretext for US Imperial Conquest." In Paul Zarembka (ed.), *Research in Political* Economy *Volume 23: The Hidden History of 9-11-2001*, pp. 261–98. Amsterdam and San Diego: Elsevier.

Ramakrishnan, S. Karthick. (2016). "Editor's Introduction." *Journal of Race, Ethnicity and Politics* 1, 1: 1–4. Available at https://www.cambridge.org/core/services/aop-cambridge-core/content/view/7F6EAD1485EF3CAF843A6FFD2C57C59C/S2056608516000027a.pdf/editors_introduction.pdf (accessed May 5, 2019).

Raphaeli, Nimrod. (2006). "The Arab Boycott of Israel in the Globalization Age." *Middle East Media Research Institute Inquiry and Analysis Series 261* (20 January). Available at https://www.memri.org/reports/arab-boycott-israel-globalization-age (accessed May 5, 2019).

Ravid, Barak. (2010). "State Archives to Stay Classified for 20 More Years, PM Instructs." *Haaretz.com* (28 July). Available at https://www.haaretz.com/1.5152655 (accessed December 17, 2018).

Razack, Sherene H. (1998). *Looking White People in the Eye: Gender, Race and Culture in Courtrooms and Classrooms*. Toronto: University of Toronto Press.

Razack, Sherene H. (2002). *Race, Space and the Law: Unmapping a White Settler Society*. Toronto: Between the Lines.

Razack, Sherene H. (2004). *Dark Threats and White Knights: The Somalia Affair, Peacekeeping and the New Imperialism*. Toronto: University of Toronto Press.

Razack, Sherene H. (2008). *Casting Out: The Eviction of Muslims from Western Law and Politics*. Toronto: University of Toronto Press.

Razack, Sherene H. (2010). "A Hole in the Wall; A Rose at the Checkpoint: The Spatiality of Colonial Encounters in Occupied Palestine." *Journal of Critical Race Inquiry* 1, 1: 90–108.

Razack, Sherene H. (2015). *Dying from Improvement: Inquests and Inquiries into Indigenous Deaths in Custody*. Toronto: University of Toronto Press.

Razack, Sherene, Malinda Smith, and Sunera Thobani, eds. (2010). *States of Race: Critical Race Feminism for the 21st Century*. Toronto: Between the Lines Press.

Rebick, Judy, and Alan Sears. (2009). "Memo to Jason Kenney: Criticism of Israel Is Not Anti-Semitism." *Rabble.ca* (1 March). Available at http://www.rabble.ca/news/memo-minister-kenney-criticism-israel-not-anti-semitism (accessed May 5, 2019).

Reddy, E. S. (1974). "Apartheid and the International Community." *Issue: A Journal of Opinion* 4, 3 (Autumn): 19–24.

Reiter, Ester. (2016). *A Future Without Hate or Need: The Promise of the Jewish Left in Canada*. Toronto: Between the Lines Press.

Reut Institute. (2010). "Building a Political Firewall Against Israel's Delegitimization Conceptual Framework" (March). Available at http://reut-institute.org/data/uploads/PDFVer/20100310%20Delegitimacy%20Eng.pdf (accessed May 5, 2019).

Reuters. (2009a). "Venezuela Expels Israel Envoy over Gaza Attacks" (6 January). Available at http://www.reuters.com/article/middleeastCrisis/idUSN06444577 (accessed May 5, 2019).

Reuters. (2009b). "Canada to Skip UN Racism Conference Due to Expected Anti-Semitism." *Haaretz.com* (24 January). Available at https://www.haaretz.com/1.4983083 (accessed December 17, 2018).

Rich, Adrienne. (2009). "Why Support the US Campaign for Academic and Cultural Boycott of Israel?" *MR Online* (3 February). Available at http://mrzine.monthlyreview.org/rich080209.html (accessed May 5, 2019).

Rich, Wilbur C. (2007). "Introduction."" In Wilbur C. Rich (ed.), *African American Perspectives on Political Science* pp. 1–4. Philadelphia: Temple University Press.

Richards, Kimberley. (2019). "Angela Davis Reoffered Award by Birmingham Civil Rights Institute." *HuffPost US* (25 January). Available at https://www.huffingtonpost.ca/entry/angela-davis-birmingham-civil-rights-award_us_5c4b50fbe4b0287e5b8a59f8?ec_carp=1826608858893581029 (accessed January 25, 2018).

Richmond, Anthony H. (2004 [1994]). *Global Apartheid: Refugees, Racism, and the New World Order*. Toronto: Oxford University Press.

Riddell, John, ed. (1993). *To See the Dawn, Baku 1920: First Congress of Peoples of the East*. New York: Pathfinder.

Roberts, Dorothy. (2011). *Fatal Invention*. New York: The New Press.

Robinson, Cedric J. (2000). *Black Marxism: The Making of the Black Radical Tradition*. Chapel Hill: University of North Carolina Press.

Robinson, Mary. (2012). *Everybody Matters: My Life Giving Voice*. New York and London: Bloomsbury Publishing.

Rodinson, Maxime. (1973). *Israel: A Colonial Settler State?*. New York: Pathfinder.

Roediger, David. (1999). *The Wages of Whiteness: Race and the Making of the American Working Class*. London: Verso.

Roediger, David. (2007). *The Wages of Whiteness*. London: Verso.

Roediger, David. (2017). *Class, Race, and Marxism*. London and New York: Verso.

Rome Statute of the International Criminal Court. (1998). Final Act of the United Nations Diplomatic Conference of Plenipotentiaries on the Establishment of an International Court. UN Doc. (A/CONF.183/13). Rome: July 15–17, 1998. Available at http://legal.un.org/icc/rome/proceedings/E/Rome%20Proceedings_v1_e.pdf (accessed May 5, 2019).

Rose, David. (2008). "The Gaza Bombshell." *Vanity Fair*. Available at https://www.vanityfair.com/news/2008/04/gaza200804.

Rose, Hilary, and Steven Rose. (2002). "The Choice Is to Do Nothing or to Try to Bring About Change: Why We Launched the Boycott of Israeli

Institutions." *The Guardian* (15 July). Available at http://www.guardian.co.uk/world/2002/jul/15/comment.stevenrose (accessed May 5, 2019).

Rose, Hilary, and Steven Rose. (2008). "Israel, Europe and the Academic Boycott." *Race and Class* 50, 1: 1–20.

Rose, John. (2004). *The Myths of Zionism*. London: Pluto Press.

Rosengarten Frank, ed. (2011). *Antonio Gramsci: Letters from Prison*. Translated by Raymond Rosenthal. New York: Columbia University Press.

Roskam, Peter J. (2017). "HR 1697, Israel Anti-Boycott Act," 115th Congress, 1st Session, Foreign Affairs Committee (introduced 23 March). Available at https://www.congress.gov/bill/115th-congress/house-bill/1697 (accessed May 5, 2019).

Ross, Oakland. (2008). "Different Worlds, Similar Problems: Native Women Head to Israel to Exchange Ideas and Improve Relationship That Has Been Strained." *The Star* (4 February). Available at https://www.thestar.com/news/2008/02/04/different_worlds_similar_problems.html (accessed December 8, 2018).

Rubenberg, Cheryl. (1983). *The Palestine Liberation Organization: Its Institutional Infrastructure*. Belmont: Institute of Arab Studies.

Rubenberg, Cheryl A. (2001). *Palestinian Women: Patriarchy and Resistance in the West Bank*. Boulder: Lynne Rienner Publications.

Ruff, Allen. (2007). "Do Zionists Run America?" *MR Online* (28 May). Available at https://mronline.org/2007/05/28/do-zionists-run-america/ (accessed May 5, 2019).

Ryan, Sheila, and Muhammad Hallaj. (1983). *Palestine Is, But Not in Jordan*. Belmont: AAUG Press.

Ryan, Sid. (2008). Speaking at Independent Jewish Voices conference, Alliance of Concerned Jewish Canadians, Toronto (29 May). Observer's Notes, A. Bakan.

Sa'ar, Amalia, and Taghreed Yahia-Younis. (2008). "Masculinity in Crisis: The Case of Palestinians in Israel." *British Journal of Middle Eastern Studies* 35, 3 (December): 305–23.

Sa'di, Ahmad H. (2000). "Israel as Ethnic Democracy? What Are the Implications for the Palestinian Minority?" *Arab Studies Quarterly* 22, 1 (Winter): 25–37.

Sa'di, Ahmad H. (2011). "Ominous Designs: Israel's Strategies and Tactics of Controlling the Palestinians During the First Two Decades." In Elia Zureik, David Lyon, and Yasmeen Abu-Laban (eds.), *Surveillance and Control in Israel/Palestine: Population, Territory and Power*, pp. 83–98. London and New York: Routledge.

Sacher, Howard M. (2005). *A History of the Jews in the Modern World*. New York: Vintage.

Sacher, Howard M. (2007). *A History of Israel from the Rise of Zionism to Our Time*. 3rd ed. New York: Alfred Knopf.

Said, Edward. (1979a). *Orientalism*. New York: Basic Books.

Said, Edward. (1988). "Introduction." In Edward W. Said and Christopher Hitchens (eds.), *Blaming the Victims: Spurious Scholarship and the Palestinian Question*, pp. 1–19. London and New York: Verso.

Said, Edward. (1992 [1981, 1979b]). *The Question of Palestine*. New York: Vintage Books.

Said, Edward. (1994). *Culture and Imperialism*. New York: Vintage.

Said, Edward. (1999). "The One State Solution." *The New York Times* (10 January). Available at http://www.nytimes.com/1999/01/10/magazine/the-one-state-solution.html (accessed May 5, 2019).

Said, Edward. (2004a). *From Oslo to Iraq and the Road Map*. New York: Vintage Books.

Said, Edward. (2004b). "Propaganda and War." In Edward W. Said, Tony Judt, and Wadie E. Said (eds.), *From Oslo to Iraq and the Road Map: Essays*, pp. 98–106. New York: Vintage Books.

Said, Edward W., Ibrahim Abu-Lughod, Janet L. Abu-Lughod, Muhammad Hallaj, and Elia Zureik. (1988). "A Profile of the Palestinian People." In Edward W. Said and Christopher Hitchens (eds.), *Blaming the Victims: Spurious Scholarship and the Palestinian Question*, pp. 235–96. London and New York: Verso.

Said, Edward W., and Christopher Hitchens, eds. (1988). *Blaming the Victims: Spurious Scholarship and the Palestinian Question*. London and New York: Verso.

Saifer, Ben. (2010). "Shalom-Salaam: Campus Israel Advocacy and the Politics of 'Dialogue.'" *Upping the Anti* 9 (November): 73–90.

Salaita, Steven. (2006). *The Holy Land in Transit: Colonialism and the Quest for Canaan*. New York: Syracuse University Press.

Salaita, Steven. (2015). *Uncivil Rites: Palestine and the Limits of Academic Freedom*. Chicago: Haymarket Books.

Salaita, Steven. (2016). *Inter/Nationalism: Decolonizing Native America and Palestine*. Minneapolis: University of Minnesota Press.

Salée, Daniel. (2004). "The Quebec State and Indigenous Peoples." In Alain G. Gagnon (ed.), *Québec: State and Society*. 3rd ed., pp. 97–124. Peterborough: Broadview Press.

Sand, Shlomo. (2009). *The Invention of the Jewish People*. London: Verso.

Sanders, Jacinta. (1999). "Honest Brokers? American and Norwegian Facilitation of Israeli-Palestinian Negotiations (1991–1993)." *Arab Studies Quarterly* 21, 2 (Spring): 47–70.

Sanyika, Mtangulizi. (2009). "Katrina and the Condition of Black New Orleans: The Struggle for Justice, Equality, and Democracy." In Robert T. Bullard and Beverly Wright (eds.), *Race, Place and Environmental Justice After Hurricane Katrina: Struggles to Reclaim, Rebuild and Revitalize New Orleans and the Gulf Coast*, pp. 87–111. Boulder, Colorado: Westview Press.

Sasson-Levy, Orna. (2002). "Constructing Identities at the Margins: Masculinities and Citizenship in the Israeli Army." *The Sociological Quarterly* 43, 3 (Summer): 357–83.

Sasson-Levy, Orna. (2003). "Feminism and Military Gender Practices: Israeli Women Soldiers in 'Masculine' Roles." *Sociological Inquiry* 73, 3 (August): 440–65.
Saul, John. (2002). "Afropessimism/optimism: The Antinomies of Colin Leys." In Abigail B. Bakan and Eleanor MacDonald (eds.), *Critical Political Studies: Debates and Dialogues from the Left*, pp. 94–112. Montreal: McGill-Queen's University Press.
Schaefer, Donald D. A. (1996). "U.S. Policy and the Arab Economic Boycott: Understanding the Origins and Dealing with Its Consequences." *The Social Science Journal* 33, 2: 168–70.
Schiffer, Sabine, and Constantin Wagner. (2011). "Anti-Semitism and Islamophobia: New Enemies, Old Patterns." *Race and Class* 52, 3: 77–84.
Schlaim, Avi. (2000). *The Iron Wall: Israel and the Arab World.* New York: W.W. Norton.
Schmidt, Andréa. (2008). "BDS Conference in Palestine: Building Solidarity, Combating Normalization." *Left Turn* (9 April). Available at http://www.leftturn.org/bds-conference-palestine-building-solidarity-combating-normalization (accessed May 5, 2019).
Schneer, Jonathan. (2010). *The Balfour Declaration: The Origins of the Arab-Israeli Conflict*. Toronto: Random House Canada.
Schwartzman, Kathleen C. (2001) "Can International Boycotts Transform Political Systems? The Cases of Cuba and South Africa." *Latin American Politics and Society* 43, 2 (Summer 2001): 115–46.
Scott, James. (1985). *Weapons of the Weak: Everyday Forms of Peasant Resistance*. New Haven: Yale University Press.
Seattle Times. (2002). "Two Peoples, One Land: Understanding the Israeli-Palestinian Conflict" (12 May). Available at http://old.seattletimes.com/news/nation-world/mideast/roots/ (accessed January 28, 2018).
Sela-Sheffy, Rakefet. (2006). "Detachment and Engagement: Israelis' Everyday Verbal Representations of 'the Israeli Person' and the Contest for the Right to Condemn a Collective Identity." *Social Identities: Journal for the Study of Race, Nation and Culture* 12, 3 (May): 3325–44.
Shafir, Gershon, and Yoav Peled. (2002). *Being Israeli: The Dynamics of Multiple Citizenship*. Cambridge: Cambridge University Press.
Shalhoub-Kevorkian, Nadera. (2006). "Negotiating the Present, Historicizing the Future: Palestinian Children Speak About the Israeli Separation Wall." *American Behavioral Scientist* 49, 8: 1101–24.
Shapiro, Talia. (2016). "Culture of Resistance: Why We Need You to Boycott, Divest and Sanction Israel." In Ghada Ageel (ed.), *Apartheid in Palestine: Hard Laws and Harder Experiences*, pp. 107–27. Edmonton: The University of Alberta Press.
Shaw, Martin. (2019). "Vote Leave Relied on Racism. Brexit: The Uncivil War Disguised the Ugly Truth." *The Guardian, International Edition* (8 January). Available at https://www.theguardian.com/commentisfree/2019/jan/08/vote-leave-racism-brexit-uncivil-war-channel-4 (accessed May 5, 2019).

Sheen, David. (2015). "The Ethnic Cleansing of Africans in Israel." *Electronic Intifada* (28 December). Available at https://electronicintifada.net/content/ethnic-cleansing-africans-israel/15099 https://electronicintifada.net/content/ethnic-cleansing-africans-israel (accessed May 5, 2019).

Shemer, Nadav. (2009). "Israel Honors Aboriginal Australian Who Protested Against Nazis." *Haaretz.com* (1 May). Available at https://www.haaretz.com/1.5045984 (accessed May 5, 2019).

Shepherd, David. (2009). "Democracy in South Africa: Examining the Heritability of a Debate." *Politikon* 36, 2: 289–313.

Shlaim, Avi. (2002). *The Iron Wall: Israel and the Arab World*. New York: Penguin Books.

Shohat, Ella. (1988). "Sephardim in Israel: Zionism from the Standpoint of Its Jewish Victims." *Social Text* 19/20 (Autumn): 1–35.

Shuraydi, Muhammad A. (2001). "Edward W. Said and His 'Beautiful Old House': A Response to Weiner." In Naseer Aruri and Muhammad A. Shuraydi (eds.), *Revising Culture, Reinventing Peace: The Influence of Edward Said*, pp. 170–78. New York and Northampton: Interlink Publishing.

Siddiqui, Haroom. (2014). "Why the Aga Khan Loves Canada and We Love Him: Siddiqu." *The Star* (26 February). Available at https://www.thestar.com/opinion/commentary/2014/02/26/why_the_aga_khan_loves_canada_and_why_we_love_him_siddiqui.html (accessed January 20, 2019).

Siegel, Paul N. (1986). *The Meek and the Militant: Religion and Power Across the World*. London: Zed Books.

Simon, Roger I., Sharon Rosenberg, and Claudia Eppert. (2000). *Between Hope and Despair: Pedagogy and the Remembrance of Historical Trauma*. New York: Rowman and Littlefield.

Sion, Liora, and Eyal Ben-Ari. (2009). "Imagined Masculinity: Body, Sexuality, and Family Among Israeli Military Reserves." *Symbolic Interaction* 32, 1: 21–43.

Slabodsky, Santiago. (2014). *Decolonial Judaism: Triumphal Failures of Barbaric Thinking*. New York: Palgrave Macmillan.

Slater, Jerome. (2011). "The Attacks on the Goldstone Report." In Adam Horowitz, Lizzy Ratner, and Philip Weiss (eds.), *The Goldstone Report: The Legacy of the Landmark Investigation of the Gaza Conflict*, pp. 360–68. New York: Nation Books.

Smith, Charles C. (2007). *Conflict, Crisis, and Accountability: Racial Profiling and Law Enforcement in Canada*. Ottawa: Canadian Centre for Policy Alternatives.

Smith, Zac. (2009). "Countering Palestine Solidarity Work in Canada." *ZSpace*. Available at www.zmag.org. Link no longer working.

Smooha, Sammy. (1997). "Ethnic Democracy: Israel as an Archetype." *Israel Studies* 2, 2: 198–241.

Soares, Joseph A. (2007). *The Power of Privilege: Yale and America's Elite Colleges*. Stanford: Stanford University Press.

Soske, Jon, and Sean Jacobs. (2015a). "Apartheid/Hafrada: South Africa, Israel, and the Politics of Historical Comparison." In Jon Soske and Sean Jacobs (eds.), *Apartheid Israel: The Politics of an Analogy*, pp. 1–12. Chicago: Haymarket Books.

Soske, Jon, and Sean Jacobs, eds. (2015b). *Apartheid Israel: The Politics of an Analogy*. Chicago: Haymarket Books.

South Africa Department of Justice and Constitutional Development Truth and Reconciliation Commission (TRC). (1998). "The TRC Final Report" (29 October). Available at http://www.justice.gov.za/trc/report/index.htm (accessed August 25, 2017).

Spector, J. B. (2004). "Non-Traditional Diplomacy: Cultural, Academic and Sports Boycotts and Change in South Africa." Conference on International Anti-Apartheid Movements in South Africa's Freedom Struggle Conference, Durban, October 10–13, 2004. Available at scnc.ukzn.ac.za/doc/AAmwebsite/AAMCONFpapers/Spector,JB.doc (accessed May 5, 2019).

Spivak, Rhonda. (2010). "Editorial: Response to Aboriginal Speaker Who Mocked Irwin Cotler During Israeli Apartheid Week" (12 May). Available http://www.winnipegjewishreview.com/article_detail.cfm?id=115&sec=1 (accessed December 17, 2018).

Srivastava, Sarita. (2005). "'You're Calling Me a Racist?' The Moral and Emotional Regulation of Antiracism and Feminism." *Signs: Journal of Women in Culture and Society* 31, 1 (Autumn): 30–62.

Stasiulis, Daiva. (1999). "Feminist Intersectional Theorizing." In Peter S. Li (ed.), *Race and Ethnic Relations in Canada*. 2nd ed., pp. 347–97. New York: Oxford.

Stasiulis, Daiva, and Abigail Bakan. (2005). *Negotiating Citizenship: Migrant Women in Canada and the Global System*. Toronto: University of Toronto Press.

Stasiulis, Daiva, and Radha Jhappan. (1995). "The Fractious Politics of a Settler Society: Canada." In Daiva Stasiulis and Nira Yuval-Davis (eds.), *Unsettling Settler Societies: Articulations of Gender, Race, Ethnicity and Class*, pp. 95–131. London: Sage.

Stasiulis, Daiva, and Nira Yuval-Davis, eds. (1995). *Unsettling Settler Societies: Articulations of Gender, Race, Ethnicity and Class*. London: Sage.

Stavenhagen, Rodolfo. (2009). "Making the Declaaration Work." In Claire Charters and Roldolfo Stavenhagen (eds.), *Making the Declaration Work: The United Nations on the Rights of Indigenous Peoples*, pp. 352–71. Copenhagen: IWGIA.

Stein, Leonard. (1961). *The Balfour Declaration*. New York: Simon and Schuster.

Stein, Rebecca L. (2008). *Itineraries in Conflict: Israelis, Palestinians, and the Political Lives of Tourism*. Durham and London: Duke University Press.

Stein, Rebecca L. (2010). "Explosive: Scenes from Israel's Gay Occupation." *GLQ: A Journal of Gay and Lesbian Studies* 16, 4: 517–36.

Stewart, Penni. (2010). "Academic Freedom in These Times: Three Lessons from York University." *Cultural and Pedagogical Inquiry* 2, 2: 48–61.

Stoil, Rebecca Shimoni. (2015). "Obama Signs Anti-BDS Bill into Law." *The Times of Israel* (30 June). Available at https://www.timesofisrael.com/obama-signs-anti-bds-bill-into-law/ (accessed January 28, 2019).

Stop the Wall Campaign. (2005). "Entire Region of Norway to Boycott Apartheid Israel" (16 December). Available at https://www.stopthewall.org/2005/12/16/entire-region-norway-boycott-apartheid-israel (accessed December 17, 2018).

Stop the Wall Campaign. (2007). "Statement in Occasion of the Workers' Boycott Call." Available at https://www.stopthewall.org/downloads/pdf/S-F2.pdf (accessed December 17, 2018).

Sullivan, Shannon and Nancy Tuana, eds. (2007). *Race and Epistemologies of Ignorance*. New York: State University of New York.

Sussman, Gary. (2004). "Is the Two-State Solution Dead?" *Current History* 103, 669 (January): 37–42.

Swedenberg, Ted. (2003). *Memories of Revolt: The 1936–1939 Rebellion and the Palestinian National Past*. Fayetteville: University of Arkansas Press.

Tafler, Sid. (2007). "Web Site Promotes Hate, B'nai Brith Members." *The Globe and Mail* (24 May). Available at https://www.theglobeandmail.com/news/national/website-promotes-hate-bnai-brith-member-says/article685986/ (accessed May 5, 2019).

Tauber, Eliezer. (1999). "The Jewish and Arab Lobbies in Canada and the UN Partition of Palestine." *Israel Affairs* 5, 4: 229–44.

Tauber, Eliezer. (2002). *Personal Policy Making: Canada's Role in the Adoption of the Palestine Partition Resolution*. Westport and London: Greenwood Press.

Tawhai, Veronica M. H. (2016). "Indigenous Peoples and Indigeneity." In Andrew Peterson, Robert Hattam, Michalinos Zembylas, and James Arthur (eds.), *The Palgrave International Handbook of Education and Citizenship for Social Justice*, pp. 97–120. London: Palgrave Macmillan.

Taylor, Charles. (1994). "The Politics of Recognition." In Amy Gutmann (ed.), *Multiculturalism: Examining the Politics of Recognition*, pp. 25–74. Princeton: Princeton University Press.

Taylor, Rupert. (1999). "Political Science Encounters 'Race' and 'Ethnicity.'" In Martin Bulmer and John Solomos (eds.), *Ethnic and Racial Studies Today*, pp. 115–23. London and New York: Routledge.

Tekiner, Roselle. (1991). "Race and the Issue of National Identity in Israel." *International Journal of Middle East Studies* 23, 1 (February): 39–55.

"The UN Resolution on Zionism." (1975). *Journal of Palestine Studies* 5, 1-2: 252–54. doi: 10.2307/2535712.

Thobani, Sunera. (2002). "War Frenzy." *Meridians: Feminism, Race and Transformation* 2, 2: 289–97.

Thobani, Sunera. (2007a). "White Wars: Western Feminisms and the 'War on Terror.'" *Feminist Theory* 8, 2: 169–85.

Thobani, Sunera. (2007b). *Exalted Subjects: Studies in the Making of Race and Nation in Canada*. Toronto: University of Toronto Press.

Thompson, Debra. (2008). "Is Race Political?" *Canadian Journal of Political Science* 4, 3: 525–47.

Thompson, Debra. (2012). "Making (Mixed-)Race: Census Politics and the Emergence of Multiracial Multiculturalism in the United States, Great Britain and Canada," *Ethnic and Racial Studies* 35, 8: 1409–26.

Thompson, Debra. (2016). *The Schematic State: Race, Transnationalism and the Politics of the Census*. New York: Cambridge University Press.

Thompson, Jon. (2011). *No Debate: The Israel Lobby and Free Speech at Canadian Universities*. Toronto: CAUT Series, James Lorimer

Thorn, Haken. (2009). *Anti-Apartheid and the Emergence of a Global Civil Society*. London: Palgrave Macmillan.

Tibawi, Abdul L. (1978). *Anglo-Arab Relations and the Question of Palestine*. London: Luzac and Co.

Tilley, Virginia. (2005a). "From 'Jewish State and Arab State' to 'Israel and Palestine'? International Norms, Ethnocracy, and the Two-State Solution." *The Arab World Geographer* 8, 3: 140–46.

Tilley, Virginia. (2005b). *The One-State Solution: A Breakthrough for Peace in the Israeli-Palestinian Deadlock*. Ann Arbor: University of Michigan Press.

Todd, Paul, and Jonathan Bloch. (2003). *Global Intelligence: The World's Secret Services Today*. London and New York: Zed Books.

Toronto Star. (2010). "Canada Skipping UN Racism 'Hatefest' Again, Ottawa Says." *The Star.com* (25 November). Available at https://www.thestar.com/news/canada/2010/11/25/canada_skipping_un_racism_hatefest_again_ottawa_says.html (accessed May 5, 2019).

Truth and Reconciliation Commission of Canada (TRC). (2015). "Honouring the Truth, Reconciling for the Future: Summary of the Final Report of the Truth and Reconciliation Commission of Canada." Available at http://nctr.ca/assets/reports/Final%20Reports/Executive_Summary_English_Web.pdf (accessed December 18, 2018).

Tully, James. (1995). *Strange Multiplicity: Constitutionalism in an Age of Diversity (The Seeley Lectures)*. Cambridge: Cambridge University Press.

Tutu, Desmond. (2002a). "Apartheid and the Holy Land." *The Guardian* (29 April). Available at https://www.theguardian.com/world/2002/apr/29/comment (accessed December 17, 2018).

Tutu, Desmond. (2002b). "Of Occupation and Apartheid: Do I Divest?" *CounterPunch* (17 October). Available at https://www.counterpunch.org/2002/10/17/do-i-divest/ (accessed December 10, 2018).

Tutu, Desmond. (2011). "Foreword: A Call to the Community of Conscience." In Adam Horowitz, Lizzy Ratner, and Philip Weiss (eds.), *The Goldstone Report: The Legacy of the Landmark Investigation of the Gaza Conflict*, pp. vii–ix. New York: Nation Books.

United Church. (2006). "General News and Announcements: Ethical Investment for Peace in Palestine and Israel" (29 June). Available at https://commons.united-church.ca/_layouts/15/WopiFrame.aspx?sourcedoc=/Documents/What%20We%20Believe%20and%20Why/Peace/Ethical%20Investment%20for%20Peace%20in%20Palestine%20and%20Israel%20(2006E735).docx&action=default&DefaultItemOpen=1 (accessed May 5, 2019).

United Church. (2012). "Report of the Working Group on Israel/Palestine Policy" (11–18 August). Available at https://commons.united-church.ca/Documents/Governance/General%20Council/41st%20General%20

Council%20(2012)/Background%20Material/Report%20of%20the%20workgroup%20on%20Israel-Palestine.pdf (accessed May 5, 2019).
United Kingdom, Foreign Office. (1917). "The Balfour Declaration." Available at https://uniteapps.un.org/dpa/dpr/unispal.nsf/0/E210CA73E38D9E1D052565FA00705C61 (accessed November 5, 2018).
United Nations. (2001). "World Conference Against Racism, Racial Discrimination, Xenophobia and Related Intolerance: Durban Declaration." (A/Conf.189/12). UN Documents. (September 8, 2001). Available at http://www.un-documents.net/durban-d.htm (accessed May 5, 2019).
United Nations. (2007). "General Assembly Adopts Declaration on Rights of Indigenous Peoples; 'Major Step Forward' Towards Human Rights for All, Says President." United Nations Meetings Coverage and Press Releases (13 September). Available at https://www.un.org/press/en/2007/ga10612.doc.htm (accessed May 5, 2019).
United Nations. (2014). "International Day for the Elimination of Racial Discrimination." Available at http://www.un.org/en/events/racialdiscriminationday/background.shtml (accessed May 5, 2019).
United Nations Archives (1977). S-1003-0006-06. World Conference to Combat Racism and Racial Discrimination. United Nations (UN), "Report of the World Conference for Action Against *Apartheid*." Vol. 1, Lagos, August 22–26, 1977.
United Nations Archives. S-0913-0019-04. (1978a). World Conference to Combat Racism and Racial Discrimination. United Nations (UN), Office of Public Information Press Section, 1978. "World Conference to Combat Racism and Racial Discrimination Ends with Adoption of Declaration and Programme of Action." (Press Release 29 August).
United Nations Archives. S-1003-0014-02. (1978b). World Conference to Combat Racism and Racial Discrimination. United Nations (UN), Office of Public Information Press Section. "Statement by Chairman of Anti-Apartheid Committee Concerning World Conference to Combat Racism" (Press Release 21 August).
United Nations Archives. S-1028-0007-02. (1983). Second World Conference to Combat Racism and Racial Discrimination. United Nations (UN), Office of Public information Press Section, 1983. "Second World Conference to Combat Racism and Racial Discrimination, Geneva, 1–13 August."
United Nations Archives. S-1055-0009-0002. (1989). "Statement by the Secretary-General on the Occasion of the International Day for the Elimination of Racial Discrimination" (21 March).
United Nations Centre Against Apartheid. (1977). *Report of the World Conference for Action Against Apartheid, Lagos, Nigeria, 22–26 August 1977*. New York: United Nations.
United Nations Economic and Social Commission for Western Asia (UN-ESCWA). (2017). *Israeli Practices Towards the Palestinian People and the Question of Apartheid: Palestine and the Israeli Occupation, Issue No. 1* (E/ESCWA/ECRI/2017/1). Beirut: United Nations. Available at https://www.middleeastmonitor.com/wp-content/uploads/downloads/201703_UN_

ESCWA-israeli-practices-palestinian-people-apartheid-occupation-english.pdf (accessed May 5, 2019).
United Nations Environment Programme (UNEP). (2009). *From Conflict to Peacebuilding: The Role of Natural Resources and the Environment*. Nairobi: UNEP. Available at https://postconflict.unep.ch/publications/pcdmb_policy_01.pdf (accessed May 5, 2019).
United Nations General Assembly. (1947). "Resolution 181(II). Future Government of Palestine." (A/RES/181(II)). 128th plenary meeting. (November 29, 1947). Available at https://unispal.un.org/DPA/DPR/unispal.nsf/0/7F0AF2BD897689B785256C330061D253 (accessed May 5, 2019).
United Nations General Assembly. (1948a). "Resolution 217 A. Universal Declaration of Human Rights." (December 10, 1948). Available at http://www.un.org/en/universal-declaration-human-rights/ (accessed May 4, 2019)
United Nations General Assembly. (1948b). "Resolution 194 (III). Palestine—Progress Report of the United Nations Mediator." (A/RES/194(III)). 186th plenary meeting. (December 11, 1948). Available at https://unispal.un.org/DPA/DPR/unispal.nsf/0/C758572B78D1CD0085256BCF0077E51A (accessed May 3, 2019).
United Nations General Assembly. (1949a). "Resolution 273 (III). Admission of Israel to Membership in the United Nations." (A/RES/273(III)). 3rd session. (May 11, 1949). https://unispal.un.org/DPA/DPR/unispal.nsf/0/83E8C29DB812A4E9852560E50067A5AC (accessed May 5, 2019).
United Nations General Assembly. (1949b). "Resolution 302 (IV). Assistance to Palestine Refugees." (A/RES/302(IV)). 4th session. (December 8, 1949). Available at https://www.unrwa.org/content/general-assembly-resolution-302 (accessed May 4, 2019).
United Nations General Assembly. (1961). "The Question of Race Conflict in South Africa Resulting from the Policies of Apartheid of the Government of the Republic of South Africa." (A/RES1663). 16th session. (November 28, 1961). Available at http://www.refworld.org/docid/3b00f1e044.html (accessed May 4, 2019).
United Nations General Assembly. (1963). "1904 (XVIII). United Nations Declaration on the Elimination of All Forms of Racial Discrimination." (A/RES/18/1904). 18th session. (November 20, 1963). Available at http://www.un-documents.net/a18r1904.htm (accessed May 4, 2019).
United Nations General Assembly. (1968). "The Policies of Apartheid of the Government of South Africa." (A/RES/2396(XXIII)). 23rd session. (December 2, 1968). Available at https://www.refworld.org/docid/3b00f1d (accessed May 5, 2019).
United Nations General Assembly. (1973). *International Convention on the Suppression and Punishment of the Crime of Apartheid* (ICSPCA). (RES/3068(XXVIII)). (November 30, 1973; entered into force July 18, 1976). Available at https://treaties.un.org/Pages/ViewDetails.aspx?src=IND&mtdsg_no=IV-7&chapter=4&clang=_en (accessed May 4, 2019).
United Nations General Assembly. (1974). "Resolution 3237 (XXIX). Observer Status for the Palestine Liberation Organization." (A/RES/3237(XXIX)). 29th

session. (November 22, 1974). https://unispal.un.org/DPA/DPR/unispal.nsf/0/512BAA69B5A32794852560DE0054B9B2 (accessed May 4, 2019).

United Nations General Assembly. (1975). "Resolution 3379 (XXX). Elimination of All Forms of Racial Discrimination." (A/RES/3379(XXX)). 30th session. (November 10, 1975). https://web.archive.org/web/20121206052903/http://unispal.un.org/UNISPAL.NSF/0/761C1063530766A7052566A2005B74D1 (accessed May 4, 2019).

United Nations General Assembly. (1978). "World Conference to Combat Racism and Racial Discrimination." (A/RES/33/99). 33rd session. (December 16, 1978). Available at https://www.refworld.org/docid/3b00f1b820.html (accessed May 4, 2019).

United Nations General Assembly. (1981). "Alternative Approaches and Ways and Means Within the United Nations System for Improving the Effective Enjoyment of Human Rights and Fundamental Freedoms: Development of Public Information Activities in the Field of Human Rights; Report of the General Secretary." (A/RES/36/133) (December 14, 1981). Available at http://www.un.org/documents/ga/res/36/a36r133.htm (accessed May 4, 2019).

United Nations General Assembly. (1983). "Second World Conference to Combat Racism and Racial Discrimination," (A/RES/38/15). 38th session. (November 22, 1983). Available at https://www.refworld.org/docid/3b00f0161c.html (accessed May 4, 2019).

United Nations General Assembly. (1992). World Public Information Campaign for Human Rights. https://www.refworld.org/docid/3b00f0ec30.html (accessed May 4, 2019).

United Nations Archives. S-1055-0009-0002 (1989). "Statement by the Secretary-General on the Occasion of the International Day for the Elimination of Racial Discrimination." (21 March).

United Nations General Assembly. (1991). "Elimination of Racism and Racial Discrimination." (A/RES/46/86). 46th session. (December 16, 1991). Available at http://www.securitycouncilreport.org/atf/cf/%7B65BFCF9B-6D27-4E9C-8CD3-CF6E4FF96FF9%7D/IP%20ARES46%2086.pdf (accessed May 4, 2019).

United Nations General Assembly. (1993). "Third Decade to Combat Racism and Racial Discrimination." (A/RES/48/91). 84th plenary meeting. (December 20, 1983). Available at http://www.un.org/documents/ga/res/48/a48r091.htm (accessed May 4, 2019).

United Nations General Assembly. (1998). "Participation of Palestine in the Work of the United Nations." (A/RES/52/250). 52nd session. (July 13, 1998). Available at https://unispal.un.org/DPA/DPR/unispal.nsf/0/162094FCBE8245D30525665E00536281 (accessed May 4, 2019).

United Nations General Assembly. (2007). "United Nations Declaration on the Rights of Indigenous Peoples." (A/RES/61/295). 61st session. (September 13, 2007). Available at https://www.un.org/esa/socdev/unpfii/documents/DRIPS_en.pdf (accessed May 5, 2019).

United Nations General Assembly. (2012). "Resolution Adopted by the General Assembly on 29 November 2012. 67/19 Status of Palestine in the United

Nations." (4 December). 1247974. Available at https://www.un.org/ga/search/view_doc.asp?symbol=A/RES/67/19 (accessed May 4, 2019).

United Nations High Commissioner for Refugees (UNHCR). (2016). *Global Trends: Forced Displacement in 2015*. Available at http://www.unhcr.org/576408cd7 (accessed May 4, 2019).

United Nations Human Rights Council (UNHRC). (2008). "Resolution Adopted by the Council at Its Sixth Special Session: Human Rights Violations Emanating from Israeli Military Incursions in the Occupied Palestinian Territory, Particularly in the Occupied Gaza Strip." (A/HRC/S-6/1). 6th special session. (January 24, 2008). Available at https://documents-ddsny.un.org/doc/UNDOC/GEN/G08/123/75/PDF/G0812375.pdf?OpenElement. Link no longer working.

United Nations Human Rights Council (UNHRC). (2018). *Report of the Special Rapporteur on the Situation of Human Rights in the Palestinian Territories Occupied Since 1967*. (A/HRC/37/75). 37th session. (14 June). Available at https://www.un.org/unispal/document/report-of-the-special-rapporteur-on-the-situation-of-human-rights-in-the-palestinian-territories-occupied-since-1967-advance-unedited-version/ (accessed January 20, 2019).

United Nations International Children's Emergency Fund (UNICEF) and Palestine Hydrology Group (PHG). (2010). *Water, Sanitation and Hygiene Household Survey Gaza* (April). Available at https://unispal.un.org/pdfs/UNICEFWS&HReport.pdf (accessed May 4, 2019).

United Nations and League of Arab States (UN and LAS). (2013). "The Arab Millennium Development Goals Report: Facing Challenges and Looking Beyond 2015." http://www.undp.org/content/dam/rbas/doc/MDGS%20publications/Arab_MDGR_2013_English.pdf (accessed May 5, 2019).

United Nations (UN) News. (2007). "United Nations Adopts Declaration on Rights of Indigenous Peoples." UN News (13 September). Available at https://news.un.org/en/story/2007/09/231062-united-nations-adopts-declaration-rights-Indigenous-peoples (accessed May 5, 2019).

United Nations Office of the Coordination of Humanitarian Affairs Occupied Palestinian Territory (UN OCHA oPt). (2012). "West Bank Movement and Access Update." UN OCHA oPt, September. Available at https://www.ochaopt.org/content/west-bank-movement-and-access-update-sep-2012 (accessed May 5, 2019).

United Nations Office of the High Commissioner for Human Rights (UN-OHCHR). (1965). "Resolution 2106 (XX) of 21 December 1965: International Convention on the Elimination of All Forms of Racial Discrimination." United Nations, Treaty Series, vol. 660, p. 195. (December 21, 1965). Available at https://www.ohchr.org/EN/ProfessionalInterest/Pages/CERD.aspx (accessed May 4, 2019).

United Nations Relief and Works Agency for Palestine Refugees in the Near East (UNRWA). (2009). "UNRWA Lifts Suspension of Aid Imports into Gaza: Press statement by Christopher Gunnes UNRWA Spokesperson." UNRWA (9 February). Available at https://www.unrwa.org/newsroom/press-releases/unrwa-lifts-suspension-aid-imports-gaza (accessed May 5, 2019).

United Nations Relief and Works Agency for Palestine Refugees in the Near East (UNRWA). (2018). "About UNRWA." Available at https://www.unrwa.org/resources/about-unrwa (accessed May 5, 2019).

United Nations Security Council (UNSC). (1949). "Resolution 69. Admission of New Members to the UN: Israel." (S/RES/69 - S/1277). 414th meeting. (March 4, 1949). https://unispal.un.org/DPA/DPR/unispal.nsf/0/CCF3096AA8F1BB8D852560C2005DA665 (accessed May 5, 2019).

United Nations Security Council (UNSC). (1968a). "Resolution 252. Question of Palestine." (S/RES/252). 1426th meeting. (May 21, 1968). https://unispal.un.org/DPA/DPR/unispal.nsf/0/46F2803D78A0488E852560C3006023A8 (accessed May 5, 2019).

United Nations Security Council (UNSC). (1968b). "Resolution 259. [Middle East]." (S/RES/259). 1454th meeting. (September 27, 1968). https://www.refworld.org/type,RESOLUTION,UNSC,ISR,3b00f20ec,0.html.

Urbina, Ian. (2002). "The Analogy to Apartheid." *Middle East Report* 223 (Summer): 58–64.

Uris, Leon. (1958). *Exodus*. Garden City: Doubleday.

US Palestinian Community Network (USPCN). (2012). "Palestinian in Solidarity with Idle No More and Indigenous Rights." *uspcn.org* (23 December). Available at https://uspcn.org/2012/12/23/palestinians-in-solidarity-with-idle-no-more-and-Indigenous-rights/ (accessed May 5, 2019).

Usher, Graham. (2005). "The Wall and the Dismemberment of Palestine." *Race and Class* 47, 3: 9–30.

Usher, Graham. (2006). "The Wall and the Dismemberment of Palestine." *Race and Class* 47, 9: 9–30.

Vally, Salim. (2008). "From South Africa to Palestine: Lessons for the New Anti-Apartheid Movement." *Left Turn* (9 April). Available at http://www.leftturn.org/south-africa-palestine-lessons-new-anti-apartheid-movement (accessed December 17, 2018).

Vancouver Sun. (2008). "Aga Khan Upholds Canada as Model for the World" (23 November). Available at http://www.canada.com/vancouversun/news/story.html?id=9c5e7816-0ee5-4ccf-b19e-441b1156cb31 (accessed July 16, 2012). Link no longer working.

Van Den Berghe, Pierre L. (1965). *South Africa: A Study in Conflict*. Berkeley: University of California Press.

Van Teeffelen, Toine. (1994). "Racism and Metaphor: The Palestinian-Israeli Conflict in Popular Literature." *Discourse and Society* 5, 3: 381–405.

Varela, Julio Ricardo. (2018). "Trump's Border Wall Was Never Just About Security. It's Meant to Remind All Latinos We're Unwelcome." *NBCNEWS Think* (28 December). https://www.nbcnews.com/think/opinion/trump-s-border-wall-was-never-just-about-security-it-ncna952011 (accessed May 5, 2019).

Vickers, Jill, and Annette Issac. (2012). *The Politics of Race: Canada, the United States and Australia*. Toronto: University of Toronto Press.

Viva Palestina. (2009). "A Lifeline from Britain to Gaza." Available at https://newint.org/blog/gaza/2009/12/17/viva-palestina (accessed February 21, 2009).

Wagner, Meg. (2017). "'Blood and Soil': Protesters Chant Nazi Slogan in Charlottesville." *CNN.com* (12 August). Available at http://www.cnn.com/2017/08/12/us/charlottesville-unite-the-right-rally/index.html (accessed September 4, 2017).

Walker, Alice. (2012). "Letter from Alice Walker to Publishers at Yediot Books." *Palestinian Campaign for the Academic and Cultural Boycott of Israel*. Available at http://www.pacbi.org/etemplate.php?id=1917 (accessed May 4, 2019).

Wallace-Wells, Benjamin. (2018). "The Pittsburgh Synagogue Shooting and the Escalating Crisis of Hate-Fuelled Violence in the Trump-Era." *The New Yorker* (27 October). Available at https://www.newyorker.com/news/current/the-pittsburgh-synagogue-shooting-and-the-escalating-crisis-of-hate-fuelled-violence-in-the-trump-era (accessed January 24, 2019).

Walton Jr., Hanes, Cheryl M. Miller, and Joseph P. McCormick, II. (1995). "Race and Political Science: The Dual Traditions of Race Relations Politics and African-American Politics." In James Farr, John S. Dryzek, and Stephen T. Leonard (eds.), *Political Science in History: Research Programs and Political Traditions*, pp. 145–74. Cambridge: Cambridge University Press.

Watson, Bruce. (2016). "The Troubling Evolution of Corporate Greenwashing." *The Guardian.com* (20 August). Available at https://www.theguardian.com/sustainable-business/2016/aug/20/greenwashing-environmentalism-lies-companies (accessed July 29, 2017).

Watts, Jerry G. (2007). "Political Science Confronts Afro-America: A Reconsideration." In Wilbur C. Rich (ed.), *African American Perspectives on Political Science*, pp. 398–433. Philadelphia: Temple University Press.

Weaver, Ole, Barry Buzan, Morten Kelstrup, and Pierre Lemaitre. (1993). *Identity, Migration and the New Security Agenda in Europe*. London: Pinter.

Weber, Max. (1977 [1905]). *The Protestant Ethic and the Spirit of Capitalism*. Englewood Cliffs, US: Prentice Hall.

Weinstock, Nathan. (1989). *Zionism: False Messiah*. London: Pluto Press.

Weiss, Martin A. (2006). "Arab League Boycott of Israel." *Congressional Research Service Report for Congress*. Library of Congress: Order Code RS22424 (19 April): 2–3.

Weiss, Suzanne. (2007). "The Holocaust and the Defense of Palestinians: Forces Responsible for Slaughter of Jews Now Oppress the Palestinian People." *Not in Our Name: Jewish Voices Against Israel's Wars*. Available at www.nion.ca. Link no longer working.

West, Cornel. (2016). "Foreward." In Angela Y. Davis, *Freedom Is Constant Struggle: Ferguson, Palestine and the Foundations of a Movement*, pp. vii–viii. Chicago: Haymarket Books

Whitaker, Reg. (2011). "Behavioural Profiling in Israeli Aviation Security as a Tool for Social Control." In Elia Zureik, David Lyon, and Yasmeen Abu-Laban (eds.), *Surveillance and Control in Israel/Palestine: Population, Territory, and Power*, pp. 371–85. London and New York: Routledge.

Whitaker, Reginald. (1999). *The End of Privacy: How Total Surveillance Is Becoming a Reality*. New York: New Press.

White, Ben. (2009). *Israeli Apartheid: A Beginner's Guide*. London: Pluto Press.

Will, Donald S. (2007). "Nonracialism Versus Ethnonationalism: Transcending Conflict in Israel/Palestine and South Africa." *Comparative Studies of South Asia, Africa and the Middle East* 27, 2: 412–22.

Will, Donald, and Sheila Ryan. (1990). *Israel and South Africa: Legal Systems of Settler Dominance.* Trenton: Africa World Press.

Williams, Eric E. (1944). *Capitalism and Slavery.* Chapel Hill: University of North Carolina Press.

Williams, Michelle Hale. (2010). "Can Leopards Change Their Spots? Between Xenophobia and Trans-Ethnic Populism Among West European Far Right Parties." *Nationalism and Ethnic Politics* 16: 111–34.

Wilson, Jason. (2017). "Charlottesville: Far-Right Crowd with Torches Encircle Counter-Protest Group." *The Guardian* (12 August). Available at https://www.theguardian.com/world/2017/aug/12/charlottesville-far-right-crowd-with-torches-encircles-counter-protest-group (accessed May 5, 2019).

Winbush, Raymond A., ed. (2003). *Should America Pay?: Slavery and the Raging Debate on Reparations.* New York: HarperCollins.

Wootliff, Raoul (2018). "Israel Passes Jewish State Law, 'Enshrining National Home of the Jewish People.'" *The Times of Israel* (19 July). Available at https://www.timesofisrael.com/knesset-votes-contentious-jewish-nation-state-bill-into-law/ (accessed August 18, 2018).

World Bank. (2009). "Assessment of Restrictions on Palestinian Water Development." Report Number 47657GZ. Washington: The International Bank for Reconstruction and Development/The World Bank (April). Available at http://siteresources.worldbank.org/INTWESTBANKGAZA/Resources/WaterRestrictionsReport18Apr2009.pdf (accessed May 5, 2019).

World Bank. (2016). "Water Situation Alarming in Gaza." *The World Bank* (22 November). Available at http://www.worldbank.org/en/news/feature/2016/11/22/water-situation-alarming-in-gaza (accessed May 5, 2019).

Wright, Joanne. (2004). *Origin Stories in Political Thought: Discourses on Gender, Power and Citizenship.* Toronto: University of Toronto Press.

Yi, Joseph E., and Joe Phillips. (2015). "The BDS Campaign Against Israel: Lessons from South Africa." *PS: Political Science and Politics* 48, 2 (April): 306–10.

Yiftachel, Oren. (2005). "Ending the Colonialism." *Haaretz* (20 July). Available at https://www.haaretz.com/opinion/1.4922809 (accessed May 4, 2019).

Yiftachel, Oren. (2006). *Ethnocracy: Land and Identity Politics in Israel/Palestine.* Philadelphia: University of Pennsylvania Press.

YouTube.com. (2014). "Through Fire and Water." Available at https://www.youtube.com/watch?v=hq8MN0OBEO4 (accessed May 4, 2019)

Young, Iris Marion. (2005). "Self-Determination as Non-Domination: Ideals Applied to Palestine/Israel." *Ethnicities* 5: 139–59.

Young-Bruehl, Elisabeth. (2004). *Hannah Arendt: For Love of the World.* New Haven: Yale University Press.

Yuval-Davis, Nira. (1997). *Gender and Nation.* London: Sage.

Yuval-Davis, Nira. (2006). "Intersectionality and Feminist Politics." *European Journal of Women's Studies* 13, 3: 193–209.

Zafer-Smith, Golda. (2003). "Anti-Semitism and Anti-Discrimination Training and Practice." *The International Journal of Human Rights* 7, 1 (Spring): 104–27.

Zangwill, Israel. (1901). "Return to Palestine." *The New Liberal Review* (December): 615–34.

Ziadah, Rafeef. (2008). "Sixty Years of Nakba: Palestinian Refugees and the New Anti-Apartheid Movement." *Left Turn* (9 April). Available at http://www.leftturn.org/60-years-nakba-%E2%80%93-palestinian-refugees-and-new-anti-apartheid-movement (accessed May 4, 2019).

Ziadah, Rafeef. (2009). "Freedom of Expression and Palestine Advocacy." *The Bullet* (19 May). Available at http://www.socialistproject.ca/bullet/bullet219.html#continue (accessed May 5, 2019).

Ziadah, Rafeef. (2010). "A View from Toronto: A Hub of 'Israel Delegitimization.'" *The Bullet* (10 March). Available at https://socialistproject.ca/2010/03/b322/ (accessed May 5, 2019).

Ziadah, Rafeef. (2016). "Palestine Calling: Notes on the Boycott, Divestment, and Sanctions Movement." In Ghada Ageel (ed.), *Apartheid in Palestine: Hard Laws and Harder Experiences*, pp. 91–106. Edmonton, Alberta: The University of Alberta Press.

Zerbisias, Antonia. (2015). "Israel Need Not Worry About Justin Trudeau." *Aljazeera* (11 November). Available at http://www.aljazeera.com/indepth/opinion/2015/11/israel-worry-justin-trudeau-151109061056908.html (accessed May 5, 2019).

Zriek, Raef. (2004). "Palestine, Apartheid and the Rights Discourse." *Journal of Palestine Studies* 34, 1 (Autumn): 68–80.

Zriek, Raef. (2008). "The Persistence of the Exception: Some Remarks on the Story of Israeli Constitutionalism." In Ronit Lentin (ed.), *Thinking Palestine*, pp. 131–47. London: Zed Books.

Zúkete, José Pedro. (2008). "The European Extreme Right and Islam: New Directions?" *Journal of Political Ideologies* 13, 3 (October): 321–44.

Zureik, Elia T. (1979). *The Palestinians in Israel: A Study in Internal Colonialism*. London: Routledge and Kegan Paul.

Zureik, Elia T. (2001). "Constructing Palestine Through Surveillance Practices." *British Journal of Middle Eastern Studies* 28, 2: 205–27.

Zureik, Elia T. (2011). "Colonialism, Surveillance and Population Control: Israel/Palestine." In Elia Zureik, David Lyon, and Yasmeen Abu-Laban (eds.), *Surveillance and Control in Israel/Palestine: Population, Territory, and Power*, pp. 3–46. London and New York: Routledge.

Zureik, Elia, and Mark B. Salter. (2005). "Global Surveillance and Policing: Borders, Security, Identity: Introduction." In Elia Zureik and Mark B. Salter (eds.), *Global Surveillance and Policing: Borders, Security and Identity*, pp. 1–11. Cullompton: Willan Publishing.

Zureik, Elia, David Lyon, and Yasmeen Abu-Laban, eds. (2011). *Surveillance and Control in Israel/Palestine: Population, Territory, and Power*. London and New York: Routledge.

INDEX

Abbas, Mahmoud 162
Abdulhadi, Rabab 135
Abella, Irving 65
Abowd, Thomas 198
Absentee Property Law of 1950 239
Abu-Laban, Baha 236
Abu-Laban, Yasmeen 4, *passim*
Abu-Lughod, Ibrahim 126, 144, 153, 236
Abunimah, Ali 234–5
Abu-Saad, Ismael 68
Achcar, Gilbert 117
Adam, Heribert 235
ADL. *see* Anti-Defamation League (ADL)
AFN. *see* Assembly of First Nations (AFN)
African Americans 30, 35
African Canadian Legal Clinic 35
African Canadians 35
African National Congress (ANC) 105, 170, 227
Afro-American politics 25
Afropessimism 227
Agamben, Giorgio 83, 84–6, 100
Ahenakew, David 134–5
Ahmadinejad, Mahmoud 36
air, in Israel/Palestine 218–22
Akenson, Donald Harman 142
Al-Aqsa Intifada 95
Alexander, Michelle 264
Al Qaeda 99, 101, 201
Altnoiland 184
American-Israeli Public Affairs Committee 156
American Jewish Congress 156
American Political Science Association (APSA) 25–6
American Studies Association 164
ANC. *see* African National Congress (ANC)
Annan, Kofi 112
Anti-Apartheid Committee 256
anti-apartheid movement 18, 150
anti-Arab racism/Islamophobia 16, 57, 125
Anti-Defamation League (ADL) 34, 156, 193–4
anti-Jewish racism. *see* anti-Semitism
anti-Judaism 61
anti-Muslim racism. *see* Islamophobia/anti-Arab racism
anti-racism 29, 35, 56, 58, 84, 112, 114, 118, 151, 164, 242, 266, 269
anti-racist feminism 11–13, 263, 269
"anti-Semitic hate fest" 2–3
anti-Semitism 2, 16–17, 29, 31–2, 34–7, 46, 52, 56–8, 61–3, 65, 97–8, 114–17, 119, 129, 141, 149, 183, 188, 208, 241, 243, 249, 259, 266
Apartheid Convention. *see* International Convention on the Suppression and Punishment of the Crime of Apartheid (ICSPCA)
apartheid system 57, 83, 105, 120, 157, 159–61, 165, 170, 257–61
  overview 225–9
  in postapartheid era 237–43
  QUAIA 189–94
  scholarship, law, and one-state advocates 229–33
  South Africa, Israel and one-state literature 233–7
  strategic implications 243–5
  UN and South Africa 250–4

Apartheid Wall ("separation barrier") 92, 98, 102, 104, 127, 159–61, 171, 220, 230, 234, 239
APSA. *see* American Political Science Association (APSA)
Arab-equals-Muslim association 41
Arab Israelis 90, 117, 155, 161, 230, 240
Arab-Israeli war. *see* Israeli-Arab War
Arab League 125, 152, 154–7
Arab Spring 209
Arafat, Yasser 74, 94
Arar, Maher 99
Arendt, Hannah 38–9, 118–19
Ashkenazi (European) Jews 15, 67–9, 116–17, 188, 195
Ashkenazi feminism 188, 195
Ashrawi, Hanan 43, 199
Assembly of First Nations (AFN) 133–4
Atlantic slavery 60, 72, 231

Baird, John 200
Bakan, Abigail 4, *passim*
Baldwin, James 30
Balfour, Arthur James 62
Balfour Declaration (1917) 8, 62, 64, 122, 142, 198, 236
Bankoff, Greg 96
Bantustanization 234
Barak, Ehud 230
Barghouti, Omar 147, 243
"Basic Law: Israel-The Nation State of the Jewish People" 2
Baum, Bruce 60
Bayefsky, Anne 249
BCRI. *see* Birmingham Civil Rights Institute (BCRI)
BDS. *see* boycott, divestment, and sanctions (BDS) movement
behavioral revolution 26
Bein, Alexander 87
Ben-Gurion, David 119, 180
Benston, Margaret 201
bicommunalism 236
Birmingham City Council 264
Birmingham Civil Rights Institute (BCRI) 264
Birmingham Holocaust Education Center 264
Bishara, Azmi 166
Bisharat, George 238, 244
Black civil rights movement 10
Blair, Tony 97
BNC. *see* Boycott National Committee (BNC)
Bowman, Glenn 38
Boyarin, Daniel 138–9, 183
Boyarin, Jonathon 139
boycott, divestment, and sanctions (BDS) movement 6–10, 46, 135, 229, 243, 248, 259, 263–4
  history and context 151–8
  Palestine solidarity 147–51
  and Palestinian civil society 158–69
  praxis and 16–20
Boycott National Committee (BNC) 150
Brexit 154, 265–6
British Mandate 64, 66, 88, 122–3, 153, 198, 211, 240
Brockman, Miguel D'Escoto 165
Brown, Michael 244, 267
Brynen, Rex 70
Bulkley, Julia E. 194–5
Bush, George H. W. 93
Bush, George W. 3, 49, 77, 96–7, 148, 162
Butler, Judith 268–9

CAIA. *see* Coalition Against Israeli Apartheid (CAIA)
Camp David Accords (1978) 92
Canada 1, 7, 16–17, 23, *passim*
  administrations of Harper 4
  and Israel/Palestine racial contract 71–6
  knowledge production 15
  multiculturalism 12–13, 27, 50, 57, 72, 266
  TRC of 131

Canadian Arab Federation 35
Canadian Jewish Congress (CJC) 133–4
Canadian Jewish News 75
Canadian Labour Congress 35
Canadian Parliamentary Coalition to Combat Antisemitism (CPCCA) 36
Canadian Political Science Association (CPSA) 6, 26
Canadian Union of Postal Workers (CUPW) 168
Canadian Union of Public Employees (CUPE) 167–8
Carter, Jimmy 104, 151–2, 161
Caterpillar 168
"the Caucasian race" 60–1
CERD. *see* Committee on the Elimination of Racial Discrimination (CERD)
Charles, Jean 101–2
Chavez, Hugo 167
Chesler, Phyllis 96–7
Chomsky, Noam 91
Chowdhry, Geeta 29
Christians/Christianity 11, 15, 32, 41, 46–7, 61–2, 64, 68, 97, 112–13, 117, 122, 138–40, 143, 157, 168, 177, 179, 183, 195
Chung, Erin Aeran 25
civil society, Palestine 158–69
CJC. *see* Canadian Jewish Congress (CJC)
"clash of civilizations" perspective 3, 17, 49, 76–7, 86
Cliff, Tony 236
Clinton, Bill 94, 95
Coalition Against Israeli Apartheid (CAIA) 78
Coastal Municipal Water Utility 217
Cobo, José Martinez 131
Cohen, Cathy J. 25
Cold War 27–8, 31, 72, 78, 83, 93, 110, 113, 231, 251, 265
"colonial amnesia" 28
colonialism 60–1, 67, 135–6, 143, 145, 153, 178, 194–200, 202, 230, 232–3, 235, 239
The Color Purple (Walker) 9–10
Committee against Torture 111
Committee on the Elimination of Racial Discrimination (CERD) 253
Committee on the Protection of the Rights of All Migrant Workers and Members of Their Families 111
Committee on the Rights of Persons with Disabilities 111
Committee on the Rights of the Child 111
Committees on Human Rights 111
Connex Ireland 165
Conservative Party 4, 7, 36–7, 210
Cook, Jonathon 229, 240
Cotler, Irwin 134
CPCCA. *see* Canadian Parliamentary Coalition to Combat Antisemitism (CPCCA)
CPSA. *see* Canadian Political Science Association (CPSA)
cultural genocide 16
cultural pluralism 12
CUPE. *see* Canadian Union of Public Employees (CUPE)
CUPW. *see* Canadian Union of Postal Workers (CUPW)

Darwish, Mahmoud 43, 268
Davis, Angela Y. 135, 244, 264, 267
Davis, Uri 17, 37, 234
Dawson, Michael C. 25
Dayan, Arie 74
Day for the Elimination of Racial Discrimination 257
DDPA. *see* Durban Declaration and Programme of Action (DDPA)
Decade of Action to Combat Racism and Racial Discrimination 254
"Declaration of Independence" 240

"Declaration on Combating Anti-Semitism" 36
de Cuèllar, Javier Pèrez 257
delegitimization 7, 45, 150, 190, 193
De Menezes, Jean Charles 100
demographic threat 185
Desmond Tutu, Archbishop 157, 166, 220
DIME weapons 221
Dreyfus Affair (1894) 116
Dugard, John 232
Durban Declaration and Programme of Action (DDPA) 257–8
Durban Review Conference (2009) 34, 36
Dutch ASN Bank 165

Economic, Social and Cultural Rights 111
economic apartheid 227, 231, 237
Edinburgh Film Festival 165
Eichmann, Adolf 38–9, 118–19
Eichmann Trial 33, 114, 118–19
Elbit 102–3
Electronic Intifada 157
Elimination of Discrimination against Women 111
Elimination of Racial Discrimination 111
El-Messiri, A. M. 74
El-Rifai, Roula 70
environmental racism
  air 218–22
  greenwashing 222–3
  in historical and regional context 207–9
  land 210–16
  Palestine and UNDRIP 205–6
  water 216–18
Eretz Israel ('the Land of Israel') 2, 87, 118, 135–6, 138, 142–3, 214, 243
ethnic democracy 55, 238
ethnicity, and race 24–31
Eurocentric/Orientalist feminism 194
European Union 36, 76
"Europe's Other" 61
Even-Ezra, Jacob 103
exceptionalism 85, 97, 120, 227
Exodus (Uris) 179–80

Falk, Richard 238
Faris, Hani 63
Farsakh, Leila 234, 241
Federation of Saskatchewan Indian Nations (FSIN) 134
feminism 186, 201, 244
  anti-racist 3, 6, 11–13
  Ashkenazi 188, 195
  Eurocentric/Orientalist 194
  Mizrahi 188
FFC. *see* Friends Fiduciary Corporation (FFC)
Financial Times 101
Finkelstein, Norman 3, 17, 34, 136
first Intifada 43, 92, 94, 169, 199
First Nations 134
First World War 64, 110, 122, 236
Fischbach, Michael R. 211
Ford, Gerald 156
Ford, Rob 191–2
Fosse, Eric 221
Foxman, Abraham 34
Fred Shuttlesworth Human Rights Award 264
French Revolution 91
Friends Fiduciary Corporation (FFC) 168
"From the Diary of an Almost-Four-Year-Old" (poem) 43
From Time Immemorial (Peters) 136
FSIN. *see* Federation of Saskatchewan Indian Nations (FSIN)
"fundamental laws" 67–8

Gainer, Terrance W. 102
Garner, Eric 244
Gaza and West Bank 55, 67, 70, 94, 98, 156, 160, 165–7, 170–1, 198–9, 207, 239–40
  air in 218–22
  Israel's war on 147–9

land in 212–16
water in 216–18
GCPEA. *see* Global Coalition to Protect Education from Attack (GCPEA)
gendered stereotypes, and settler colonialism 194–200
gender politics and rebranding
gendered stereotypes and settler colonialism 194–200
homonationalism after 9/11 178–81
overview 177–8
QUAIA 189–94
women's equality 182–8
General Union of Palestinian Women (GUPW) 198–9
George, David Lloyd 122
Gilbert, Mads 221
Glaser, Daryl 239
Global Coalition to Protect Education from Attack (GCPEA) 241
Global Feminist Conference (1992) 199
Golan Heights 160
Golda Meir Mount Carmel Training Centre 134
Goldberg, David Theo 45–6, 86, 226
Goldstone, Richard 221–2
Goldstone Report 220–1
Gordon, Neve 92, 98, 170, 214, 216, 218
Gramsci, Antonio 6, 14, 50, 59, 76, 104, 137, 244, 247–8, 265
Greater Serbia 238
Greek Cinematography Centre 165
Green Line 76, 214, 216, 240, 243
Green Party 163, 167
greenwashing 222–3
G4S company 267
Gulf War (1991) 93
GUPW. *see* General Union of Palestinian Women (GUPW)
Gurion, Ben 39

Ha'aretz 230
Haifa Cinema Festival 165
Haifa Film Festival 162
Halbertal, Moshe 186
Halper, Jeff 170
Halperin-Kaddari, Ruth 184
Hamas rocket fire 170
Hammer, Juliane 71
Hanchard, Michael 25
Harle, Vilho 60
Harper, Stephen 1, 4, 36, 49–50, 54–5, 75, 100, 124, 200, 210
Harper's Magazine 3
Hawking, Stephen 163
Hebrew Bible (Old Testament) 139, 143
hegemonic discourse 11
hegemony 55, 76, 130, *passim*
Gramscian notion of 19, 55, 86, 137
and racial contract 13–16
Herzl, Theodore 38, 61–3, 116, 135, 142, 236
Hitler, Adolf 65, 135
Hobsbawm, Eric 137
Holocaust 11, 20, 33, 36, 39–40, 58, 65, 67, 109–10, 113–14, 116–20, 182–3
Holy Land 179
homonationalism 178–81
House of Commons 28
House of Representatives 263
human rights revolution 179
description 110–20
overview 109–10
and Palestine redux 121–8
Human Sciences Research Council of South Africa 232
Humphrey, John 50
Huntington, Samuel 3, 17, 49, 77
Hurricane Katrina 205–6, 209
Hussein, Saddam 154
Hussein, Sharif 122
Hussein, Sherif 64

IAW. *see* Israeli Apartheid Week (IAW)
ICCA. *see* Interparliamentary Coalition for Combating Anti-Semitism (ICCA)

ICERD. *see* International Convention on the Elimination of All Forms of Racial Discrimination (ICERD)
ICJ. *see* International Court of Justice (ICJ)
ICSPCA. *see* International Convention on the Suppression and Punishment of the Crime of Apartheid (ICSPCA)
"the idea of Palestine" 19
Identity Card (poem) 43
IDF. *see* Israeli Defence Force (IDF)
IHL. *see* International Humanitarian Law (IHL)
IJV. *see* Independent Jewish Voices (Canada) (IJV)
imperialism 61, 181
Independent Jewish Voices (Canada) (IJV) 35, 78
Indigeneity, Palestinian
  articulating contentious origin stories 144–5
  in historic Palestine and diaspora 141–4
  overview 129–30
  and UN 130–2
  Zionist claims 133–43
Indigenous Arab 40–1
The Indonesian Tennis Federation 167
International Conference on Human Rights 254
International Convention on the Elimination of All Forms of Racial Discrimination (ICERD) 126, 254
International Convention on the Suppression and Punishment of the Crime of Apartheid (ICSPCA) 231–2
International Court of Justice (ICJ) 75–6, 98, 127, 159–60
International Criminal Court 44, 213, 232
International Day for the Elimination of Racial Discrimination 242, 253
International Humanitarian Law (IHL) 213, 232
international relations (IR) 28
International Year for Action to Combat Racism and Racial Discrimination 254
Interparliamentary Coalition for Combating Anti-Semitism (ICCA) 36
IR. *see* international relations (IR)
Irgun 88
The Irish Joint Committee on Foreign Affairs 165
Islamic Human Rights Commission of the UK 101
Islamofascism 96–7
Islamophobia/anti-Arab racism 16, 82, 84, 171, 194
"Is Race Political?" (Thompson's article) 27
Israel 1–8, *passim*
  anti-racist feminism 11–13
  idea of 31–40
  praxis and BDS movement 16–20
  racial contract and hegemony 13–16
  rebranding and politics of gender (*see* gender politics and rebranding)
  traditions of academic 23–4
Israeli Apartheid Week (IAW) 1, 166–7
Israeli-Arab War
  1967 114, 117
  1973 155
Israeli Defence Force (IDF) 186, 189, 219
Israeli High Court of Justice 189
Israeli Practices towards the Palestinian People and the Question of Apartheid 151, 238
Israelization 82, 95, 99, 119

The Israel Lobby and US Foreign Policy (Mearsheimer and Walt) 79
Israel/Palestine
during 1948–67 87–90
during 1967–91 90–3
during 1992–2000 93–5
during 2001–08 95–103
air in 218–22
environmental racism 207–9
greenwashing 222–3
and human rights revolution 109–28
land in 210–16
sites of resistance 104–5
social sorting and 81–4
as state of exception 84–7
water in 216–18
Israel/Palestine racial contract 15–20, 23–4, 32–4, 36, 40, 42, 44–5, 263–4, *passim*
and Canada 71–6
as category of analysis 52–9
civil society and BDS 158–69
description 67–71
emergence of 59–66
and hegemony 13–16
overview 49–52
and Palestine solidarity 147–51
theorizing 84–7
"Israel's gay decade" 189
Israel's Ministry of Environmental Protection 222
Israel Studies (journal) 225

Jamal, Amal 132
Jerusalem Conference on International Terrorism (1979) 93
Jewish Americans 30, 32
"Jewish councils" *(Judenrate)* 39
Jewish Federations of North America 193
Jewish National Fund (JNF) 211
Jewish Question 59, 65
Jewish Voice for Peace 264
Jews/Jewish people *passim*
Jihad and Jew Hatred: Islamism, Nazism and the Roots of 9/11 (Küntzel) 98
JNF. *see* Jewish National Fund (JNF)
Journal of Race, Ethnicity and Politics (journal) 26
Judaism 37, 58–9, 116, 136, 138–9, 166
Judaization 212, 214

Kahn, Susan Martha 185
Karmi, Ghada 182, 229
Katrina Bill of Rights 209
Kenney, Jason 2, 55
Khan, Aga, IV 12
kibbutzim tradition 201, 241
King, Martin Luther 264
King, William Lyon Mackenzie 113
Kipling, Rudyard 60
Klein, Naomi 3, 102, 147, 153
the Knesset (Israeli parliament) 1–2, 4, 54, 166
Korn, Alina 90
Krieger, Joel 77
Küntzel, Matthias 98
Kurdi, Aylan 265
Kurdi, Tima 265
Kymlicka, Will 27, 145

The Lancet (journal) 220
land, in Israel/Palestine 210–16
"Land Day" 212
Larry and Judy Tanenbaum Foundation Fellowships 134
Lavie, Smadar 188
Law of Return 70, 184
League for Human Rights of B'nai Brith Canada 192
League of Arab States. *see* Arab League
League of Nations 64, 66, 73, 110, 113, 121
Lentin, Ronit 153, 182

lesbian, gay, bisexual, transgender/transsexual, and queer/questioning (LGBTQ) 178, 181, 190–1, 194, 200–2
LGBTQ. *see* lesbian, gay, bisexual, transgender/transsexual, and queer/questioning (LGBTQ)
Liberal Party 4, 7, 54, 134, 263
Loach, Ken 162
Locomotive Drivers Union 164
London Conference 115
London Review of Books 79
London Underground bombings 100
Long Range Acoustic Device (LRAD) 219
LRAD. *see* Long Range Acoustic Device (LRAD)
Lyon, David 82

MacDonald, David 119
McCulloch, Jude 100–1
McMahon, Henry 64
McSweeney, Bill 28
MacMillan, Margaret 142
Magal 102–3
"Management Committee" 56
Mandela, Nelson 105, 227, 238
Maple Leaf Sports and Entertainment 134
Marie, Eva 180
Marshall, Mark 239–40
Martin, Paul 75
Masalha, Nur 46, 143, 208
Massad, Joseph 195–6
mass nonviolent movement 263
Mbembe, Achille 19, 236
Mearsheimer, John 79
Meir, Golda 40, 41
Merkel, Angela 266
Mills, Charles 6, 13–14, 17, 19, 50–4, 58–9, 78, 247
Ministry for Immigrant Absorption 193
Mizrahi feminism 188
Mizrahi/Sephardic Jews 68–9, 117
Mohanty, Chandra 135
Moodley, Kogila 235
Moon, Ban Ki 265
Morales, Evo 167
Morgan, Ed 133
Morris, Benny 137
Mubarak, Hosni 209
multiculturalism 12–13, 27, 37, 50, 57, 72, 266
Muslim Brotherhood 98

Nadeau, Mary-Jo 40
Nadel, Ira 179
Nair, Sheila 29
Nakba 33, 41–2, 44, 90, 109, 123, 137, 143, 153, 157, 182, 195, 198, 240
Nationalist Party 230
National Organization for Women 199
National Party 249
National Post (newspaper) 40
Nazi Holocaust. *see* Holocaust
Nazis/Nazism 65–7, 97, 113–15, 118–20, 231
neo-Gramscian approach 14, 32
Netanyahu, Binyamin 71, 93, 95
new anti-Semitism 16, 34, 36, 97, 120
The New Anti-Semitism: The Current Crisis and What We Must Do About It (Chesler) 96
"New Jew" 183
New Liberal Review 63
Newman, Paul 180
New Testament 139
The New Yorker (magazine) 39
The New York Times 186, 229, 264
NGO. *see* nongovernmental organization (NGO)
Noble, David 140
nongovernmental organization (NGO) 35, 188, 199, 243
"non-white" groups 60
Norwegian Civil Service Union 165
Nuremburg Trials 39, 114–15, 118–19
Nzima, Sam 255

Obama, Barack 49, 77, 148
Occupied Palestinian Territories 13, 55, 57, 73, 92, 94–5, 120, 134, 149, 165, 168, 205, 211–14, 217–18, 232–4, 243, 248
OISE. *see* Ontario Institute for Studies in Education (OISE)
Old Testament (Hebrew Bible) 139, 143
Olmert, Ehud 161, 230
Omar, Ilhan 263
One Dimensional Woman (Power) 201
one-state literature, and apartheid system 229–37
"The One State Solution" 229
The One-State Solution: A Breakthrough for Peace in the Israeli-Palestinian Deadlock (Tilley) 233
Ontario Institute for Studies in Education (OISE) 39
Operation Cast Lead 148–9, 170, 215–16, 220
Operation Kratos 102
Operation Protective Edge 216
Order of Canada distinction 134
Orientalism 17, 41, 58, 63, 69, 71, 121–2, 125, 142, 171, 177, 183, 194, 202, 259
Orientalized Middle East 103
Oslo Accords 71, 94–5, 155, 171, 218, 234
Oslo II Accord of 1995 218
Oslo process 67, 83, 94, 127, 198, 229, 233, 235
Ostjude ("Eastern Jew") 38

PA. *see* Palestinian Authority (PA)
Padnan-Eisenstark, Dorit D. 201
Palestine 1–8, *passim. see also* Israel/Palestine racial contract
  anti-racist feminism 11–13
  articulating contentious origin stories 144–5
  civil society and BDS 158–69
  historic and diaspora 141–4
  narratives and discourses 129–30
  political science and 24–31
  praxis and BDS movement 16–20
  race and ethnic studies 24–31
  racial contract and hegemony 13–16
  traditions of academic 23–4
  and UNDRIP 205–6
Palestine: Peace not Apartheid (Carter) 104, 151
Palestine Liberation Organization (PLO) 67, 73, 91–4, 125, 127, 141
Palestinian Arabs 15, 42, 63, 66, 68, 88–91, 95, 141–2, 153, 182, 199, 216
Palestinian Authority (PA) 94
Palestinian Grassroots Anti-Apartheid Wall Campaign 160
Palestinianization 82–3, 86, 90, 93, 95, 99, 100, 105, 260
Palestinian National Charter (1964) 195–6
Palestinian terrorist 83, 90–1, 102
"the Palestinian voice" 42
Palestinian Women's Charter (1994) 198
Pappe, Ilan 17, 31, 42, 70, 84, 87–8, 137, 207
The Partition Plan 66, 73, 87, 121–2, 179
Pearson, Lester B. 179
Peled-Elhanan, Nurit 69
Peleg, Yaron 183
Peters, Joan 136
Peto, Jennifer 39–40
Philistines 46
Pieterson, Zollie Hector 255
pinkwashing 178, 189–94, 202
Piterberg, Gabriel 239
Plan Dalet 88
PLO. *see* Palestine Liberation Organization (PLO)
"Political Economy of Women's Liberation" (article) 201
political science and race 24–31

postapartheid era 237–43
Power, Nina 201
Presbyterian Church 168
Press Ordinance of 1933 240
Pride Coalition for Free Speech 191
Pride Toronto event 191–2
pro-Israel orientation 4
Puar, Jasbir K. 177, 181, 190, 200

QS. *see* Québec Solidaire (QS)
Québec Solidaire (QS) 163
Queers Against Israeli Apartheid (QUAIA) 178, 189–94
"the question of Palestine" 59, 109–10, 121–8, 171, 202
The Question of Palestine (Said) 41

Rabbinical Courts 184
Rabin, Yitzhak 94
race/racism/racialization 2–7
  anti-Jewish (*see* anti-Semitism)
  Palestine and ethnic studies 24–31
  reified race 25
  traditions of academic 23–4
  world conferences to combat 254–7
racial contract, Israel/Palestine 15–20, 23–4, 32–4, 36, 40, 42, 44–5, 67–71, 263–4, *passim*
  and Canada 71–6
  as category of analysis 52–9
  civil society and BDS 158–69
  description 67–71
  emergence of 59–66
  and hegemony 13–16
  overview 49–52
  and Palestine solidarity 147–51
  theorizing 84–7
The Racial Contract (Mills) 50, 52–3, 59
"racial Palestinianization" 86
racial Southafricanization 226
Ransby, Barbara 135
Razack, Sherene 196
Reagan, Ronald 93
reified race 25
Report of the Special Rapporteur on the Situation of Human Rights in the Palestinian Territories Occupied Since 1967 238
"Resolution 50" 167–8
"The Return of Palestine" (article) 63
Rhodes, Cecil 116, 236
Rich, Wilbur 25
Robinson, Mary 36
Roosevelt, Eleanor 251
Roosevelt, Franklin D. 113, 251
Rose, Hilary 170
Rose, Steven 170
Rosenberg, Charnie 237
Rothschild, Walter 122
Rubenberg, Cheryl A. 197–8

Sa'di, Ahmad H. 144, 153
Said, Edward 3, 19, 41–2, 45, 61, 109, 122, 180, 229, 268
Sand, Shlomo 118, 137–8, 140
San Francisco Conference 115
Sanyika, Mtangulizi 209
Saskatoon Star Phoenix 134–5
SATAWU. *see* South African Transport and Allied Workers Union (SATAWU)
"Scream" (*Tze'aka* in Hebrew) 219
Sears, Alan 40
second Intifada 98
Second World War 4, 11, 15, 24, 31–3, 50, 58–9, 65–6, 72, 91, 99, 109–10, 113–14, 116, 118–21, 130, 140–1, 148, 226, 231, 238, 242–3, 247, 251, 265, 268
self-determination 64, 67, 75, 121, 131, 142, 144–5, 159, 169, 198, 200, 202, 235, 243
"self-hating Jew" 34, 37–9
"Semites" 61
Sentas, Vicki 100–1
Sephardic/Mizrahi Jews 68–9, 117
settler colonialism 60–1, 67, 135–6, 143, 145, 153, 194–200, 202, 230, 232–3, 235, 239

Shadareh, Massoud 101
Sharon, Ariel 161
Sharpeville Massacre 220, 242, 251–3
Shoa. see Holocaust
Six-Day War (1967) 33, 119, 161, 212, 216
Smith, George P. 165
Smuts, Jan 236
social sorting 81–8, 90, 95, 97, 99, 101, 103–5, 260
solidarity, Palestine 147–51
South Africa, apartheid system in 233–7, 250–4, 257–61
South African Transport and Allied Workers Union (SATAWU) 164
South West Africa People's Organisation (SWAPO) 92
Stalinism 65–6
Stern Group 89
Stop the Wall Campaign 78
sui generis 82, 228, 259
Sullivan, Shannon 19
surveillance 81–3, 85–6, 89–90, 92–3, 95, 99–105, 190–1, 193, 197, 200, 212, 219, 248, 260
SWAPO. *see* South West Africa People's Organisation (SWAPO)

Tanenbaum, Larry 134
Taylor, Charles 27
Telos Press 98
terra nullius 135, 208
terrorism/terrorist 81–4, 86, 91–3, 96–7, 99–102, 105, 125, 149, 206, 237, 240
Third World 117
Thobani, Sunera 96
Thompson, Debra 26–7
"Through Fire and Water" (video) 54
Tilley, Virginia 85, 233, 238
Tlaib, Rashida 263
Toronto City Council 191–2
The Toronto Star 2
TRC. *see* Truth and Reconciliation Commission (TRC)
Troper, Harold 65
Trudeau, Justin 7–8, 54, 75, 124, 200, 265–6
Trump, Donald J. 7–8, 49, 77–8, 124, 148, 265–6
Truth and Reconciliation Commission (TRC) 15, 131, 242, 252–3, 255
Tuana, Nancy 19
"Turtle Island" 47 n.2

UAVs. *see* unmanned air vehicles (UAVs)
UNCHR. *see* UN Commission on Human Rights (UNCHR)
UN Commission on Human Rights (UNCHR) 112
UN Declaration on the Rights of Indigenous Peoples (UNDRIP) 130–2, 179, 210
  and Palestine 205–6
UNDRIP. *see* UN Declaration on the Rights of Indigenous Peoples (UNDRIP)
UNESCO. *see* United Nations Educational, Scientific and Cultural Organization (UNESCO)
UN FAO. *see* UN Food and Agricultural Organization (UN FAO)
UN Food and Agricultural Organization (UN FAO) 216
UNHRC. *see* United Nations Human Rights Council (UNHRC)
United Church of Canada's Toronto Conference 168
United Methodist Church 168
United Nations Educational, Scientific and Cultural Organization (UNESCO) 12
United Nations Human Rights Council (UNHRC) 55, 112
United Nations Relief and Works Agency (UNRWA) 124

United Nations (UN) 2, 33, 35–6, *passim*
- and apartheid South Africa 250–4
- Charter 115, 213, 232, 254
- Commission on Human Rights 232, 251
- Declaration of Human Rights 32, 50, 109, 111, 113, 115, 123, 126, 151, 226, 250, 253–4, 265
- Declaration on the Rights of Indigenous Peoples 20
- Economic and Social Commission for Western Asia 151, 238
- Economic and Social Council 75
- Fact-Finding Mission 220–1
- General Assembly 66, 75–6, 112, 117, 123–7, 162, 165–6, 231–2, 249–55
- and Palestinian Indigeneity 130–2
- Relief and Works Agency for Palestine Refugees 70, 132
- Resolution 194 42
- Security Council 213, 253–4, 257

United States 2–3, 12, 15–17, 23–5, 30–6, 39, 44, *passim*
- Black civil rights movement 10
- November 2016 presidential election 7
- 2018 US Congressional election 263

unmanned air vehicles (UAVs) 99, 219
UNSCOP. *see* UN Special Committee on Palestine (UNSCOP)
UN Special Committee on Palestine (UNSCOP) 116
Uris, Leon 179–80
Usher, Graham 90, 92

Van Teeffelen, Toine 71
Venessa, David 101

Walker, Alice 9–11
Walt, Stephen 79
"war of independence" 118
war on terror 3, 49, 77, 83–4, 86, 95–6
The Washington Post 222
water, in Israel/Palestine 216–18
Watts, Jerry G. 25
WCAR. *see* World Conference on Racism, Racialization, Xenophobia and Related Intolerance (WCAR)
We Can Have Peace in the Holy Land: A Plan That Will Work (Carter) 151–2
Weisman, Eyal 218
Weizmann, Chaim 62–3
West Bank and Gaza. *see* Gaza and West Bank
Whitaker, Reginald 29
"White Australia" project 238
White Paper (report) 64–5
white supremacy 14, 50
Wolfensohn, James D. 223
Women's Affairs Technical Committee 198
women's equality 182–8
World Bank 218, 223
The World Conference Against Racism 265
World Conference on Racism, Racialization, Xenophobia and Related Intolerance (WCAR) 2–3, 15, 34–6, 46, 56, 110, 127, 249–50, 254, 257–9, 268
World Conferences to Combat Racism and Racial Discrimination 242, 255–6
World Health Organization 217
World Pride event (2006) 190–2
World Public Information Campaign for Human Rights 111
World Social Forum (WSF) 164
World Trade Organization 153, 155
World Zionist Congress 61
World Zionist Organization 230
- Jewish Agency (Status) Law 68

WSF. *see* World Social Forum (WSF)

Yadgar, Yaacov 184
Yiftachel, Oren 212
Young, Iris Marion 145
Young-Bruehl, Elisabeth 39
YouTube 54

Zangwill, Israel 63
Zerbisias, Antonia 7
Zionism/Zionist movement 17, 29, 37–41, 52, 56–9, 61–7, 69, 74, 79, 85, 87–8, 91, 97–8, 114–18, 122–3, 126–7, 129–30, 132–43, 150, 152, 155–6, 158, 164, 166–7, 169, 171, 179–84, 187–8, 196, 207–8, 210–11, 222, 235–7, 239–43, 268
Zionist Congress 182, 184
Zreik, Raef 239